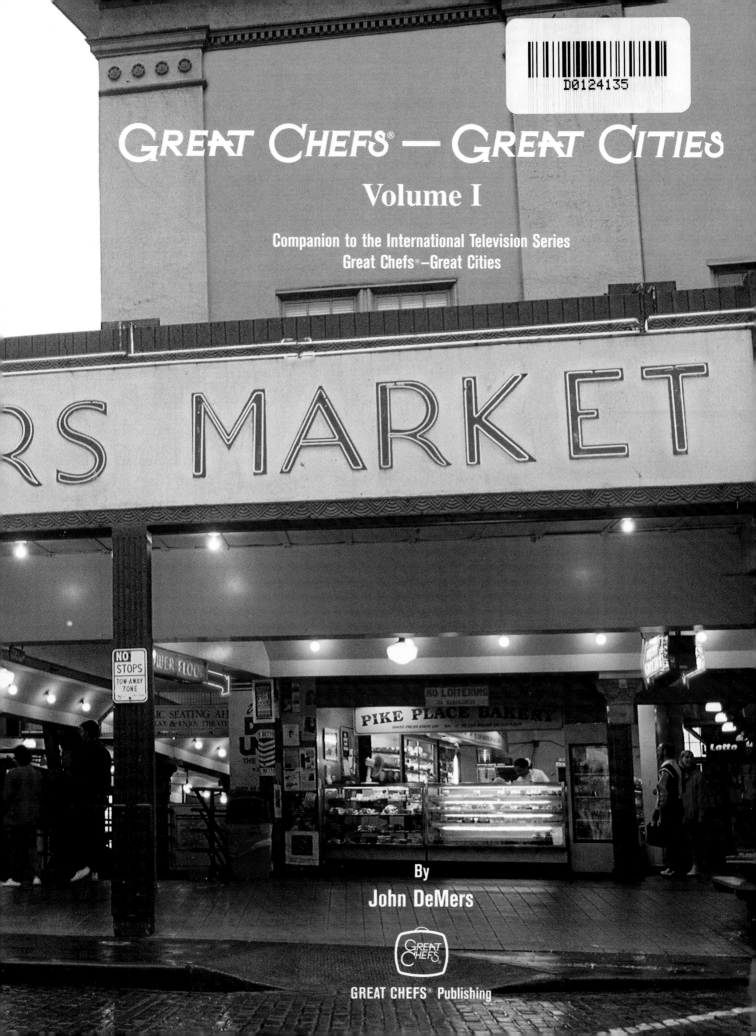

GREAT CHEFS® — GREAT CITIES

Volume I

Companion to the International Television Series
Great Chefs®—Great Cities

By
John DeMers

GREAT CHEFS® Publishing

Other Great Chefs®
companion cookbooks
are available:

Great Chefs of New Orleans I
Great Chefs of New Orleans II
Great Chefs of San Francisco
Great Chefs of Chicago
Southwest Tastes
Great Chefs: the Louisiana new Garde
Great Chefs of the East
Great Chefs Cook Italian
Great Chefs Cook American

All series now available on home video, including
Great Chefs—Great Cities

Additional home videos available:

Great Chefs: Appetizers	*Great Outdoor Cooking*
Oriental Obsessions	*Great Chefs, Great BBQ*
A New Orleans Jazz Brunch	*Great French Fest*
Chocolate Passion	*Down Home Cookin'*
Great Chefs: The Women	*Great Chefs Cook American*
Seafood Sampler	*Great Chefs Cook Italian*
Great Chefs: Desserts	*Great Chefs Halloween Treat*
Mexican Madness	*Great American Inns*
Chocolate Edition	*A Southwest Thanksgiving Feast*
Great Southern Barbecue	*An International Holiday Table*

Published by
  Great Chefs Publishing
  G.S.I., Inc.
  P.O. Box 56757
  New Orleans, LA 70156
  1-800-321-1499

Printed in China

First Printing 1996

Library of Congress Cataloguing-in-Publication Data

John DeMers
Great Chefs®—Great Cities

Library of Congress Catalogue Card Number 95-078445
Includes index
        1. Cooking in America
                I. Great Chefs—Great Cities
                II. Title
ISBN   Hardbound 0-929714-31-8
                Softbound 0-929714-32-6
UPC   Hardbound 0-490092-318-1-7
                Softbound 0-490092-326-1-6

W9-BMO-845

GREAT CHEFS® — GREAT CITIES

Volume I

CONTENTS

GREAT CHEFS — GREAT CITIES
Volume 1

The Chefs and Their Cities

These outstanding Great Chefs, listed by the major city nearest their restaurants, have contributed the more than 290 recipes which comprise the 120 creative dishes contained in this book. The recipes reveal both the ingredients and the techniques necessary to recreate fine cuisine in the home kitchen. All of these dishes have been presented on the first forty programs of the television series, GREAT CHEFS—GREAT CITIES.

Christian Gille
  Le Jardin
  The Westin Canal Place

Feuillant of Fresh Berries with
  Mango-Raspberry Coulis, page 216

Emeril Lagasse
  Emeril's/Nola

Scallop and Leek Flan, page 84

Susan Spicer
  Bayona

Smoked Duck Hash, page 112

John Wong
  Trey Yuen

Alligator Stir-fry, page 90

Tommy Wong
  Trey Yuen

Crawfish with Spicy Black Bean Sauce, page 90

New York, New York

Lynne Aronson
  Lola

Grilled Rack of Lamb with Risotto, Fava Beans,
  and Cardamom Sauce, page 130

Lidia Bastianich
  Felidia

Gamberoni alla Griglia, page 82
Brutti Ma Buoni, page 177

Daniel Boulud
  Restaurant Daniel

Crabmeat Salad, page 48
Sweetbreads with Camomile and Morels, page 122

Antoine Bouterin
  Le Périgord

Almond Heart, page 198

David Burke
  Park Avenue Cafe

Corn Flan with Smoked Salmon, page 26

Bobby Flay
  Mesa Grill

Grilled Swordfish Tostada, page 42

Larry Forgione
  An American Place

Veal Steak Sauté with Jerky Sauce, page 120
Lemon Angel Food Chiffon, page 191

Paul Ingenito
  The Russian Tea Room

Grilled Scallops on Silver Dollar Blini, page 46

Michael Lomonaco
  The '21' Club

The '21' Club Crab Cakes, page 10
Rum Banana and Maple Ice Cream Sandwich, page 164

Charles Palmer
  Aureole

Carpaccio of Tuna, page 58

Debra Ponzek
  Montrachet

Pasta with Mushrooms and Foie Gras, page 14

Alain Sailhac
  L'École/French Culinary Institute

Eggplant and Roasted–Red Pepper Terrine, page 34

André Soltner
  Lutèce

Ballottine of Sole Sauce Émeraude, page 22

Emily Luchetti Stars	Mascarpone Caramel Cream with Berries and White Chocolate–Raspberry Brittle, page 152
George Morrone Aqua	Tuna Tartare, page 28
Janet Rikala Postrio	Passion Fruit Cheesecake, page 194
Julian Serrano Masa's	Lobster Salad on a Bed of Potato, with Confit of Crispy Leek and Truffle Vinaigrette, page 60 Medallions of Venison with Caramelized Green Apples, page 149
Jeremiah Tower Stars	Ballottine of Braised Duck, Chicken, Veal, and Foie Gras, page 114

Seattle, Washington

Monique Andrée Barbeau Fullers Sheraton Seattle Hotel & Towers	Salmon Salad with Avocado Vinaigrette and Corn Salsa, page 104
Kaspar Donier Kaspar's	Earl Grey Sorbet with Fresh Berries, page 162
Shelley Lance Dahlia Lounge	Apple Dumplings with Cinnamon-Rum Sauce, page 210

Washington, District of Columbia

Jeffrey Buben Vidalia	Baked Vidalia Onion with Chive Blossom Vinaigrette, page 14 Lemon Chess Pie, page 184
Patrick Clark Hay-Adams Restaurant The Hay-Adams Hotel	Roasted Rack of Lamb with Ratatouille Polenta and Black Olive Lamb Juice, page 132
William C. Greenwood The Jefferson	Lamb Chops with Goat Cheese–Macaroni Soufflé, page 135 Sun-dried Cherry Charlotte with Green Tea Ice Cream, page 192
Klaus Helmin Tivoli	Terrine of Squab Breast and Wild Mushrooms, page 51 Braised Rabbit with Black Olives, page 129
Patrick O'Connell The Inn at Little Washington	Rhubarb Pizza, page 172
Jean-Louis Palladin Jean-Louis at the Watergate	Strawberry Crème Fouette, page 208
Francesco Ricchi i Ricchi	Italian Flat Bread, page 19

All chefs and restaurants are listed in this book as they were taped for the television series, GREAT CHEFS —GREAT CITIES. Chefs and restaurants do change; if you wish to dine with a particular chef or restaurant, Great Chefs suggests you call the restaurant when planning your trip.

ACKNOWLEDGEMENTS

First and foremost, I must thank the great chefs in all these great American cities, whose tireless efforts inspire whatever good things can be said between the covers of a book. To compose a work such as this is an adventure in reflected light; it is an opportunity to share for a moment in the illumination provided by these glowing careers in the nation's best kitchens.

Thanks are certainly due the entire Great Chefs team, both those who traveled to produce the television series and those who stayed behind to wrestle with this book. My gratitude goes out particularly to John Shoup and John Beyer, who invited me to participate, and Linda Nix, who helped me live to tell the tale.

Also involved in making this book the wonder that it is were talents as diverse as photographer Eric Futran, designer Larry Escudier and artist Dwain Richard, editor Carolyn Miller in San Francisco, and recipe tester Carolyn Buster in Chicago. The final look and feel of any book is as much about these contributions as about any turn of phrase in which its author might take special pride.

Finally, I must thank my wife Sandra and our children Sara, Michael, Amanda and Tessa. They have put up with a guy who, for the most part, "eats for a living," and they have done so with the sense of humor such putting-up-with requires.

—John DeMers
  New Orleans

PREFACE

In San Francisco as a young executive chef was leading the Great Chefs crew through a swanky hotel's labyrinthine kitchen, he mused, "you've probably been in more kitchens then I have." He was probably right. In over a decade we have taped eleven hundred and fifty dishes, in three hundred and eighty restaurant kitchens, while featuring over four hundred chefs. That's a lot of béarnaise sauce under the bridge.

The latest series, GREAT CHEFS—GREAT CITIES, now begets this companion cookbook. It is a digest of marvelous recipes drawn from Honolulu to New York, San Francisco to Miami, and Chicago to Seattle.

A high proportion of the country's greatest restaurants are in cities (or in a city's orbit) because it is there that you find not only concentrated population, but a financial base broad enough to support upscale restaurants. With the best dining cities, other characteristics are evident. Many are proximal to high quality indigenous product, or can access a transportation system to acquire it. Also though many are tourist-oriented, a large number of locals regularly dine at the restaurants. For these and other reasons, most of the best chefs find their way to the cities.

When Great Chefs Television is working in a city we generally view it with periscopic vision (bordering perhaps on tunnel vision). There is little or no sightseeing and minimal, if any, contact with other elements that stamp an urban area. What we do get is a paradigmatic view of the dining scene, since we spend most of our time taping and/or talking to chefs. Therefore, knowing it is a parlous undertaking, I offer a sort of culinary snapshot of a few of the cities in the new series.

ATLANTA: the restaurant scene here was on the uptick before the '96 Olympics. Any city where Jean Banchet is opening a restaurant is ascending

BOSTON: serious in most things and certainly about good food. For example, a line of diners waiting an hour in sub-zero weather to eat at Todd English's Olives

CHICAGO: during the eighties it was propelled into a front-line food city, principally by the infusion of a group of talented new chefs

DALLAS: high-end restaurants have grown, but the Southwestern theme is still predominant

HOUSTON: enjoys a number of new and impressive spots often located in the suburbs. The problem, of course, is getting there

LOS ANGELES: one city where the stars aren't cooking; they're out front, eating

MIAMI: here and all over southern Florida chefs are developing a real regional identity with local product and Caribbean flavors

NEW ORLEANS: with deep food roots it has somehow survived a rollercoaster economy and boasts a disproportionate number of remarkable restaurants

NEW YORK: like marriage, anything you say about it is probably true. The city is still the centrosphere of American cuisine. Unlike most areas, the cooking is not regionally oriented, but you can find anything in New York

PORTLAND/SEATTLE/HONOLULU: the Northwest is finally actualizing James Beard's panegyric to its natural bounty, and, with Hawaii, is developing Pacific Rim cuisine

SAN FRANCISCO: often erroneously compared to New Orleans. They are, however, similar when ratio of good restaurants to population is a factor

WASHINGTON, D.C.: although Jean-Louis Palladin is still the culinary *force majeure,* a number of fine new chefs have elevated that city's dining.

In America it appears that anything can be celebritized, and in the nineties (you'll pardon the expression) the salad days are here for restaurants and chefs. Sirio Maccione, the owner of Le Cirque, was designated a "Living Landmark" by the New York Landmarks Conservancy. Moreover, chefs appear quite often on network morning and late shows, while several even host their own series. Further, there are now companies that teach chefs 'television performance technique'. I personally believe that societal rectitude would be better served if some of the people who make TV shows would go to Chefs school.

Be that as it may, *Great Chefs—Great Cities* offers a unique opportunity to sample a cooking cross-section from some of the most talented chefs in the country. As we are indebted to them for sharing their gifts, so it is hoped that you will enjoy partaking of those gifts.

—John Beyer
  Producer/Director
  Great Chefs Television

FOREWORD

by Ella Brennan
Commander's Palace
New Orleans

I'm a city girl. No apologies. Great cities offer all the things I love in life: the arts, the theater, the music, and—of course—the food!

In New Orleans the favored form of entertainment has always been the food. Now if you can combine the foods and the music—say in a jazz brunch—now you're talking about a little bit of heaven on earth.

America is starting to catch on to this, starting to understand what we have always known in New Orleans—that food and dining are so much more than just sustenance. First there is the pleasure of the food itself. Not many of life's pleasures top a Vidalia onion and Creole tomato salad, a just-in-season perfectly cooked fat soft shell crab, and a Ponchatoula strawberry shortcake. Then there is something special that happens when people break bread together. Eating is so personal. Savoring a great meal with good conversation is nourishing and life-giving in another way altogether.

To me this is a pleasure that abounds in America's great cities today. So my friends John Beyer and John Shoup's work, GREAT CHEFS—GREAT CITIES, is a brilliant addition to the collection of "foodies" everywhere. This book by John DeMers helps the home cook join the fun.

Great Chefs programs and cookbooks have been a great part of spreading the word across the country about what great chefs and great restaurants do. The original *Great Chefs of New Orleans* series was one of the first times many Americans were able to see what goes on behind the scenes in restaurants. Obviously, people were intrigued and the Great Chefs were on to something. I had people from all over the country telling us they had seen the show and loved it.

These gentlemen know a great chef when they see one, and they have a way of capturing that essence.

Passion Fruit Cheesecake; *Janet Rikala, Postrio*

America's Cities: Cradles of Fine Cuisine

Like fine wine, which draws its complexity and goodness from the mingling of climate and soil, America's great cities draw their cuisines from the interweaving of two basic factors. Ask to know a city's cuisine and its chefs will speak of two influences: where it is and who built it there.

Location molds a city in a thousand ways. It gives a city a climate, and that in turn gives it a mood. Location largely determines what a city does for a living, and as a result what type of people live there. And location dictates what kind of food the people of a city eat. Nearly every American city was formed before airplanes were available to fly in food—and before the simplest types of refrigeration were available. That meant that people subsisted on what the local terrain could give them.

Nearly every American city had a bounty of some kind: from the sea harvest of the Atlantic, Pacific and Gulf coasts to the game and wild foods of the Midwest and South. To say that people on water ate fish and people on land ate meat and vegetables is to over-simplify. But in city after city, location did tell the tale.

The second factor in the cuisine of America's cities is the unique mixture of peoples who live in each one. Thanks to its rich natural resources, the United States became an overflowing cornucopia and a symbol of hope to the rest of the world, drawing an unprecedented mingling of races and nationalities to its shores.

New York, New York

Italian and Irish, Germans, Dutch and Scandinavian, French, Spanish, Italians and Greeks—they poured onto these shores in wave after wave, decade after decade. They brought little in the way of material goods, yet no one would deny that what they brought with them helped to create a new country. They brought ideas and ideals. They brought history and culture and values. They brought their faith, their music, their books (sometimes even when they couldn't read)—and they brought their food.

The foods of this new country turned up first in the great cities, for that is where the first settlers congregated, where the air was filled with the smells of home. Indeed, cooking and serving food became entry-level jobs that many claimed as their first in the New World. Its components were familiar in the group's chosen (or mandated) neighborhood, and its language was nearly always that of the old country.

In the beginning, European immigration laid the foundation of the new culture. Yet the quirky twists of commerce and history meant that the new nation would draw immigrants from all points of the compass.

Despite the vastness of the Pacific Ocean, it was only a matter of time before the West Coast would find its natural partner in the Far East. As had the peoples of the Mediterranean three thousand years earlier, the countries on the rim of the Pacific came to see their similarities as well as their differences. Chinese first, next Japanese, then Thai and Korean and Filipino and Indonesian and Vietnamese would bring valuable cuisines with them.

Meanwhile, the cooking of Latin America merged with Native American cuisine, to produce a unique style of cooking that would eventually affect nearly every region of the country. Its basic foods—corn, beans, tomatoes and chilies—would form the culinary foundations of Texas, New Mexico, Arizona and southern California before being embraced by the rest of the nation and the world.

South Florida
conch • spiny lobster fresh vegetables • citrus fruit • stone crabs • Key limes • rum • pompano

Hawaii
pork • macadamia nuts crabs • coconuts pineapples • bananas guavas • passion fruit opakapaka • poi yellowfin ahi

The South and Gulf Coast
corn • pork • greens peas and beans • grits chicken • rice • pecans bourbon • Vidalia onions filé • oysters • shrimp cayenne • red snapper crabs • crawfish

Unlike the immigrants who came eagerly, seeking their fortune, the Africans were brought against their will as objects of trade. Yet they too brought their culture, their rich treasure of religion, dance and song. And they too brought their foods and cooking techniques, recreating the tastes of home in an alien land.

In the big cities of the North, African-inspired food remained a buried treasure, "soul food" rarely sampled by non-Africans. In the rural South, this cooking became the food of black and white alike (especially among the poor). And in Europeanized New Orleans, Africa spoke most forcefully, mingling with French and Spanish behind kitchen doors to become Creole cuisine. African tastes even influenced the Cajun cooking of the Louisiana countryside, giving it a different heart and a different soul from anything in its French or French Canadian past.

Call it whatever you will—American food, New World cuisine, New American cuisine or fusion cooking—the cooking of today's chefs is a continuation of the story we've just told. Some of the chefs are native born, others came from one "old country" or another. Each one brought the cooking techniques and foods of his or her home to a land already rich in native and imported culinary traditions

Keep our natural abundance and rich mix of cultures in mind as you browse, read, cook and feast your way through this book. This is a pilgrimage from which you will emerge well-fed and immeasurably wiser about the bounteous land and great cities that so many great chefs have learned, in one language or another, to call home.

The Far West
avocados • artichokes sourdough • Dungeness crab • grapes and wine fresh vegetables and fruit • prawns • razor clams • salmon • oysters berries • cheese • apples mushrooms

Southwest
piñon nuts • chilies • beef beans • wild game • corn cactus pear • pecans tomatoes

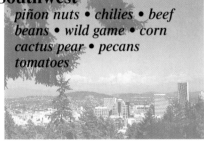

The Breadbasket
corn • beef • grains • duck fruit • butter • trout lamb • pike • wild rice dove • cheese • beer

The East Coast
molasses • lobster • maple sugar • lamb • crabs fresh vegetables • clams root vegetables • cod apples • oysters • chicken pork • duck

Oysters Béarnaise; *Daniel Bonnot, Chez Daniel*

Little Tastes: Appetizers and First Courses

No part of the meal has proven as ripe for innovation by chefs in America as the first course. The "little taste" of an appetizer seems a slot uniquely filled by light, fresh tastes.

In the past decade or so, restaurants in some cities have devoted themselves to appetizers exclusively, replacing the traditional meal structure with a free-form flow of small dishes. Appetizers have an enormous potential for creativity.

In the following pages, our chefs turn that potential into dazzling reality. Whether traditional openers like crab cakes, or such exotics as Peruvian-style sweet and sour quail or Asian-Southwestern lobster with avocado and tangy honey-radish sauce, the willingness to rewrite the rules is written all over these recipes.

New Orleans, Louisiana

STAN FRANKENTHALER
The Blue Room / East Coast Grill, Boston, Massachusetts

Stan Frankenthaler started his cooking career at the age of seven, shelling peas and snapping beans at his grandmother's side. He's been enamored of the rituals of food ever since.

At seventeen, Frankenthaler began turning an avocation into a career. Cooking his way through the University of Georgia led to a pilgrimage to the Culinary Institute of America. After graduating with high honors in 1984, Frankenthaler took a working tour of Boston, first at the Meridien, then at Jasper White's, ending with a year as that kitchen's celebrity sous-chef. Happily for Frankenthaler, White was working on a cookbook at the time, so he was given the opportunity to run the kitchen.

After a six-month educational tour of the wine regions of France and Italy, Frankenthaler had a chance to pinch-hit once again. This time it was at Hamersley's Bistro, where sous-chef Jody Adams was on a lengthy maternity leave and the Hamersleys were occupied with the birth of their first child. As if running the store were not enough, Frankenthaler found himself dreaming more and more of a first-rate home-catering business. This Choice Catering Company would eventually earn top honors in its field from Boston's print and broadcast media.

Finally, it was time for an eatery of his own. With Chris Schlesinger and Cary Wheaton of the East Coast Grill and Jake and Earl's Dixie Barbecue, Frankenthaler opened the Blue Room at One Kendall Square in Cambridge. The menu is as unusual as it is dramatic, featuring open-fire cooking from around the world. From Mongolian to Mexican to Middle Eastern, the Blue Room literally sizzles.

And it's all because Frankenthaler spent those hours with his grandmother, snapping beans and falling in love with food.

Sweet and Sour Quail Peruvian Style

Stan Frankenthaler
The Blue Room/East Coast Grill
Boston, Massachusetts

An exotic mix of spices, vinegar, red wine, dried fruit, and vegetables makes a dark, tangy marinade and sauce for quail, which are served on a bed of salad and garnished with homemade potato chips. Plan to begin this dish 2 days before serving.

Serves 4

Spices
2 teaspoons coriander seeds
1 teaspoon cumin seed
½ teaspoon red pepper flakes
4 allspice berries

Sauce
2 tablespoons olive oil
1 white onion, diced
1 small carrot, peeled and diced
2 garlic cloves, chopped
½ cup packed brown sugar
½ cup balsamic vinegar
½ cup dry red wine
1½ cups reduced veal or beef stock
  (see page 228)
8 whole dried figs
2 tablespoons golden raisins
2 tablespoons chopped dried apricots
1 red bell pepper, roasted, peeled,
  seeded, and diced (see page 235)
1 tomato, peeled, seeded, and diced
  (see page 234)
1 to 2 teaspoons peeled and minced
  fresh ginger
Salt and freshly ground black pepper
  to taste

4 semi-boneless quail

Potato Chips
Peanut oil for frying
2 unpeeled red potatoes, thinly sliced
Kosher salt and cayenne pepper to taste

Salad
½ bunch watercress
½ cup shredded radicchio
½ cup julienned haricots verts or baby
  Blue Lake green beans, blanched

¼ cup fresh parsley leaves
½ cup extra-virgin olive oil
¼ cup fresh lemon juice
½ teaspoon kosher salt
½ teaspoon freshly ground black
  pepper

Peanut oil for frying

To prepare the spices: In a medium sauté pan or skillet over medium heat, toast the spices, stirring frequently, until they are fragrant and begin to smoke, 5 to 7 minutes. Remove the pan from heat and grind the spices in a spice grinder, a well-washed coffee grinder, or in a mortar with a pestle. Set aside.

To make the sauce: In a medium sauté pan or skillet over medium heat, heat the olive oil. Add the onion, carrot, and garlic and sauté until mixture begins to brown, 10 to 15 minutes. Add the brown sugar and stir, allowing the sugar to melt and caramelize. Add the balsamic vinegar and stir; add the red wine and veal or beef stock. Add the figs, raisins, apricots, and bell pepper, and tomato. Bring the mixture to a boil and cook to reduce slightly, then add the toasted spices and ginger and continue to cook to reduce until the liquid is syrupy, about 10 minutes. Taste and adjust the seasoning with salt and pepper.

Place the quail in the sauce and, once the sauce returns to a boil, turn the quail to coat with the sauce. Remove from heat and let the quail cool in the pan. Place the quail and the sauce in a shallow nonaluminum pan, cover, and refrigerate for 2 days.

To make the chips: Pour peanut oil to a depth of 2 inches in a large heavy sauté pan or skillet. Heat over medium-high heat to 375°F, or until a submerged crumb of bread immediately floats to the top and begins to sizzle. Fry the potato slices in batches until golden brown and crisp, about 5 minutes. Remove from the oil with a slotted spoon, drain on paper towels, and season with the kosher salt and cayenne pepper.

To make the salad: Toss the greens and vegetables with the olive oil and lemon juice, and season to taste with salt and pepper.

Pour peanut oil to a depth of ½ inch in a medium, heavy sauté pan or skillet. Heat over medium-high heat. Remove the quail from the sauce and scrape off any dried fruit. Pan-fry the quail, turning once, until crisp, 3 to 4 minutes. Transfer the quail to a warm platter.

Pour the sauce into a small pan and heat over medium heat. If the sauce is thin, cook to reduce until syrupy; if it is too thick, thin it slightly with a bit of water.

To serve: Place ¾ cup of salad off-center on each serving plate. Place 1 quail to one side of the salad and spoon some of the sauce around the quail. Top the salad with a few potato chips.

Sweet and Sour Quail Peruvian Style;
Stan Frankenthaler, The Blue Room/East Coast Grill

The '21' Club Crab Cakes

Michael Lomonaco
The '21' Club
New York, New York

Everyone loves crab cakes. This classy version adds cilantro, Old Bay seasoning, and a pungent chili mayonnaise to make an irresistible starter.

Serves 8

1 pound fresh jumbo lump crabmeat
2 tablespoons olive oil
2 tablespoons diced red bell pepper
2 tablespoons diced yellow bell pepper
1 tablespoon minced jalapeño chili
2 teaspoons minced garlic
3 to 6 tablespoons mayonnaise, preferably homemade
¼ cup fresh cilantro leaves, coarsely chopped
2 tablespoons dried bread crumbs
1½ tablespoons Old Bay seasoning mix
Salt and freshly ground pepper to taste

Chili Mayonnaise
½ cup mayonnaise, preferably homemade
1 to 2 teaspoons Thai chili sauce, or to taste
1 tablespoon Dijon mustard
1 tablespoon prepared horseradish
½ cup dried bread crumbs
⅓ cup olive oil
1 tablespoon butter

Garnish
1 large tomato, peeled, seeded, and diced (see page 234)
1½ tablespoons snipped fresh chives

Clean the crabmeat carefully to remove all shell fragments, but try to keep the lumps intact. In a medium sauté pan or skillet over high heat, heat 1 tablespoon of the oil and sauté the bell peppers, chili, and garlic for 1 minute; set aside. In a large bowl, combine the crabmeat, 3 tablespoons of the mayonnaise, cilantro, bread crumbs, and the sautéed mixture. Add the seasoning mix, salt, and pepper. Mix well, and if mixture is dry, add more mayonnaise to bind. Cover and refrigerate for 20 minutes.

To make the chili mayonnaise: In a small bowl, combine all of the ingredients and mix well. Place in a squeeze bottle and set aside.

Form the crab mixture into 8 equal-sized balls and pat each into a disc. Place the bread crumbs in a shallow dish and press each crab cake into the crumbs, one at a time, to coat all sides evenly.

Preheat the oven to 375°F. In a large skillet over high heat, heat the olive oil until it is almost smoking. Add 4 of the crab cakes. Lower the heat slightly, add half of the butter to the pan, and fry the cakes for about 1 minute per side, or until light and golden colored. Remove the fried cakes to a baking sheet and place in the oven for 5 to 6 minutes to finish cooking. Repeat to fry all the remaining cakes.

To serve: Place 1 crab cake in the center of each serving plate and drizzle some of the chili mayonnaise around the edges. Garnish each plate with 3 small piles of diced tomatoes, then sprinkle with the snipped chives.

Grilled Chinese Eggplant with Balsamic Vinaigrette

Susanna Foo
Susanna Foo Chinese Cuisine
Philadelphia, Pennsylvania

Vodka, soy sauce, and balsamic vinegar are some of the surprising ingredients of this East-meets-West appetizer, which is garnished with diced tomatoes combined with Bloody Mary mix.

Grilled Chinese Eggplant with Balsamic Vinaigrette;
Susanna Foo, Susanna Foo Chinese Cuisine

4 Asian eggplants
¼ cup soybean oil or olive oil
1 tablespoon soy sauce
1 tablespoon vodka or gin

Balsamic Vinaigrette
1 teaspoon minced garlic
1 tablespoon finely shredded
 fresh ginger
2 tablespoons soy sauce
2 tablespoons balsamic vinegar
1 tablespoon soybean or olive oil

Seasoned Tomato
¼ cup Bloody Mary mix
2 tablespoons fresh lemon juice
2 tablespoons minced fresh cilantro

Garnish
8 radishes, with leaves
Fresh cilantro sprigs, (optional)

Halve the eggplants lengthwise.
Score each with ½-inch-wide
crosshatching cuts, going halfway
through the eggplant. Cut each eggplant
into 2-inch diagonal slices. In a shallow
dish, combine the oil, soy sauce, and
vodka or gin, and marinate the eggplant
at room temperature for 1 hour.

Preheat the broiler with a heavy
baking pan under it. Using a slotted
spoon, transfer the eggplant from the
marinade to the pan. Broil until the
eggplant is soft and tender, turning
once, 4 to 5 minutes.

To make the balsamic vinaigrette: Place
all the ingredients in a small bowl and
combine with a wire whisk.

To make the seasoned tomato: Combine
all the ingredients in a small bowl, and
stir together.

To serve: Divide the eggplant, cut-side
up, among the serving plates and top
each piece with some of the balsamic
vinaigrette and tomato mixture. Garnish
each plate with radishes and some
cilantro sprigs.

SUSANNA FOO
Susanna Foo Chinese Cuisine, Philadelphia, Pennsylvania

Susanna Foo was born in Inner Mongolia and has been on a
journey outward ever since. Few Chinese-born chefs have proven as
innovative or as courageous as Foo in rethinking, reworking, and sometimes reinventing the tastes and textures of their native cuisine.

Most cases of "fusion" cuisine today involve Western chefs adopt-
ing techniques and ingredients from Asia. Foo handles her fusion the
other way around, reinterpreting Chinese classics from a French
perspective. She emphasizes sauces made from stocks in the French
manner, finishing her sauces with herbs and spices from every point
on the globe.

The result, she believes, is a lighter, brighter, more velvety
and more flavorful rendition of the dishes she grew up enjoying.
Obviously, her customers at Susanna Foo Chinese Cuisine in
Philadelphia agree.

Another major departure from Chinese cuisine is Foo's love of
raw vegetables. The Chinese don't eat them at all, but Foo finds her
inspiration in Italy, dressing up her popular water chestnut salad with
none other than olive oil and balsamic vinegar.

Raised in Taiwan, Foo came to the United States in 1967 and
earned a master's degree in library science from the University of
Pittsburgh. Though she had no real restaurant experience, she and
husband E-Hsin joined his family in opening Hu-Nan of Philadelphia
in 1979. By 1987, the couple felt ready to strike out on its own,
launching Susanna Foo Chinese Cuisine.

Two years later, Foo was named one of the Ten Best New Chefs
by *Food & Wine* magazine. Perhaps even more notably, according to
the *Zagat Survey*, her restaurant has received the highest scores of any
Chinese restaurant in any city in the country.

MICHAEL KORNICK
Aujourd'hui, Four Seasons Hotel, Boston, Massachusetts

"People yearn for simple cuisine. I really believe in preserving the natural integrity of the product one is working with. Chicken should taste like chicken."

Michael Kornick, named executive chef at the Four Seasons Hotel at age twenty-nine, hails from the American Midwest and shows a heartland affinity for the basics. Still, Kornick can and does call on a number of ethnic influences as he cooks, from Japanese and Thai to French and Italian.

The chef's ambition blossomed at age thirteen. Three years later, he started his own catering company. Kornick admits that his first catering clients were his parents' friends, who took pity on the aspiring entrepreneur. Many, however, could recognize the beginnings of a chef in Kornick's venture.

After receiving his associate degree from the Culinary Institute of America, Kornick headed home, setting the pattern for his early career: globe-trotting jaunts for experience and further education, broken by extended stints of working in Chicago.

The Metro Restaurant provided Kornick his first real job, as a line cook for the 120-seat restaurant. Later he worked as a line cook at the Quilted Giraffe in New York, then as executive sous-chef at the Windsor Court Hotel in New Orleans. Next it was back to Chicago, where Kornick revitalized Gordon's before joining the creative restaurateurs at Lettuce Entertain You Enterprises.

Over the next two years, he served as consulting chef for Un Grande Cafe; as executive chef for the Pump Room in the Ambassador East Hotel (overseeing special events for its fiftieth anniversary); and as executive chef and opening partner at The Eccentric, partially owned by Oprah Winfrey. In Kornick's spare time, he tasted his way through England and France and spent thirteen weeks in Asia, working some of the time at a hotel in Bangkok.

"I'm really into product," says Kornick, summarizing the message of his ongoing self-education. "I survey the markets all the time so I can see what is fresh and what isn't. I ask our vendors a lot of questions, like where it was grown, how it ripened, and how it will be shipped. In this business, it's essential to insist upon the best."

Peppered Salmon Niçoise

Michael Kornick
Aujourd'hui
Four Seasons Hotel
Boston, Massachusetts

The flavors of the south of France — fennel, tomatoes, garlic, olives, and basil — adorn a dish of salmon fillets coated with cracked pepper and served with a salad of curly endive.

Serves 4

Vegetable Vinaigrette
1 whole garlic head, cloves separated and peeled
1 tablespoon plus 1 cup olive oil
Salt and freshly ground black pepper to taste
2 plum (Roma) tomatoes, cored and seeded
1 fennel bulb, cored, quartered, and cut into 1/2-inch dice
4 ounces haricot verts or baby Blue Lake green beans, cut into 1-inch pieces
1 red bell pepper, seeded and deribbed
1 yellow bell pepper, seeded and deribbed
1 tablespoon fennel seeds
6 tablespoons balsamic vinegar
1 tablespoon snipped fresh chives
1 cup Kalamata olives, pitted
1/2 cup basil leaves, cut into fine shreds

Peppered Salmon
Four 3-ounce salmon fillets
Salt to taste
1 1/2 tablespoons fresh-cracked black pepper
2 tablespoons olive oil

1 head frisée (curly endive), leaves separated
1/2 cup fresh basil leaves, cut into fine shreds

To prepare the vegetable vinaigrette:
Preheat the oven to 225°F. Coat the
garlic cloves with the 1 tablespoon olive
oil and season with salt and pepper.
Place in a pie tin and roast uncovered for
35 to 45 minutes, or until soft and
golden brown. Set aside.

In a medium saucepan of boiling
lightly salted water, blanch the tomatoes
for about 20 seconds. Remove from
water with a slotted spoon, drop into ice
water to cool, and remove from the ice
water with a slotted spoon. Peel, seed,
and set aside. In the same pan of boiling
water, blanch the fennel and the beans
for 30 seconds, then drop into ice water.
Drain. Neatly dice the tomatoes and
peppers into ½-inch pieces and set
aside.

Preheat the oven to 325°F. Lightly
crush the fennel seeds in a mortar with
a pestle or grind for a few seconds in a
spice grinder or a well-washed coffee
grinder. Spread out on a baking sheet
and place in the oven for 1 minute, or
until they are aromatic. In a medium
bowl, whisk together the fennel seeds,
1 cup olive oil, and balsamic vinegar,
and season with salt and pepper to taste.
Add the diced vegetables, chives,
olives, and roasted garlic. Toss together
and add the basil.

To prepare the salmon: Sprinkle the
salmon on both sides with the salt and
press the cracked pepper into the flesh.
In a large sauté pan or skillet over high
heat, heat the olive oil and cook the
fish 1 minute on the first side, then
turn and cook for 2 minutes on the
second side. The fish should remain
rare in the center.

To serve: On each serving plate,
mound some of the frisée to one side
and place 1 piece of the salmon on the
opposite side. Spoon some of the vinaigrette and the vegetables around and
over the greens and the salmon. Garnish
with the basil.

Peppered Salmon Niçoise; *Michael Kornick, Aujourd'hui, Four Seasons Hotel*

Pasta with Mushrooms and Foie Gras

Debra Ponzek
Montrachet
New York, New York

Two extraordinary culinary pleasures — forest mushrooms and foie gras — are combined in this elegant pasta dish.

Serves 4

Sauce

12 ounces shiitake mushrooms or a
  combination of wild and domestic
  mushrooms, plus 4 *each* shiitake
  and black trumpet mushrooms
  (about 4 ounces)
2 tablespoons olive oil
1 cup 1/4-inch diced celery
1 cup 1/4-inch diced peeled carrot
1 1/2 teaspoons minced shallot
2 1/2 cups chicken stock (see page 228)
2 cups heavy (whipping) cream
Salt and freshly ground black pepper
  to taste

2 tablespoons olive oil
1 teaspoon salt, plus salt to taste
8 ounces tricallini (tiny bow-tie) pasta
4 ounces 1-inch-thick fresh foie gras
Truffle juice (optional)
1 tablespoon snipped fresh chives or
  minced fresh parsley
Freshly ground black pepper to taste

To prepare the sauce: Remove and reserve the stems of all the mushrooms. Thinly slice and set aside the 4 shiitake and 4 black mushroom caps. Mince or grind the stems and enough of the caps to measure 1 cup; set aside. Chop the remaining mushroom caps.

In a large sauté pan or skillet over high heat, heat the oil and sauté the celery, carrot, and shallot until the vegetables are soft but not browned, about 3 to 4 minutes. Add the 1 cup minced or ground stems and caps, the chopped mushroom caps, and the chicken stock. Lower the heat to medium and cook for 20 minutes. Add the cream, stir and cook over

medium heat until slightly thickened, 10 to 15 minutes. Strain the sauce and season with salt and pepper. Set aside.

To cook the pasta: Bring 2 quarts of water to a boil. Add olive oil, 1 teaspoon salt, and the pasta and cook until al dente, 3 to 5 minutes. Drain and rinse under cold water to stop the cooking. Drain again and set aside.

Meanwhile, to prepare the foie gras: Season the foie gras with salt and pepper and cut it into 1/2-inch dice. Heat a large, dry, nonstick pan over high heat and cook the foie gras until browned on all sides, a total of about 1 minute. Remove from the pan and drain on paper towels. Keep warm in a low oven.

In a medium sauté pan or skillet over medium heat, warm the strained cream sauce until bubbly, add the sliced mushroom caps and cooked pasta, and continue to cook over low heat, stirring, until warmed throughout, 2 to 3 minutes. Add the truffle juice (if using) and chives or parsley, and adjust the seasoning.

To serve: Spoon the pasta into shallow pasta bowls and place some of the foie gras on top of each serving.

Baked Vidalia Onion with Chive Blossom Vinaigrette

Jeffrey Buben
Vidalia
Washington, D.C.

The less done to mask the sweet flavor of Vidalia onions the better. This recipe enhances the taste but does nothing to disguise it.

Serves 4

4 large untrimmed Vidalia onions or
  other sweet white onions
1 cup cold rich veal stock
  (see page 228, 231)
8 fresh thyme sprigs
4 fresh rosemary sprigs

Baked Vidalia Onion with Chive Blossom Vinaigrette; *Jeffrey Buben, Vidalia*

½ cup (1 stick) unsalted butter, cut into
  8 pieces
Salt and freshly ground black pepper
  to taste
4 tablespoons raw sugar

Chive Blossom Vinaigrette
2 tablespoons minced garlic
2 plum (Roma) tomatoes, peeled,
  seeded, and cut ¼-inch dice
  (see page 234)
2 tablespoons snipped fresh chives
4 fresh chive blossoms, petals separated
Salt and freshly ground black pepper
  to taste
½ cup olive oil
3 tablespoons red wine vinegar
Juice from baked onions, above

Fresh chive blossoms, petals separated,
  for garnish

To prepare the onions: Preheat the oven
to 400°F. Cut one thin slice from the top
of each onion to form a flat surface.
Score through the dry outer skin from
top to bottom, leaving the root intact.
Peel back the outer skin, pulling it
toward the stem, and form it into
a "plume."

Cut four 12-inch squares of aluminum foil and place 1 onion on each,
cut-side down. Pull up the edges of the
foil slightly and place ¼ cup of the veal
stock around each onion. Place 2 thyme
sprigs and 1 rosemary sprig around each
onion, add 2 pieces of butter, and sprinkle with salt, pepper, and 1 tablespoon
of the sugar. Gather the foil up around
each onion, completely enclosing the
"plume." Place the onions in a shallow
baking pan, and bake for 40 to 50
minutes, or until they are very tender.

To make the vinaigrette: In a medium
bowl, combine the garlic, tomatoes,
chives, and chive blossoms. Add the salt
and pepper and whisk in the olive oil
and vinegar.

To serve: Open the foil packets and
place 1 onion in the center of each serving plate. Pour the juices from the foil
into the vinaigrette, whisk, and adjust
the seasoning. Spoon 4 pools of vinaigrette around each onion and garnish
with chive petals between the pools.

DEBRA PONZEK
Montrachet, New York, New York

Debra Ponzek had some advance training in presentation before
coming into the culinary field: She spent two years studying engineer-
ing at Boston University before deciding the restaurant kitchen was
where she really wanted to be.

"My food is modern French," Ponzek declares. "It's not typically
classic, but it is based on French technique. I favor bold seasonings
and enjoy lots of herbs in my dishes." She further describes her
cooking as "more modern than classical, and more Provençal and
Mediterranean, with lighter sauces, broths and vinaigrettes."

Ponzek, who at age twenty-eight was selected as one of *Food &
Wine* magazine's Ten Best New American Chefs, switched her school
when she switched her major, trading BU for the CIA. After graduation in 1984, she followed up on her Institute externship by working at
the Tarragon Tree in Chatham, New Jersey, not too far from her native
Morristown. It wasn't long before she moved into a chef position at
Toto, a steakhouse in Summit, New Jersey.

Eventually, practice did make perfect, and Ponsek was ready when
opportunity knocked, in the form of Drew Nieporent and his restaurant
Montrachet in Manhattan's TriBeCa neighborhood. Beginning as sous-
chef in 1986 and rising to chef ten months after that, Ponzek blossomed at Montrachet, gathering the attention of diners and restaurant
critics alike.

She soon received the *Food & Wine* recognition, was selected as
Chef of the Year by the Chefs in America Association, and was chosen
Rising Chef of the Year by the James Beard Foundation. Ponzek took
particular satisfaction in receiving the prestigious Moreau Award,
becoming the first American so honored.

SCOTT CHEN
Empress of China, Houston, Texas

Scott Chen is proud of the menu he serves in Houston's Empress of China, but he is every bit as proud of his wine list. Empress of China's list showcases no fewer than 850 labels, with more than twenty thousand French and California wines in the cellar.

Most diners would recognize this bounty as almost unheard of in a Chinese restaurant. When forced to apply a name, however, Chen calls his cooking "Franco-Chinese Pacific Rim," so all the usual bets are off. He has worked for several years to combine the pure flavors of the Pacific Rim with a decidedly French influence, while defying virtually all the stereotypes of Chinese cuisine.

A native of Taiwan, Chen began his career at the Taipei Hilton after college and military service. He came to the United States in 1980 and spent five years working in restaurants in San Francisco, Los Angeles, New York, and Houston, all the while expanding his knowledge of world cuisine. He opened Empress of China in 1985, emphasizing nouvelle Chinese dishes – all natural, low calorie, and low cholesterol. It was "East meets West" food all the way, and that was good enough for Scott Chen.

Then the wine boom hit town. Suddenly, every fine diner in Houston was spending hours each week reading about, talking about, and tasting wines. Chen was one of them, studying on his own and also hosting tastings at Empress of China. The restaurant's wine list grew with each tasting, with each book he read, and with each excited report shared by a regular patron.

Along the way, Chen's cooking began to evolve toward dishes better suited to fine wines. The French influence on Chen's cuisine grew, as did the broadest outlines of Pacific Rim cooking.

The James Beard Foundation, for whom Chen has cooked several dinners, praised the chef in its publications. "His unique Franco-Asian cuisine left diners in awe," a food writer for the Foundation said. "His striking presentations, startling flavor combinations, and cross-cultural wine pairings defied every stereotype."

While gaining this kind of praise, Chen is active in seeking approval for his cooking from both the American Heart Association and the Pritikin movement. At the same time he also greatly values his membership in the Confrérie de la Chaîne des Rôtisseurs, L'Ordre Mondial des Gustateurs and the Palm Beach, Florida, chapter of the Brotherhood of Knights of the Wine, which has dubbed him a Master Knight.

Lobster with Avocado and Tangy Honey Sauce

Scott Chen
Empress of China
Houston, Texas

There's a clear blending of Asian delicacy with Southwestern flare in this starter of lobster tails with a corn salsa and a sweet-hot sauce.

Serves 4

Four 4-ounce lobster tails
Salt for sprinkling

Tangy Honey Sauce
½ cup honey
1 tablespoon hot mustard
1 tablespoon fresh lemon juice
1 tablespoon olive oil
1 teaspoon sugar

Corn Salsa
½ cup cooked corn kernels
½ cup finely diced white onion
1 large tomato, peeled, seeded, and finely chopped (see page 234)
½ cup chopped fresh cilantro
2 fresh jalapeño chilies, seeded and minced
1 tablespoon fresh lemon juice
Salt to taste

Garnish
1 ripe avocado
2 tablespoons heavy (whipping) cream
4 fresh dill sprigs

To prepare the lobster: Preheat the oven to 400°F. Place the lobster tails on a lightly greased baking sheet and sprinkle lightly with salt. Bake for 15 minutes, or until the meat is opaque. Immediately plunge the lobster into ice water to chill, then remove the meat from the shell, cut into medium chunks, and set aside.

To make the sauce: Combine all of the sauce ingredients in a medium bowl and whisk to mix. Place the sauce in a squeeze bottle and set aside.

To make the salsa: In a medium bowl, combine the corn, onion, tomato, cilantro, and jalapeños. Season with the lemon juice and salt. Set aside.

To serve: Place a 3-inch-diameter ring mold in the center of each of 4 serving plates. Peel, halve, and seed the avocado. Trim all 4 sides of each half, making a rectangular shape. Cut each half into lengthwise slices and arrange in an overlapping circle around the sides of each mold. Place a lobster tail in the center of the avocado circle and top with a spoonful of the corn salsa. Drizzle the salad with the honey sauce, then make decorative circles of additional sauce around the edge of the plates. Garnish the top of the lobster with a sprig of dill. Serve at room temperature.

Lobster with Avocado and Tangy Honey Sauce; *Scott Chen, Empress of China*

Rabbit Ravioli in a Potato Crust with Red Pepper Oil

Jean-Georges Vongerichten
JoJo's/Vong
New York, New York

The filling is rabbit confit, and the "pasta" is paper-thin slices of potato. Fried until crisp and golden, the Asian-style ravioli are served with a vinaigrette made with bell peppers.

Serves 8

Rabbit Confit

1 carrot, peeled
1 celery stalk
1 leek split lengthwise, washed, and outer tough green leaves removed
1 onion
3 garlic cloves
2 legs and 2 loins of rabbit
Salt to taste
1 tablespoon cracked black pepper
½ cup dry white wine
1 bunch fresh thyme (about ½ ounce) separated into sprigs
2 cups olive oil

Red Bell Pepper Oil

2 large red bell peppers, seeded, deribbed, and coarsely chopped
½ cup water (optional)
2 tablespoons sherry vinegar
¼ cup olive oil
¼ teaspoon kosher salt

Ravioli

2 large Idaho potaotes, peeled
¼ cup olive oil
2 eggs, beaten with 1 tablespoon water
1 cup clarified butter (see page 223)
½ cup peanut oil
Kosher salt to taste

Herb Salad

1 head frisée
½ bunch arugula
1 tablespoon *each* snipped fresh chives and fresh dill
1 tablespoon *each* minced tarragon, fresh parsley, and fresh chervil

5 tablespoons olive oil
3 tablespoons sherry vinegar
Salt and freshly ground black pepper to taste

To prepare the rabbit: Preheat the oven to 350°F. Finely chop the carrot, celery, leek, onion, and garlic, and place into a 4-inch-deep baking pan. Add the rabbit, season with salt and pepper, add the wine and thyme, then cover with olive oil. Seal the pan with aluminum foil and bake for 2 hours, or until the meat is tender.

Remove the rabbit from the pan to cool, then remove the meat from the bone and coarsely chop. Drain the oil and juices from the vegetables, then remove the thyme and discard. Mix together the rabbit meat with vegetables and season with salt and pepper. Set aside. This mixture may be covered and refrigerated for up to 24 hours.

To prepare the pepper oil: Put the peppers through an electric juice extractor. Or, place the peppers in a food processor or blender with the ½ cup water and process to a puree. This should yield about 1½ cups of juice. Place the juice in a small saucepan over medium-high heat and cook to reduce the liquid to 1 cup. Strain this syrup through a fine-meshed strainer, add the vinegar and oil, season with salt, and set aside.

To make the ravioli: Preheat the oven to 450°F. Cut the potatoes lengthwise into paper-thin slices using a mandoline or V-slicer. Line a baking sheet with parchment paper or aluminum foil, brush the paper or foil with olive oil, and lay the potato slices on the pan in a single layer. Brush the slices with olive oil. Cover with another sheet of paper or foil and set another baking sheet on top to keep the potatoes flat as they bake.

Bake for 3 to 5 minutes, or until soft, but not colored. Remove the potato slices and drain and blot with paper towels. Immediately begin to make and fry the ravioli to prevent the potatoes from discoloring.

Brush the potato slices lightly with the beaten eggs. Put 1 mounded teaspoon of the rabbit mixture on one

half of each potato slice, fold the potato over, and press firmly around the edges to seal.

In a large sauté pan or skillet over medium-high heat, heat the butter and oil until fragrant. Drop in the ravioli in batches and fry, turning once, for 2 to 3 minutes, or until golden and crispy. Remove from the oil with a slotted spoon and drain on paper towels. Sprinkle with salt while the ravioli are still warm.

To make the salad: Use scissors to cut the frisée and arugula into 1-inch pieces. Place the greens in a large bowl with the herbs, and toss with the olive oil, vinegar, salt and pepper.

To serve: Place some of the herb salad on each serving plate. Overlap several ravioli along the edge of the plate and spoon some of the red pepper oil onto the plate.

Note: *The ravioli can be made in advance and reheated in a preheated 325°F. oven for 2 to 3 minutes just before serving.*

Italian Flat Bread;
Francesco Ricchi, i Ricchi

Italian Flat Bread

Francesco Ricchi
i Ricchi
Washington, D.C.

Here's a reminder (as though we needed one) that sometimes the simplest things are the best. One of the breads is covered with tomato while the other is left plain, for variation in taste as well as color.

Makes 48 pieces

Sponge
3 packages active dry yeast
1 cup warm (105° to 115°F) water
2 cups unbleached all-purpose flour

Dough
2 cups warm (105° to 115°F) water
Sponge, above
3 tablespoons olive oil
1 teaspoon salt
3 to 4 cups unbleached all-purpose flour

Topping
Kosher salt for sprinkling
Extra-virgin olive oil for drizzling
2 ripe plum (Roma) tomatoes, peeled,
   seeded and thinly sliced
1 teaspoon dried oregano

To make the sponge: Stir the yeast into the warm water, and let sit until foamy, about 10 minutes. Place the flour in a large bowl and, using a wooden spoon, stir the yeast mixture into the flour, mixing very well. Cover the bowl with a towel and let sit in a warm place overnight.

To make the dough: Add the warm water to the sponge, mixing with a wooden spoon. Stir in the oil and salt, then stir in the flour 1/2 cup at a time. Turn the dough out onto a floured surface and knead for 7 to 8 minutes, or until smooth. Divide the dough into 2 pieces, form each into a loaf, cover with a towel, and let rise in a warm place for 20 minutes.

Preheat the oven to 350°F. Place each loaf onto a 13-by-17-inch baking sheet and roll it with a rolling pin to fill the pan. Cover again and let stand for 20 minutes.

Final preparation: Using your fingers, press evenly spaced holes into the surface of the dough and sprinkle with kosher salt. Drizzle olive oil all over the surface. Arrange the tomato slices in a single layer on one pan of dough. Sprinkle the tomatoes with oregano, then lightly sprinkle with kosher salt and drizzle with more olive oil. Bake both breads for 30 minutes, or until light golden brown. Cut into triangles or rectangles and serve warm.

FRANCESCO RICCHI
i Ricchi, Washington, D.C.

Francesco Ricchi admits that his cooking style has become slightly more complex since coming to this country in 1988. But Ricchi's strength remains the pure, country tastes of his native Tuscany.

The chef, who runs Ristorante i Ricchi in Washington, D.C., with his American wife Christianne, grew up around great cooking in the town of Cercina just outside Florence. The family had for generations served the *cucina rustica* for which Francesco would become famous.

When he and Christianne staked their claim in the nation's capital, it was Ricchi's goal to recreate the warmth of his family's personal service as well as the wonders of Tuscan cooking. Within a very short time, two important visitors verified that they were doing a terrific job. George Bush visited i Ricchi shortly after he took the presidential oath of office in January 1989. And *Washington Post* restaurant critic Phyllis Richmond dined there also, later declaring that nowhere in the United States had she tasted such authentic Tuscan cuisine.

For Americans familiar only with the red-sauced standards of southern Italy, and even for those who know the buttery-lemony classics of northern Italy, it's a safe statement that Tuscan food tastes like neither. It uses tomatoes, as well as butter and lemon, and stresses the hearty flavors of roasted meats, savory broths and soups, filled pastas, and coarse-textured breads.

Awards have followed Ricchi's dedication to his special region of Italy, including *Esquire* magazine's Best New Restaurant honor in 1989, and a listing by *Food & Wine* as one of the 25 finest restaurants in North America. In the spirit of Francesco Ricchi, Washingtonians keep things simpler than that: They call it the city's best Italian restaurant year after year.

HUBERT KELLER

Fleur de Lys, San Francisco, California

Chef Hubert Keller's career has been a tour of the cooking of his native France, a tour whose souvenirs he is happy to share with diners at his San Francisco restaurant. It's important to note here that in French, *souvenirs* are not mere trinkets from the road but profound memories.

Since opening Fleur de Lys with Maurice Rouas in 1986, Keller's French cuisine has drawn wide praise as the best in San Francisco. Those who've shared this opinion have included John Mariani in *Esquire*, Bryan Miller in the *New York Times* and Michael Bauer in *Food & Wine*.

If the student is, to some degree, a measure of the master, then both Keller and his teachers have much for which to be grateful. His training began at the École Hôtelière in Strasbourg, then continued under the Haeberlin brothers at the Auberge de l'Ill in Alsace. After additional training with Paul Bocuse at Collonges, Keller spent time with pastry expert Gaston Lenôtre in Paris and cooked aboard the *Mermoz*, one of the stars of the French Paquet Line. Experience at the Domaine de Châteauneuf in Nans les Pins led to an assignment with Provençal celebrity Roger Verge at Moulin de Mougins.

Famed restaurant followed famed restaurant for Keller, including stints at the Hotel Negresco in Nice and the Hotel Prieuré in Saumur. Finally, though, Verge called the chef back into the family to open his La Cuisine du Soleil in São Paulo, Brazil. After two years in this very different world, Keller moved to San Francisco to manage the kitchen at Verge's Sutter 500. When Keller opened Fleur de Lys with Rouas, it too was on Sutter Street.

Though he can thank a lifetime of great chefs for teaching him so many things, today Keller considers Verge his mentor. It was under his influence that Keller developed his own style of combining the classics of French cuisine with the sun-struck foods of Provence.

Corn Pancake with Thinly Sliced Salmon, Caviar, and Watercress Sauce

Hubert Keller
Fleur de Lys
San Francisco, California

What an elegant surprise! Each corn pancake holds a treasure of fresh salmon and caviar, and is beautifully balanced by a vivid green watercress sauce.

Serves 6

1 eight-ounce piece fresh Norwegian
  salmon, cut from the tail end
3 ounces golden sturgeon or
  salmon caviar
Salt and freshly ground black pepper
  to taste

Corn Pancakes
4 ears fresh corn
3 eggs
2 tablespoons flour
1 teaspoon salt
½ teaspoon freshly ground black pepper

Watercress Sauce
2 cups firmly packed watercress leaves
  (about 2 bunches)
3 cups water
Salt to taste
3 tablespoons unsalted butter
2 tablespoons minced shallots
½ cup dry white wine
½ cup heavy (whipping) cream
2 tablespoons vegetable oil

Garnish
18 asparagus tips, blanched for
  30 seconds
White and black sesame seeds, toasted
  (see page 236)
2 large tomatoes
2 tablespoons sour cream
1 tablespoon minced fresh chives

To prepare the salmon: Run your finger over the salmon meat from head to tail end to find any small hidden bones and remove them before slicing. Using a very thin sharp knife and slicing toward the tail end, cut 6 thin lengthwise slices of salmon. Spoon 1 generous teaspoon of caviar on one half of each piece of salmon and fold the opposite half over. Season the salmon lightly with salt and pepper on both sides. Set aside and keep cool until ready to cook.

To make the pancake batter: In a large pot of lightly salted boiling water, cook the corn for 3 minutes, then drain and cut kernels from the cobs. You should have about 2 cups of corn. Place the corn, eggs, flour, salt, and pepper in a blender or food processor and process until coarsely pureed, leaving some bits of corn kernels. Pour the batter into a bowl and set aside.

To make the sauce: In a medium saucepan over high heat, bring the water to a boil, lightly salt, and cook the watercress until tender, about 3 minutes. Drain and reserve ½ cup of the cooking liquid. Plunge the leaves into the ice water to stop the process. Drain again and squeeze tightly in a cotton towel to remove all of the moisture. There should be about ½ cup of cooked watercress.

In a small saucepan over medium-high heat, melt the butter and cook the shallots until translucent, about 1½ minutes. Add the wine, stir, and cook to reduce until very little liquid remains. Add the cream to the pan and simmer for 5 minutes, then add the watercress and cook an additional 5 minutes. Pour the mixture into a blender or food processor and blend until the sauce is completely smooth. Return the sauce to the pan to keep warm.

To cook the pancakes: Heat a large sauté pan or skillet over medium heat, brush the surface of the pan with vegetable oil and spoon 1½ tablespoons of the pancake batter into the pan. Set 1 salmon packet on top of the batter and spoon more batter on top to cover the salmon. Repeat to make 2 more pancakes. Cook until the pancakes are a golden brown color on one side, about 1½ minutes. Before the pancakes are set, push in the edges with a spatula to make each a uniform "cake" shape.

Turn and cook the pancakes on the second side until brown, about 1½ minutes. The total cooking time will be about 3 minutes. Place the cooked pancakes in a 200°F oven and repeat to cook the remaining pancakes.

To serve: Check the watercress sauce and, if it is too thick, thin with a bit of the liquid reserved from poaching the watercress. Dip the tip of the asparagus into the sesame seeds to coat. Core and cut each tomato into 8 wedges, then slide each wedge to form a fan.

Place 1 pancake on each serving plate and surround with the asparagus tips and tomato fans. Place 1 teaspoonful of sour cream on each pancake and additional caviar on top the cream. Spoon watercress sauce around the cake between each vegetable and garnish with a sprinkling of the chives.

Corn Pancake with Thinly Sliced Salmon, Caviar, and Watercress Sauce; *Hubert Keller, Fleur de Lys*

Ballottine of Sole Sauce Émeraude

Ballottine of Sole Sauce Émeraude; *André Soltner, Lutèce*

André Soltner
Lutèce
New York, New York

In this classic preparation, the white flesh and mild flavor of Dover sole is combined with the pink flesh and assertive taste of salmon. The dish is served cold, with an emerald-colored sauce.

Serves 8

9 Dover sole fillets (about 3 pounds), skinned
3 eggs
½ cup heavy (whipping) cream
1 teaspoon salt
Freshly ground black pepper to taste
One 8-ounce salmon fillet, cut into three 4-by ½-by-½-inch "fingers"
1 bay leaf
2 fresh thyme sprigs

Émeraude Sauce
½ cup fresh parsley sprigs, minced
½ cup spinach leaves, finely chopped
½ cup watercress leaves, finely chopped
1½ cups homemade mayonnaise prepared with salt, pepper, and cayenne pepper

Garnish
Carrot curls
Tomato roses

To make the mousseline: Cut 3 of the sole fillets into small chunks and place them in a blender or food processor with the eggs, cream, salt, and pepper. Process for 1½ to 2 minutes, or until the mixture is completely smooth. Cover and refrigerate the mousseline if not using immediately.

Using the side of a cleaver, gently flatten the remaining 6 fillets until they are of a thin, even thickness. Spread some of the mousseline on a fillet, top with another fillet, and spread again with a thin layer of mousseline. Add one of the salmon fingers and roll the entire assembly into a tight coil. Spread some mousseline on each end of the roll and set aside. Repeat until all of the fish is rolled into 3 cylinders.

Wet a clean cloth kitchen towel, squeeze out all of the excess moisture, and spread it on a work surface. Place a sheet of parchment paper on top of the towel and lightly brush it with olive oil. Arrange the cylinders of sole on the paper end to end across the narrow edge of the paper, fitted snugly together without any space between them. Using the edges of the towel and paper to push, roll the fish tightly, then wrap it inside the paper and cloth and tie the ends and middle of the bundle with cotton string.

To cook the ballottine: Use a deep sauté pan or skillet wide enough to hold the ballottine without bending. Place the pan over high heat, and place the ballottine into it with enough lightly salted water to cover the ballottine. Add the bay leaf and thyme, and when the water has come to a boil, lower the heat and gently simmer for 30 minutes. Remove the ballottine from the water and drain. Cut the strings and, while it is still encased in the paper and towel, roll the ballottine tighter. Retie it in the same 3 places and place the ballottine back into the poaching liquid for 2 hours, then refrigerate overnight.

To prepare the sauce: Wrap the chopped herbs tightly in a cloth kitchen towel and twist it tightly until all of juices are extracted. In a small bowl, stir the juices into the mayonnaise and let it sit to intensify flavor.

To serve: Unwrap the chilled ballottine and slice into ½-inch-thick slices. Place 2 slices on each serving plate, surround with some of the sauce, and garnish with carrot curls and tomato roses.

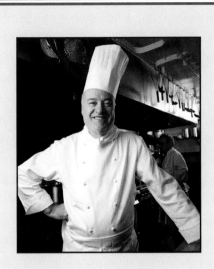

ANDRÉ SOLTNER
Lutèce, New York, New York

For thirty-five years, André Soltner has been a chef with a message for those breaking into his profession. The greatest achievement in cooking is making food taste like the world's best version of itself.

First-time diners at Soltner's Lutèce find themselves left speechless by the flavor of the least dramatic things. In this chef's hands, roast chicken, tomato soup, or country paté can pack a wallop that sets a standard for those dishes for the rest of the diner's life. Most often, it's a standard that is never equalled.

Lutèce has, over the decades, been a tale of two philosophies, both of which have been successful. Its original owner, who hired Soltner as chef, believed in high prices for high prices' sake. The goal was simple: to be New York's most expensive restaurant, a mission that, of course, required considerable vigilance and a certain amount of pretension.

When Soltner became the owner of Lutèce in 1972, everything changed except the glorious food. Pretension went out the window, with the chef's wife Simone personally greeting and seating diners. The prices reflected the quality of the food, yet there was absolutely no effort to charge more for the sake of charging more.

Today, Soltner has sold Lutèce but remains its master on a consulting basis. It still turns away about thousands of disappointed diners a year, including national and international luminaries.

Other than cooking at Lutèce and cooking at home, Soltner's other passion is skiing. He found his way onto skis while working at restaurants in Switzerland. His abilities propelled him into the French Alpine troops when it was time for military service. He kept his cooking skills to himself, however, listing his profession as cabinetmaker. When Soltner took up a chef's ladle again, it would not be for army food.

STEPHAN PYLES
Star Canyon, Dallas, Texas

"I've taken the ingredients and recipes inherent in the many different cultures and historical eras of Texas and created original dishes," says fifth-generation Texan Stephan Pyles, making it all sound simple.

At Star Canyon in Dallas, Pyles is still creating and still capitalizing. Who better to do so than the chef *Bon Appétit* praised for "almost single-handedly changing the cooking scene in Texas"? Not bad for a kid who started by helping out at his family's Truck Stop Cafe in West Texas at the age of eight.

For nine glittering years, Pyles won accolades from all over the world for his then-signature restaurant in Dallas, Routh Street Cafe. For six years, he reveled too in praise for its casual spinoff, Baby Routh. He even opened Goodfellow's and Tejas way up north in Minneapolis, the home of his partner.

For all of that, in January 1993, Pyles dissolved the partnership. That meant closing Routh Street and selling his interest in the three remaining places. It was time for a change, and the seven-thousand-square-foot showpiece called Star Canyon was it.

As designed by Wilson & Associates, the new place features a 130-seat dining room, a 50-seat outside patio, a 30-seat private dining room and culinary center, a ten-seat wine room and an eight-seat counter surrounding the exposed kitchen. It also features a Pyles' vision of new Texas cuisine: part cowboy, part southern, and part Latino and Southwestern. And Pyles couldn't be happier.

"This is the ultimate restaurant for me," he says. "It is the culmination of my many years and all my experiences in the hospitality industry."

A strange and wondrous journey it has been. From that first gig at the Truck Stop Cafe, Pyles went on to earn a degree in music while cooking in his spare time. Spare time evolved toward full time during a post-graduation trip to France, which introduced Pyles to such masters as Alain Chapel and Roger Verge.

Pyles made his way to Dallas in 1980, working in a series of small restaurants while perfecting his technique in his "leisure" hours. Then he happened on a job as chef's assistant at the Great Chefs of France Cooking School at the Robert Mondavi Winery in Napa. There he worked closely with Michel Guerard, the Troisgros brothers, and George Blanc.

Tamale Tart with Roasted–Garlic Custard and Crabmeat

Stephan Pyles
Star Canyon
Dallas, Texas

In this variation on the classic tamale, a dough very similar to tamale dough is used to make the tart shell. The tart is then steamed and served with pico de gallo.

Serves 8

Ancho Chili Puree
4 ancho chilies
1 cup hot water
1 tablespoon olive oil
Pinch of salt

Roasted Red Pepper Puree
1 large red bell pepper, roasted, peeled, and seeded (see page 235)
1 tablespoon olive oil
Pinch of salt

Tart Dough
2 cups masa harina
   (available in Latino markets)
1/4 cup yellow cornmeal
2 teaspoons salt
2 teaspoons ground cumin
1/4 teaspoon cayenne pepper
6 tablespoons vegetable shortening
6 tablespoons Ancho Chili Puree, above

Roasted Garlic Custard
2 teaspoons olive oil
4 large garlic cloves
1 1/2 cups heavy (whipping) cream
2 egg yolks
3/4 teaspoon salt
Freshly ground white pepper to taste

Crabmeat Topping
2 tablespoons olive oil
1/4 cup diced onion
10 ounces lump crabmeat, carefully picked over to remove shell fragments
1/2 cup diced mixed red and yellow tomato
2 tablespoons minced fresh cilantro
2 serrano chilies, seeded and minced
2 teaspoons fresh lime juice

Garnish
Pico de Gallo (recipe follows)
Fresh cilantro sprigs

To make the chili puree: Soak the ancho chilies in hot water for 1 hour or longer, until they have softened. Strain and reserve the soaking liquid. Remove the stems, seeds, and ribs of the chilies and place the chilies in a blender. Add the oil, salt, and ¼ cup of the soaking liquid and puree until a thick sauce is formed. Remove from the blender and set aside.

To make the red pepper puree: Place the roasted pepper in a blender, add the oil and salt, and puree until smooth; set aside.

To make the tart dough: In a medium bowl, combine the masa harina, cornmeal, salt, cumin, and cayenne pepper. In the bowl of an electric mixer, whip the shortening on medium-high speed until light and fluffy, about 1 minute. Gradually add the dry ingredients and continue to mix until well blended. With the machine running, add the chili and pepper purees and mix until the mixture begins to hold together.

Transfer the dough to a work surface, press it together, and knead once or twice or until the dough is smooth. Shape the dough into a log and cut it into 8 equal pieces. Press each portion into a 3-by-1-inch tart pan (or use one 8-inch pan with a false bottom), making a ¼-inch thickness on the bottom and pressing the dough up the sides of the pan(s).

To make the custard: Preheat the oven to 300°F. In a small sauté pan or skillet over high heat, heat the olive oil and add the garlic. Place the pan in the oven and roast until the garlic is golden brown, about 15 minutes. Place the garlic and oil in a blender and process until smooth.

In a medium saucepan over medium heat, cook the cream until it is reduced to 1 cup. Add the reduced cream to the blender and blend for 1 minute. In a medium bowl, beat the egg yolks, then drizzle in the garlic-cream mixture, whisking constantly. Season with the salt and white pepper.

Fill the shell(s) three-fourths full with the custard and wrap the entire tart pan(s) tightly in plastic wrap. Fit a trivet and a bamboo steamer or a metal steamer basket in a wok or large pan of simmering water and place the tart(s) in the steamer. Cover and steam until the custard is set, about 20 minutes. Make sure the water is simmering, not boiling; if the heat is too high the mixture may curdle.

To make the crabmeat topping: In a medium sauté pan or skillet over high heat, heat the olive oil until just smoking. Add the onion and sauté for 1 minute. Add the remaining ingredients and heat through, about 2 minutes.

To serve: Remove the tart(s) from the steamer and remove the plastic wrap. Remove small tarts from their pans and set one in the center of each serving plate, or cut the large tart into 8 wedges.

Spoon a portion of the crabmeat topping onto each serving and garnish with pico de gallo. Tuck a few cilantro sprigs under the edge of each tart and serve immediately.

Pico de Gallo
Makes 1½ cups

1 tomato, peeled, seeded, and cut into
  ¼-inch dice (see page 234)
½ white onion, cut into ¼-inch dice
1 tablespoon minced serrano or jalapeño
  chili (with or without the seeds)
1 tablespoon fresh lime juice
1 tablespoon chopped fresh cilantro
1 tablespoon olive oil
1 teaspoon minced garlic
Salt to taste

In a small bowl, combine all ingredients and let sit for about 30 minutes before serving.

Tamale Tart with Roasted-Garlic Custard and Crabmeat; *Stephan Pyles, Star Canyon*

Corn Flan with Smoked Salmon

▪▪▪▪▪▪▪▪▪▪▪▪▪▪

David Burke
Park Avenue Cafe
New York, New York

Corn is a popular vegetable among young American chefs, because of its indigenous roots and also because of its versatility. In this recipe, a corn custard is served in an egg shell and topped with smoked salmon.

Serves 6

Corn Flan

¼ cup fresh or frozen corn kernels
1 cup chicken stock (see page 228)
½ cup heavy (whipping) cream
½ teaspoon kosher salt
12 eggs
Freshly ground black pepper to taste

Salmon Topping

1 tablespoon butter
Reserved corn kernels from flan, above
¼ cup reserved stock from flan, above

4 ounces smoked salmon, cut into thin slivers
¼ cup snipped fresh chives
1 tablespoon coriander seeds, lightly crushed
¼ teaspoon ground cumin
Salt and freshly ground black pepper to taste

6 Herbed Potato Chips (recipe follows) or 12 toast triangles for garnish

To make the flan: Into each of 2 small saucepans, place half of the corn kernels. Add the stock to one of the pans and the cream and salt to the other. Place both pans over medium heat and poach the kernels for 4 to 5 minutes. Set aside.

Remove a small circle from the small end of each eggshell with an egg cutter, emptying 2 of the eggs into a medium bowl and the remaining eggs into a container with a lid. Reserve the 10 eggs for another use. Clean the edges of the eggshells of any shell fragments and set them in a cardboard egg carton that has been placed into a deep baking pan.

Preheat the oven to 325°F. Strain the corn from the stock and add about ½ cup of the stock to corn and cream mixture; reserve the remaining stock. Puree the corn and cream in a blender or food processor, then slowly pour the hot liquid into the eggs, whisking constantly. Strain the mixture and extract all of the juices from the kernels; reserve the kernels. Pour the strained mixture into a small pitcher and carefully fill the eggshells three-fourths full. Pour 1 inch of boiling water into the baking pan, cover the pan with aluminum foil, and place the eggshells in the oven to bake until set, about 45 minutes. Or, place the baking pan over a medium-low burner and simmer on top of the stove for about 15 minutes.

To make the salmon topping: In a small sauté pan or skillet over medium heat, melt the butter and add the reserved corn kernels and about ¼ cup of the reserved stock. Add the salmon, chives, coriander, and cumin, tossing just until heated through. Season with salt and freshly ground black pepper.

Corn Flan with Smoked Salmon; *David Burke, Park Avenue Cafe*

To serve: Place each eggshell in an egg cup and spoon some of the salmon topping into each shell. Serve each with 1 herbed potato chip or 2 toast triangles.

Herbed potato chips
Makes 12 chips
1 large unpeeled baking potato
2 tablespoons olive oil
6 whole chive stems, plus 1 tablespoon snipped fresh chives.

Preheat the oven to 425°F. Line a baking sheet with parchment paper or grease it. On a mandoline or V-slicer, slice the potato lengthwise into 12 very thin slices. Place the slices on the prepared pan and brush the slices lightly with olive oil. Sprinkle the snipped chives over the potato slices and arrange one chive stem on each. Top with another slice of potato and brush again lightly with olive oil.

Cover the potatoes with a sheet of parchment paper and set another baking pan on top, or grease the pan and place it on top, and bake until the potatoes are crisp and browned, about 20 minutes.

DAVID BURKE
Park Avenue Cafe, New York, New York

David Burke is sometimes called New York's most imitated chef, but he takes the honor with a grain of sea salt. His creativity is a natural process, involving his daily tasks, his mood on any given day, and not infrequently suggestions from his kitchen and service staffs.

"Occasionally, I see my dishes being duplicated," he observes. "Garnishes, ideas and techniques. And that's all right with me. It happens with other chefs too." And the creativity itself? "Well, I get an idea, I come up with a style, and one thing leads to the next."

At Park Avenue Grill, which Burke created with veteran New York restaurateur Alan Stillman, one thing has been leading to another since the sophisticated American country restaurant opened its doors in early 1992. Burke has even produced the first cut of fish ever trademarked, the signature "swordfish chop."

For all the imitation of this dish or that, what most chefs would like to duplicate is Burke's experience cooking in some of the most distinguished kitchens in the United States and in Europe.

After graduation from the Culinary Institute of America, Burke cooked in restaurants in Burgundy and southwest France. Later highlights included service as personal chef to shipping magnate Stolt Neilson in Oslo, Norway; two years as sous-chef at La Crémaillière in Banksville, New York; and work as a seafood chef for New York's Hotel Plaza Athénée.

After a stint at Larry Forgione's highly regarded River Cafe, Burke returned to Europe, where his work history reads like a tour of the continent's best restaurants. The study of pastry with Lenôtre in Paris gave way to cooking with Troisgros in Roanne, with Marc Meneau at L'Espérance, with Georges Blanc in Vonnas, at Maison Blanche with José Lampreia, at Fauchon and Moulin de la Vierge.

With all this experience in his pocket, Burke was ready to run the kitchen at River Cafe, which he did until he and Stillman opened Park Avenue Cafe.

By the way, the swordfish chop was born when Burke noticed that the piece of trout that is attached to the collarbone looks like a miniature veal chop. This same piece, on a swordfish, is the same size as a veal chop.

So a legend, and a trademark, were born. Like the famous tagged duck at Tour d'Argent in Paris, each Park Avenue Cafe swordfish chop is numbered. Now, if only Burke could find a way to sign his creation, he would have a true collectible.

GEORGE MORRONE
Aqua, San Francisco, California

Since the day he opened Aqua with Michael Mina, chef George Morrone has been on a roll. House-smoked salmon, for instance, are rolled like cannelloni with dressed baby greens bursting out of each end. Trout is rolled around chanterelles, encased in a crisp potato crust.

Not everything at Aqua is rolled, of course. But everything has earned the excited applause of San Francisco. Michael Bauer of the *San Francisco Chronicle* weighs in with a full four stars. The city's mayor chose to have his wedding reception at Aqua, a sure sign that the restaurant has arrived.

Morrone himself arrived from his native New Jersey by way of New York. He did a youthful apprenticeship at a neighborhood bakery before moving on to the Culinary Institute of America. Hyde Park was close enough to Manhattan to land him a job at Charles Palmer's River Cafe.

After three years of gazing at New York's skyline from the shores of the East River, Morrone attracted the attention of Bradley Odgen at San Francisco's Campton Place Hotel. There, Morrone's classical training from the CIA was a good match with Ogden's innovative, regional American style.

All of age twenty-six, on the strength of his work at Campton Place, Morrone was tapped to serve as executive chef at the posh Hotel Bel-Air in Los Angeles. Paul Zuest, the demanding general manager of that property, had had to hire and fire three top chefs before finding the right one in Morrone.

At the end of five years at the Bel-Air, Morrone's heart called him home. From the day of its opening, Aqua has been at the top of the city's seafood restaurant list for the creativity of its cuisine and the beauty of its high-ceilinged dining room.

From the mussel soufflé to the Hawaiian swordfish coated with pepper and served with pancetta-wrapped shrimp and port wine sauce Morrone was, until his departure, a force that helped Aqua do swimmingly.

Tuna Tartare

George Morrone
Aqua
San Francisco, California

In this elegant takeoff on classic steak tartare, raw tuna is diced and molded in a ring, then topped with a quail egg yolk and served with toast triangles.

Serves 4

12 ounces sashimi-grade tuna
Salt and freshly ground white pepper
 to taste
½ cup pine nuts
4 quail eggs
8 thin slices bread, lightly toasted and
 trimmed of crust
3 garlic cloves, minced
2 red serrano, Scotch bonnet (habanero),
 or jalapeño chilies, or any combination, seeded and minced
1 plum or pear, pitted and very finely
 diced
16 fresh mint leaves, cut into fine shreds
1 tablespoon toasted sesame oil
1 tablespoon chili oil

To prepare the tuna: Trim all skin and veins from the tuna. Using a sharp knife dipped in water, slice the tuna and cut it into ¼-inch dice. Season the fish with salt and pepper and place it in a small bowl set in another bowl filled with ice. Cover and refrigerate.

Preheat the oven to 350°F. Place the pine nuts on a baking sheet and toast, shaking occasionally to brown evenly, 5 to 8 minutes. Let cool slightly, then roughly chop the nuts and set them aside.

Gently top the narrow end of each quail eggshell by cutting with a sharp, small knife. Carefully remove the top and separate each egg. Discard the white and place the yolk back into each reserved eggshell. Cut each slice of toast into 4 triangles.

To serve: Place a 2-inch-diameter stainless-steel ring mold in the center of each serving plate. Spoon one fourth of the tuna into each ring mold and press lightly with the back of a spoon. Combine the garlic and chilies. Around each mold place 3 mounds of one-fourth of the nuts, the chili mixture, and the fruit. Gently press a quail egg into the center of each serving of tuna and carefully remove the ring mold. Arrange 8 toast triangles around the edge of each plate. Sprinkle the plates with mint and drizzle with the sesame and chili oils.

Tuna Tartare; *George Morrone, Aqua*

Stone Crab Salad with Baby-Tomato Confit; *Marc Lippman, Raleigh Hotel*

Stone Crab Salad with Baby-Tomato Confit

Marc Lippman
Raleigh Hotel
Miami Beach, Florida

For many, nothing says Miami better than the sweet, succulent meat of the stone crab. The layering of red tomato with yellow makes a tropical banquet for the eyes, as does the drizzle of tomato sauce and sprinkle of snipped chives.

Serves 4

Baby Tomato Confit
8 ounces (about 20) yellow tear-drop
   tomatoes
8 ounces (about 20) red cherry tomatoes
2 bay leaves
2 small fresh rosemary sprigs
About 2 cups olive oil

Stone Crab Salad
2 pounds cooked stone crabs, or 2 cups
   fresh stone crabmeat
3 tablespoons champagne vinegar
Salt and freshly ground black pepper
   to taste
3 tablespoons snipped fresh chives
1 tablespoon fresh lime juice

Tomato Sauce
1 large tomato, peeled, seeded, and
   chopped (see page 234)
2 tablespoons fresh lime juice
Salt and freshly ground black pepper
   to taste
1/2 cup reserved oil from Baby Tomato
   Confit, above

Garnish
1/2 avocado, peeled, pitted, and diced
8 fresh chive stems, cut into 3-inch
   lengths
2 tablespoons snipped fresh chives
Roasted yellow pepper sauce, optional
   (see Note)
Fresh chive sauce, optional (see Note)

To make the confit: Preheat the oven to 200°F. Place the tomatoes in 2 small baking pans, separated by color. Divide the herbs between the pans and add oil to cover. Cover the pans tightly with aluminum foil and roast for 5 hours. Strain the oil from the roasted tomatoes through cheesecloth or a coffee filter. Remove and discard the herbs and reserve the tomatoes. Reserve the oil for the sauce.

To make the crab salad: Crack the crab claws with the back of a knife and remove all of the meat. Add the remaining ingredients. Mix with a fork and taste for seasoning. Cover and refrigerate until ready to serve.

To make the tomato sauce: Place the tomato in a blender or food processor and add the lime juice, salt, and pepper. Add the reserved oil and blend until smooth. Taste and adjust the seasoning, then set aside in a small bowl or squeeze bottle. (You will have about 1½ cups of the tomato oil left; cover and keep in a cool place for other uses.)

To serve: Place a 3-inch-diameter stainless-steel ring mold in the center of each serving plate. Place one-fourth of the red tomatoes in the bottom of each ring, add a layer of yellow tomatoes, and top with one-fourth of the crabmeat. Press down gently with the back of a spoon and remove the rings. Top each serving with diced avocado and arrange 2 chive stems on top. Drizzle some of the sauce around the edges of the plates and sprinkle with snipped chives.

Note: *The two additional sauces used to garnish the plate can be made by following the recipe for the tomato sauce. In place of the tomato, use 1 seeded large yellow bell pepper for the first sauce, and 1 cup snipped fresh chives for the second.*

MARC LIPPMAN
Raleigh Hotel, Miami Beach, Florida

Like many of his peers, Marc Lippman felt honor-bound to master the traditions of French haute cuisine before exploring his own American heritage. In his case, La Varenne in Paris provided the diploma to place beside his B.S. in hotel management from the Rochester Institute of Technology in New York.

By the time he studied at La Varenne, the chef-to-be had already worked as a line cook at the Montauk Yacht Club on Long Island and at the Plaza Hotel's famed Oak Room. He had also served as a seafood chef at El Dorado Petit in New York. After La Varenne, he could raise his sights even higher.

Lippman was selected by the Michelin-starred Apicus of Jean Pierre Vigato to complete an internship with further hands-on training. From foie gras to salmon in phyllo, Lippman mastered the mysteries of French cuisine, first at Apicus, then with J. M. Bouvier at Pavillion Montsouris and with Philippe Delacourcelle at Le Clos Morillons.

He returned to New York to serve as assistant pastry chef at Bouley, then moved on to the Hudson River Club. His province there was roasting meats, including lamb, veal, venison, and beef, and creating a meat special every day.

Then Lippman heard the song of New York's version of the south: Miami. First at the Blue Star on chic South Beach and then at the Raleigh, he worked wonders combining such south Florida foods as stone crabs with French cooking techniques. All this taste and a suntan too!

REED HEARON
LuLu, San Francisco, California

One of a new breed of diversely educated American chefs, Reed Hearon picked up his college degree before turning to the stove. And he chose to do so with a double major not known for its expediency: philosophy and mathematics.

Fresh from the University of Texas, Hearon joined Jimmy Schmidt and Michael McCarty in opening the Rattlesnake Club in Denver – an ambitious project named one of America's best new restaurants within only fourteen days of its opening.

A year after launching Rattlesnake, Hearon joined Mark Miller to start Coyote Cafe and eventually provided assistance on Miller's *Coyote Cafe Cookbook* (Ten Speed Press). Two years after taking on the Santa Fe restaurant scene, Hearon was off to San Francisco to serve as chef at the Corona Bar and Grill.

San Francisco appealed to Hearon, but he took a side trip to join Harley Baldwin for a stint at Aspen's prestigious Caribou Club. Back in the Bay Area in January 1993, Hearon and partner Louise Clement opened the doors of LuLu.

Located near the dynamic Yerba Buena Center for the Arts, LuLu's Riviera cuisine, dramatic interior, and lively crowd earned the place rave reviews as well as a loyal local following. His success inspired Hearon to write his own cookbook, *Salsa* (Chronicle Books). After all, with five to seven hundred diners each day, he had a built-in readership. Within three months of publication, *Salsa* went back for a second printing.

Hearon and Clement have since collaborated on new restaurants as distinct as Cafe Marimba in San Francisco and Burlingame, California, (featuring the chef's first love, authentic Mexican cuisine from Oaxaca and the Yucatán), and LuLu Bis, next door to LuLu and a calmer counterpart to the bigger restaurant's bustle.

Fresh-cracked Conch with Vanilla-Rum Sauce and Spicy Black Bean Salad

Mark Militello
Mark's Place
Miami, Florida

The conch is pounded for tenderness before it is delicately fried and served with a *picante* salad of black beans and mango. The vanilla-rum sauce is a decidedly tropical treat.

Serves 6

Black Bean Salad
¼ cup dried black beans
1 garlic clove
1 tomato, peeled, seeded; and finely diced (see page 234)
1 mango, peeled, seeded, and finely diced
3 green onions, thinly sliced, including some green
½ Scotch bonnet (habanero) chili, seeded and minced
3 tablespoons extra-virgin olive oil
2 tablespoons fresh lime juice
1 tablespoon minced fresh cilantro
1 tablespoon minced fresh mint
1 tablespoon minced red onion
Salt and freshly ground black pepper to taste

Vanilla-Rum Sauce
¼ cup white Bacardi rum
¼ cup dark Bacardi rum
3 tablespoons sugar
1 tablespoon fresh lime juice
1 small shallot, minced
½ vanilla bean
1 cup (2 sticks) unsalted butter, cut into ½-inch pieces
Salt and freshly ground black pepper to taste

4 to 5 shelled conch (1 to 1½ pounds)
Salt and freshly ground black pepper to taste
2 eggs, beaten
¼ cup milk
1 cup unbleached all-purpose flour
1 cup fresh bread crumbs
½ cup clarified butter (see page 223)

Garnish

3 tablespoons finely diced red bell
    pepper
3 tablespoons finely diced green onion
    (white and tender green part)
6 Key lime wedges

To make the bean salad: Two days
before serving, rinse and carefully pick
over the black beans, cover them with
cold water, and let soak overnight. In a
medium saucepan, combine the beans
and garlic and add enough water to
cover. Bring the beans to a boil over
high heat, reduce heat, and simmer until
the beans are tender, 1 to 1½ hours.

Drain the beans and rinse with cool
water. Drain again and place them in a
medium bowl. Add the tomato, mango,
green onions, chili, oil, lime juice,
cilantro, mint, and onion. Season with
salt and pepper, mix well, and adjust the
seasoning as necessary. Cover and chill
overnight.

To make the sauce: In a heavy, medium
nonaluminum saucepan over medium
heat, combine the rums, sugar, lime
juice, and shallot. Split the vanilla bean
in half lengthwise and scrape the seeds
into the pan. Add the vanilla pod to the
pan and boil the mixture, stirring so that
the sugar melts but does not caramelize.
When the mixture has reduced to 3
tablespoons, whisk in the butter a few
pieces at a time. Do not let the sauce
boil; if the pan gets too hot, pull it off
the heat as the final butter is added.
Strain the sauce into a bowl, season
with salt and pepper, and keep warm
over barely tepid water.

To prepare the conch: Cut the conch on
the diagonal into ¼-inch-thick slices.
Place a sheet of plastic wrap over each
medallion and use a mallet to pound the
meat as thin as possible. Season the
conch with salt and pepper. In a shallow
bowl, combine the eggs and milk and
whisk until blended. Place the flour in
another shallow bowl, and place the
bread crumbs in a third shallow bowl.

Just before serving, heat the clarified
butter in a heavy large sauté pan or skillet over medium heat. Dip each slice of

conch into the flour, then into the egg
mixture, and finally into the bread
crumbs; the breading should be only
a light, thin layer. Fry the conch until
lightly golden brown on both sides,
about 45 seconds on the first side, and
30 seconds on the second. Drain the
conch on paper towels and lightly salt it.

To serve: Place about 2 tablespoons of
the bean salad in the center of each
serving plate. Spoon 3 pools of vanilla
sauce around the salad and place 3
slices of conch between the pools of
sauce. Sprinkle some of the red pepper
and green onion over the sauce, and
place a wedge of lime on each plate.

Iron Skillet-Roasted Mussels

Reed Hearon
LuLu
San Francisco, California

Mussels and clams deserve the respect,
some chefs would argue, of being left

pretty much alone. Here's a recipe that
does almost nothing to alter their sea-
fresh flavor.

Serves 4

48 mussels, scrubbed and debearded
Salt and freshly cracked black pepper
    to taste
1 cup clarified unsalted butter
    (see page 223), heated

Heat a large dry cast-iron skillet over
high heat until smoking hot. Place the
mussels in the skillet in a single layer
and continue to heat until they open, 2
to 3 minutes. Remove the mussels as
they pop open, and keep warm. Discard
any mussels that do not open. Return
all mussels to the skillet and generously
sprinkle them with the salt and pepper,
and spoon some of the butter over each.

Serve the mussels directly from the
hot skillet, with remaining butter in a
small bowl set in the center of the skillet
for dipping.

Fresh-cracked Conch with Vanilla-Rum Sauce and Spicy Black Bean Salad;
Mark Militello, Mark's Place

Eggplant and Roasted–Red Pepper Terrine;
Alain Sailhac, L'École/French Culinary Institute

Eggplant and Roasted-Red Pepper Terrine

▼▼▼▼▼▼▼▼▼▼▼▼▼

Alain Sailhac
L'École/French Culinary Institute
New York, New York

Serve this elegant terrine at the height of summer. The tomato vinaigrette and the tomatillo and tomato garnish add even more color to this vibrant appetizer.

Serves 4

Terrine
½ cup olive oil
1 large unpeeled eggplant, cut into thin
    lengthwise slices
4 tablespoons butter
8 ounces spinach, washed, drained, and
    stemmed
Salt and freshly ground black pepper
    to taste
¼ teaspoon ground nutmeg
1 *each* large red and yellow bell pepper,
    roasted, peeled, quartered, and seeded
    (see page 235)
1 garlic clove
1 tablespoon chopped fresh basil
2 ounces Swiss cheese, sliced paper thin
1 teaspoon fresh thyme leaves

Viniagrette and Garnish
2 tablespoons red wine vinegar
Salt and freshly ground black pepper
    to taste
¼ cup olive oil
1 small tomato, peeled, seeded,
    and julienned (see page 234)
2 fresh tomatillos, husked
Fresh flat-leafed (Italian) parsley sprigs
Fresh thyme sprigs

To make the terrine: Preheat the oven to 400°F or preheat the broiler. Brush a baking sheet lightly with some of the olive oil and brush the eggplant slices on both sides with the rest of the oil. Arrange the slices in one layer on the baking sheet and bake them until they are lightly colored, about 10 minutes, or broil for 3 to 4 minutes.

In a large sauté pan or skillet over medium heat, melt the butter and sauté the spinach leaves, tossing them until the spinach is wilted and the liquid has evaporated, about 2 minutes. Add the salt, pepper, and nutmeg, and set aside. Salt and pepper the bell peppers. Crush the garlic and mince it with the basil.

Lightly brush a 3-by-5-inch mini-loaf pan or similar-sized mold with olive oil and line it with lengthwise slices of the eggplant, allowing the ends to hang over the edges of the pan. Spoon in a thin layer of the spinach and top with 1 slice of cheese, cut to fit the pan. Add a layer of yellow bell pepper, then half of the garlic mixture, spreading it with the back of a spoon. Add a layer of eggplant slices and sprinkle with some salt and pepper. Layer again with spinach, cheese, red bell pepper, garlic mixture, cheese, and the thyme. End with a layer of eggplant and fold in the overhanging edges. Press gently on the top of the terrine with your fingers to be sure that the corners are filled completely and the top is flat.

Lightly brush the shiny side of a sheet of aluminum foil with olive oil and wrap the terrine tightly with it. Place the terrine into a slightly larger deep pan and add boiling water to halfway up the side of the terrine. Place in the preheated oven for 30 minutes, or bring to a gentle boil on top of the stove, cover, and simmer for 30 minutes.

Place the cooked terrine on a wire rack and let cool until just slightly warmer than room temperature. Unwrap the terrine and invert onto a cutting board. Using a very sharp knife, cut it into eight $\frac{1}{2}$-inch-thick slices.

To make the vinaigrette: In a small bowl, combine the vinegar, salt, and pepper. Slowly whisk in the olive oil until the mixture is emulsified. Cut about half of the julienned tomato into fine dice and add it to the vinaigrette; reserve the remaining julienned tomato. Let the vinaigrette sit until ready to serve.

To serve: Place 2 slices of the terrine on each serving plate, surround them with some of the vinaigrette, and garnish the plate with thin slices of the tomatillo, a tiny heap of julienned tomato, and sprigs of parsley and thyme.

ALAIN SAILHAC
L'École / French Culinary Institute, New York, New York

Alain Sailhac is profound proof that there's not necessarily a discrepancy between those who do and those who teach.

Sailhac has spent four decades learning how to "do" French cuisine. Today, at the French Culinary Institute in New York, he teaches with a mix of generosity and authority that surely will be one reason his art lasts into the next generation.

Sailhac began his education early, peddling his bicycle at dawn each day to a restaurant in his native Millau. There he would sweep the floors, shovel coal for the fires, then cook until 11 at night. He was all of fifteen at the time.

Later positions introduced Sailhac to the rest of his country and its regional styles. He worked at several places in Paris, including the Hotel Claridge, with a two-year side trip involving combat in the Algerian War. Islands also played a role in the chef's development: Corfu and Rhodes among the Greek Islands, Guadeloupe in the French Caribbean, even New Caledonia in the South Pacific.

For most of the next twenty years, Sailhac's career mirrored the evolution of fine French dining in the United States. Some of that evolution, in fact, was his handiwork. Chef jobs took him from Le Perroquet in Chicago to Le Cygne and Le Cirque in New York during their first golden ages, then on to the '21' Club and the Plaza Hotel.

After going on to consult for New York's Regency Hotel, Sailhac was named dean of culinary studies at the French Culinary Institute. At the Institute, his courses are based on a lifetime of cooking—and that's quite a subject indeed.

FRANK BRIGTSEN
Brigtsen's, New Orleans, Louisiana

In the beginning, there was Chef Paul. And for Frank Brigtsen, as for several other Louisiana chefs who trained with Paul Prudhomme, that association would prove both an asset and a liability through the early years of their careers, when they were inevitably known as Prudhomme's protégés.

Brigtsen was the first of Prudhomme's students to succeed on his own. Some of the newest up-and-coming chefs have cooked with Prudhomme and then spent time cooking with Brigtsen, a sure sign that all the best students are called to be teachers someday.

Brigtsen met Prudhomme before K-Paul's became a mecca in New Orleans' French Quarter. Prudhomme was executive chef at the Brennan family's Commander's Palace, where Brigtsen started an apprenticeship in 1971. Brigtsen continued to cook while attending Louisiana State University in Baton Rouge and eventually returned to Prudhomme and the bustle of K-Paul's.

Brigtsen blackened innumerable redfish during that time, while learning a lifetime of culinary skills from the Cajun master. At K-Paul's, Brigtsen was named the first-ever night chef, finally rising to the position of executive chef as Prudhomme's cookbooks and globe-trotting appearances kept him out of town more and more.

With the acceptance and encouragement of Prudhomme, Brigtsen went out on his own in 1986. He found a charming, multiroomed old house in the Carrollton section of New Orleans, just a few steps from a bend in the Mississippi River, and hung out a shingle that read simply "Brigtsen's."

At the start, everyone talked about the Prudhomme connection and the Prudhomme influence, even as this protégé established his own style. As sometimes happens, it was the national media that took Brigtsen seriously first: *Food & Wine* magazine, the *Zagat Survey*, *Gault-Millau*, *Travel/Holiday*, Champagne Mumm's *Order of the Cordon Rouge*. The local media listened, finally giving Brigtsen's the coveted "five beans" in the *Times-Picayune*.

Today, with his wife and partner Marna, Brigtsen keeps his eyes (and his mind) open for whatever idea, whatever ingredient, whatever ethnic combination earns a voice somewhere in the nation. After that, it's up to him to apply his own judgment, his own hand – and to keep on cooking.

Cheese Grits Cake

Frank Brigtsen
Brigtsen's
New Orleans, Louisiana

These cheese grits cakes are served with a relish of bell pepper, corn, and mirliton, a pale green pear-shaped vegetable popular in New Orleans cuisine and also known as chayote.

Serves 6

Grits Cakes
5 cups water
3 tablespoons minced jalapeño chilies
1 tablespoon salt
2 teaspoons unsalted butter
1½ cups grits (not instant type)
2 cups (8 ounces) grated sharp Cheddar
  cheese

Mirliton-Corn Relish
1 large fresh ear corn, husked
1 medium-large mirliton, halved
2 tablespoons minced red onion
2 tablespoons minced red bell pepper
½ teaspoon distilled white vinegar
½ teaspoon minced fresh basil
¼ teaspoon salt
¼ teaspoon Tabasco sauce

Tomatillo Sauce
¼ cup vegetable or peanut oil
One 6-inch corn tortilla
1 tablespoon olive oil
1 cup finely chopped yellow onions
8 tomatillos, husked
  and quartered
½ teaspoon minced fresh garlic
½ teaspoon salt
¼ teaspoon minced jalapeño chile
¼ teaspoon ground cumin
¼ teaspoon dried whole-leaf oregano
1¼ cups shrimp stock (see page 230)
½ teaspoon minced fresh cilantro

Seasoning Mix
1 tablespoon salt
2 teaspoons sweet Hungarian paprika
1 teaspoon dried whole-leaf oregano
½ teaspoon onion powder
½ teaspoon garlic powder
½ teaspoon ground black pepper
½ teaspoon ground white pepper
¼ teaspoon cayenne pepper

2 cups olive oil
1 cup unbleached all-purpose flour
4 teaspoons Seasoning Mix, above
1 whole egg
1 cup milk
2 cups fine dried bread crumbs
2 tablespoons unsalted butter
24 medium shrimp, peeled and deveined
6 fresh cilantro sprigs

To make the grits cakes: In a medium saucepan, bring the water to a boil. Add the jalapeño, salt, and butter. Slowly stir in the grits, reduce the heat to very low, cover the pan, and cook until the grits are tender and thick, 5 to 7 minutes. Remove from the heat and add the cheese, stirring until it is melted and thoroughly incorporated.

Pour the grits mixture into an 8-by-12-by-2-inch baking pan and smooth the top, then refrigerate until chilled, about 1 hour. Use a 3¼-inch cookie cutter or the top of a glass to cut out 6 cakes. Keep them chilled until ready to finish and serve.

To make the mirliton-corn relish: In a large pot of boiling water, cook the ear of corn for 10 minutes. Remove from the heat and cut the corn from the cob. Break apart the kernels with your fingers and place them in a large bowl. In the same pot of boiling water, boil the mirliton until fork tender, about 12

minutes. Remove from the water, remove the peel, seed, and cut the mirliton into ¼-inch dice. Add the mirliton and remaining ingredients to the bowl and toss thoroughly. Set aside until ready to serve.

To make the tomatillo sauce: In a large, heavy saucepan or skillet over medium heat, heat the vegetable or peanut oil. Add the tortilla and fry until both sides are crisp and golden brown, about 2 minutes. Drain the tortilla on paper towels and crumble it with your fingers.

In a medium saucepan over medium-low heat, heat the olive oil and cook the onions until they begin to brown, 1 to 2 minutes. Reduce heat to low, add the tomatillos, and cook until they begin to soften, 4 to 5 minutes. Add the garlic, salt, jalapeños, cumin, and oregano. Cook for 1 minute, stirring constantly. Add the shrimp stock and cilantro, and bring the mixture to a boil. Reduce the heat to low and add the crumbled tortilla. Place the mixture in a blender and puree, then set aside and keep warm until ready to use.

To make the seasoning mix: In a small bowl, combine all ingredients.

To cook the grits cakes: In each of 2 large, heavy sauté pans or skillets over medium heat, heat 1 cup oil to 375°F,

or almost smoking. Mix the flour with 2 teaspoons of the seasoning mix and place in a shallow dish. Mix the egg and milk in another shallow dish. Mix the bread crumbs with 2 teaspoons of the seasoning mix in a third shallow dish. Lightly coat each grits cake with some of the flour, dip it into the egg mixture, then coat with some of the bread crumbs. Fry the cakes in the hot oil, turning once or twice, until they are crisp and browned, about 4 minutes total. Remove the cakes from the oil, drain on paper towels, and keep warm in a low oven.

Discard the oil and return one of the pans to the stove over high heat. Add the butter, shrimp, and ½ teaspoon of the seasoning mix. Cook, stirring constantly, until the shrimp turn pink, about 2 minutes. Add the mirliton-corn relish and cook just until heated, 1 more minute.

To serve: Ladle about ¼ cup of the sauce onto each serving plate and place a grits cake in the center. Place 3 shrimp around the cake and 1 on top. Spoon some of the relish around the cake and between the shrimp, and a small amount on top. Garnish each plate with a sprig of cilantro and serve immediately.

Deviled Oysters with Sour Mango Slaw and Tabasco Butter Sauce

▼▼▼▼▼▼▼▼▼▼▼▼▼▼▼▼▼▼▼▼

Dean Fearing
the Mansion on Turtle Creek
Dallas, Texas

These spicy baked oysters are given unexpected flavor and texture by a tart slaw of mango and cabbage. The mango should be just slightly underrripe, so that it is full of flavor, yet able to be grated easily.

Serves 4 to 6

8 to 12 fresh oysters
¼ cup minced shallots
3 tablespoons minced garlic
¼ cup cooked and crumbled bacon (about 3 slices)
2 tablespoons minced fresh parsley
2 tablespoons minced fresh thyme
1 tablespoon fresh-cracked black pepper
2 tablespoons mayonnaise, preferably homemade
1 tablespoon Dijon mustard
3 hard-cooked eggs, whites and yolks separated and each finely chopped
¾ cup bread crumbs
1 teaspoon Tabasco sauce
1 teaspoon Worcestershire sauce
1 teaspoon fresh lime juice
½ teaspoon salt

Tabasco Butter Sauce
2 tablespoons vegetable oil
¼ cup minced shallots
¼ cup finely diced leeks
¼ cup finely diced celery
¼ cup finely diced red bell pepper
3 tablespoons minced garlic
2 fresh thyme sprigs
1 teaspoon freshly ground black pepper
2 to 3 chilies de árbol or other small dried hot chilies
¼ cup chopped parsley stems
¼ cup champagne or white wine vinegar
¼ cup dry white wine
1 tablespoon Tabasco sauce, or more to taste
½ cup heavy (whipping) cream
1 cup (2 sticks) unsalted butter at room temperature
1 teaspoon fresh lemon juice
Salt to taste

Garnish
Sour Mango Slaw (recipe follows)
Fresh parsley sprigs

To prepare the oysters: Shuck the oysters, reserving and straining all liquor. Clean and reserve the deeper halves of the shells for serving. Check the oysters and remove any sand, cut them into quarters, and place in a large bowl with the shallots, garlic, bacon, parsley, thyme, and cracked pepper.

Add the mayonnaise and two-thirds of the chopped egg whites and egg yolks. Add ¼ cup of the bread crumbs and season with the Tabasco and Worcestershire sauces, lime juice, and salt. If the oysters are especially juicy, you may need to add up to ¼ cup more bread crumbs to bind the mixture and absorb moisture. Mix well, cover, and refrigerate.

To make the Tabasco butter sauce: In a large sauté pan or skillet over medium-high heat, heat the oil and add the shallots, leeks, celery, and bell pepper. Cook the mixture for 2 minutes, tossing frequently, then add the garlic, thyme, black pepper, chilies, and parsley stems. Add the vinegar and wine and cook to reduce for 2 to 3 minutes. Add the reserved oyster liquor, the Tabasco sauce, and cream, and cook to reduce for 4 to 5 minutes.

Deviled Oysters with Sour Mango Slaw and Tabasco Butter Sauce;
Dean Fearing, the Mansion on Turtle Creek

Remove from heat and slowly whisk in the butter, then add the lemon juice. Strain the sauce through a fine-meshed sieve, pushing down on the solids with a ladle to release all of the juices. Taste and add salt. This sauce is an emulsion and must be kept warm over hot, but not boiling, water; reheating the sauce will cause it to "break" or curdle. If the sauce is being made well in advance, it could be held in a Thermos until serving time.

To finish the oysters: Preheat the broiler. Divide the oyster mixture among the reserved shells and place them on a baking sheet. Coat the top of the oysters lightly with ¼ cup bread crumbs and broil for 3 to 5 minutes, or until they are hot, bubbly, and well browned on top.

To serve: Place 2 or 3 oysters on each serving plate. Make a mound of the sour mango slaw at the top of each plate. Spoon some Tabasco butter sauce between the oysters and a little around each shell. Garnish the plates with parsley sprigs and sprinkle the remaining chopped egg whites and yolks over the oysters.

Sour Mango Slaw
Makes 1 quart

1½ tablespoons fresh lime juice
2 teaspoons mayonnaise, preferably homemade
1 tablespoon extra-virgin olive oil
1½ teaspoons finely grated fresh ginger
1½ teaspoons minced garlic
Salt to taste
½ cup julienned partly green peeled mango
¼ cup finely shredded green cabbage
¼ cup finely shredded red cabbage
¼ cup julienned peeled carrot
¼ cup julienned red onion

In a large bowl, combine the lime juice and mayonnaise and whisk in the olive oil. Add the ginger, garlic, and salt and let the dressing sit for 5 to 10 minutes to combine the flavors. Add the remaining ingredients and toss well to coat. Adjust the seasoning if necessary. Cover and refrigerate until ready to serve.

DEAN FEARING
the Mansion on Turtle Creek, Dallas, Texas

Some traditional chefs take a hard line on writing cookbooks, fearing that by giving away their recipes they're giving away the kitchen. At the Mansion on Turtle Creek, Dean Fearing harbors no such fears. After filling two cookbooks with his dazzling Southwestern recipes, he says, "I can always create another one."

The calm conviction that there's no limit to his culinary creativity has been at the heart of Fearing's success for more than a decade. More than any other chef, Fearing can claim the authorship of today's Southwestern cuisine. Yet Fearing is less concerned with that authorship than with working on new recipes. Every week he creates 24 new dishes at the Mansion, and he still approaches the task with exuberance.

The ideas come from anywhere and everywhere: from travel, from reading, from childhood memories. One day Fearing caught himself recalling the backyard barbecues from his childhood in Kentucky. By a delightfully tangled route, this momentary nostalgia evolved into rack of wild boar with watermelon glaze, basil mashed potatoes and cucumber relish. That menu became almost as popular as such Fearing signature dishes as lobster tacos and tortilla soup.

Classically trained at the Culinary Institute of America, Fearing began his career at Maisonette in Cincinnati, followed by some notable work at the Pyramid Room of the five-star Dallas Fairmont Hotel.

When the Mansion on Turtle Creek opened in 1980, Fearing signed on as sous-chef, a position he held until becoming part owner (with fellow Fairmont veteran Tom Agnew) of the successful Agnew's. This restaurant was the first in Dallas to present new American cuisine, and the first to draw attention to Southwest cuisine from as far away as the *New York Times*.

When Agnew's shut its doors, it was time for Fearing to "come home." After a brief stint at the Verandah Club at the Anatole Hotel, he was named executive chef at the Mansion.

Fearing's main task now is developing new recipes, rather than cooking them on the line. But as we noted, this doesn't intimidate him at all. As long as there are sunsets in the Southwest, as long as there is progressive country to strum on his guitar, as long as there are chilies, cilantro, jícama and tomatillos, Dean Fearing should have no problem.

LYDIA SHIRE AND SUSAN REGIS
Biba, Boston, Massachusetts

Lydia Shire, one of the bright lights of the culinary renaissance in New England, is famous in food circles for selling her wedding ring to pay for her tuition at London's Cordon Bleu. But it *was* after her divorce.

Together with chef Susan Regis, who has worked with her for many years, Shire operates Biba as a personal statement of her love of food. It is one of only a handful of new restaurants that have introduced a new kind of cooking to Bostonians.

After graduation from Cordon Bleu in 1970, Shire headed back to Boston to cook at Maison Robert before moving on to the Harvest Restaurant in Cambridge and Cafe Plaza at the Copley Plaza Hotel. In 1981, she cooked at Parker's at the Parker House Hotel before helping Jasper White open Seasons at the Bostonian. Throughout its first year with White, and then for five years with Shire as executive chef, Seasons exceeded its projected revenues.

In 1986, Shire left Boston to open the Four Seasons Hotel in Beverly Hills, remaining on the West Coast for several years. Working as a chef consultant, she opened Langan's Brasserie and the Beverly Restaurant and Market. Eventually, though, her own dreams took her back to Boston in 1989 to open Biba. It has won awards and prospered ever since.

Regis joined Shire back at Seasons, starting as *garde-manger* and working her way up to head cook. She too made the move to California, cooking at the Four Seasons and serving as restaurant chef at Langan's Brasserie. When it was time to open Biba, Regis returned to Boston; she wouldn't have missed this for the world.

Roasted Foie Gras Risotto
▀▙▀▙▀▙▀▙▀▙▀▙▀▙▀▙▀▙▀▙▀

Lydia Shire, with Susan Regis
Biba
Boston, Massachusetts

This creamy risotto with its topping of sliced baked foie gras is the height of luxury, even if you choose to simplify the garnish by deleting the crisp slices of potato and beet.

Serves 4

12 ounces fresh foie gras
Salt and freshly cracked black pepper to taste
1 tablespoon olive oil
1 tablespoon minced peeled carrot
1 tablespoon minced leek, white part only
1 tablespoon minced fresh flat-leaf (Italian) parsley leaves
1 teaspoon minced shallot
1 teaspoon minced fresh thyme
Four 6-by-6-inch sheets pork caul fat (see directions)
2 tablespoons clarified butter (see page 223)

Risotto:
1³/₄ cups chicken, duck, or veal stock (see page 228, 231)
¹/₄ cup clarified unsalted butter (see page 223)
1 tablespoon olive oil
¹/₂ Spanish onion, finely diced
2 shallots, minced
1¹/₂ cups Arborio rice
1 teaspoon minced fresh herbs such as thyme, sage, parsley, or oregano
2 tablespoons freshly grated Parmesan cheese
Salt and freshly ground black pepper to taste

Garnish
1 baking potato
4 tablespoons clarified unsalted butter (see page 223)
Reserved sautéed vegetables from foie gras, above
Salt and freshly ground black pepper to taste
Kosher salt for sprinkling
1 beet, peeled
1 quart vegetable oil
1 tablespoon flour
8 fresh sage leaves
2 garlic cloves, sliced

1 tablespoon "ice" wine vinegar or champagne vinegar, plus more for sprinkling
1 cup chicken, duck, or veal stock (see page 228, 231)
Freshly ground black pepper to taste

To prepare the foie gras: Place the foie gras in warm water to cover and let it stand 20 minutes to soften and warm, which makes it easier to work with. Remove the foie gras from the water and place it, flat side up, on a work surface. Gently separate the lobes and pull out the veins. Turn over, cut the foie gras into 4 equal portions, and season with salt and pepper.

In a small sauté pan or skillet over medium-high heat, heat the olive oil and lightly sauté the carrot, leek, parsley, shallot, and thyme until they are aromatic, 2 to 3 minutes.

Soak the caul fat in warm water for 20 minutes. Drain and pat the sheets of caul fat dry with paper towels and lay them on a work surface. Sprinkle each with some salt and pepper, then 1/2 tablespoon of the sautéed vegetables (reserve the remaining sautéed vegetables). Place 1 portion of the foie gras, rounded side down, on top of the vegetables and tightly wrap the caul fat around the foie gras to make neat packages. Chill for 1 hour before cooking.

To make the risotto: In a small saucepan over medium heat, bring the stock to a simmer. Reduce heat to maintain the stock at a bare simmer. In a heavy, medium saucepan over medium-high heat, heat the clarified butter with the oil. Add the onion and shallots, and cook over medium heat until they are translucent, about 3 minutes. Add the rice, and stir to coat the grains with the oil mixture. Slowly add 3/4 cup of the stock and reduce the heat to medium low. Continue to cook, stirring frequently, until all of the liquid has been absorbed. Add an additional 3/4 cup stock and continue to stir over medium-low heat until the rice is tender but firm to the bite and liquid is absorbed. The total cooking time should be 18 to 20 minutes.

At this point, the rice may be held in a warm place for up to 1 hour before finishing and serving. Set the remaining stock aside. To finish the risotto, add the herbs and cheese, and season with salt and pepper. Reheat as much of the remaining 1/4 cup stock, as necessary to maintain the creamy texture of the rice.

To prepare the garnish: Preheat oven to 425°F. Using a mandoline or V-slicer, cut the potato into extremely thin lengthwise slices. Place the slices on a baking sheet lined with lightly oiled parchment paper or aluminum foil. Brush the slices with 2 tablespoons of the clarified butter and sprinkle with reserved sautéed vegetables, salt, and pepper. Place another oiled sheet of parchment paper or foil over potato slices, then place another baking sheet on top. Bake in oven until crisp, about 30 minutes. Remove from the oven, remove the top pan and paper or foil, sprinkle with kosher salt, and set aside.

Using a mandoline or V-slicer, slice the beet into the longest, thinnest slices possible. In a large sauté pan or skillet, heat the vegetable oil to 375°F, or until almost smoking. Lightly dust the beet slices with flour and fry them until crisp, about 1 minute. Drain on paper towels, sprinkle with kosher salt and set aside.

In a small sauté pan or skillet over medium-high heat, heat the remaining 2 tablespoons clarified butter and fry the sage leaves and garlic slices until they are crisp and lightly browned, 45 to 60 seconds. Drain on paper towels and set aside.

To make the sauce: Remove the foie gras from the pan it was cooked in and slice on the diagonal into 1/2-inch-thick slices. Drain off any fat remaining in the pan and place the pan over high heat. Deglaze the pan with the 1 tablespoon vinegar and 1/2 cup of the stock, and stir to scrape up the browned bits from the bottom of the pan. Cook to reduce the liquid to about 2 tablespoons. Add the remaining 1/2 cup stock and whisk until it forms a slightly thickened sauce.

To serve: Place 1 slice of the foie gras in the center of each serving plate. Spoon a portion of the risotto next to the foie gras, then ladle some sauce over the foie gras. Arrange the fried sage and garlic around the plate and splash a bit of vinegar over each serving. Grind pepper over the plate, including the edges, then garnish with the slices of potato and beet.

Note: *The chef uses a special ice wine vinegar from Germany, which she describes as sweet and an especially good counterpoint to the richness of the foie gras and sauterne wine they serve with it. Champagne vinegar can be substituted.*

Roasted Foie Gras with Risotto; *Lydia Shire with Susan Regis, Biba*

Grilled Swordfish Tostada; *Bobby Flay, Mesa Grill*

Grilled Swordfish Tostada

Bobby Flay
Mesa Grill
New York, New York

Seared swordfish, avocado vinaigrette, and black bean-mango salsa take the tostada to a new height.

Serves 6

2 cups peanut oil
Six 4-inch flour or corn tortillas

Avocado Vinaigrette
1/4 avocado, peeled and seeded
1/4 jalapeño chili, seeded
1 tablespoon finely chopped red onion
2 tablespoons fresh lime juice
1/4 cup olive oil
1/2 tablespoon honey
Salt and freshly ground black pepper
   to taste
Six 6-ounce swordfish steaks
Olive oil for brushing
Salt and freshly ground black pepper
   to taste
6 tablespoons julienned jícama
1 cup Black Bean and Mango Salsa,
   (recipe follows)

Garnish
6 tablespoons jícama, julienned
1/2 avocado, peeled, pitted, and sliced
1/2 *each* red and yellow bell pepper,
   seeded, deribbed, and julienned
2 tablespoons chopped fresh cilantro

   To prepare the tortillas: In a medium heavy sauté pan or skillet over high heat, heat the peanut oil to 375°F, or until a piece of tortilla sizzles when it is immersed. Fry each tortilla, turning once, about 1 1/2 minutes on each side, or until crisp. Drain on paper towels and keep warm in a low oven.

To make the vinaigrette: Place the avocado, jalapeño, onion, and lime juice in a blender and puree until smooth. With the motor running, add the oil in a slow steady stream until the mixture emulsifies. Add the honey, salt, and pepper. This can be prepared ahead, stored in a covered nonaluminum container, and refrigerated. Bring to room temperature before using.

To prepare the swordfish: Preheat a broiler or prepare a grill. Brush the swordfish lightly with olive oil, season with salt and pepper and broil or grill over hot coals for 1 1/2 minutes. Turn and cook on the second side for 30 seconds, or until just seared.

To serve: Scatter some of the jícama on each serving plate, top with a tortilla, add a thin layer of salsa, and top with 1 piece of swordfish. Use a squeeze bottle to pipe some of the avocado vinaigrette over the fish and the plate. Garnish each plate with a slice of avocado, some of the peppers, and cilantro.

Black Bean and Mango Salsa
Makes 2 cups

1/2 cup cooked black beans, drained
1/2 mango, peeled and coarsely chopped
1/2 cup finely chopped red onion
1/2 jalapeño chili, seeded and finely
   minced
1/4 cup coarsely chopped fresh cilantro
1/4 cup fresh lime juice
2 tablespoons olive oil
Salt and freshly ground black pepper
   to taste

In a medium bowl, combine all of the ingredients and adjust the seasonings with salt and pepper. This can be prepared and refrigerated 3 to 4 hours in advance. Bring to room temperature before serving. Fresh papaya may be substituted for the mango.

BOBBY FLAY
Mesa Grill, New York, New York

Barbecued duck and wild mushroom quesadilla with spicy mango salsa. Grilled swordfish tostada with black bean and mango salsa. Barbecued ribs with chipotle-peanut sauce and corn-tomatillo relish. This is the stuff that Mesa Grill's dreams are made on, and Bobby Flay is the chef they're made by.

When Mesa Grill opened in 1991, Flay promised, "I'm going to put a new and colorful twist on Southwestern cuisine." He has not only succeeded in doing this but in riding the wave of the style's popularity to fame in New York, a long way from Arizona and New Mexico. As critic Gael Greene states the case, "the sassy fare at Mesa Grill surpasses anything of its kind elsewhere in New York."

Flay began cooking at age 17, when he took a job at Joe Allen's in New York. The management here was so impressed by his talent that it paid his tuition to that city's French Culinary Institute, where Flay was a member of that school's first graduating class in 1984.

It was restaurant owner Jonathan Waxman who first introduced Flay to Southwestern cooking. The chef-to-be was mesmerized by the region's foods and set about exploring the possibilities of Southwestern cuisine.

From 1988 to 1990, Flay followed his passion at New York's Miracle Grill, where something of a cult following gathered around his innovative and flavorful creations. These dishes became the basis for *Bobby Flay's Bold American Food*, published by Warner Books.

Semolina and Goat Cheese Dumpling

▀▖▀▖▀▖▀▖▀▖▀▖▀▖▀▖▀▖▀▖▀▖▀▖

Todd English
Olives
Boston, Massachusetts

The robust flavors of the Italian countryside are featured in these filled dumplings, which are topped with a tomato-mushroom ragout and garnished with grilled fennel.

Serves 6

Roasted Tomatoes

6 plum (Roma) tomatoes
1 tablespoon olive oil
Salt and freshly ground pepper to taste
2 teaspoons chopped fresh flat-leaf (Italian) parsley
2 teaspoons chopped fresh basil

Dumplings

4 ounces fresh mild goat cheese at room temperature
2 tablespoons sour cream
1 tablespoon minced fresh flat-leaf (Italian) parsley
1 tablespoon minced fresh rosemary
$1/2$ tablespoon minced fresh sage leaves
3 cups water
1 teaspoon salt, plus salt to taste
$1\frac{1}{2}$ cups fine semolina flour
$1/4$ cup freshly grated Parmesan cheese
4 tablespoons unsalted butter
Freshly ground black pepper to taste
About $1/2$ cup unbleached all-purpose flour

Portobello Ragout

2 to 3 tablespoons olive oil
$1\frac{1}{2}$ to 2 pounds portobello mushrooms, stemmed and sliced $1/2$-inch thick, or a combination of wild mushrooms such as chanterelles, shiitakes, hedgehogs, and black trumpets

1 teaspoon salt
1 tablespoon butter
$1/2$ cup chopped onion
2 large garlic cloves, thinly sliced
$1/2$ cup dry white wine, or more if necessarry
Roasted Tomatoes (above)

1 large fennel bulb
Olive oil for coating
2 tablespoons butter

Garnish

1 bunch watercress
2 tablespoons minced fresh flat-leaf (Italian) parsley
2 tablespoons freshly grated Parmesan cheese

To make the roasted tomatoes: Preheat the oven to 180°F. Line a baking sheet with aluminum foil. Core and cut the tomatoes in half lengthwise and squeeze out most of the seeds. Place the tomatoes in a small bowl and add the olive oil, salt, and pepper. Place the tomatoes skin-side down on the prepared pan and bake for $2\frac{1}{2}$ hours, or until slightly dried but still soft.

Remove the tomatoes from the pan and place them on a paper towel-lined baking sheet to drain. Chop the tomatoes in $1/2$-inch pieces and toss with the parsley and basil. Refrigerate the tomatoes if not using them immediately.

To make the dumplings: In a bowl of an electric mixer, whip the cheese and sour cream with the herbs until smooth, 1 minute. Chill in the refrigerator for at least 10 minutes to blend the flavors and firm the cheese.

In a large saucepan over high heat, bring the water to a boil, add the 1 teaspoon of salt, then slowly add the semolina, whisking constantly. When

the semolina has begun to pull away from the sides of the pan, add the Parmesan and butter, and stir briskly. Remove from heat and season with salt and pepper. Let sit about 5 minutes until cool enough to handle, or hold in a warm place if not finishing immediately.

Lightly dust a work surface with some of the flour and spoon out 2 generous tablespoonfuls of the semolina mixture onto the work surface. Press the dough into a disc approximately $1/4$ inch thick. Hold the dough in the palm of one hand and place 1 generous teaspoonful of the goat cheese mixture in the center of the dough. Fold the dough in half and pinch the edges to seal. Press and roll the dumpling in your hand to shape it into a small log shape with flat ends, being sure the filling is sealed securely in the center. Place the completed dumpling on a baking sheet. Repeat to use the remaining dumpling mixture. Chill the dumplings until ready to finish and serve.

To make the portobello ragout: In a large sauté pan or skillet over medium-high heat, heat 2 tablespoons olive oil, add the sliced mushrooms, and sauté until they are browned, 2 to 3 minutes. If using a variety of mushrooms, cook the heaviest first and gradually add the lighter varieties, cooking until all are lightly browned. If the pan becomes crowded, remove some of the mushrooms and continue to sauté the remainder in batches until all of them are lightly browned. Return all of the mushrooms to the pan to proceed.

Sprinkle the mushrooms with the salt. Add the butter to the pan, then the onion and garlic, and cook until the onion is translucent, about 2 minutes, adding 1 tablespoon olive oil if necessary. Add the wine, then the roasted tomatoes. Lower the heat and maintain the mixture at a simmer while proceeding with the recipe, and adding more wine if necessary to keep the mushrooms moist.

To prepare the fennel: Prepare a grill, or preheat a broiler. Trim the fennel bulb and cut it into 6 wedges. In a large saucepan of lightly salted water over high heat, blanch the fennel until almost tender, about 10 minutes. Remove the fennel and place it in a bowl of ice water to stop the cooking process, then drain and pat dry. Lightly rub the fennel with olive oil and grill or broil until browned and completely tender. Set aside and keep warm.

To cook the dumplings: Preheat the oven to 400°F. In a large sauté pan or skillet over medium-high heat, heat the butter until the foam subsides. Add some of the dumplings and cook, rolling them around the pan, until lightly browned, 2 to 3 minutes. Do not crowd the pan. Repeat until all of the dumplings are browned. Place the browned dumplings into the oven until warmed through, 8 to 10 minutes.

To serve: Spoon some of the mushroom ragout with its juices into each of 6 shallow soup plates. Place 1 piece of grilled fennel and a small bouquet of watercress around the edge. Place 2 dumplings into the center of each bowl. Lightly sprinkle each serving with minced parsley and Parmesan cheese.

Semolina and Goat Cheese Dumpling; *Todd English, Olives*

PAUL INGENITO
The Russian Tea Room, New York, New York

Paul Ingenito is not Russian, but some of his best dishes are: Blini, kakuska, karsky shashlik, and borscht, classics of the Russian Tea Room.

Still, Ingenito expresses his own eclectic tastes at regular intervals. Calling his style "refined country cooking" and fitting it comfortably within the Russian tradition, the chef has created such dishes as borscht with braised duck and grilled sea scallops with silver dollar blini. Ingenito is also inspired by his memories of his Italian grandmother's soups and stews.

A 1984 graduate of the Culinary Institute, Ingenito cooked with Larry Forgione at An American Place. There, he was an active participant in the American food revolution, joining Forgione in creating signature dishes of the new cuisine and exploring the native ingredients that fueled it.

He also traveled with Forgione, cooking at benefits and fund raisers in every corner of the United States, and sharing kitchen space with the likes of Wolfgang Puck, Dean Fearing and Jonathan Waxman. This broadened his exposure to California and Southwestern cuisine, as well as other ethnic and regional foods.

Ingenito brought this background to the table – quite literally – when he joined the Russian Tea Room as executive sous-chef in 1989. Less than a year later, he rose to executive chef, taking one of New York's most beloved half-century traditions squarely onto his well-traveled shoulders.

Grilled Scallops on Silver Dollar Blini

Paul Ingenito
The Russian Tea Room
New York, New York

Here's a dish that captures the elegance of czarist Russia in both content and presentation. Keep in mind that the lemon vodka mignonette is an excellent sauce for any grilled fish or shellfish.

Serves 4

Blini Batter
1/2 cup buckwheat flour
1/4 cup unbleached all-purpose flour
1/4 cup sugar
1 cup milk
2 eggs, slightly beaten
4 tablespoons unsalted butter, melted
1/2 teaspoon active dry yeast
1 tablespoon melted butter

Lemon Vodka Mignonette
3 dried apricots, finely diced
1 red bell pepper, seeded, deribbed, and finely diced
1 lemon, peeled, seeded, sectioned, and finely diced
6 chive stems, snipped
1 tablespoon lemon vodka
1 tablespoon sherry vinegar
1 teaspoon balsamic vinegar
Salt and freshly ground black pepper to taste

Lemon Beurre Blanc
1/2 cup dry white wine
1/2 cup chopped parsley stems
4 teaspoons fresh lemon juice
1 tablespoon minced shallots
3/4 cup heavy (whipping) cream
1 cup (2 sticks) cold unsalted butter, cut into tablespoon-sized pieces
Salt and white pepper to taste

Vegetable Gâteau
2 tablespoons unsalted butter
1/2 cup finely diced leek, white part only
1/4 cup finely diced peeled carrot
1/4 cup finely diced celery
4 large shrimp, peeled, poached, and finely diced

Salt and freshly ground black pepper
  to taste
About ⅓ cup Lemon Beurre Blanc,
  (above)

1 tablespoon unsalted butter, melted
12 large sea scallops
2 tablespoons olive oil
Salt and freshly ground black pepper
  to taste

Garnish
¼ cup sour cream
4 ounces osetra caviar
4 fresh chervil sprigs

To make the blini batter: In a large bowl, combine the flours and sugar. In a medium saucepan, combine the milk, eggs, butter, and yeast, and stir. Place the pan over low heat and warm gently to not more than 150°F. Remove the pan from the heat and whisk in the dry ingredients, mixing well. Strain the mixture through a fine-meshed sieve and set aside for 1 hour at room temperature to allow the yeast to "ferment."

Grilled Scallops on Silver Dollar Blini; *Paul Ingenito, The Russian Tea Room*

To make the mignonette: In a small nonaluminum bowl, combine the apricots, bell pepper, lemon, and chives, and mix well. Add the vodka and vinegars, season with salt and pepper, and set aside.

To make the lemon beurre blanc: In a small heavy nonaluminum saucepan over medium-high heat, cook the wine, parsley stems, 3 teaspoons of the lemon juice, and shallots until the liquid is almost evaporated, about 10 minutes. Add the cream and continue to cook over medium-high heat to reduce the liquid to ½ cup. Whisk the butter into the reduced cream 1 tablespoon at a time, whisking constantly until all of the butter is used and the sauce has a velvety consistency. Strain the sauce through a fine-meshed sieve and season it with the remaining 1 teaspoon lemon juice and salt and pepper. Set aside and keep warm over barely tepid water until ready to use.

To make the vegetable gâteau: In a large sauté pan or skillet over low heat, melt the butter and cook the leek for about 2

minutes. Add the carrot and celery, and cook for about 1 minute. Add the shrimp, season with salt and pepper, and remove from heat. Add just enough of the lemon beurre blanc to bind the shrimp mixture. Keep in a warm place until ready to assemble the dish.

To cook the blini: Heat a large griddle or nonstick skillet over medium heat. Lightly brush the surface of the griddle with half of the melted butter. Stir the batter briskly and spoon 12 tablespoon-sized portions onto the griddle to form the "silver dollar" blini. Cook until the top is bubbly and the bottom is golden, about 1 minute, then turn with a spatula and cook on the second side until golden, about 30 seconds. Remove from the heat and set aside in a warm place. Repeat, making 12 slightly larger blini, about 2 inches across, using 2 tablespoons of batter for each. Cut these blini with a 1½-inch-diameter ring mold or cookie cutter to form perfect circles. The blini may be made ahead of time and held, covered, until ready to assemble the plates.

To prepare the scallops: Brush the scallops with olive oil, season with salt and pepper, and cook them in a hot sauté pan or skillet until they are firm and translucent, 1½ minutes on each side.

To serve: Place a 1½-inch-diameter stainless steel ring mold in the center of each serving plate. Place 1 trimmed blini in the bottom, and spoon in 1 tablespoon of the gâteau mixture. Layer with a second trimmed blini and 1 tablespoon of the gâteau mixture, and top with another trimmed blini. Press the top down gently.

Arrange three of the "silver dollar" blini around each ring and spoon some of the vodka mignonette between each one. Place 1 scallop on each of the "silver dollars." Carefully remove the ring mold and pipe a rosette of sour cream on top of the tower. Spoon some caviar on top of the sour cream and on top of each scallop. Garnish each serving by drizzling some of the remaining beurre blanc around the edges of the plate, then add a sprig of fresh chervil.

Crabmeat Salad; *Daniel Boulud, Restaurant Daniel*

Crabmeat Salad

Daniel Boulud
Restaurant Daniel
New York, New York

Fresh crab is combined with cucumber and cilantro and sparked with mango and mint in this delightful mixture of tastes, colors and textures.

Serves 4

Crabmeat Salad
16 ounces fresh crabmeat, carefully
  picked over to remove shells
2 tablespoons fresh lime juice
2 tablespoons olive oil
Salt and freshly ground black pepper
  to taste

Cucumber-Mango Salad
1/2 cup finely diced cucumber
1/2 cup finely diced mango
1 teaspoon fresh lime juice
1 teaspoon olive oil
1/2 teaspoon minced fresh cilantro
1/4 teaspoon minced fresh mint
Salt and freshly ground black pepper
  to taste

Cucumber Coulis
1 unpeeled fresh cucumber, seeded
  and chopped
1 tablespoon olive oil
1 teaspoon fresh lime juice

Mango Coulis
1 very ripe mango, peeled, pitted, and
  chopped
1 tablespoon olive oil
1 tablespoon fresh lime juice

Garnish
1/2 cucumber, peeled, seeded, and cut
  into matchsticks
1/2 mango, peeled, pitted, and cut into
  matchsticks
1 teaspoon olive oil
1 teaspoon fresh lime juice
Salt and freshly ground black pepper
4 fresh mint sprigs
4 fresh cilantro sprigs

To make the crabmeat salad: Carefully pick over the crabmeat, removing any bits of shell. Place the crabmeat into a small bowl and mix with the lime juice and olive oil, and lightly season with salt and pepper. Cover and refrigerate until ready to use.

To make the cucumber-mango salad: In a medium bowl, combine all the ingredients and mix well. Cover and refrigerate until ready to use.

To make the cucumber coulis: Place the cucumber in a blender or food processor and puree. Transfer to a fine-meshed sieve and allow the excess moisture to drain off. Place the cucumber pulp back in the blender or food processor, add the remaining ingredients and puree until smooth. Place coulis in a squeeze bottle and set aside.

To make the mango coulis: In a blender or food processor, combine all the ingredients and puree until completely smooth. Strain the coulis through a fine-meshed sieve. Place into a squeeze bottle and set aside.

To prepare the garnish: In a medium bowl, toss the cucumber and mango with the olive oil, lime juice, and salt and pepper.

To serve: In the center of each serving plate, place a 3-inch-diameter stainless-steel ring and spoon one-fourth of the crabmeat salad into each, pressing it down with the back of a spoon. Spoon some of the cucumber-mango salad on top of the crabmeat and again smooth the top and gently press down. Remove the rings. Squeeze 5 dots of each coulis, evenly spaced, around the edge of the plate. Arrange a few matchsticks of mango and cucumber around the plate, and garnish with a sprig of mint and cilantro.

DANIEL BOULUD
Restaurant Daniel, New York, New York

True to the French tradition of earning your stripes each step of the way, Daniel Boulud cooked for more than thirty years with some of the world's most famous chefs before hanging his own name above a door. Since 1993, Restaurant Daniel on the Upper East Side has been one of the hottest restaurants in town.

Boulud doesn't attach any fancy name to his cuisine; he is content to call his food "contemporary French." The rest of the message, he believes, has to be on the plate. That's a lesson he learned from his grandfather, who ran a small cafe in southeastern France. Boulud grew up on a nearby farm (one of the best apprenticeships for any chef), then went to work at Nandro, a Michelin two-star in Lyons.

From 1973 to 1981, Boulud cooked with some of France's brightest lights, including Georges Blanc at La Mère Blanc in Vonnas, Roger Verge at Le Moulin de Mougins in Mougins, and Michel Guerard at Les Près d'Eugénie in Eugénie-les-Bains. Boulud eventually became chef at Les Étoiles, the finest restaurant in Denmark.

The European Commission brought Boulud to the United States to serve as chef to Ambassador Roland de Kergorlay; then Boulud headed for New York. Years at the Westbury Hotel and the Plaza-Athénée prepared Boulud for his most famous stint before opening Restaurant Daniel: executive chef at Le Cirque from 1986 to 1992.

During this extraordinary era for the hyper-chic eatery, Boulud's cooking picked up four stars from the *New York Times* and won praise as the best restaurant in the nation from *Gault-Millau*. In fact, Boulud's Le Cirque was named the No. 3 restaurant in the world by the television show "Lifestyles of the Rich and Famous."

Now, Boulud is earning superlatives for a restaurant of his own.

LAWRENCE CHU
Chef Chu's, Los Altos, California

When Lawrence Chu opened a fast-food outlet called Chef Chu's with only a dozen takeout items on the menu, he was a self-described Ph.D.: "poor, hungry and determined."

A quarter century later, lovers of Chinese cuisine all over America have heard of Chu and many have tasted his cooking; for the twelve-item takeout joint has evolved into a full-service dining spot serving up to eight-hundred customers a day.

Chu was born in the Szechwan region of China during the dark days of World War II. He grew up in Shanghai, Taiwan and Hong Kong, getting a taste of three other regional cuisines. After Hong Kong, he moved to the United States and cooked at Trader Vic's in San Francisco, where he experienced Asian cooking, American style.

Chu worked his way through school in San Francisco, cooking in restaurants with cuisines as diverse as his adopted home. Even when he was struggling to keep his fast-food outlet afloat, he made sure to offer a range of dishes with origins from Shanghai to Peking to Szechwan to Canton.

All this time, Chu was exercising his newly adopted all-American trait: the willingness to experiment. He was among the first to understand concerns about healthfulness, preparing his dishes with less saturated fat and less salt than they would have in China. He also began an ongoing project to introduce Chinese vegetables to his customers.

Chu has combined two of his great loves with aspects of his profession. A passion for travel has inspired him to lead small groups on culinary adventures through China, while his passion for teaching has taken root in his restaurant, where he has set up a home kitchen for classes.

Larry Chu realizes that to continue growing, Chinese cuisine needs to strive for new levels of experience. Happily, he can draw in this mission from a national menu that includes a lot more than 12 fast-food dishes.

Minced Chicken in Lettuce Cups

Lawrence Chu
Chef Chu's
Los Altos, California

This refreshing appetizer also makes a good party dish. Cut the lettuce cups smaller, top with 1 tablespoon of the chicken, garnish with rice sticks and peanuts, and serve as an hors d'oeuvre.

Serves 6 to 8

4 or 5 dried black mushrooms (shiitakes)
1 whole chicken breast, halved, boned, and skinned
1 head iceberg lettuce
2 cups vegetable oil for deep-frying
1 ounce rice stick noodles, broken into small pieces (about ½ cup)
1 green onion, minced, including tender greens
½ cup coarsely chopped bamboo shoots
¼ cup coarsely chopped water chestnuts

Sauce
1 tablespoon Chinese rice wine or dry sherry
1 tablespoon oyster sauce
3 tablespoons hoisin sauce
½ teaspoon salt
Pinch of white pepper
2 teaspoons toasted sesame oil

2 tablespoons roasted peanuts, crushed, for garnish

To prepare the mushrooms: In a small bowl, soak the mushrooms in warm water to cover for 20 minutes. Remove the mushrooms, pat them dry with paper towels, and coarsely chop them.

To prepare the chicken: Mince or dice the chicken into ½-inch pieces.

To prepare the lettuce cups: Cut about 1 inch off the stem end of the lettuce, peel off 6 to 8 of the largest leaves and, using scissors, cut them into neat cups 4 to 5 inches in diameter.

To prepare the rice sticks: In a wok or deep-fryer, heat the oil to 350°F, or until a noodle dropped in the oil puffs and comes to the surface. Add the rice sticks to the oil in small batches and fry until completely puffed, about 15 seconds. Remove the noodles from the oil with a slotted spatula and drain on paper towels.

Remove all but 1 to 2 tablespoons of oil from the wok. Reheat the wok over high heat and add the chicken, stirring quickly to separate the pieces. Stir-fry until the chicken turns opaque, then add, one at a time, the mushrooms, green onion, bamboo shoots, and the water chestnuts. Continue to stir-fry for 30 seconds. Add the sauce ingredients one at a time, in this order: rice wine or sherry, oyster sauce, hoisin sauce, salt, pepper, and sesame oil. Toss lightly for 5 seconds.

To serve: Arrange the lettuce cups around the edges of a large serving platter. Mound the chicken in the center of the platter and sprinkle with rice sticks and peanuts. Diners will each spoon some of the chicken mixture into a lettuce cup, add a few rice sticks and some of the peanuts, and eat the lettuce cup out of hand.

Minced Chicken in Lettuce Cups;
Lawrence Chu, Chef Chu's

Terrine of Squab Breast and Wild Mushrooms

Klaus Helmin
Tivoli
Rosslyn, Virginia

This terrine is notable not only for its use of squab but for its separate layering of the kinds of wild mushrooms, using gelatin to preserve the juices of each.

Serves 6 to 8

4 whole squab breasts
Freshly ground black pepper to taste
4 tablespoons canola oil
1 tablespoon brandy
4 ounces shiitake mushrooms, stemmed
4 ounces oyster mushrooms, stemmed
4 ounces chanterelle mushrooms, stemmed
Salt to taste
9 tablespoons dry Pinot Grigio wine
2 tablespoons plain gelatin

Garnish
1 1/2 cups mâche or baby greens
1 small tomato, peeled, seeded, and finely diced (see page 234)
1 tablespoon snipped fresh chives

To prepare the squab: Bone and skin the squab breasts and rub them with the pepper. In a large sauté pan or skillet over high heat, heat 1 tablespoon of the oil and sauté the breasts, turning to brown all sides, about 3 minutes. Add the brandy to the pan, and ignite it with a match. Shake the pan until the flames subside. Continue to cook the breasts, turning them in the juices, until they are browned but still rare, about 8 minutes.

To prepare the mushrooms: Place 3 large sauté pans or skillets over medium-high heat, and add 1 tablespoon of the oil to each pan. Place one kind of mushroom in each pan and sauté, tossing quickly, until the mushrooms are beginning to brown, about 2 minutes. Sprinkle all of the mushrooms with salt and pepper and add 2 tablespoons of the wine to each pan. Toss and cook for an additional 3 to 4 minutes. Set aside.

In a small bowl, dissolve the gelatin in the remaining 3 tablespoons of the wine until it softens, about 1 minute. Set the bowl over a pan of hot water and warm over low heat, stirring, for 1 minute, or until the gelatin is completely dissolved. Add one-third of the gelatin-wine mixture to each pan, tipping the pan to let the gelatin completely mix with the juices. Continue to cook over medium heat, stirring for 1 to 2 minutes; remove from heat and set aside to cool slightly.

To prepare the terrine: Line a standard 8-by-4-inch loaf pan or a 3-cup terrine mold with plastic wrap, leaving a 6-inch overhang all around. Spoon the chanterelle mushrooms and all of their juices into the bottom of the mold and smooth with back of a spoon. Place in the refrigerator for 20 minutes to let the gelatin firm.

Remove the mold from the refrigerator and place 2 squab breasts, end to end, on top of the mushroom layer. Spoon the oyster mushrooms and their juices over the squab and return the mold to the refrigerator for 20 minutes.

Remove the mold from the refrigerator and place the remaining 2 squab breasts into the mold, then spoon the shiitake mushrooms and their juices on top. Fold the excess plastic wrap tightly over the top of the mold and press down with your fingers to compress the mushrooms to be sure the mixture reaches into all of the corners. Return the mold to the refrigerator and chill for 6 to 8 hours.

To serve: Using the excess plastic wrap as a handle, pull the terrine from the mold, remove the plastic wrap, and using a serrated knife, slice the terrine into 1/2-inch-thick portions. On each serving plate, place 1 slice of the terrine just off center. Arrange some of the mâche or baby greens on the side and lightly sprinkle the plate with tomato and chives.

Onion Tart; *Jean Claude Poilevey, Le Bouchon*

Onion Tart

Jean Claude Poilevey
Le Bouchon
Chicago, Illinois

One of the great French classics, this onion tart is a favorite bistro dish in Paris and Lyons.

Makes one 10-inch onion tart; serves 6

Savory Tart Crust
1½ cups unbleached all-purpose flour,
¼ teaspoon salt
¾ cup (1½ sticks) unsalted butter at
  room temperature, cut into pieces
¼ to ⅓ cup lukewarm water

Onion Filling
¾ cup ¼-inch-diced bacon
  (about 6 to 8 slices)
3 cups thinly sliced onions
  (about 2 medium-large onions)
½ cup (2 ounces) finely diced or
  grated cheese
1 egg yolk
½ cup heavy (whipping) cream
1 teaspoon salt
½ teaspoon ground white pepper
Pinch of ground nutmeg
6 parsley sprigs for garnish (optional)

To make the crust: Combine the flour and salt in the large bowl of a heavy-duty electric mixer fitted with a paddle. With the mixer running on the slowest speed, add the butter and continue to mix until mixture resembles a coarse meal and the butter is completely incorporated into the flour, about 10 minutes. Increase the speed to medium and gradually add the water until the dough sticks together and no dry flour is visible. Do not overwork the dough. Or, to make by hand, cut the butter into the flour and salt with a pastry cutter or 2 forks until the mixture resembles coarse meal. Gradually mix in the water with a fork until the dough pulls together into a ball.

Shape the dough into a compact ball, wrap in a cloth or plastic wrap, and let sit for at least 30 minutes at room temperature. The dough can be made 1 day ahead.

Preheat the oven to 350°F. On a floured board, and using a floured rolling pin, roll the dough into a thin 12-inch circle. Fold the dough in half, then into quarters, transfer it to a 10-inch tart pan, and unfold it. Press the dough into the sides and bottom of pan and roll a rolling pin over the top, cutting off the excess from the edges. Cut a piece of parchment paper or aluminum foil into a 14-inch circle. Place the paper or foil over the dough and fill with dried beans or pie weights.

Bake for about 30 minutes, or until the crust is set and the edges are lightly browned. Carefully remove the beans and paper or foil. Return to the oven and bake the crust another 1 or 2 minutes, or until dough is golden brown. Let cool slightly before filling.

To make the filling: In a 12-inch sauté pan or skillet over medium-high heat, cook the bacon just until the fat begins to melt. Add the onions and continue to cook, stirring or shaking the pan, until they are golden in color, about 15 to 20 minutes. As they begin to brown, reduce the heat and stir more frequently to make sure the onions do not burn. Drain the onions in a colander. Let cool slightly.

In a large bowl, whisk together the egg yolk, cream, salt, pepper, and nutmeg. Add the cheese and onions. Fill the shell with the mixture, smoothing it evenly with a rubber spatula. Bake for 18 to 20 minutes, or until set and golden brown. Let cool slightly before cutting into wedges.

To serve: Place 1 wedge on each serving plate and garnish with a sprig of parsley if desired.

JEAN CLAUDE POILEVEY
Le Bouchon, Chicago, Illinois

For twenty years, the last five as sole owner, Jean Claude Poilevey was responsible for the exquisite French cuisine at Chicago's La Fontaine. So when that restaurant closed its doors in 1993, Poilevey felt drawn to something a good deal simpler.

His forty-seat Le Bouchon, a quintessential bistro, has garnered considerable praise since opening in the neighborhood known as Bucktown in June 1993. The warmth of the surroundings and the excellence of its simple food keep drawing patrons back.

Born in the Burgundy region of France, Poilevey started learning his trade at age fourteen in a series of local restaurant kitchens. In the mid-1960s, he moved to London and worked at the Cafe Royale and the Colony Club. In 1968, he was recruited (along with Jean Banchet and four other French chefs) to open the Playboy Club in Lake Geneva, Wisconsin. Several years later he moved to the Chicago area, where he opened La Fontaine with two partners in 1973.

Patrons at Le Bouchon, which filled the space once housing Gavroche, look for no culinary innovations. The signature dish, in fact, is Poilevey's onion tart, a classic blend of crispy pastry and carmelized onions. The other favorites are traditional bistro dishes as well: sautéed wild mushrooms, lentil soup, hunter-style rabbit.

Since French chefs wrote the book on world-class fussy dining in this country, it's only fair that they have a chance to show that some of the world's best "home cooking" hails from their homeland as well.

ROY YAMAGUCHI

Roy's Restaurant, Honolulu, Hawaii

Roy Yamaguchi's love of cooking has taken him a long way – initially from Tokyo to the Culinary Institute of America in Hyde Park, New York. What he learned there would transform everything he knew about food.

"Even as a boy I loved to cook," says Yamaguchi, "whether it was fried Portuguese sausage and eggs or a full-on Thanksgiving dinner – which I once prepared for my family – growing up in the middle of Tokyo, Japan." He ponders a moment. "I first took up Home Ec in high school because I liked the odds of being the only boy in the class."

After graduating from the CIA in 1976, Yamaguchi found his way to Los Angeles. According to the young chef, in the years that followed he was enrolled in the school of hard knocks, with twelve-hour days in the kitchen seven days a week. But L'Escoffier, L'Ermitage and Michael's were no ordinary kitchens. A fast learner, Yamaguchi was soon elevated to full "boy wonder" status and stints as executive chef at Le Serene and Le Gourmet.

In 1984, Yamaguchi put together a partnership and opened 385 North in West Hollywood, specializing in what the chef called "Euro-Asian" cuisine. His Asian presentations of predominantly French tastes were embraced by Hollywood foodies and California critics alike.

Still, Yamaguchi yearned for something more. In 1988, he moved to the original home of his father and grandparents: the Hawaiian islands. He opened Roy's that year and went on to develop Hawaii regional cuisine.

Since then, Yamaguchi has opened four more Roy's restaurants, including one in Tokyo and one in Guam. But he can still be found cooking seven days a week in the Roy's five minutes from his home in Honolulu's Hawaii Kai district.

"I still start each day as if I had to prove myself all over again," says the star of the Hawaii public television series "Hawaii Cooks With Roy Yamaguchi." "I'm constantly in search of new ideas. Cooking is my life. When I'm in the kitchen and I look out the window, I can't help but think I must be one of the luckiest persons in the world."

New 'Kine' Smoked Nairagi Sashimi with Fresh Ogo Salad

▾▾▾▾▾▾▾▾▾▾▾▾▾

Roy Yamaguchi
Roy's Restaurant
Honolulu, Hawaii

This recipe carries us deep into the heart of Japanese-influenced Hawaiian cuisine. Since it asks the cook to cure and smoke striped marlin, as well as to whip up a seaweed salad, it must be considered a rather ambitious adventure in the kitchen.

Serves 4

Cured and Smoked Nairagi

6 ounces sashimi-grade loin of nairagi (striped marlin) or yellowfin or bluefin tuna fillet
1 tablespoon black sesame seeds, toasted (see page 236)
2 tablespoons packed brown sugar
1/4 cup granulated sugar
1 tablespoon kosher salt
1 tablespoon chopped Maui or other sweet white onion
1 teaspoon minced fresh basil
1 teaspoon snipped fresh dill

Ogo Salad

6 ounces ogo (seaweed), red and green if available
1 small Maui or other sweet white onion, cut into 1/4-inch julienne
1 small tomato, seeded and cut into 1/4-inch julienne
1 tablespoon 1/4-inch diagonally-cut green onion, including some of the green top
3 ounces fresh bean sprouts
1/4 cup finely julienned Japanese cucumber
1 tablespoon finely julienned carrot
1 tablespoon minced fresh cilantro
2 tablespoons toasted sesame oil
2 tablespoons soy sauce
2 tablespoons olive oil
2 teaspoons minced fresh ginger
1 teaspoon red pepper flakes
1 teaspoon minced garlic
1 teaspoon chili oil
1 teaspoon fresh lemon juice

Salad Dressing

¼ cup soy sauce

2 tablespoons toasted sesame oil

1 tablespoon rice wine vinegar

1 tablespoon Black Peppercorn–Wasabi
 Vinaigrette (recipe follows)

1 tablespoon fresh lemon juice

1 tablespoon extra-virgin olive oil

1 tablespoon Lingham brand Thai chili
 sauce (available at Asian markets)

⅛ teaspoon red pepper flakes

Garnish

2 cups baby greens

2 ounces enoki mushrooms

¼ fresh mango, cut into ¼-inch-thick
 julienne

Whole fresh chive stems

Shichimi pepper
 (available at Asian markets)

White sesame seeds

Lingham brand Thai chili sauce

Soy sauce

To cure the fish: Two days before
serving, coat the fish with the sesame
seeds, pressing them firmly into the
flesh on all sides, and wrap the fish
tightly in a double square of cheesecloth. In a small bowl, combine the
sugars, salt, onion, basil, and dill. Place
about half of the curing mixture on a
piece of plastic wrap, put the wrapped
fish on top, and add the rest of the
curing mixture. Wrap the fish tightly in
the plastic wrap and chill for at least
4 or up to 24 hours.

Remove plastic wrap, lightly wash
off the curing mixture, and remove the
fish from the cheesecloth, leaving the
sesame seeds in place. Place the fish in
a deep baking pan and brush the fish
with olive oil. Cover and refrigerate for
24 hours.

To smoke the fish: Prepare a cold
smoker by placing the fish on a wire
rack over a baking pan filled with ice
cubes. Place this in the smoker (see
Note) and smoke at 75°F for 45 to 60
minutes. The fish will have smoky taste,
but will remain raw.

To make the ogo salad: In a large bowl,
combine the seaweed, onion, tomato,
green onion, bean sprouts, cucumber,
carrot, and cilantro. In another bowl,
combine the remaining ingredients.

Mix well and adjust the seasoning as
necessary; the flavor should be
pleasantly salty and spicy. Toss the
seaweed mixture with this dressing and
chill until ready to assemble and serve.

To make the salad dressing: In a small
bowl, combine all of the ingredients.
Place into a squeeze bottle and set aside.

To serve: Using a very sharp knife,
slice the smoked fish paper thin. In the
middle of each chilled salad plate,
arrange a mound of the ogo salad.
On top, place a few leaves of the baby
greens and add 4 to 5 slices of the fish
fanned out over the top. Add some of
the enoki mushrooms and some of the
mango. Drizzle the salad and edge of
the plate with the salad dressing. Add
the remaining slices of mango and 1 or
2 chive stems. Sprinkle Shichimi pepper
and sesame seeds over the salad and
around the edge of the plate. Drizzle
with Lingham chili sauce, some of the
remaining dressing, and soy sauce.

Note: *If a commercially built smoker
is not available, you may make a
smoker by building a low fire in a
kettle-type grill. Push the coals to the
side, add a pan of soaked wood chips,
and set the fish with the rack and ice
cubes on the grill. Cover and smoke
for about 45 minutes. Or, place soaked
wood chips in the bottom of a heavy
wok, then place a rack or perforated
pan over the coals. Set the fish with
the rack and ice cubes on top.*

Black Peppercorn–Wasabi Vinaigrette
Makes 1 cup

¼ cup wasabi powder (available in
 Asian markets)

2 tablespoons hot water

½ cup grated peeled fresh ginger

¼ cup extra-virgin olive oil

2 tablespoons toasted sesame oil

1½ teaspoons fresh lemon juice

¼ cup rice wine vinegar

¼ cup grated Maui or other sweet white
 onion

½ tablespoon minced fresh cilantro

½ teaspoon soy sauce

1 tablespoon fresh-cracked black pepper

1 tablespoon honey

Salt to taste

In a small bowl, combine the wasabi
powder with the hot water to make a
thick paste. The mixture should be thick
enough that it stays in the bottom of the
bowl when the bowl is inverted. Set the
paste aside.

Press the ginger through a fine-
meshed sieve or squeeze it in your hand
over a bowl to extract the juice. In a
blender, combine 1 tablespoon of the
ginger juice with all the remaining
ingredients except the salt and blend
well. Slowly add the wasabi paste until
the desired taste and consistency is
reached. Season with salt. Cover and
refrigerate for up to 1 week.

New 'Kine' Smoked Nairagi Sashimi with Fresh Ogo Salad;
Roy Yamaguchi, Roy's Restaurant

Spicy Shrimp with Avocado Salsa and Fried Tortilla Chips;
Robert Del Grande, Rio Ranch

Spicy Shrimp with Avocado Salsa and Fried Tortilla Chips

Robert Del Grande
Rio Ranch
Houston, Texas

All the colors, tastes, and textures of the Southwest seem to find a place somewhere in this dish. The salsa cools even as it adds a bit of zing.

Serves 4

Roasted Vegetables
4 plum (Roma) tomatoes
6 tomatillos, husked
4 garlic cloves, threaded on a soaked
   wooden skewer
1 yellow bell pepper
1 red bell pepper
1 or 2 jalapeño chilies
1 small white onion, quartered

Shrimp
1 pound medium shrimp in the shell
1 teaspoon chili powder
1 teaspoon salt

Avocado Salsa and Garnish
Roasted Vegetables, above
1 cup fresh cilantro leaves
2 teaspoons coarse salt
$1/4$ to $1/2$ cup tomato juice
2 avocados, peeled, seeded, and diced
4 teaspoons fresh lime juice
Freshly ground black pepper to taste
$1\frac{1}{2}$ teaspoons maple syrup (optional)
4 lime wedges
4 cilantro sprigs
Fried Tortilla Chips (recipe follows)

To roast the vegetables: Over a very hot charcoal fire, grill the vegetables until they are lightly charred and tender but not mushy. Remove all vegetables from the grill. Place the peppers and chili(es) in a paper bag, close it, and let them cool. Remove the skins and seeds from the peppers and the seeds from the jalapeño(s). Set all the vegetables aside.

To prepare the shrimp: In a medium saucepan, place the shrimp and add enough cold water to just cover them. Add the chili powder and salt to the pan and, over high heat, bring the water to a boil. Immediately remove the pan from the heat and set aside for 1 minute, then drain, place the shrimp in a single layer on a baking sheet, and let cool to room temperature. Set aside 8 shrimp for the garnish and dice the remainder.

To make the salsa: In a blender or food processor, place all of the roasted vegetables, along with any juices collected while they are cooled. Add the cilantro leaves, coarse salt, and process them adding enough of the tomato juice to produce a chunky salsa. Pour the salsa into a large bowl. Reserve ¼ cup of the diced avocado for garnish, and gently stir the remainder into the salsa along with the diced shrimp. Add the lime juice and pepper. Taste for seasoning. If it is too spicy or tart, add maple syrup to balance the flavors.

To serve: Spoon the salsa into large Margarita glasses and garnish the top with 2 reserved shrimp, a lime wedge, some of the reserved diced avocado, and a sprig of cilantro. Serve the salsa with the tortilla chips.

Fried Tortilla Chips
Makes 32 chips

4 flour or corn tortillas, each cut into
  eighths
Oil for frying
Chili powder and salt, optional

In a heavy saucepan over high heat, heat 1 inch of oil until smoking. Add the tortilla triangles in batches and fry until golden and crisp, about 2 minutes. Using a slotted spoon, remove and drain on paper towels. Lightly season with chili powder and salt, if you like.

ROBERT DEL GRANDE
Rio Ranch, Houston, Texas

No one can accuse Robert Del Grande of not knowing what goes on in the pan or on the plate. After all, he picked up a B.S. in chemistry and biology in 1976 and earned a Ph.D. in biochemistry five years later. While best known nationally as the chef-owner of Cafe Annie in Houston, Del Grande is currently investing his time in a place called Rio Ranch.

Considering that he counts Albert Einstein and Bertrand Russell as two of his primary influences, it should come as no surprise that Del Grande is both scientific and philosophical about what he does.

"Each dish on the plate should be the manifestation of one single thought," he explains. "It all fits exactly like a puzzle – and a tight, singular thought squeezes errors out. The main item, the technique, the vegetable, and the sauce equal the whole. So the more complicated you make the sauce, the simpler you make the vegetable."

Del Grande is a native Californian, and he also points to a dinner at Michael's in Santa Monica in 1980, as another major inspiration for his cooking. The excitement of that dinner began to turn Del Grande's mind toward a career in food.

In the summer of 1981, he went to Houston to visit his future wife Mimi. He had worked in restaurants a bit while getting his Ph.D., but nothing had prepared him for the epiphany he would experience at Cafe Annie. It was a French bistro at the time, and Mimi's sister and brother-in-law were general partners. And they needed a cook.

Del Grande's plan included starting postdoctoral work in the fall, but the summer flirtation with Cafe Annie took hold. After a year, he was executive chef, slowly evolving the menu toward new American cuisine, with an emphasis on the Southwest. Del Grande approached cooking as a scientist goes at science, reading about and mastering the subject, then pushing out the boundaries on his own.

At Rio Ranch since 1992, Del Grande seems quite satisfied with his career choice. As far as he's concerned, you can create much more exciting things in the kitchen than in the chemistry lab.

CHARLES PALMER
Aureole, New York, New York

Charles Palmer may be the chef and co-owner of one of Manhattan's most stylish restaurants, but he got his start in a home economics class in Smyrna, New York. It was there that the "joy of cooking" became a reality to him and he began to learn the basic skills that placed him in the right place at the right time.

When the Swiss chef at the Colgate Inn left abruptly one day, there was a young man in his kitchen ready to take over. He was only sixteen, but he was already a pro. His name was Charles Palmer.

Palmer would eventually found two major restaurants in Manhattan: Aureole in 1988, consistently ranked among the top twenty-five restaurants in the entire United States, and the Chefs Cuisiniers Club in 1990, born from the practice of late night dining among chefs. Now known as Alva, the latter place is notable for the menus from around the world that adorn its walls and for staying open until 2 A.M. A huge mural of famous chefs is behind the bar.

After training at the Culinary Institute of America, Palmer found his first home at La Côte Basque, joining the team led by Jean-Jacques Rachou that reopened that famed eatery. Before heading to La Côte Basque each day, he made sauces at Lavandou. At the end of each day, he made pastries at Le Petite Marmite.

In 1983, Palmer was named executive chef at the River Cafe, following in the famous footsteps of Larry Forgione. While in this hotbed of innovative American cuisine, Palmer constructed a smoke-house, became a partner in a duck farm, and set up his own network of small farmers to provide 70 percent of his produce. Palmer increased the River Cafe's profits, and raised it from one to three stars in the eyes of Bryan Miller of the *New York Times*.

This chef loves to travel—especially from restaurant to restaurant and kitchen to kitchen. In search of personnel and fresh inspiration, Palmer pays regular visits to France, Italy, Belgium, Germany, and every significant culinary region of the United States.

Carpaccio of Tuna

Charles Palmer
Aureole
New York, New York

Here's a fresh, light appetizer: thin slices of raw tuna on spicy greens dressed with a lemony vinaigrette.

Serves 4

Four 3-ounce, 1/4-inch-thick cross-cut
   slices yellowfin or bluefin tuna
3 tablespoons olive oil
Salt and freshly ground black pepper
   to taste

Vinaigrette
2 tablespoons extra-virgin olive oil
3 shallots, minced
2 tablespoons white wine vinegar
Grated zest and juice of 1/2 lemon
1 teaspoon snipped fresh chives
Kosher salt and freshly ground black
   pepper to taste
3 cups spicy baby greens, such as
   purslane, watercress, or arugula

Garnish:
1 1/2 tablespoons finely diced celery
1 1/2 tablespoons finely diced tomato
Grated zest of 1/2 lemon
1 tablespoon caperberries (see Note)

To prepare the fish: Place 1 slice of tuna on a sheet of plastic wrap rubbed with some olive oil. Top with another piece of oiled plastic wrap and use the smooth side of a meat mallet or the side of a heavy bottle to pound the fish to a sheet $1/16$-inch thick, turning it with each stroke to make a uniformly round piece. Season with salt and pepper. Repeat with the remaining pieces of fish.

To make the vinaigrette: In a small sauté pan or skillet over medium heat, heat the olive oil and sauté the shallots until they are translucent, about 2 minutes. Place the shallots and oil in a small bowl, and add the remaining ingredients. Place $1/4$ cup of the vinaigrette in a squeeze bottle and set aside.

To serve: Toss the greens with the remaining vinaigrette. Place some of the greens on each of the serving plates and place 1 piece of carpaccio in the center. Garnish with the celery and tomato, drizzle with the vinaigrette in the bottle, then add the lemon zest and caperberries.

Note: *Caperberries are a product of Spain. They are about the size of an olive and come with a 1-inch stem attached.*

Carpaccio of Tuna; *Charles Palmer, Aureole*

Lobster Salad on a Bed of Potato, with Confit of Crispy Leek and Truffle Vinaigrette

▛▜▛▜▛▜▛▜▛▜▛▜▛▜

Julian Serrano
Masa's
San Francisco, California

A lobster salad based on French techniques and exquisite ingredients makes a showstopper first course.

Serves 4

Truffle Vinaigrette
3/4 cup extra-virgin olive oil
1/2 cup truffle oil
3 tablespoons sherry vinegar
2 tablespoons truffle juice
Salt and freshly ground black pepper to taste
2 red potatoes
1/4 teaspoon saffron
1 tablespoon diced shallot
1 tablespoon snipped fresh chives
Two 1-pound chicken (female) lobsters
1 large leek, white part only
Vegetable oil for deep-frying
Salt to taste
1 teaspoon truffle shavings

Garnish
Truffle oil
Lobster or salmon roe
2 tablespoons snipped fresh chives
4 fresh chervil sprigs

To make the truffle vinaigrette: In a large bowl, combine the oils, vinegar, and truffle juice and whisk until emulsified. Season with salt and pepper, and set aside.

To prepare the potatoes: Peel the potatoes and carve them into 1-inch-diameter cylinders. Place a medium saucepan of lightly salted water over high heat and bring to a low boil. Add the saffron and stir until dissolved. Add the potatoes and cook until tender, about 10 minutes. Slice the potatoes into 1/4-inch-thick medallions and place them into a small bowl with the shallot, chives, and 3 tablespoons of the vinaigrette.

To prepare the lobsters: Place a large stockpot of lightly salted water over high heat and bring it to a boil. Kill each lobster by using the point of a large knife to make a small incision in the back of the shell where the chest and tail meet. Place a long flat stick such as a chopstick against the underside of each lobster tail and tie it securely in place; this prohibits the tail from curling while the lobster cooks, and makes the meat easier to slice. Plunge the lobsters into the boiling water and cook until the shells turn bright red, 2 to 3 minutes.

Drain the lobsters and remove the strings and sticks. To clean the lobsters, hold the lobster over a medium plate and twist body (head) from the tail, shaking any roe out of the body cavity and tail section onto the plate (not all lobsters will have this coral-colored roe). Twist off claws and large knuckles and the legs where they join the body.

Lobster Salad on a Bed of Potato, with Confit of Crispy Leek and Truffle Vinaigrette;
Julian Serrano, Masa's

Reserve the bodies, large knuckles, legs, and shells for stock. Lightly crush each tail shell with your hands and carefully remove the meat. Pull the black strip out of the tail and discard it. Slice the tail into ½-inch-thick medallions. Use the back of the knife to crack the claws and remove the meat from them.

Place the lobster meat in a medium bowl and toss with the remaining vinaigrette. Place the bowl over a pan of warm water and keep warm over low heat for no more than 10 to 15 minutes.

To prepare the leek: Cut the leek in half lengthwise, and plunge into cold water to clean. Drain the leek and pat it very dry with paper towels, then cut the leek into thin lengthwise strips.

In a heavy medium saucepan or skillet, heat a 2-inch depth of oil until it reaches 350°F, or is fragrant. Drop in the leek and stir with a fork to separate the strands and keep the oil moving. Cook until crisp, 1 to 2 minutes. Remove the leek from the oil with a slotted spoon and drain on paper towels, again separating the strands with a fork. Sprinkle the leek with salt.

To serve: Add the truffle shavings to the potatoes and toss. Arrange 4 slices of potato in a circle in the center of each serving plate. Place 1 lobster medallion on each slice of potato and spoon some of the dressing on top. Mound some of the crisp leeks on top of the salad, and add the meat of 1 claw to each plate. Drizzle the plate with truffle oil, scatter some of the lobster roe or salmon caviar and snipped chives around the edges, and garnish with a sprig of fresh chervil.

JULIAN SERRANO
Masa's, San Francisco, California

Born in the Spanish capital of Madrid, Julian Serrano cooked his way through several sections of the world before finding his home in a San Francisco French restaurant founded by a chef from Japan. In fact, you might say that Masa's, the inspiration of the late Masa Kobayashi, has helped Serrano find himself.

In the spirit of Masa, Serrano has taken French cuisine in San Francisco to a decidedly new level, using the freshest of ingredients, classic sauces, and artistic presentation. This follows naturally enough, since it was Masa himself who hired Serrano in May 1984 and taught him to fulfill his vision.

"Masa gave my life to me," Serrano reflects today. "I finally realized that I could be a creative chef, that I could make beautiful things with talented people, that I could strive for perfection."

That desire for perfection was basic to Kobayashi's vision, but it was also a factor in Serrano's upbringing and apprenticeship in the European system. A graduate of Escela Gastronomie PPO, the hotel management school in Marbella on Spain's Costa del Sol, Serrano worked in some of Europe's most celebrated kitchens: Lucas-Carton in Paris, Hotel de France in Auch in southwest France, and Chez Max in Zurich.

The United States became his home port when Serrano embarked on a series of positions with Caribbean cruise liners sailing out of Miami. He next cooked in a Spanish restaurant in Nashville and a German restaurant called Beethoven in San Francisco before being hired at Masa's.

After the death of that widely praised establishment's founder, the top job was taken by William Galloway, with Serrano as his sous-chef. After a year, Serrano took a five-month trip to the Continent, honing his skills further with the likes of André Daquin, Alain Senderens, and Max Kehl. By the time he returned to Masa's, it was time to take on the ultimate challenge as its executive chef.

In addition to acclaim from *Gourmet* magazine, the *San Francisco Examiner* and the *San Francisco Chronicle*, under Serrano Masa's has received the highest rating ever given by his adopted city's *Zagat Restaurant Survey*.

If it was indeed Masa Kobayashi who gave Julian Serrano his life, it is Julian Serrano who breathes new life each day into the restaurant that is Masa's legacy.

DANIEL BONNOT

Chez Daniel, New Orleans, Louisiana

"There is an evolution in learning the way to cook, and it takes years of working for tough chefs." Daniel Bonnot ponders his own career for a moment, then pushes on. "The principles of cooking come first, at school. The learning part started with my apprenticeship, and it takes years."

For Bonnot, the unofficial dean of French chefs in New Orleans, the learning has never ended. Today, at his bistro, Chez Daniel, Bonnot is exploring the simplest dishes of his homeland, the kinds of foods he was rarely able to cook as chef at a long series of groundbreaking upscale restaurants.

Starting at age fourteen, Bonnot cooked his way through posts in several Paris restaurants, thus earning an assignment as personal chef to the minister of the French army. After military service, he worked at the famous Savoy Hotel in London, then at the Auberge de la Vielle Tour on the island of Guadeloupe in the French West Indies.

The Caribbean experience proved important to the twenty-three-year-old Bonnot, since it opened his eyes to a style of French cooking that would play a role in the rest of his career.

"It was my first experience with Creole food, and I couldn't believe the fish and vegetables and fruit, or the fresh spices and herbs that were available," Bonnot recalls. "After three years, I wanted to go to New Orleans because it seemed very French, but I wanted to cook classic French cuisine in New Orleans."

That mission became the foundation of the years that followed. Indeed, when Bonnot opened the restaurant Louis XVI in 1971 as the twenty-six-year-old *chef de cuisine*, it was a revelation for New Orleans. While French-flavored Creole food was everywhere in the city, most patrons had never tasted such classics as beef Wellington, rack of lamb, lobster in sauce américaine.

In time, Bonnot expanded his work and his frame of reference, overseeing Louis XVI as it became the training ground for much of New Orleans' restaurant industry.

Today, Bonnot has created the opposite of a huge "white table-cloth" restaurant: his own classic French bistro. Everybody who knows New Orleans knows about Daniel Bonnot, and everybody loves his food. Chez Daniel is suave and savvy; for Bonnot, it is clearly fun. It is a new chapter in his development as a chef. Like the best kind of artist, Bonnot is still growing.

Oysters Béarnaise

Daniel Bonnot
Chez Daniel
New Orleans, Louisiana

Here's a fresh spin on oysters baked in their shells. These are baked in scooped-out potato skins and topped with sautéed onions and leeks and béarnaise sauce.

Serves 6

3 unpeeled red potatoes
2 tablespoons unsalted butter
Tender green mid-section of 1 leek, sliced very thinly
1 onion, thinly sliced
Salt and fresh ground black pepper to taste
2 tablespoons Pernod
2 teaspoons minced fresh tarragon
6 large oysters, shucked, with their liquor reserved

Béarnaise Sauce
1/3 cup tarragon vinegar
1/2 cup dry white wine
2 tablespoons minced shallots
3 tablespoons minced fresh tarragon
3 egg yolks
1 cup (2 sticks) unsalted butter, melted
Salt and freshly ground black pepper to taste

Garnish
1 ounce prosciutto, cut into fine slivers
2 fresh tarragon sprigs

To prepare the potatoes: Preheat the oven to 350°F. Place a large pot of lightly salted water over high heat, bring to a low boil, and cook the potatoes until tender, about 10 minutes. Drain and cut the potatoes in half lengthwise. Scoop out the inside, leaving a 1/2-inch-thick shell. Place the potatoes in the oven for 3 to 4 minutes to dry slightly. Set aside. Leave the oven set at 350°F.

In a large, deep sauté pan or skillet over medium-high heat, melt 1 tablespoon of the butter and sauté the leek and onion, stirring often, until they are tender and most of the juices have evaporated, 10 to 15 minutes. Add the salt, pepper, and the remaining 1 tablespoon butter to the pan and cook for 5 minutes. Add the Pernod, warm it, and light it with a match. Shake the pan until the flames subside. Add the tarragon and cook for 3 minutes. Spoon some of the leek and onion mixture into each potato shell and top with one of the oysters and a little of the oyster liquor.

To prepare the béarnaise sauce: In a heavy medium nonaluminum sauté pan or skillet, combine the vinegar, wine, shallots, and 2 tablespoons of the tarragon. Bring the mixture to a boil and cook to reduce to ¼ cup. Remove from heat and let cool.

One at a time, whisk the egg yolks into the vinegar mixture, then return the pan to low heat and, whisking constantly, gradually add the butter to make a thick sauce. Strain the sauce through a fine-meshed sieve into a bowl and add the remaining 1 tablespoon tarragon, salt, and pepper. Keep warm over barely tepid water.

To serve: Bake the potatoes until the oysters inside plump and their juices have been absorbed by the potatoes, about 5 minutes. Spoon some of the béarnaise sauce over each of the oysters. Place the oyster-filled potatoes on a layer of rock salt in a serving platter, garnish each with some of the prosciutto, and place the tarragon sprigs among the oysters.

Oysters Béarnaise;
Daniel Bonnot, Chez Daniel

Smoked Trout Cake with Celery Juice

Jose Gutierrez
The Peabody
Memphis, Tennessee

New American chefs love smoked trout, a food more widely indigenous than smoked salmon from the Pacific Northwest. These terrific fried fish cakes are balanced by a fresh celery juice sauce and a fennel puree.

Serves 6

6 potatoes (12 ounces)
2 cups chicken stock (see page 228)
Pinch of saffron
Salt to taste

Celery Juice Sauce
½ bunch celery
2 tablespoons Colman's dry mustard
½ tablespoon fresh lemon juice
Salt and freshly ground black pepper
2 tablespoons olive oil

Fennel Puree
1 large fennel bulb, topped and coarsely
    chopped
¾ to 1 cup chicken stock (see page 228)
Salt and freshly ground black pepper
    to taste

Smoked Trout Cakes
3 small whole smoked trout (about 1½
    pounds total)
4 eggs
1 tablespoon snipped fresh chives
1⅓ cups diced celery (about 4 stalks)
¼ cup diced red bell pepper
Salt to taste
2 cups fine dried bread crumbs
1 tablespoon olive oil

Garnish
18 Belgian endive leaves
18 red oak lettuce leaves
18 curly endive leaves

To prepare the potatoes: Peel the potatoes and cut them into 2-inch cubes. With a melon baller, remove the center from each cube. In a medium saucepan over medium-high heat, bring the stock to a low boil. Stir the saffron into the stock, add the salt, then add the potatoes. Cook until the potatoes are just tender, 6 to 8 minutes. Remove them from the stock with a slotted spoon, drain them upside down on paper towels, and set aside.

To make the celery juice sauce: Using an electric juice extractor, process the celery to obtain ½ cup of juice. In a blender, combine the juice, mustard, lemon juice, salt, and white pepper. With the motor running, slowly add the olive oil to obtain a thick, creamy sauce. Set aside.

To make the fennel puree: In a small, deep pan or skillet over medium-high heat, place the fennel and enough stock to cover it. Cook until the fennel is tender, about 8 minutes. In a blender, puree the fennel with just enough stock to make a puree that is smooth but thick enough to mound in a spoon. Season with salt and pepper. Set aside and keep warm.

To prepare the trout cakes: In a large bowl, beat 3 of the eggs. Remove the skin and bones from the fish and break up the meat with your fingers. Place the fish in the bowl with the beaten eggs and add the celery, red pepper, chives, and salt. Mix with a fork and add just enough of the bread crumbs to bind the mixture together.

Form the mixture into 6 balls, then pat and shape them into 1-inch-thick cakes. Place the remaining egg in a separate shallow bowl and beat the egg. Place the remaining bread crumbs in another shallow bowl. Dredge the cakes in the egg, and then in the bread crumbs. Cover and refrigerate for at least 30 minutes.

In a large sauté pan or skillet over medium heat, heat the oil and fry the trout cakes, turning once, until golden brown, a total of about 4 minutes.

To serve: In the center of each serving plate, spoon a mound of the fennel puree. Lay 1 trout cake against this mound. Place 1 potato cube at the edge of the cake and fit one of each of the decorative greens into the potato to form a "bouquet." Spoon some of the celery juice sauce on each side of the plate and serve immediately.

Roast Bahamian Lobster with Chili, Saffron, Vanilla, and Rum;
Allen Susser, Chef Allen's

Roast Bahamian Lobster with Chili, Saffron, Vanilla, and Rum
■■■■■■■■■■■■■■■■■■■■

Allen Susser
Chef Allen's
Miami Beach, Florida

Bahamian lobsters, unlike their kin hailing from northern waters, have no claws. Either type of lobster will work in this recipe, in which Caribbean cooking establishes a beachhead in south Florida.

Serves 6

6 Bahamian lobsters, or 6-ounce lobster
  tails
1 teaspoon fresh thyme leaves
Salt and freshly ground black pepper
  to taste
¼ cup olive oil

Glaze
1 cup dry white wine
2 shallots, minced

1 vanilla bean, split lengthwise
1 teaspoon minced Scotch bonnet
  (habanero) chili
Pinch of saffron
3 tablespoons Myers's dark rum

1 tablespoon Myers's dark rum
Green Papaya Slaw (recipe follows)

To prepare the lobsters: Light a wood or charcoal fire in a grill. (The lobsters may also be broiled under a preheated broiler or baked in a 350°F oven until the meat is opaque.) Kill each lobster by using the point of a large knife to make a small incision in the back of the shell where the chest and tail meet. Twist the body (head) and tail apart, and twist off the legs where they join the body. Reserve the legs to use for stock another time. With a large, heavy knife, cut through each tail shell on the top side, spread it open, and pull out the meat, leaving it attached to the shell at the tail end. Remove and discard the black strip. Lay the meat on top of the shell and sprinkle with the thyme, salt,

and pepper. Drizzle the olive oil over the lobster and set the lobster aside for 15 minutes.

To make the glaze: Heat a medium sauté pan or skillet over high heat, add the wine and shallots, and cook to reduce for 1 minute. Add the vanilla bean, chili, saffron, and 3 tablespoons of the rum. Continue to cook over medium heat until the glaze is thick, syrupy, and reduced to ½ cup, about 10 minutes.

Preheat the oven to 350°F. Place the lobsters, meat-side down, on the grill, and cook until they are nicely charred and have absorbed some of the smoky flavor of the grill, about 5 minutes. Transfer the lobsters to a heavy roasting pan and brush with glaze. Place the pan into the oven and roast for 8 minutes. Remove from the oven and brush the lobsters with the remaining glaze. Add the 1 tablespoon rum to the pan, warm it over medium heat and light it with a match. Shake the pan until the flames subside, then turn the lobsters in the pan to coat them.

To serve: Place a mound of papaya slaw in the center of each serving plate. Remove the lobster from each shell and lay the tail over the slaw on each plate. Brush with any remaining glaze and serve.

Green Papaya Slaw
Serves 6
1 large green papaya, peeled and seeded
1 large red bell pepper, seeded, deribbed
  and cut into fine julienne
1 carrot, peeled and cut into fine
  julienne
1 white onion, julienned
3 tablespoons shredded fresh ginger
Juice of 1 large lime or more to taste
3 tablespoons olive oil
1 teaspoons celery seeds
1 tablespoon kosher salt
1 teaspoon white pepper

Shred the papaya using the large holes of a grater. In a medium bowl, combine all the ingredients and toss well. Let sit for 1 hour before serving to let the flavors blend. Adjust the seasoning.

Charred Rare Tuna with Radish Salad and Soy-Ginger Vinaigrette

🔲🔲🔲🔲🔲🔲🔲🔲🔲

Anne Gingrass
Postrio
San Francisco, California

Coat and sear the tuna for this beautiful Asian-flavored salad 1 day in advance and chill it overnight. The tuna is then cut into very thin slices.

Serves 4

Tuna
3 tablespoons fresh-cracked pepper
1 tablespoon minced fresh ginger
One 8-ounce piece sashimi-grade
    yellowfin tuna, trimmed into
    an even rectangle
Peanut oil for frying

Soy-Ginger Vinaigrette
1/4 cup soy sauce
1/4 cup fresh lime juice
2 teaspoons minced shallots
1 teaspoon minced fresh ginger
1 teaspoon minced garlic
1/2 cup peanut oil
2 teaspoons toasted sesame oil
Salt and freshly ground black pepper
    to taste

Radish Salad
1 1/2 cups julienned peeled carrots
    (about 2 to 3 carrots)
1 cup thinly sliced red onion (1 onion)
1 cup julienned daikon (available in
    Asian markets)
1/2 cup julienned leek, white part only
1/4 cup thinly sliced red radishes
1/4 cup minced fresh cilantro
Soy-Ginger Vinaigrette, above

To prepare the tuna: On a sheet of waxed paper, combine the pepper and ginger. Roll the tuna in the mixture and press to evenly coat the tuna. Brush a large sauté pan or skillet with oil, heat it over high heat, and sear the tuna on each side for 30 to 45 seconds, or just until the outside is seared. Remove the tuna from heat, cover, and refrigerate until serving time.

ANNE GINGRASS
Postrio, San Francisco, California

For Anne Gingrass and her husband David, cooking is literally a labor of love. After their meeting at the Culinary Institute of America in 1983, the two chefs moved to California and haven't been apart since.

For a time, though, they hopped back and forth so often between Los Angeles and San Francisco it was hard to tell who was going in which direction. Anne found herself going from Spago in Southern California to Stars in Northern California, then back again. At the same time, David was moving from Mudd's and the San Francisco Tennis Club to the Hotel Bel-Air, then Spago.

One constant of their life emerged: an amiable relationship with chef Wolfgang Puck. Anne held the post of chef at Spago for three years, while David developed the restaurant's signature homemade breads, sausages, and smoked salmon.

Anne and David married in 1986 and welcomed the opportunity to return to San Francisco to help establish Puck's first restaurant in that city. Postrio, named after its Post Street location and the trio of chefs in the kitchen, opened to rave reviews in April 1989. An elegant and thoroughly contemporary restaurant just off the city's busy Union Square, Postrio showcases local products and exciting interpretations of ethnic cuisines, particularly those of the Italian and Chinese cultures so prevalent in San Francisco.

Recently, it was time for the Gingrasses to hop again. In 1995 they left Postrio to open their own restaurant, Hawthorne Lane, on a secluded street near the city's new Museum of Modern Art.

To make the vinaigrette: In a blender or food processor, combine the soy sauce, lime juice, shallots, ginger, and garlic. Process for 1 minute and strain the mixture into a medium bowl. Slowly whisk in the oils and season with salt and pepper.

To make the salad: In a large bowl, combine the carrots, onion, daikon, leek, red radishes, and cilantro. Mix well, then toss with just enough of the vinaigrette to moisten the salad.

To serve: Use a very sharp knife to slice the cold charred tuna horizontally into sixteen 1/8-inch-thick slices. Toss the salad and mound one-fourth of it in the center of each of the serving plates. Fan 4 slices of tuna around the salad and drizzle it with some of the remaining vinaigrette.

MICHEL RICHARD
Citrus, Los Angeles, California

Michel Richard is a rarity: a French chef in the United States who is as concerned about diet as he is about flavor. Of course, after working with Michel Guerard, the father of *cuisine minceur*, at Eugénie-les-Bains, he's convinced that the two concerns need not be mutually exclusive.

"There is definitely a French tradition that is based on fresh flavors," says the chef-owner of the chic California-style Citrus in Los Angeles. "We use the term *pointu*, meaning they have an edge that enlivens them. The minute you add butter and cream, that changes, and the honest flavors are dulled."

Richard's cuisine is vibrant with flavor, as anyone who has tasted his Muscovy duck with Pinot Noir and bacon sauce, his chicken ravioli with herb sauce or his sautéed salmon with beet sauce and green beans will attest. In fact, many body-conscious Californians would be surprised to know that Richard got his start, and still excels, not in carrot sticks but in French pastry.

A classically trained chef from Rheims in the Champagne district, Richard worked first with dessert master Gaston Lenôtre. In 1975, he traveled to New York with Lenôtre to open a pastry shop. Then he spent a decade in Los Angeles running his own pastry shop, making his signature light desserts. Eventually, he opened Citrus, where he serves the same sort of desserts, plus a complete menu to match.

"I was tired of hearing how French food is heavy," he says. "And I was tired of seeing the French open the same restaurants here as they would in France."

Richard wanted his restaurant to be classy but not stuffy, and the light, bright decor mirrors both the name of the place and the style of the cooking. The sunny patio is covered with white canvas awnings and umbrellas, and both the outdoors and indoors are furnished with white wicker chairs and pale yellow linens.

The cooking is mostly done without using butter, cream, or flour, yet even the sauces are smooth and substantial, their consistency achieved with herb and vegetable purées. Guilt-free desserts are offered, including an excellent fruit mousse, although Richard also turns out more decadent pleasures, such as the chocolate cake with orange slices.

The idea is not one of deprivation, Richard insists, but of moderation. "You have to adapt to the lifestyle of your customers," he says. "This is California, not Normandy."

Swordfish Porcupines and Chayote Rémoulade

Michel Richard
Citrus
Los Angeles, California

Kataifi, or shredded phyllo dough, is available in the refrigerator or freezer section of Middle Eastern markets. When swordfish cubes are dipped in egg and kataifi, then fried, the crisp shreds of phyllo resemble the spines of a porcupine.

Serves 4

1 pound fresh or thawed frozen kataifi
1/3 cup all-purpose flour
1 egg at room temperature
1 tablespoon water
Salt and freshly ground black pepper
  to taste
Four 1-inch-thick 6-ounce swordfish
  steaks
Vegetable or peanut oil for frying
Salt to taste
1/4 cup snipped fresh chives
Chayote Rémoulade (recipe follows)

Remove the kataifi from the package and, over a shallow bowl, cut it with scissors into 1-inch pieces. Using your fingers, pull the dough apart, tossing and fluffing it in the bowl until it is completely separated into individual threads.

Place the flour in a small shallow bowl. In another shallow bowl, beat the egg and add the water, salt, and pepper. Line a baking sheet with parchment paper or grease the baking sheet; set aside.

To prepare the swordfish: Cut each swordfish steak into 4 large cubes and remove any large veins from the fish. Dip 1 swordfish cube into the flour and shake off any excess. Dip the cube into the egg mixture, then place it in the kataifi. Pick up the coated cube and press it firmly into the palms of your hands until it forms a package about 2½ inches in diameter. Shake to remove any excess kataifi, and place the fish on the prepared pan. Repeat with the remaining swordfish cubes. If not cooking immediately, cover and refrigerate for 1 hour, or until ready to use. Bring to room temperature before frying.

To cook the swordfish: Line a baking sheet with several layers of paper towel. In a large, heavy sauté pan or skillet, heat 1 inch of oil to 350°F, or until bubbles form around a wooden spoon immersed in the oil. Using tongs, dip 1 swordfish portion into the oil and cook until the bottom is set, then immerse the entire portion. Repeat to add the remaining swordfish in batches without crowding. Cook the "porcupines" until golden on both sides, about 3 minutes total. Using tongs or a slotted spoon, remove each piece from the oil and drain well on the prepared pan. Sprinkle the hot fish with salt and some of the snipped chives.

To serve: Spoon a mound of chayote rémoulade in the center of each serving plate. Arrange 4 "porcupines" on top of the rémoulade, sprinkle with more chives, and serve immediately.

Chayote Rémoulade
Makes 2 cups

2 chayotes, peeled and seeded
2 tablespoons orange juice
1 tablespoon Dijon mustard
1 tablespoon mayonnaise, preferably
  homemade
1 tablespoon minced shallot
1 teaspoon sugar
1 teaspoon Tabasco sauce
Salt and freshly ground black pepper
  to taste

Shred the chayotes on a mandoline or V-slicer. In a medium bowl, combine the shredded chayote with the orange juice, mustard, mayonnaise, shallot, sugar, and Tabasco. Mix well and add salt and pepper. Serve within 30 minutes.

Swordfish Porcupines and Chayote Rémoulade; *Michel Richard, Citrus*

Goat Cheese Cobbler

▀▄▀▄▀▄▀▄▀▄▀▄▀▄▀▄▀▄▀▄

Bruce Molzan
Ruggles Grill
Houston, Texas

Though it borrows the name of a popular dessert, this is a savory appetizer from start to finish. The sauce of fresh fruit juices in balsamic vinegar provides a perfect contrast to the creamy cheese filling.

Serves 8

Crust
3 cups sifted unbleached all-purpose
 flour
1 tablespoon sugar
1 teaspoon salt
1 cup (2 sticks) unsalted butter at room
 temperature, cut into pieces
3 to 4 tablespoons ice water

Filling
1 pound cream cheese at room
 temperature
3/4 cup sour cream
1 teaspoon salt
Freshly ground black pepper to taste
3 eggs
8 ounces fresh white goat cheese at
 room temperature

Ginger Paste
1/2 cup and sliced, peeled fresh ginger
2 cups rice wine vinegar
1/2 cup dry white wine
1/2 cup sugar
Salt to taste
1 tablespoon freshly ground
 black pepper

Verjus Sauce
2 1/2 pounds green grapes
1 pound red grapes
1 pear, cored, peeled, and chopped
1 apple, cored, peeled, and chopped
1 orange, peeled, seeded, sectioned, and
 chopped

1 cup balsamic vinegar
1 cup (2 sticks) cold butter, cut into
 1-inch pieces
Ginger Paste (above)

Salad
4 cups baby greens (a combination of
 red oak lettuce, baby spinach, fresh
 arugula, and watercress)
1/2 cup Verjus Sauce (above)
1 tablespoon balsamic vinegar
1 tablespoon olive oil
1/3 cup freshly grated Parmesan cheese
1 cup (5 ounces) hazelnuts, toasted,
 skinned, and coarsely chopped
 (see page 236)

Garnish
1 unpeeled Granny Smith apple, cored
 and cut into 1/8-inch-thick matchsticks
1/2 cup (2 1/2 ounces) hazelnuts, toasted,
 skinned, and coarsely chopped
 (see page 236)
1/4 cup freshly grated Parmesan cheese

Goat Cheese Cobbler; *Bruce Molzan, Ruggles Grill*

To make the crust: In a large bowl, combine the flour, sugar, and salt. Using a pastry blender or 2 forks, cut in the butter until the mixture resembles cornmeal. Remove 1 cup of this mixture and set aside. Gradually add the ice water to the remaining mixture, stirring with a fork, until the dough holds together when pressed between the fingers.

Divide the dough into 8 portions and roll each between 2 sheets of parchment paper or waxed paper to a thickness of 1/8 inch. Remove 1 sheet of the paper and fit the dough into 3-inch tart pans. Reserve left-over dough crumbs. Remove the remaining paper. Cut a 5-inch circle of parchment or aluminum foil and press into the tart pans over the dough. Pierce the dough through the paper or foil with the tip of a knife, then fill the shells with dried beans or pie weights. Refrigerate the unbaked shells for 20 minutes or more.

Preheat the oven to 425°F. Bake the tart shells for 15-20 minutes, or until beginning to brown. Remove from the oven and remove the paper or foil and beans. Let cool completely.

To make the filling: Preheat oven to 375°F. In the bowl of an electric mixer, combine the cream cheese, sour cream, and salt, and beat on medium speed until blended. With the mixer running, add the eggs one at a time, then add the salt and pepper. Stop the mixer and scrape down the sides, then add the goat cheese and mix until blended. Spoon the filling into the tart shells and sprinkle the top with the reserved dough crumbs.

Immediately bake the tarts for 1 hour. (Or, the tarts may be refrigerated and baked later.)

To make the ginger paste: In a heavy, medium saucepan, combine all ingredients except the black pepper. Cook over medium-low heat until all the liquid has evaporated and only a paste remains. Puree the mixture in a blender or food processor, then add the pepper. Set aside to cool.

To make the verjus sauce: Use an electric juice extractor to juice the grapes, pear, apple, and orange. Add the balsamic vinegar and measure the quantity; you should have about 7 cups. Place the juices into a small, heavy saucepan and cook over medium-high heat to reduce to about 1 cup. Still over medium-high heat, but without boiling, whisk in the butter a few pieces at a time, stirring constantly to completely incorporate each batch. Whisk in the ginger paste.

To make the salad: In a large bowl, combine the greens and add the verjus, vinegar, and oil. Toss to coat the greens with the dressing, then add the Parmesan and nuts.

To serve: Place 1 cobbler on each of 8 large serving plates. Ladle some of the remaining verjus sauce around the edge of each cobbler and place approximately 1/2 cup salad on one side of each plate. Garnish each salad with the apple matchsticks, then sprinkle each plate, including the edges, with some of the nuts and Parmesan cheese.

Roasted-Vegetable Terrine

▀▄▀▄▀▄▀▄▀▄▀▄▀▄▀▄▀▄▀▄

Gene Bjorklund
Aubergine
Memphis, Tennessee

Clever garnishes add a spark to this classic French dish: curls of deep-fried eggplant skins and crispy wafers of Parmesan.

Serves 4

6 plum (Roma) tomatoes
6 tablespoons olive oil
Salt and freshly ground black pepper
   to taste
2 large eggplants
2 zucchini
1 *each* red and green bell pepper,
   roasted, peeled, seeded and cut into
   ¹/₄-inch strips (see page 235)
Peanut oil for deep frying

Parmesan Wafers
5 tablespoons sifted finely grated
   Parmesan cheese
1 tablespoon all-purpose flour

2 cups baby mixed greens for garnish

Preheat the oven to 180°F. Core and cut the tomatoes in half lengthwise and shake out most of the seeds. Place the tomatoes in a small bowl and add 2 tablespoons of the olive oil, the salt, and pepper. Place the tomatoes, skin-side down, on a baking sheet and bake until dried but still soft, 2¹/₂ hours. Remove the tomatoes and place them on a paper towel-lined baking sheet to drain. Cover the tomatoes with a towel and refrigerate if not using them immediately.

Peel the eggplant in wide strips and reserve the peel. Slice the eggplants lengthwise into ¹/₄-inch-thick slices, lay them on a baking sheet in a single layer,

and sprinkle both sides lightly with salt. Slice the unpeeled zucchini lengthwise into ¹/₄-inch-thick slices, lay them on a baking sheet in a single layer, and sprinkle the slices lightly with salt. Let the vegetables stand for 20 minutes to render the water from them. Dry the slices with paper towels. Cut the peppers into ¹/₄-inch-wide strips.

In a large sauté pan or skillet over medium-high heat, heat 1 tablespoon of the olive oil and fry a few of the eggplant slices slowly in one layer, turning them often, until they are golden brown, 2 to 3 minutes on each side. Repeat to cook the remaining eggplant slices, then the zucchini slices. As the vegetables brown, remove them from the pan and lay them on paper towel-lined baking sheets. Add more olive oil to the sauté pan or skillet as necessary. Pat the slices dry with paper towels and chill if not assembling the terrine immediately.

To prepare the terrine mold: Line four 3-inch-wide ramekins, 2 inches deep, with plastic wrap, leaving a 3-inch overhang all around. Place one-fourth of the eggplant slices in each of the molds, letting the ends hang over the sides. Press the zucchini slices around the sides of the molds, pressing them into place with your fingers. Sprinkle the layers with salt and pepper. Layer one-fourth of the red pepper strips around the sides of the mold, pressing the peppers against the sides with your fingers. Next, layer one-fourth of the green pepper strips around the sides, pressing them against the red pepper. Sprinkle with salt and pepper.

Fit pieces of the roasted tomato into the center of the mold and lay 1 tomato half on top. Press down to compact the layers and check to see that the mold is packed full; if not, fill in the spaces with small pieces of the appropriate color of vegetable. The terrine should be very tightly packed, with all of the vegetables pressed tightly against the sides.

Roasted-Vegetable Terrine; *Gene Bjorklund, Aubergine*

Pull the overhanging slices of eggplant over the top of the mold and press, then pull the plastic wrap tightly over the mold. Place the terrines on a baking sheet and place another baking sheet on top of them. Add a 5-pound weight to the top pan and chill the terrines in the refrigerator for 24 hours.

To make the eggplant-skin curls: Cut the reserved eggplant skin into very fine julienne. Fill a heavy, medium saucepan to a depth of 2 inches with peanut oil, and heat over high heat to 350°F or until a bread crumb immediately sizzles and floats to the top when dropped in. Fry the strips until they crisp and curl, about 2 minutes. Drain on paper towels and set aside.

To make the Parmesan wafers: In a small bowl, combine the cheese and flour. In a medium nonstick sauté pan or skillet over medium-high heat, sprinkle about 1½ tablespoons of the mixture in an oval shape and spread it evenly with the back of a spoon. As the cheese melts and forms a wafer it will turn golden brown, about 1½ minutes. Turn the wafer carefully and let it brown on the second side, about 45 seconds.

Carefully remove the wafer from the pan with a wide spatula and curl it over a glass placed on its side to give it a curved shape. Repeat to make 4 wafers. The wafers will become more crisp as they dry and can be made up to 4 hours ahead of time; set them aside in a cool, dry place until ready to serve.

To serve: Open the plastic wrap on the top of each terrine and pat the vegetables with a paper towel to remove any excess moisture. Invert each terrine onto the center of a serving plate and remove the plastic wrap completely. Top the terrine with some of the deep-fried eggplant-skin curls, place a Parmesan wafer on one side of the terrine, and add a garnish of baby greens on the other side of the plate.

GENE BJORKLUND
Aubergine, Memphis, Tennessee

Memphis has some claims to food fame. Barbecue would have to top any list, followed by fried catfish. But a European chef coming to the banks of the Mississippi from cooking stints in France, Monte Carlo, Key West, Copper Mountain, and Morocco might seem like a fish out of water.

Not so, insists Gene Bjorklund, who received his primary training at the Lycée Technique d'Hotelière in Nice and cooked under more than one Michelin three-star chef before setting his sights on Memphis. With Bjorklund in the kitchen at Aubergine, the city famous for Graceland now cooks with grace as well.

At Aubergine, Bjorklund's province is Provence, that herb-kissed and sun-drenched blending of France and Italy, with memories of Greece strewn about in between. Bjorklund has been chef-owner here since June 1993, having earned his Memphis stripes at places as diverse as Bosco's Pizza Kitchen and Brew Pub, Anthony's, La Tourelle, and Chez Philippe at the Peabody Hotel.

This chef's encounters with France, primarily its southern exposure, go back as far as his 1980 apprenticeship at Chez Antoine in Aix-en-Provence. Other formative experiences included work with Alain Ducasse at the three-star Restaurant Le Louis XV in Monte Carlo, with Marc Meneau at the three-star L'Espérance in St-Père-sous-Vézelay, and, early on, at Club Med in Tetuan, Morocco, and Arc 2000 in the French Alps.

Today, however, Bjorklund seems mighty pleased to find himself in Memphis. Though the city may still be better known for music on Beale Street, Bjorklund can be proud to have created a famed bit of Provence in the heart of Tennessee.

Shrimp and Corn Rellenos; *Kevin Rathbun, Nava*

Shrimp and Corn Rellenos

Kevin Rathbun
Nava
Atlanta, Georgia

A traditional Latin American finger food gets a serious upgrading: Anaheim chilies are stuffed with a corn, shrimp, and cheese filling, then coated, fried, and served with cilantro sour cream and golden tomato sauce. Rattlesnake bean relish provides the final touch.

Serves 6

Filling
2½ tablespoons butter
½ cup minced onion
1 jalapeño chili, seeded and minced
1 tablespoon minced garlic
¾ cup fresh or frozen corn kernels
4 ounces shrimp, peeled, deveined, and
    chopped
1 tablespoon chopped fresh basil
1 tablespoon chopped fresh cilantro
¾ cup (3 ounces) grated Chihuahua or
    Monterey jack cheese
¼ cup crumbled fresh white goat cheese
Salt and freshly ground black pepper
    to taste

Cilantro Sour Cream
2 tablespoons safflower oil
3 shallots, minced
1 garlic clove, minced
¾ cup fresh cilantro leaves, chopped
2 tablespoons water
¼ cup sour cream
Salt and freshly ground black pepper
    to taste

Golden Tomato Sauce
4 tablespoons unsalted butter
2 large golden tomatoes, chopped
2 tablespoons minced shallots
1 tablespoon minced garlic
1 cup chicken stock (see page 228)
¼ cup fresh lime juice
Coarse salt and freshly ground black
    pepper to taste
1 tablespoon sugar, or to taste

Tortilla Crust
Peanut oil for frying
4 red chili corn tortillas (see Note)
3 tablespoons flour

2 teaspoons ancho chili powder (see Note)
2 shallots, roughly chopped
1 jalapeño chili, with or without seeds
2 tablespoons minced fresh cilantro
2 tablespoons dried white bread crumbs

1/2 cup unbleached all-purpose flour
2 eggs
3/4 cup buttermilk
6 Anaheim chilies, roasted and peeled, but left whole (see page 235)
Peanut oil for frying

Garnish
Rattlesnake Bean Relish (recipe follows)
6 fresh cilantro sprigs

To make the filling: In a large sauté pan or skillet over high heat, melt the butter and sauté the onion and jalapeño until the onion is translucent, about 3 minutes. Add the garlic and sauté for 2 minutes. Add the corn and shrimp and sauté until the shrimp are pink, about 2 minutes. Add the basil and cilantro and remove the pan from the heat. Stir in the cheeses and add salt and pepper. Cover and chill completely before using.

To make the cilantro sour cream: In a small sauté pan or skillet over high heat, heat the oil and sauté the shallots and garlic until they are translucent, about 2 minutes. Place the contents of the pan in a blender, add the cilantro and water, and blend until smooth. With the motor running, gradually add the sour cream. Add salt and pepper to taste and set aside.

To make the golden tomato sauce: In a large saucepan over high heat, melt 2 tablespoons of the butter and sauté the tomatoes, shallot, and garlic for 3 to 4 minutes. Add the lime juice and chicken stock, reduce heat, and simmer for 10 minutes. Add the salt and pepper and simmer another 3 to 5 minutes. Place the mixture in a blender or food processor and blend until completely smooth, add-ing the remaining 2 table-spoons of butter in chunks. Strain the sauce and add sugar as necessary to balance the acidity of the tomatoes. Set aside and keep warm.

To make the tortilla crust: In a deep

sauté pan or skillet over medium-high heat, heat 1 inch of peanut oil to almost smoking and fry the tortillas until they are very crisp, turning once or twice. Set them aside to cool. In a blender or food processor, combine the flour, ancho powder, shallots, jalapeño, and cilantro. Crumble the tortillas and add them to the blender or food processor with the bread crumbs, continuing to process until the mixture is evenly crushed.

To assemble the rellenos: Place the crust ingredients into a shallow bowl. Place the flour in another shallow bowl. In a third shallow bowl, beat the eggs with the buttermilk. Slit each roasted chili completely down one side, remove the seeds, and fill with some of the cold filling. Wrap the chili around the filling; depending on the size of the chili, it may not cover the filling completely. Lightly dust a relleno with flour, then dip it into the egg wash. Place the relleno in the crust mixture and use your hands to press and pack the crust onto the relleno. Repeat until all the rellenos are coated.

To finish the rellenos: In a large deep sauté pan or skillet over medium-high heat, heat 1 inch of peanut oil until it begins to smoke. Fry the rellenos, turning gently and only as often as necessary to completely brown them on all sides, 2 to 3 minutes. Drain the rellenos on paper towels.

To serve: Spread a circle of tomato sauce in the center of each serving plate and swirl in some of the cilantro sour cream. Place 1 relleno in the center of the plate and spoon some rattlesnake bean relish over the top. Garnish the plate with a sprig of cilantro.

Notes: *If red chili corn tortillas are not available, yellow corn tortillas plus 1 teaspoon paprika can be substituted. To make ancho chili powder, toast 2 ancho chilies in a 250°F oven for 20 minutes, then remove the stem and seeds and grind the pods into a fine powder in a spice grinder.*

Rattlesnake Bean Relish
Makes 3 cups

2 cups dried rattlesnake beans or substitute pinto beans
6 cups chicken stock (see page 228)
1/2 cup minced red onion
1/4 cup minced red bell pepper
1/4 cup finely chopped yellow bell pepper
1 jalapeño chili, seeded and minced
2 tablespoons chopped fresh cilantro
1/2 cup fresh lime juice
1/4 cup vegetable oil
1/4 teaspoon Tabasco sauce
Salt and freshly ground black pepper to taste

Pick over the beans to remove any stones. Rinse the beans and soak them in water to cover for 6 to 8 hours or overnight. Drain and rinse the beans. In a large saucepan, combine the beans and chicken stock. Bring to boil, reduce heat, cover, and simmer until tender, about 45 minutes. Drain the beans and place them in a large bowl. Add the remaining ingredients and let sit for 10 to 15 minutes to blend flavors.

Shrimp Enchiladas on Black Bean Sauce; *Stephan Pyles, Star Canyon*

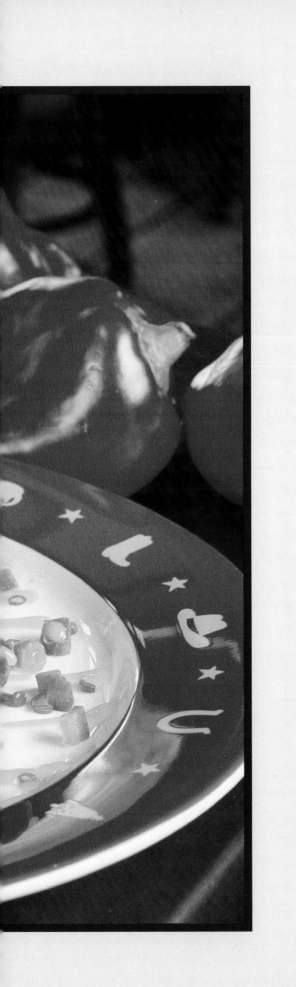

Fish and Shellfish

Thanks to modern methods of distribution and transportation, every fine restaurant in America can now serve first-rate fish and shellfish, even though many chefs prefer to highlight that of their region.

The popularity of fish and shellfish has grown along with the increasing awareness of their healthfulness. Restaurants have also contributed to this trend by emphasizing the careful cooking of fish and shellfish: not overcooking, then serving them simply.

Many of the recipes in this chapter use grilling or pan-searing, two cooking techniques that combine healthfulness and simplicity. In place of heavy butter-based sauces, you will find dishes that make use of fresh salsa or low-fat sauces. Fish and shellfish cooking in America is reaching new levels of art, and more and more people are becoming patrons.

Honolulu, Hawaii

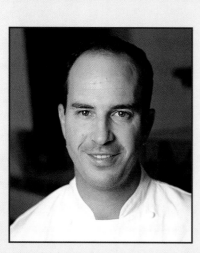

MARK MILITELLO
Mark's Place, Miami, Florida

Before Mark Militello, it was much harder to locate south Florida on the American culinary map. After all, with the exception of a plateful of stone crabs, a Cuban sandwich, and a handful of Eastern European dishes from New York, Miami food had little to recommend it.

Militello initiated something new in south Florida: an indigenous cuisine born of Caribbean ingredients, California techniques, and a keen awareness of ethnic influences from around the globe.

"I love this job because it affords me a lot of freedom," Militello says. "It is a great creative outlet." In his role of culinary pioneer, he has flown all over the country to cook south Florida cuisine, participating in the Rising Chefs dinner series at the James Beard House in New York, Meals on Wheels in Chicago, and the American Harvest Workshop at Cakebread Cellars in Napa Valley.

When Ethel and Bobby Kennedy's son Max was married in Philadelphia in 1991, Militello was flown to that city to oversee the banquet. That same year, he helped cook for the James Beard Holiday Auction.

Born in El Paso and raised in Buffalo, Militello began his education in Milwaukee, later earning an associate degree in hotel and restaurant management from New York State University and a bachelor of science in hospitality management from Florida International University.

He achieved prominence as a chef at Cafe Max in Pompano Beach, which he developed into three restaurants. Eventually, he became both executive chef and co-owner of one of these eateries, which was renamed Mark's Place.

The chef and his restaurant, not surprisingly, have picked up their share of honors and awards over the years. Militello was named to *Food & Wine* magazine's list of Ten Best New Chefs in America, and Mark's Place received a DiRona award as one of the nation's twenty-five best restaurants and distinguished restaurant honors from *Condé-Nast Traveler*. In 1992, Militello was named by the James Beard Awards committee as the best chef in the American Southeast.

Creole Spiny Lobster

Mark Militello
Mark's Place
Miami, Florida

In this wildly festive Caribbean dish, spiny lobsters are marinated in a lime-tinged Antilles marinade, sautéed, and served with a spicy mixture of island vegetables and a garnish of plantains and salt cod.

Serves 6

Six 1½-pound fresh spiny (rock)
  lobsters, preferably Caribbean

Antilles Marinade
½ cup extra-virgin olive oil
½ cup dry white wine
6 tablespoons fresh lime juice
3 tablespoons minced shallots
Salt and freshly ground black pepper
  to taste

Sauce
2 tablespoons extra-virgin olive oil
2 tablespoons minced garlic
½ cup finely diced onion
½ cup fresh or frozen corn kernels
½ cup diced red bell pepper
1 Scotch bonnet (habanero) chili, seeded
  and minced
3 tablespoons dry sherry
1½ tablespoons curry powder
2 large (8 ounces) tomatoes, peeled,
  seeded, and finely chopped
  (see page 234)
2 cups lobster or fish stock
  (see page 230)
½ cup finely diced christophine
  (chayote)
½ cup finely diced calabaza or acorn
  squash
½ cup finely diced yellow yam or sweet
  potato
½ cup cooked pigeon peas or black-
  eyed peas
2 tablespoons fresh thyme leaves
2 tablespoons chopped fresh flat-leaf
  (Italian) parsley
Salt and freshly ground black pepper
  to taste

Garnish

3 unpeeled plantains
Vegetable oil for frying
Salt to taste
1 tablespoon olive oil
1 bunch calaloo or spinach, washed, stemmed, and roughly chopped
2 tomatoes, peeled, seeded, and cut into 1/4-inch dice (see page 234)
1 garlic clove, minced
2 ounces salt cod, soaked in 4 changes of warm water for 15 minutes and rinsed each time, then drained and separated into flakes
Salt and freshly ground pepper to taste
6 dal puri* or flour tortillas
Lime wedges, preferably Key limes

To prepare the lobster: Separate the tail from the head of the lobsters, then split the tail in half lengthwise, leaving the end attached at the fins. Loosen the meat from the shell, but leave it slightly attached. Place the lobster tail halves, shell-side down, in a shallow dish or nonaluminum pan. Combine all the marinade ingredients and spoon the marinade over the lobster. Let sit at room temperature for 15 minutes. (If it sits longer, the lime juice will begin to cook the lobster meat.) Reserve the heads and bodies for other use, such as stock.

To make the sauce: In a large sauté pan or skillet over medium-high heat, heat the olive oil and add the garlic and onion, then add the corn, pepper, chili, 2 tablespoons of the sherry, and the curry powder, and sauté for 2 to 3 minutes. Add the tomatoes and stock and bring to a boil, then lower the heat and simmer for 15 minutes. Pass the sauce through a fine food mill or a fine-meshed sieve and return the sauce to the pan. Add the remaining sauce ingredients. Over low heat, simmer the mixture for 15 minutes, or until the vegetables are tender.

To make the vegetable garnish: In a small saucepan over high heat, boil the plantains in lightly salted water until they are tender, about 15 minutes. Peel the plantains and cut one of them into 1/4-inch-thick slices.

In a large sauté pan or skillet over high heat, heat the olive oil and sauté the calaloo or spinach, tomatoes, garlic, and salt cod flakes until the vegetables are tender, 3 to 5 minutes. Add the plantain slices and stir until they are heated through. Add salt and pepper. Set aside and keep warm.

Slice the remaining plantain into very thin lengthwise slices. In a heavy, medium sauté pan or skillet, heat 1 inch vegetable oil to 350°F, or until a bread crumb immediately sizzles and comes to the top when dropped in. Fry the plantain slices, turning once, until they are lightly browned and crisp, about 3 to 5 minutes. Using a slotted spoon, remove the plantains from the oil and drain on paper towels. Sprinkle the slices with salt while they are still warm. Set aside.

To cook the lobsters: Preheat the oven to 350°F. Pat the lobsters dry with paper towels. In a large sauté pan or skillet over medium-high heat, heat the oil and sear the lobsters, cut-side down, until lightly colored, about 2½ minutes, then turn and cook on the shell side for 1 minute. Make sure the heat is not too

high in order to prevent the lobster meat from becoming tough. Drain the oil from the pan, return the pan to the heat, and add the remaining 1 tablespoon sherry. Ladle the sauce over the lobsters and place the pan in the oven to finish cooking, 7 to 8 minutes.

To serve: Preheat the broiler. Fold the dal puri or tortillas into quarters. Place under the broiler for a few minutes on each side until lightly toasted.

Meanwhile, remove the lobster meat completely from the shell and dip the meat briefly into the sauce, then return it to the shells for presentation. Place some of the vegetable garnish in the center of each serving plate and add 1 split lobster tail to each plate. Spoon the sauce over the lobster and onto the plate.

Serve with the grilled dal puri or tortillas and the lime wedges, and place a fried plantain slice in the center of each dish.

* Dal puri are flat breads made from lentil flour and are available in Indian markets.

Creole Spiny Lobster; *Mark Militello, Mark's Place*

Langoustine Purse with Mango, Leeks, and Ginger, with a Port Wine Sauce; *Hans Röckenwagner, Röckenwagner*

Langoustine Purse with Mango, Leeks, and Ginger, with a Port Wine Sauce

Hans Röckenwagner
Röckenwagner
Los Angeles, California

Langoustines receive an elegant treatment here: Sautéed with chopped leeks, layered with blanched leek and spinach leaves, and tied into "purses" of rice paper. They are then served with an ambrosial port wine reduction and an intense curry oil.

Serves 3

Curry Oil
2 tablespoons best-quality curry powder
½ tablespoon water
1 cup soybean oil

Langoustine Purses
12 langoustines (giant prawns), cleaned
Salt and freshly ground black pepper
  to taste
1½ tablespoons extra-virgin olive oil
4 tablespoons unsalted butter
4 cups coarsely chopped leeks (white
  and light green part only)
2 garlic cloves, thinly sliced
¼ cup minced fresh ginger
½ cup lobster stock (see page 230)
¼ cup finely shredded fresh basil
18 large spinach leaves
Tender green part of 1 or 2 leek leaves,
  cut into ¼-by-8-inch strips
Six 8-inch round rice paper sheets
  (available in Asian markets)

Port Wine Reduction
4 cups ruby port
2 shallots, thinly sliced
1 pod star anise
¼ cup veal stock (see page 228)

3 tablespoons butter
2 mangoes, peeled, seeded, and
  thinly sliced

To make the curry oil: In a small bowl, combine the curry powder and water, and stir to form a paste. Whisk the paste into the oil and let stand at room temperature for 24 hours, then strain it through cheesecloth into a bowl without pressing any solids into the resulting oil.

To make the purses: Season the langoustines with salt and pepper. In a large sauté pan or skillet over high heat, heat the olive oil and sear the langoustines for 30 to 45 seconds, then remove from the pan and set aside.

In the same pan over low heat, melt the butter and add the leeks. Cook the leeks until they are softened, 8 to 10 minutes, then add the garlic and ginger and cook for 3 more minutes. Add the lobster stock, increase the heat to medium, and cook to reduce the liquid by half, about 10 minutes. Remove from heat, season to taste with salt and pepper, and add the basil. Set aside.

Bring a medium saucepan of lightly salted water to a boil and blanch the spinach leaves for 15 seconds, then remove them with a slotted spoon and plunge them into ice water. Drain the spinach well. Blanch the leek strips for 1 minute in the boiling water and plunge them into ice water. Drain the leek strips.

Dip the sheets of rice paper into lukewarm water for a few seconds until they are softened and pliable, and place them on the work surface. Lay 3 of the blanched spinach leaves over each of the rice papers and mound 2 tablespoons of the leek mixture into the center. Top each with 2 langoustines, then top the langoustines with 1 tablespoon of the leek mixture. Bring the sides of the rice paper up and gather them together at the top to form the "purse." Wind 1 of the blanched leek strips around the top of each purse and tie the ends. Set the completed purses on a baking sheet and place in the refrigerator.

To make the wine reduction: In a small, heavy nonaluminum saucepan, combine the port, shallots, and star anise and cook over medium heat to reduce by three-fourths, about 30 minutes. Add the veal stock, stir to blend, and continue to cook to reduce to just under 1 cup of syrupy liquid, about 30 to 40 minutes. Strain the sauce through cheesecloth into a clean saucepan and set aside to keep warm.

To serve: Preheat the oven to 425°F. Brush the bottom of a large nonstick baking pan with some of the melted butter and place the purses in the pan. Drizzle the remaining butter over the purses and bake in the oven until they are golden and crisp, 8 to 10 minutes.

On each of the serving plates, arrange a circle of overlapping mango slices. Place 2 purses in the center of each plate and drizzle the wine reduction and the curry oil around the edges of the plate.

HANS RÖCKENWAGNER
Röckenwagner, Los Angeles, California

If this chef's last name seems like a modern version of the revolutionary German opera composer's, the allusion is apt. Hans Röckenwagner has spent the better part of his career creating new culinary ideas. And he has done so in a hotbed of such ideas, southern California.

In the space of ten years, Röckenwagner opened his namesake restaurant in Venice, then traded it in on a larger location in Santa Monica; created a casual, California-Mediterranean eatery called Fama; opened a sophisticated sandwich shop and bakery cleverly dubbed Röcken Roll; and finally premiered a wildly innovative restaurant in the Beverly Prescott Hotel, this time under the name Röx.

The story begins in Germany, where young Hans cooked his way around the restaurant run by his parents in Schlingen, Holaschoff. He was formally trained and received his apprenticeship in the Black Forest, followed by a cooking tour of France and Switzerland. Highlights included Zum Adler, a two-star near Basil, the Hotel Beau Rivage in lovely Lausanne and Le Coq au Vin in Triel-sur-Seine, just outside Paris.

Röckenwagner was introduced to the United States by Jovan Trboyevic, who brought the chef to Chicago to cook at Le Perroquet. He opened his first version of Röckenwagner in 1985, and hasn't really slowed down since.

Over the years, his restaurants have been awarded stars and toques and forks, yet Röckenwagner seems proudest of the less typical accolades. For example, he was one of only five American chefs chosen to cook the first-ever American dinner at the Seperi e Sapori gastronomic festival in Italy. And his bakery-deli was named by *Los Angeles* magazine as one of the five best places to pick up a picnic basket for the Hollywood Bowl.

With such honors coming his way on a regular basis, it's a given that Röckenwagner will continue his innovative work in the kitchen — or rather, in the many kitchens that await him in the future.

JEAN-GEORGES VONGERICHTEN
JoJo's / Vong, New York, New York

Born in Alsace (which explains his French first name and German surname), Jean-Georges Vongerichten not only had the chance to work under acclaimed Michelin chef Louis Outhier, he got to work above him as well. As a member of Outhier's "flying squadron of chefs," Vongerichten was sent to open ten restaurants around the world, including Bangkok, Singapore, Hong Kong, Portugal, London, Boston and New York.

Even before he took to the skies, Vongerichten was well along on his voyage of culinary discovery. Deciding to become a chef at age fifteen, he started close to home – and as close to glory as you can get in Alsace. His apprenticeship at the three-star Auberge de l'Ill taught him much about his native region's foods, yet propelled him outward at the same time. His next job, under Paul Bocuse at his three-star near Lyons, moved Vongerichten south, a process that pointed him toward Outhier and L'Oasis in the south of France.

The chef was lured to New York to run the kitchen at the Drake Hotel's Restaurant Lafayette. During this extraordinary period, he was forced to confront the traditional bias against hotel restaurants. The top rating of four stars from the *New York Times* was the result, making the Lafayette the city's only hotel dining room to be so honored.

The message was clear: Vongerichten should open his own place. As it turned out, he opened not one but two. The first, called JoJo, evoked his highly personal style of cooking with a nouvelle reliance on vegetable juices, vinaigrettes, flavored oils, and broths.

Vongerichten's second entrepreneurial outing, opening two years after JoJo, is called Vong. Though taken from his own, the name has an appropriately Asian sound, for Vong combines the ingredients of Thailand and Vietnam with the refinement of classic French techniques.

Through it all, Vongerichten has continued to develop his trademark simple style. His cookbook, in fact, is titled *Simple Cuisine* (Prentice Hall Press) and is devoted to dishes at their most basic and most flavorful.

The menus at JoJo are unique. In a world in which chefs practically pen novellas about each dish, giving the life history of each berry in the sauce, JoJo's are given such names as Codfish, Salmon, Chicken, Duck, or Lamb. It requires a certain faith in the chef to order here. Vongerichten has earned precisely such faith.

Roast Lobster with an Orange Zest Crust

Jean-Georges Vongerichten
JoJo's/Vong
New York, New York

A colorful and unusual treatment of roast lobster: A broth of artichokes and arugula serves as the base for the lobster, which has been pan-roasted with a coating of powdered orange zest.

Serves 4

Orange Zest Powder
2 oranges
1 cup sugar
1½ cups water

Lobsters
6 quarts water
1 tablespoon salt
Four 1½-pound lobsters
Salt and freshly ground black pepper
  to taste

Artichoke Broth
4 large artichokes
2 tablespoons fresh lemon juice
2 tablespoons olive oil
½ cup chopped onion
1 teaspoon salt
3 to 4 cups dry white wine

2 tablespoons olive oil
1 bunch arugula, stemmed and julienned

To prepare the orange zest powder:
Preheat the oven to 275°F. Line a baking sheet with parchment paper or aluminum foil. Using a small knife or zester, remove the zest (outer colored skin) of the oranges without picking up any of the bitter white pith underneath. If you have used a knife, cut the zest into fine julienne.

In a small, heavy nonaluminum saucepan, cook the sugar and water together over medium-high heat until the sugar is dissolved, 2 minutes. Add the orange zest and cook for 10 minutes. With a slotted spoon, remove the zest from the syrup and place it in a single layer in the prepared pan.

Bake until the zest is very crisp, about 20 minutes. Let the zest cool and grind it in a food processor or spice grinder to a very fine powder. Set aside.

To prepare the lobsters: In a very large stockpot over high heat, bring the water to a boil and add the salt. Kill the lobsters by inserting the point of a large knife into the back of the shell where the tail meets the body. Add the lobsters to the boiling water and blanch for 2 minutes. Remove the lobsters and drain them. Remove the claws and pull the meat from the shell, cut through the head and tail lengthwise, and pull out the tail meat in 2 whole pieces. Season the tail and claw meat with salt and pepper and set aside.

To make the artichoke broth: Cut off the leaves from the artichokes, cut off the stem, and remove the choke with the tip of a spoon. Trim the artichoke heart and cut it into 4 pieces. Place the artichoke pieces in a small bowl, add water to cover, and stir in the lemon juice to prevent discoloration while the remaining hearts are being trimmed.

In a small sauté pan or skillet over medium heat, heat the olive oil. Cook the onion in the oil for 5 minutes, then add the artichoke pieces, salt, and enough of the white wine to cover the artichokes. Over medium-high heat, simmer until the artichokes are tender, about 20 minutes. Strain the broth through a fine-meshed sieve and return it to the pan. Reserve the artichoke pieces.

To roast the lobsters: Preheat the oven to 350°F. Spread the powdered orange zest on a plate and press the cut sides of the lobster tail and one side of the claw meat into the zest to coat them. Reserve the leftover powdered zest.

In a large sauté pan or skillet over medium-high heat, heat the olive oil and sauté the lobster pieces, cut-side down, until they are lightly browned, 2 to 3 minutes. Turn them over and cook for 1 more minute, then place the pan in the oven and cook until the lobster meat is opaque, about 3 minutes. Slice the lobster pieces into medallions and keep warm.

To serve: Reserve ½ cup julienned arugula leaves for garnish. Reheat the artichoke broth if necessary, add the arugula, and cook over medium heat just until the arugula is wilted, about 2 minutes. Spoon the arugula and broth into shallow soup bowls, add some of the artichoke pieces to each bowl, and top with the lobster medallions. Garnish each bowl with some fresh arugula leaves and sprinkle some of the reserved powdered zest on the rim of the plates.

Roast Lobster with an Orange Zest Crust; *Jean-Georges Vongerichten, JoJo's/Vong*

Gamberoni alla Griglia

Lidia Bastianich
Felidia
New York, New York

Shrimp baked and grilled with bread crumbs are paired with a delightfully different sauce and "smothered spinach" with an unexpected touch of Worcestershire.

Serves 6

Shrimp
2 pounds jumbo shrimp in the shell
2 tablespoons olive oil
Salt and freshly ground black pepper
 to taste
½ cup dried fine bread crumbs,
 preferably homemade
1 tablespoon minced fresh thyme

Sauce
2 tablespoons olive oil
¼ cup chopped onion
4 garlic cloves, minced
4 shallots, minced
⅓ cup dry white wine
2 tablespoons unsalted butter
1½ tablespoons Worcestershire sauce
1 tablespoon tarragon vinegar
1 tablespoon fresh lemon juice
2 thyme sprigs
1 tablespoon minced fresh flat-leaf
 (Italian) parsley

Smothered Spinach
1 pound spinach, washed and stemmed
3 tablespoons olive oil
6 garlic cloves, minced
1½ tablespoons Worcestershire sauce
½ teaspoon salt
Freshly ground black pepper to taste

To prepare the shrimp: Preheat the oven to 475°F. Peel the shrimp, leaving the tail attached. Using a sharp paring knife, carefully slit each shrimp down the back and one third of the way to the tail. Remove the vein. Rinse the shrimp under cool water, drain well, and pat dry.

In a shallow baking dish, toss the shrimp with the oil, salt, and pepper. Place the bread crumbs and thyme in another shallow dish and toss the shrimp with the crumbs. Shaking off any excess crumbs, place each shrimp, split-side down and tail curled up and over the shrimp, in the baking dish. Wrap each tail section with a bit of foil and bake for 5 minutes. Place the dish under a broiler and broil for 1 minute; remove the foil and keep the shrimp warm.

To make the sauce: In a medium nonaluminum sauté pan or skillet over medium-high heat, heat the oil and sauté the onion, garlic, and shallots until they are translucent, 2 minutes. Add the

Gamberoni alla Griglia; *Lidia Bastianich, Felidia*

wine, butter, Worcestershire sauce, vinegar, lemon juice, and thyme. Lower the heat and simmer for 3 minutes. Strain the sauce through a fine-meshed sieve and stir in the parsley. Set aside and keep warm.

To make the spinach: Wash the spinach twice in cool water and drain. In a large sauté pan or skillet over medium heat, heat the oil and sauté the garlic until golden but not browned, 2 minutes. Add the spinach, Worcestershire sauce, salt, and pepper. Cover and cook over medium-low heat until the spinach is wilted, 3 minutes, stirring occasionally. Remove from the heat and discard the garlic.

To serve: Spoon some of the spinach on each serving plate, spoon some of the sauce around the spinach, and arrange 4 or 5 shrimp in the center.

LIDIA BASTIANICH
Felidia, New York, New York

When writing about Lidia Bastianich, it's hard to top what Jay Jacobs said in *Gourmet*, reviewing the restaurant Felidia in 1991. Bastianich, wrote the critic, "radiates the sort of beauty that comes straight from a loving heart... She is wedded nunlike to her calling. As she talks of food and its preparation, it becomes obvious that for her the service of a meal is an act of love."

The restaurant's name is a combination of Lidia's name with that of her husband Felice. The pleasure these two take in their work is evident in every aspect of the restaurant, from the decor to the cuisine.

Felidia has consistently been ranked as one of the best Italian restaurants in New York, a city with a vast number of Italian restaurants. The region it represents is Istria, a peninsula that juts out into the Adriatic. Once a part of Italy, Istria now belongs to Croatia, and its cuisine is an intriguing combination of Italian, Austrian and southern Slavic dishes.

The couple has been operating restaurants in and around New York for many years, ever since Felice's arrival in the United States in 1958. He is a familiar figure in the city markets in the mornings, seeking out the finest and freshest foods for Felidia's menu.

As a chef, Lidia is as demanding of herself as she is of her ingredients. She learned the secrets of the Istrian kitchen at her grandmother's knee, then embellished them through extensive study and first-hand experience. Her imprint on Felidia's menu is obvious in its emphasis on simple seasonal dishes.

Most important, perhaps, Bastianich has introduced New York diners to the cooking of her native Istria, first at the popular Buonavia and Villa Secondo for 10 years in Queens, then finally at Felidia from the day it opened in 1981.

With her unique area of knowledge, Bastianich has proven a popular teacher and lecturer. She serves as vice president of the Ordine Ristoratori Professionisti Italiani of New York and has given a course on the anthopology of food at Pace University. Bastianich has been a guest lecturer on Istrian cuisine at numerous cooking schools around the country, sharing her love in a manner that comes most naturally.

EMERIL LAGASSE
Emeril's/Nola, New Orleans, Louisiana

"I don't use customers as guinea pigs." Emeril Lagasse seems momentarily amused by the image this statement conjures up, then presses on. "You're not going to come in and find braised lobster with strawberry sauce."

He's right about that—yet no chef has done more to push out the boundaries of Louisiana's Creole and Cajun cuisines than this young man of Portuguese descent from Fall River, Massachusetts.

In his namesake restaurant in New Orleans' Warehouse District, you're likely to dine on grilled andouille with homemade Worcestershire sauce, sautéed crawfish over jambalaya cakes, fried oysters with roasted garlic sauce and warm potato salad, and desserts ranging in decadence from the simplest strawberry shortcake to the world's best banana cream pie.

After spending more than seven years as executive chef for Ella and Dick Brennan at Commander's Palace, Lagasse took the big step of opening a place of his own. According to Lagasse, no one encouraged him more in this than the Brennans, who have a tradition of understanding such yearnings and laboring to help them become a reality.

Since Lagasse enjoyed almost free rein in the Commander's kitchen, the transition to running his own restaurant was a smooth one. Over time, he has refined (and keeps refining) his style of cooking and has motivated his staff to share his enthusiasm through daily tastings and discussions.

"We will never rest on our laurels," vows Lagasse. "We get up every day and try a little harder than yesterday. If you provide great food and great service in a good clean environment, you can be successful." This credo has obviously rung true, for by the chef's estimate more than 90 percent of his 120 seats are filled by New Orleanians.

Lagasse began shaping his future by earning a doctorate from Johnson and Wales cooking school in Rhode Island. One of that institution's most esteemed graduates, he practiced his art initially in New York, Boston, and Philadelphia.

Commander's Palace was still being touted as the former home of Paul Prudhomme when Lagasse arrived in the Big Easy. That kind of talk stopped quickly once Lagasse took over the kitchen. He helped to establish Commander's not only as a sterling dining establishment but as a leader in the reinvention of Creole cuisine.

Scallop and Leek Flan

Emeril Lagasse
Emeril's/Nola
New Orleans, Louisiana

In this savory flan, a filling of scallops, cream, leeks, and potatoes is baked in a crust and served with a cool cream made with fresh chives.

Serves 6 to 8

1¼ cups unbleached all-purpose flour
½ teaspoon salt
⅓ cup (⅔ stick) cold unsalted butter or vegetable shortening, cut into small pieces
3 to 4 tablespoons ice water

Filling
3 bacon strips, cut into ½-inch pieces
¾ cup thinly sliced leeks
1 tablespoon minced garlic
1 tablespoon plus 1 teaspoon Creole seasoning
½ teaspoon salt
8 large sea scallops, cut in half crosswise
3 eggs
1 cup heavy (whipping) cream
1 cup (4 ounces) grated Parmigiano Reggiano cheese
2 tablespoons minced fresh parsley
2 tablespoons snipped fresh chives
2 tablespoons minced shallots
Salt and freshly ground black pepper to taste

2 unpeeled red potatoes, thinly sliced

Garnish
Chive Cream (recipe follows)
Snipped fresh chives
Chive blossoms, separated into petals

To make the crust: In a large bowl, combine the flour and salt. Add the butter and work it into the flour with your fingers until the mixture resembles coarse crumbs. Using a fork, stir in the water 1 tablespoon at a time, then press the mixture together with your fingers until the dough forms a smooth ball. Wrap the dough in plastic wrap and refrigerate for 20 minutes.

Preheat the oven to 375°F. Lightly dust a 9-inch pie pan with flour and set aside. On a lightly floured surface, roll the chilled dough into a 1/8-inch-thick circle. Fold the circle in half, then in half again to assist in lifting and moving it to the pie pan. Unfold the dough into the pan and press it in place to remove any air bubbles under the dough. Trim off the excess dough and crimp the edges into a decorative border.

To prepare the filling: In a large sauté pan or skillet over medium heat, sauté the bacon until crisp, about 3 minutes. Add the leeks, garlic, and 1 tablespoon Creole seasoning, and sauté for 2 minutes. Add the salt. Remove the bacon mixture from the pan. Place the pan over high heat and sear the scallops for 30 seconds on each side, then sprinkle lightly with the remaining Creole seasoning and set aside to cool.

In a medium bowl, whisk together the eggs, cream, 3/4 cup of the cheese, the parsley, chives, and shallots. Season with salt and pepper.

Arrange the scallops in a single layer in the bottom of the prepared crust. Add the potato slices in a layer over the scallops, then spoon in the bacon mixture. Pour the cream mixture over the top and sprinkle the tart with the remaining 1/4 cup cheese. Bake for 15 minutes, then turn the oven down to 350°F and continue to bake until the tart is puffy and brown, about 15 more minutes. Let cool slightly, 10 to 15 minutes, before cutting.

To serve: Cut the flan into 6 or 8 wedges and place 1 wedge in the center of each serving plate. Spoon some of the chive cream over the top of the wedge and onto the plate. Garnish the plate with snipped chives and chive petals.

Chive Cream
Makes 1 cup

3/4 cup sour cream
2 tablespoons finely snipped fresh chives
2 tablespoons Chardonnay or other
  dry white wine
1 tablespoon minced shallots
1/2 teaspoon salt
1/2 teaspoon freshly ground black pepper

In a small bowl, combine the sour cream with the chives, wine, and shallots, and mix well. Season with salt and pepper.

Scallop and Leek Flan; *Emeril Lagasse, Emeril's/Nola*

Pan-seared Scallops with Polenta

▼▼▼▼▼▼▼▼▼▼▼▼

Tim Keating
La Reserve
Omni Houston Hotel
Houston, Texas

A dish for lovers of mushrooms, which are blended into the polenta, used to garnish the dish, and are an integral part of the nage, or sauce, that tops the seared scallops and sautéed polenta diamonds.

Serves 6

30 sea scallops, preferably in the shell
2 tablespoons extra-virgin olive oil
1 tablespoon minced fresh flat-leaf
   (Italian) parsley, chives, tarragon,
   and chervil
½ teaspoon sea salt
Freshly ground black pepper to taste

Polenta

4 tablespoons olive oil
½ cup (2½ ounces) mixed wild
   mushrooms, such as morels, shiitakes,
   oysters, and porcini
1 cup polenta, preferably white
4 cups cold water
2 tablespoons butter, cut into bits
¾ cup (3 ounces) freshly grated
   Parmesan cheese
¼ cup julienned sun-dried tomatoes
2 tablespoons minced fresh flat-leaf
   (Italian) parsley, chives, tarragon,
   and chervil
Salt and freshly ground black pepper
   to taste

Mushroom-Corn Nage

2 tablespoons extra-virgin olive oil
4½ tablespoons butter
12 ounces fresh white or field
   mushrooms, sliced
8 dried shiitake mushrooms, soaked 15
   to 20 minutes, drained, and sliced
Sea salt and freshly ground black pepper to taste
1 elephant garlic clove, halved and
   crushed
3 large shallots, minced
3 cups chicken stock (see page 228)

1½ tablespoons chopped fresh flat-leaf
   (Italian) parsley
1 ear fresh corn
Uncooked polenta for dusting
4 tablespoons olive oil

Garnish

½ cup chicken stock (see page 228)
8 ounces fresh morel mushrooms,
   stemmed
4 ounces fresh oyster mushrooms
4 ounces fresh shiitake mushrooms,
   stemmed
2 tablespoons olive oil
2 tablespoons dry white wine
6 baby carrots, trimmed to 1-inch tops
12 ears baby corn, preferably fresh
8 ounces haricots verts or baby
   Blue Lake green beans
1 tablespoon butter
1 ear fresh corn
6 fresh rosemary sprigs

To prepare the scallops: Remove the scallops from their shells if necessary and clean all tissue from around the scallops. In a medium bowl, combine the scallops with the olive oil, herbs, salt, and pepper, and let sit for 20 to 30 minutes.

To make the polenta: In a large sauté pan or skillet over medium-high heat, heat 2 tablespoons of the olive oil and sauté the mushrooms until they are tender, about 4 minutes. Set aside.

Pan-seared Scallops with Polenta;
Tim Keating, La Reserve, Omni Houston Hotel

In a large saucepan, stir the polenta into the cold water. Cook over medium heat, stirring constantly and scraping down the sides of the pan until the mixture is thick and no longer grainy, about 25 minutes. Add the butter and Parmesan cheese and mix well. Fold in the sautéed mushrooms, dried tomatoes, and the herbs, and mix thoroughly. Season with salt and pepper.

Line a 1-inch-deep sided baking sheet (a jelly roll pan) with parchment paper or aluminum foil, and lightly brush the paper or foil with 1 table-spoon of the olive oil. Spread the polenta in the pan and smooth with a rubber spatula. Brush another sheet of parchment paper or foil with the remaining 1 tablespoon olive oil and place oil-side down on the polenta. Let cool to room temperature, then refrigerate to chill completely, at least 2 hours or up to 24 hours.

To make the nage: In a large sauté pan or skillet over high heat, heat the olive oil and butter until the butter foams. Add the fresh and soaked dried mushrooms, and sauté until they are a rich brown, about 12 to 15 minutes. Season with salt and pepper. Add the garlic, shallots, stock, and parsley, and stir until well combined. Place this mixture in a medium saucepan.

Cut the kernels from the ear of corn, scraping the cob with a knife to remove all of the milk. Add to the saucepan. Place the saucepan over medium heat, bring the mixture to a boil, and cook for 15 to 18 minutes. Strain the sauce through a fine-meshed sieve, return it to the pan, and cook over medium heat to reduce it by one-half, about 15 minutes. Set the sauce aside and keep warm.

Cut the polenta into 2-inch diamond shapes and dust them on both sides with some of the uncooked polenta. In a large sauté pan or skillet over high heat, heat 1 tablespoon of the olive oil and sauté the polenta quickly in batches, adding 2 more tablespoons of oil as needed, until golden brown, 2 to 3 min-utes on each side. Place the sautéed polenta on a baking sheet and place in a warm oven until ready to arrange on serving plates.

In a large, heavy sauté pan or skillet over medium-high heat, heat the remaining 1 tablespoon olive oil and sauté the scallops in batches, turning to sear on all sides, until they are golden brown, 3 to 4 minutes.

To prepare the garnish: In a small saucepan over medium heat, bring the stock to a boil. Blanch the morels in the stock for 1 minute. Drain, reserving the blanching liquid.

In a large, heavy sauté pan or skillet over high heat, heat the olive oil and sauté the shiitake and oyster mushrooms, tossing constantly, until they are browned and tender, about 12 to 15 minutes. Add the morels, reduce heat to medium, and toss with the herbs and reserved blanching liquid. Continue to cook for 10 to 12 minutes. Add the white wine to the pan and stir. Set aside.

In a small saucepan of lightly salted boiling water, blanch the carrots, baby corn, and haricots verts or baby green beans until just tender, about 6 to 8 minutes; drain. In a medium sauté pan or skillet over medium heat, melt the butter. When the butter foams, sauté the vegetables for 2 minutes. Set aside and keep warm.

Preheat the oven to 400°F. Roast the ear of corn, in its husk, for 12 minutes. Remove the husk and, using a large knife, cut off the kernels in long sections. Set aside.

To serve: Place 5 diamonds of polenta in the center of each serving plate with the points touching in the center. Place 1 scallop on top of each polenta diamond. Arrange some vegetables in the center, standing them upright as much as possible. Sprinkle each plate with the mushrooms and ladle some of the nage over the scallops, polenta, and mushrooms. Add strips of corn kernels and sprigs of fresh rosemary to each plate.

TIMOTHY KEATING
La Reserve, Omni Houston Hotel, Houston, Texas

At a height of six feet eight inches, Tim Keating can really keep an eye on everything going on around him. And as executive chef at the Omni Houston Hotel, he has taken its restaurants – particularly the elegant La Reserve – to, dare we say, new heights.

Guests in La Reserve can still find many of the complicated dishes of the recent past, such as charred tomato gnocchi with lobster hash and yellowfin tuna tartare with tomato compote. Keating also has worked to lower both the prices and the complexity of many of the dishes. And he has laid down the law that, in the end, whatever the customer wants is the best food to serve.

"If someone wants a blackened ribeye," the chef says, trying not to grimace, "we will prepare it."

Keating played basketball for two years at William Paterson College in New Jersey. Once settled on a cooking career, however, he went at it with a culinary full-court press. Moving to California, Keating cooked at a series of posh hotels and restaurants.

At places like Rancho Mirage, the Ritz-Carlton resort, and Le Meridien, he had the opportunity to watch and learn from a number of terrific visiting chefs, the most memorable being Jacques Maximin and Claude Poissonieux. He also operated his own catering company in San Diego.

In 1983, Keating accepted the top chef's position at the Omni after helping Christian Delouvrier reopen Nikko Hotel's Essex House in New York City. Today, he oversees the food served in La Reserve, the Cafe on the Green, the Palm Court, and the Black Swan. In all of these eateries, his presence is felt in even the smallest details.

"Several things are a religion with me," he admits, "such as all-butter croissants, well-made stocks, and properly worked mashed potatoes. We use only the best russet potatoes, cook them in salted water, dry them in an oven until the excess moisture is gone, then put them through a ricer or food mill."

Another priority for Keating is serving on the regional steering committee for the Chefs Collaborative 2000, an educational initiative of Old Ways Preservation and Trust Exchange, which organizes chefs to advance sustainable food choices. He is also a dedicated member of the Houston chapter of the American Heart Association's committee on heart-healthy restaurant dining.

TODD ENGLISH
Olives, Boston, Massachusetts

Like any former baseball player who finds himself owning his own restaurant after studying at the Culinary Institute of America and cooking at La Côte Basque, Todd English viewed the American food revolution of the 1980s with mixed emotions. The same trends that had opened the doors for him were, in a sense, making him wonder if he really wanted to go in.

"I couldn't see myself doing all that nouvelle, prissy stuff," he recalls. "I mean, no offense, but it just wasn't full-bodied enough for me." The search for "full-bodied" cuisine would eventually become a pilgrimage for English.

Growing up in Amarillo, Texas, English was a baseball catcher when he went to the University of North Carolina, and the main thing he wanted to catch was a career in the major leagues. Then he found that cooking good food was even better than winning both halves of a double header. He was hooked.

The CIA training and work at La Côte Basque started him on his career, but English was still troubled by the nouvelle trend in American cuisine. So he set off on a tour of Italy, tasting the rustic dishes of village after village. He also spent time working in several kitchens, including Dal Pescatore in Canto sull Olio and Paruccuchi in Locando D'Angello.

Returning to the United States, he spent three years cooking in Boston at a popular northern Italian restaurant called Michela's. In 1989, English and his wife Olivia opened Olives in the shadow of the Bunker Hill Monument. Before long, the Charlestown neighborhood was known as the place where Olives was.

Here, English mixes rustic Italian and rustic American flavors, using a brick-hearthed, wood-fired grill to produce pizza topped with figs and prosciutto then drizzled with olive oil; wood-grilled lobster and roasted chicken; and Parmesan pudding with a sauce of New England sweet peas.

English has since spread his wings even more, expanding the dining room from the original fifty, and opening Figs Pizzeria, also in Charlestown. The second place delights a local crowd with the chef's dizzying vision of traditional and not-so-traditional pizzas. Around Bunker Hill, it turns out, the one-time catcher from Amarillo is quite a catch.

Roasted Eggplant and Scallop Pie Provençal

Todd English
Olives
Boston, Massachusetts

Each "pie" is really an individual round of sautéed eggplant, topped with roasted eggplant and sautéed vegetables, then a layer of sliced scallops and a sprinkling of bread crumbs. Potato aïoli is the final touch.

Serves 4

1 pound jumbo sea scallops
  (12 to 16 scallops)

Roasted Eggplant Mixture
One 12-ounce can plum tomatoes, drained (reserve juice), seeded, and roughly chopped
2 globe eggplants, 3 to 4 inches in diameter
Salt for sprinkling
About ³/₄ cup olive oil
Salt and freshly ground black pepper to taste
1 cup ¹/₄-inch-diced zucchini
1 cup ¹/₄-inch-diced yellow squash
¹/₂ cup ¹/₄-inch-diced fennel
1 cup ¹/₄-inch-diced red onion
Puree from 3 roasted garlic cloves (see page 234)
¹/₂ cup chopped fresh basil
1 tablespoon chopped fresh rosemary
¹/₂ cup chopped fresh flat-leaf (Italian) parsley

Potato Aïoli
1 large Idaho potato, peeled and cut into 6 pieces
¹/₄ cup fresh lemon juice
2 tablespoons balsamic vinegar
¹/₂ cup water
1 egg yolk (optional)
Puree from 3 roasted garlic heads (see page 234)
¹/₂ teaspoon cayenne pepper
1 cup virgin olive oil
Salt and freshly ground black pepper to taste

Toast and Topping
4 thin slices country-style bread
½ cup fresh bread crumbs
1 tablespoon olive oil
Salt and freshly ground black pepper
  to taste

To prepare the scallops: Rinse and remove the muscle from the scallops, then slice each scallop into 3 rounds. Cover and refrigerate until needed.

To prepare the eggplant and make the eggplant mixture: Place the tomatoes on a baking sheet and bake in a 250°F oven until dry, about 1 hour. Set aside.

Cut 1 eggplant into ¼-inch dice. Cut the second eggplant into four ½-inch rounds. Sprinkle salt over both the diced and sliced eggplant and let sit for 30 minutes on paper towels, then rinse and pat dry.

In a medium sauté pan or skillet over medium-high heat, heat ¼ cup of the olive oil, add the diced eggplant, and cook until the edges begin to brown. Season with salt and pepper, then transfer the eggplant to a baking sheet with a slotted spoon. In the same way, sauté the zucchini, squash, and fennel separately in turn, adding olive oil as needed, and transfer to the baking sheet.

Add 2 tablespoons olive oil to the pan and sauté the diced onion with the roasted garlic puree for 2 to 3 minutes. Add the tomatoes, basil, rosemary, and half of the parsley. Reduce the heat to low and cook for 5 minutes, then set aside.

In a medium sauté pan or skillet over medium heat, heat ¼ cup of the olive oil. Place the eggplant rounds in the hot oil and brown on both sides, about 3 to 5 minutes per side. Remove from pan, drain, and let cool.

To make the aïoli: Boil the potato in salted water until soft, 8 to 10 minutes, then pass it through a ricer or sieve. Place the riced potato in a blender or food processor and add the lemon juice, balsamic vinegar, water, egg yolk, garlic puree, and cayenne pepper. Pulse to blend, then with the motor running, slowly add the olive oil to make a thick sauce. Set aside.

Preheat the oven to 400°F. Toast the bread slices in a preheated oven for 3 to 5 minutes, or until slightly toasted. Set aside. In a small sauté pan or skillet over medium heat, heat the olive oil and toast the bread crumbs until golden, about 3 minutes, tossing constantly. Set aside.

To assemble: Place the toast slices 1 inch apart in a lightly oiled baking pan. Place the eggplant rounds on top, and spoon equal amounts of the eggplant mixture on each of the eggplant rounds. Evenly divide the sliced scallops among the rounds, placing them on top of the eggplant mixture in an overlapping pattern. Bake for 15 to 20 minutes. Remove and sprinkle with the remaining parsley before serving. Serve with the potato aïoli.

Roasted Eggplant and Scallop Pie Provençal; *Todd English, Olives*

Crawfish with Spicy Black Bean Sauce

■▼■▼■▼■▼■▼■▼■▼■▼■▼■

Tommy Wong
Trey Yuen
Mandeville, Louisiana

Louisiana crawfish (known elsewhere as crayfish) with an Asian accent: It's stir-fried with pork, garlic, fermented black beans, and ginger, sauced with Asian seasonings and Worcestershire sauce, then stirred with beaten eggs and green onions. Try this quick dish for brunch.

Serves 4

2 tablespoons peanut oil
8 ounces pork butt (smoked optional), finely chopped
1½ tablespoons fermented black beans, well rinsed and drained
4 tablespoons minced garlic
1½ tablespoons minced fresh ginger
¼ teaspoon red pepper flakes, or more to taste
3 tablespoons dry sherry
3 tablespoons mirin (sweet sake) or sweet sherry
2 tablespoons sherry vinegar
1 large white onion cut in half lengthwise, then cut into ¼-inch-thick slices

1 cup ½-inch diagonally sliced green onions (white part only)
1 pound cooked crawfish tails

Seasoning Mix
½ cup chicken stock (see page 228)
1 tablespoon toasted sesame oil
¼ cup soy sauce
2 tablespoons oyster sauce
1 tablespoon Worcestershire sauce
1 tablespoon cornstarch

2 whole eggs, beaten
½ cup ¼-inch-diced green onion tops
Salt and freshly ground black pepper to taste
4 cooked whole crawfish

In a wok heated over high heat, heat the peanut oil and cook the pork until the redness disappears, 2 to 3 minutes. Mash the drained black beans with 1 tablespoon of the garlic. Spread the pork around the upper sides of the wok and add the remaining 3 tablespoons garlic and the ginger to the center. Stir together quickly with the pork, then add the mashed beans. Sprinkle in the pepper flakes, then add the wines and vinegar. Add the white and green onions, then the stock. Quickly cover and let the flavors mingle for 2 to 3 minutes.

Uncover the wok and add the crawfish tails. Combine all the

seasoning mix ingredients, add to the wok, and stir until the sauce thickens. Add the eggs and green onion tops, stir to cook the eggs, then quickly transfer to a serving platter and garnish with the whole crawfish. Serve at once.

Alligator Stir-fry

John Wong
Trey Yuen
Mandeville, Louisiana

Alligator meets its match in this Chinese-Louisiana dish. The sweet white meat is a beautiful contrast to the spicy, salty, and earthy Asian seasonings.

Serves 4

Alligator and Marinade
1 pound alligator meat (tail loin preferred), completely trimmed
2 tablespoons cornstarch
2 tablespoons peanut oil
½ teaspoon salt
3 tablespoons egg white

½ cup peanut oil
12 shiitake mushrooms, stemmed and halved on the diagonal

½ teaspoon red pepper flakes

2 cups pearl onions, peeled, or
   1-inch pieces of the white part of
   green onions

1 cup 1-inch-diagonal-cut celery slices

½ cup sliced shallots

1 tablespoon minced garlic

½ cup miso

3 tablespoons oyster sauce

2 teaspoons toasted sesame oil

1 cup chicken stock (see page 228)

2 tablespoons dark soy sauce

⅓ cup coarsely chopped green onion
   tops or fresh chives

Garnish

½ cup sliced almonds

½ cup thinly sliced cucumber

1 tablespoon chopped green onion tops
   or snipped fresh chives

To marinate the alligator: Cut the alliga-tor loin into ⅛-inch-thick slices. Place the meat in a medium bowl and sprinkle with the cornstarch, then add the peanut oil and salt. Mix thoroughly, then add the egg white, coating well (this helps to retain the moisture when frying). Let sit at room temperature for 20 minutes.

Heat a wok or large, heavy skillet over high heat until very hot. Add the peanut oil, then add the marinated alligator. Stir-fry for 3 to 4 minutes, then add the mushrooms and stir-fry for 2 more minutes.

Using a slotted spoon, remove the alligator and mushrooms from the pan and set aside. Remove all but 3 tablespoons of peanut oil from the pan. Add the red pepper flakes to the hot peanut oil, then the onions, celery, shallots, and garlic. Stir-fry for 1 to 2 minutes. Add the miso and return the alligator and mushrooms. Cover and steam for 2 minutes. Uncover and add the oyster sauce, sesame oil, chicken stock, and soy sauce, and stir-fry over high heat for 1 to 2 more minutes. Add the green onion tops and stir-fry for 1 to 2 minutes.

To serve: Mound the stir-fry on a serving platter, sprinkle with sliced almonds, and surround with slices of cucumber. Sprinkle with chopped green onion tops or chives.

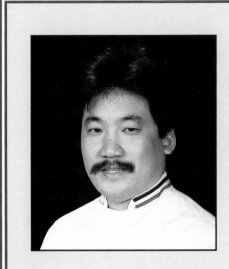

TOMMY AND JOHN WONG
Trey Yuen, Mandeville, Louisiana

The Wong brothers have been an influence on the Louisiana din-ing scene for more than fifteen years. Their restaurant, Trey Yuen in Mandeville on the north shore of Lake Pontchartrain, has taught the local dining public just how far Chinese cuisine can travel.

A crucial part of the Wongs' achievement has been the incorpora-tion of local ingredients such as crawfish and alligator into some of the most elegant presentations in the Asian repertoire. The result has been world-class cooking that has wowed diners since the day Trey Yuen opened its doors.

"We actually draw people from a sixty- to eighty-mile radius, from Louisiana and Mississippi," says Tommy Wong. "That says a lot. People on the north shore are quite well-traveled eaters. They know good food. I always say you can't be mediocre and survive in this area. We're just so spoiled by good food here."

There was a time when the Wong brothers were anything but spoiled. Tommy and John Wong, along with brothers James, Joe, and Frank, were all born in Hong Kong after their parents escaped from Canton province during the Chinese civil war. And all five worked in restaurants, doing every job from dishwasher to cook. Cooking held a special appeal for the brothers, growing out of their love of grocery shopping with their mother.

The Wong show went on the road some time later, traveling from Hong Kong to Vancouver to Amarillo to San Francisco, with the five brothers working in restaurants in each city. The family finally settled in tiny Hammond, Louisiana, put all five thousand dollars of their savings into a small lunchtime eatery named the China Inn, and began building their reputation with two woks and a mere eleven tables.

Their mission was clear: to resurrect Chinese dining from its image as quick, cheap food and reveal it for what it truly was, a cuisine of graceful techniques and fresh flavors. At the China Inn, people began to talk about the Wongs. When they opened Trey Yuen, "jade-green garden," in 1980, the talking evolved into loud applause from a loyal customer base.

More recently, the Wongs returned to their local roots in Hammond, but they've traveled a long way from the China Inn. Now they have opened a second location of Trey Yuen. As much a peaceful sanctuary as the original, it is also as much a culinary mecca as the five brothers can make it.

JASPER WHITE
Jasper's, Boston, Massachusetts

In 1983, an 1802 molasses warehouse on Boston's waterfront was transformed into Jasper's. Jasper White and his wife Nancy set out there to do something New England had not witnessed before: to create a menu that included every ingredient and technique that set New England apart from any other region.

"I'm proud of my simplest dishes," the New Jersey farm-born White says. "I didn't invent lobster and corn chowder. I'm proud to serve that. It was probably made 350 years ago, and it works. It's still good. What I'm proud of is, I buy the best lobsters I can get. I get the sweetest corn I can get. We do everything properly."

Although White is a creative chef, creativity is not his ultimate goal.

"Obviously, I'm creative. There are hundreds of dishes that I've done somewhat out of thin air, often due to necessity or whatever. But that's not my approach. There's very little that's really truly original. What little of it there is, is often just garbage. That's true for other art forms also."

Since White arrived in Boston in 1978, he has focused on New England cuisine. Everywhere he went in Boston, he found Europeans in the kitchen, cooking mostly European food. In a city that had served as an incubator for the American experiment, he wanted to explore the dishes that were uniquely American.

With his cooking partner Lydia Shire, White created a New England menu and an American ambience. One reason White was so insistent that his waterfront place have a bar is that bars are so American. "You come in," he says simply, "there's a bar."

Over the years, along with the best chefs in other cities, White became a crusader for small farms, which he believes are the best source of good foods. And he fights tirelessly against the pollution that is, among other things, threatening the seafood on which so much New England cuisine is based.

With his restaurant and philosophy solidly established, White distilled both into a permanent legacy: a highly praised cookbook titled *Jasper White's Cooking From New England* (Harper & Row). It offers three hundred of his best recipes, along with his thoughts on New England cuisine. After his sabbatical from the day-to-day operations of a restaurant, White has returned with new approaches to American cuisine.

Portuguese Mussels
▼▼▼▼▼▼▼▼▼▼▼▼▼

Jasper White
Jasper's
Boston, Massachusetts

This is a typical dish prepared by Portuguese families on the beach after harvesting mussels on the New England coast. The combination of spicy sausage and seafood is traditional in Portuguese cuisine.

Serves 4

Sauce
¼ cup olive oil
4 small whole bay leaves
1 tablespoon minced garlic
1 onion, diced
1 small bell pepper, seeded, deribbed, and diced
2 tomatoes, peeled, seeded, and diced (see page 234)
1 cup dry white wine
4 ounces chouriço or linguiça sausage, thinly sliced
Freshly ground black pepper to taste

Mussels
48 to 50 fresh mussels, scrubbed and debearded
2 tablespoons chopped fresh flat-leaf (Italian) parsley
2 tablespoons chopped fresh cilantro

To make the sauce: In a very large sauté pan or skillet over high heat, heat the olive oil and add the bay leaves. Cook the bay leaves until they are lightly browned and fragrant, 1 to 2 minutes. Add the garlic, onion, and pepper, and cook until the vegetables are tender but not browned, about 2 minutes. Add the tomatoes, wine, and sausage. Season with pepper, lower the heat, and simmer the mixture for 5 minutes.

Meanwhile, to prepare the mussels: Add the mussels to the pan, cover, and cook until the mussels have opened, 4 to 6 minutes. Remove from heat and open the mussels over the pan to retain their juices. Discard any mussels that do not open. Remove and discard one-half of the shell and place the mussels with their half shell in soup bowls. Return the pan to heat, add the cilantro and parsley, and sauté for 1 minute. Season again with pepper if desired.

To serve: Spoon some of the sauce over the mussels in each dish and serve immediately.

Portuguese Mussels; *Jasper White, Jasper's*

Moroccan-Style Sea Bass in a Golden Balloon

▼▼▼ ▩▩▩▩▩▩▩▩▩ ▼▼▼

Andrew Wilkinson
The Rainbow Room
New York, New York

At the Rainbow Room, the "golden balloon" is made from a special gold-colored foil, but you can make your own spectacular presentation by wrapping the sea bass in aluminum foil. The fish are served with a Moroccan-flavored sauce of tomatoes and harissa, a simple eggplant compote, and couscous with fresh herbs.

Serves 4

Tomato-Harissa Sauce
2 tablespoons olive oil
½ cup finely chopped onion
1 tablespoon minced fresh garlic
2 tablespoons tomato paste
1 cup dry white wine
2 large tomatoes, peeled, seeded, and roughly chopped (see page 234), or 2 cups canned plum tomatoes, drained, seeded, and chopped
¼ cup finely diced peeled carrot
½ cup finely diced celery
½ teaspoon dried oregano
2 to 3 bay leaves
½ teaspoon cumin seeds
One 3-inch cinnamon stick
About 2 tablespoons harissa, or 1 tablespoon Thai chili paste

Eggplant Compote
1 large globe eggplant
2 tablespoons olive oil
1 teaspoon ground cumin
½ cup dry white wine

Four 6-ounce sea bass fillets, skin removed
Salt and freshly ground black pepper to taste
1 tablespoon butter at room temperature
1 cup dry white wine

Couscous (recipe follows)

To make the tomato-harissa sauce:
Preheat the oven to 350°F. In a medium sauté pan or skillet over medium heat, heat the oil and sauté the onion and garlic until tender, about 5 minutes. Add the tomato paste and continue to cook and stir over high heat until the tomatoes are caramelized and all of the moisture is removed from the paste. Add the wine to the pan and bring it to a boil. Stir in the tomatoes, carrot, celery, and oregano and set aside.

Make a bouquet garni by tying the bay leaves, cumin seeds, and cinnamon stick in a square of cheesecloth with a cotton string. Add the bouquet garni to the tomato mixture, cover, and bake for 1 hour. Let cool slightly, then remove the bouquet garni and gradually stir in the harissa or chili paste to taste.

To prepare the eggplant compote: Preheat the oven to 350°F if necessary. Cut the unpeeled eggplant lengthwise into ½-inch-thick slices, then into ¼-inch julienne. In a large sauté pan or skillet over medium-high heat, heat 1 tablespoon of the olive oil and fry the eggplant strips, adding the remaining olive oil as necessary. Sprinkle the eggplant with the cumin, add the wine, and bring the mixture to a boil. Cover and bake for 15 minutes.

To prepare the sea bass: Preheat the oven to 400°F. Season the fish fillets on both sides with salt and pepper. Cut four 12-inch squares of aluminum foil and spread the non-shiny side of each with some of the butter.

Moroccan-Style Sea Bass in a Golden Balloon; *Andrew Wilkinson, The Rainbow Room*

Place a portion of the eggplant compote halfway between the center of a foil square and one of its points. Top with some of the tomato-harissa sauce. Top with 1 fish fillet. Fold one corner of the foil over to meet the opposite corner, forming a triangle with the fish inside. Tightly fold and crimp the edges to form a half circle, leaving a small opening at one end. Into this opening, carefully pour about ¼ cup of wine, then tightly crimp the foil so that no steam will escape during the cooking process. Repeat to make 4 packets.

Place each foil packet in a large sauté pan or skillet over high heat and cook until the foil puffs, about 1 minute. Place the packets on a baking sheet and bake for 8 to 10 minutes for 1-inch-thick fish (adjust the time if the fish is thicker or thinner).

To serve: Bring the puffed "balloons" to the table and open them in front of the guests to let them appreciate the aromas. Spoon the fish onto serving plates, surround each serving with the sauce and eggplant compote from the packet, and serve with couscous.

Couscous
Makes 4 cups

1 cup chicken stock (see page 228)
1 cup couscous
3 tablespoons minced fresh parsley
½ cup finely diced cucumber
2 tablespoons minced fresh mint
2 tablespoons unsalted butter
Salt and freshly ground black pepper
   to taste

In a medium saucepan, bring the stock to a boil. Place the couscous in another medium saucepan and pour the boiling stock over the couscous. Stir to mix well, cover, and set aside until the liquid is completely absorbed, about 10 minutes. Stir in the remaining ingredients and serve.

ANDREW WILKINSON
The Rainbow Room, New York, New York

At New York's Rainbow Room, Andrew Wilkinson's job is "to add to the romance of Rainbow by building new memories." For a place that's been building memories since it opened in 1934, that is quite a task.

The Rainbow Room, floating sixty-five stories above midtown Manhattan, is considered the crowning jewel of New York City's pre-eminent business and entertainment complex, Rockefeller Center. It was conceived as a formal supper club, with headliners ranged from Edgar Bergen and Charlie McCarthy to Judy Holliday and Mary Martin. The Rainbow Grill opened a short time later, as an informal counterpart to the Room.

The Rainbow Room has closed a handful of times over the decades and in recent years had gone into decline. Now, however, the place is clearly in the midst of a renaissance. Not least of all, Wilkinson's cooking has made the Rainbow Room a place to go for exciting and innovative cuisine.

After working on the docks and in the restaurants of Portland, Oregon, as a young man, Wilkinson crossed America to the Culinary Institute, then the Atlantic to the Michelin two-star Kur Hotel Traube in Germany's Black Forest. Back from the Continent, Wilkinson took up a post at Boston's Polcaris, until restaurateur Joe Baum brought him to New York as sous-chef at his New American showpiece, Aurora.

In 1989, Wilkinson worked in Japan at the Hotel Clio Court in Hakata, then returned to Aurora, where he was promoted to chef. In resurrecting the Rainbow Room, Baum was attracted to Wilkinson's managerial and culinary skills, as well as to his understanding of the Rainbow's classic elements and the need for the scale of the food to fit the grand traditions of the room.

BRUCE MOLZAN
Ruggles Grill, Houston, Texas

Bruce Molzan has worked hard for more than a decade to make sure no one takes Texas cooking for granted. Texas food, Molzan argues from the kitchen at Ruggles Grill, is a lot more than barbecue and chili.

"My menu has down-to-earth appeal," Molzan says. "I have sandwiches on the menu, grilled liver and steak, mashed potatoes, pastas and pizzas – something for everyone. I believe in being creative, but I know I have to cook what people want to eat – and that's substantial, good food."

For all of his love of Southwestern tastes, therefore, Molzan is also a chef in love with "comfort foods," those dishes that we remember fondly from childhood. Most of Molzan's creations pay homage to Americana: smoked salmon and warm potato cake, corn chowder, corn breaded catfish with corn salad and pickled onions, black pepper pasta with sweet garlic cream and grilled chicken.

As for American desserts, Molzan's wife Susan is in the pastry kitchen, spinning such variations on old-fashioned sweets as white chocolate bread pudding, Oreo cheesecake, cherry pie with homemade ice cream, and chocolate fudge pie.

Both Bruce and Susan are graduates of the restaurant management program at James Madison University in Virginia, after which Bruce went on to the Culinary Institute of America and Susan managed the food service at Neiman-Marcus Town & Country in Dallas. Bruce later cooked at Houston's downtown Hyatt Regency, at the Warwick Post Oak, and at SRO restaurant developed by a group of local businessmen.

After spending some time studying with Wolfgang Puck, Molzan and his wife joined forces at Ruggles Grill. The couple came in as part owners and, by December 1987, emerged as sole proprietors. More recently, Bruce found himself working with the Brennan family of New Orleans to revamp the menu at a place called Third Coast in Houston.

It would appear that Bruce Molzan, despite his love of comfort food, never allows himself to get too comfortable – not when there's so much good work to do.

Redfish with Shrimp and Crab Roasted-Pepper Butter and Pumpkin Seeds

▼■▼■▼■▼■▼■▼■▼■▼■▼

Bruce Molzan
Ruggles Grill
Houston, Texas

A shrimp and crab butter made with beurre blanc, and a roasted-pepper puree with pumpkin seeds combine the glories of two great cuisines—French and Mexican—in this colorful dish.

Serves 4

Roasted Tomato Garnish
1 tablespoon olive oil
2 plum (Roma) tomatoes, halved
 lengthwise

Four 6-ounce redfish or red snapper
 fillets, skinned
Salt and freshly ground black pepper
 to taste
2 tablespoons olive oil

Roasted Pepper Puree and Pumpkin Seed Garnish
1 yellow bell pepper
1 red bell pepper
2 poblano chilies
1 Scotch bonnet (habanero) chili
1 red onion
5 small unpeeled garlic heads
3 tablespoons olive oil
3/4 cup pumpkin seeds
1/2 cup chopped fresh cilantro
Salt and freshly ground black pepper
 to taste

Beurre Blanc
2 tablespoons minced shallots
3/4 cup dry white vermouth
2 tablespoons white wine vinegar
3/4 cup heavy (whipping) cream
1/2 cup (1 stick) unsalted butter, cut into
 tablespoon-sized pieces
1 tablespoon fresh lemon juice
Salt and freshly ground black pepper
 to taste

Shrimp and Crab Roasted-Pepper Butter
2 tablespoons olive oil
2 tablespoons minced shallots

1 small jalapeño chili, seeded and minced

8 medium shrimp

2 plum (Roma) tomatoes, peeled, seeded, and finely diced (½ cup); (see page 234)

8 ounces fresh jumbo lump crabmeat

½ cup roasted pepper puree, above

1 cup beurre blanc, above

Salt and freshly ground black pepper to taste

Garnish

2 zucchini, cut into 8 pieces and trimmed into ovals

8 baby carrots

12 asparagus spears

½ cup (2 ounces) grated Italian Fontina cheese

4 fresh cilantro sprigs

To prepare the tomatoes: Preheat the oven to 250°F. Oil a low-sided baking sheet and place the tomatoes on it, cut-side up. Bake until dry, about 1 hour. Set aside.

Season the fillets on both sides with salt and pepper, then coat with olive oil and place in the refrigerator. Remove from the refrigerator 30 minutes before cooking.

To make the puree and pumpkin seed garnish: Preheat the broiler. Roll the peppers, chilies, onion, and garlic in 2 tablespoons of the olive oil and broil until charred, turning frequently, about 10 minutes for the peppers and chili, 20 minutes for the garlic, and 30 minutes for the onion.

Transfer the pepper and chili to a paper or plastic bag, close the bag, and let cool to the touch. Transfer the onion and garlic to a plate and let cool. Peel and seed the peppers and chili. Peel the onion and squeeze the garlic puree from the roasted heads. You should have about 5 tablespoons of puree.

In a medium sauté pan or skillet over medium heat, heat the remaining 1 tablespoon oil and toss the pumpkin seeds until they begin to pop and are lightly toasted, about 4 to 5 minutes.

Place the peppers, chilies, onion, garlic, ¼ cup of the pumpkin seeds, and the cilantro in a blender or food processor and blend to a smooth paste. Season with salt and pepper and set aside. Reserve the remaining pumpkin seeds for garnish.

To make the beurre blanc: Combine the shallots, vermouth, and vinegar in a small saucepan and bring to a boil over medium heat. Cook to reduce the liquid to about ¼ cup. Add the heavy cream and cook to reduce to about ⅓ cup. Whisk in the butter 1 tablespoon at a time to make a thick sauce. Add the lemon juice, salt, and pepper.

To make the shrimp and crab roasted-pepper butter: In a large sauté pan or skillet over medium heat, heat the olive oil and sauté the shallots and jalapeño for 1 minute. Add the shrimp and sauté for 1 minute. Add the tomato, sauté for 30 seconds, then add the crabmeat. Add the pepper puree and cook over medium-high heat for 1 more minute, then add the beurre blanc. Stir and remove from heat. Adjust the seasoning as necessary and keep warm over barely tepid water.

Preheat the broiler and broil the fish for 2 minutes on one side, then turn and grill for 1 to 2 minutes, or until the fish is opaque throughout.

To serve: Preheat the broiler. Place a fish fillet in the center of each serving plate. Arrange the zucchini, carrots, asparagus spears, and tomatoes around the fish. Ladle the sauce over the fish, top each with some of the grated cheese, and sprinkle the remaining ½ cup pumpkin seeds over and around the plates. Place under the broiler to melt the cheese, about 1 minute. Garnish each plate with a cilantro sprig.

Redfish with Shrimp and Crab Roasted-Pepper Butter and Pumpkin Seeds; *Bruce Molzan, Ruggles Grill*

Yellowtail Snapper with Melon Relish and Orange Vinaigrette

▼■▼■ ■ ■ ■ ■ ■ ■ ■

Hubert Des Marais
The Ocean Grand
Palm Beach, Florida

South Florida cuisine at its tropical finest showcases butterflied snapper fillets with a cool-spicy relish and an intense vinaigrette.

Serves 4

Annatto Oil
2 tablespoons annatto seeds
½ cup olive oil

Melon Relish
¾ cup ½-inch-diced cantaloupe
¾ cup ½-inch-diced honeydew melon
¾ cup ½-inch-diced watermelon
1 tablespoon minced fresh ginger
2 teaspoons minced Scotch bonnet (habanero) chili
2 tablespoons fresh Key lime juice
1 teaspoon minced fresh thyme
1 tablespoon minced fresh cilantro

Orange Vinaigrette
2 cups fresh orange juice, cooked over medium-high heat to reduce to 1 cup, or ½ cup orange juice concentrate
1 tablespoon Dijon mustard
2 teaspoons champagne vinegar
½ cup vegetable oil
2 teaspoons toasted sesame oil
1 tablespoon water (optional)
Salt and freshly ground black pepper to taste

Four 1-pound whole yellowtail snappers, scaled
Olive oil for brushing
8 fresh lemon thyme sprigs
16 fresh cilantro sprigs
Salt and freshly ground black pepper to taste

Garnish
2 tablespoons molasses, preferably Jamaican
4 fresh cilantro sprigs
4 fresh rosemary sprigs

To make the annatto oil: Crush the annatto seeds in a spice grinder or mortar and place them in the oil. Let steep at room temperature for at least 1 hour. Strain through a fine-meshed sieve.

To make the melon relish: In a medium bowl, toss the cantaloupe, honeydew, and watermelon with the ginger and chili. Add the lime juice, thyme, and cilantro. Toss again. Let sit at room temperature for up to 1 hour.

To make the orange vinaigrette: In a small bowl, blend the orange juice, Dijon mustard, and vinegar. Slowly whisk in two-thirds of the vegetable oil. Check and adjust the seasoning with vinegar, salt, or pepper. Add the remaining

Yellowtail Snapper with Melon Relish and Orange Vinaigrette;
Hubert Des Marais, The Ocean Grand

vegetable oil and the sesame oil. Add the water if necessary to thin the vinaigrette. Let sit at room temperature until serving.

To prepare the snapper: Remove the heads from the snappers. Using a sharp flexible knife, make an incision down the back of the snapper from the head to the tail, following the spine, on both sides of the fish. Use the knife to cut between the flesh and the rib cage down to the tail, leaving the flesh attached at the tail end. Cut through the spine of the fish at the tail and remove the spine. Open the two halves of the fish flat like a book. You should have 2 butterfly-cut fillets attached to the tail.

Carefully remove all pin bones from the fillets with a pair of needlenose pliers. Brush the flesh side of each fish with olive oil. Season with salt and pepper, and place 1 thyme sprig and 2 cilantro sprigs in the center of each butterfly. Fold the sides of the fillets over the sprigs and press them together. Repeat for each fish. Using a sharp knife, cut several X marks in the skin side of the fillets. This prevents the fish from curling during cooking.

In a large sauté pan or skillet over high heat, heat the annatto oil and brown the snappers on both sides, 2 to 3 minutes per side.

To serve: Divide the melon relish among the plates. Surround the relish with the orange vinaigrette. Using a squeeze bottle, drizzle the relish and vinaigrette with the molasses. Place the snapper in the center of the relish and garnish the plate with fresh herb sprigs.

HUBERT DES MARAIS
The Ocean Grand, Palm Beach, Florida

Hubert Des Marais attributes much of his success to the joy of working for a privately owned hotel, where he has the freedom to create his own south Florida cuisine.

A graduate of the Culinary Institute of America, Des Marais says his cooking style (and that of Palm Beach's Ocean Grand) is exemplified by the menu he prepared for the James Beard Foundation and its Great Hotel Chefs series in New York.

The dinner included yucca-crusted oysters with caviar, grilled yellowfin tuna with smoked pink swordfish, swamp cabbage and roast pepper essence, and Florida venison with Haden mango.

"Even though this is a thrilling, fantastic time for both my team and me," says Des Marais, "I never want to fall into the trap of resting on my laurels. In fact, I'm working very hard to make sure that none of this attention affects the way that I live my life. My main objectives are to keep experimenting with new concepts and try to improve upon what I've done before."

Like several other leaders of the regional cuisine movement, Des Marais is a zealot for new and flavorful ingredients. The Ocean Grand, which he joined just prior to its opening in 1990, has its own garden, with trees bearing Hawaiian guavas, Meyer and Ponderosa lemons, and carambola, plus a wide variety of fresh herbs and the chilies known as pili pili.

Another side to Des Marais' mission is establishing and keeping good relationships with small farmers, ranchers, and fishermen all across south Florida. This is the chef's support group, the source of those special touches that set his cuisine apart.

Prior to joining the Ocean Grand, Des Marais honed both his cooking and administrative skills at several of the South's most luxurious hotels. These included the Ritz-Carlton in Houston, where he was executive sous-chef; Hawk's Key Resort in the Florida Keys, where he was executive chef; and South Carolina's famed Kiawah Island, where he served as a *garde-manger* and a chef.

A true traveling gourmet, Des Marais enjoys venturing with his wife Evangeline (the Ocean Grand's former catering director) to new and exotic locales. Not long ago, they toured remote areas of Africa and Asia, sampling the food at every stop. Needless to say, it wasn't long before elements of that experience found their way into the recipes at the Ocean Grand.

ELKA GILMORE
Elka, San Francisco, California

Elka Gilmore knew she wanted to work in a restaurant when she was only eleven, and she wasn't about to let little things like labor laws stand in her way. "I lied about my age to get the job," she says of her dishwashing stint at Cafe Camile, a small French restaurant in her hometown of San Antonio. "I loved the excitement of the kitchen, and once I discovered good food, I found that I had a natural inclination to cook."

Charity may begin at home, but Gilmore's culinary career began with that first underage dishwasher's job. "My mother was talented in many ways but a terrible cook. She was always trying to do strange things with organ meat."

The gifted daughter of a military historian father and an artist mother, Gilmore entered the accelerated studies program at the University of Wisconsin at age fourteen. Her major was chemistry, but it was her unofficial minor as the cafeteria cook's assistant that said more about her vocation.

After Cafe Camile, Gilmore was all set to make fresh pasta sheets and prepare ravioli for a horde at the cafeteria. Only when the head cook instructed her to open twenty No. 10 cans of the stuff did she realize her skills were a little elevated for the job.

By the end of college, Gilmore had graduated to an afternoon cook position at L'Étoile, Madison's version of a cutting-edge restaurant. This propelled her, after graduation, to positions in Boston at Romagnoli's Table and Rebecca, then at the Summer House on Nantucket.

After a six-month apprenticeship in the south of France, cooking at the Lou Callen Inn in the village of Cotignac, Gilmore felt she was starting to understand French cuisine.

"The French love for food began to make sense," she says. "The cuisine is fresh and exciting. I began to understand why the French so often talk enthusiastically about what they ate at their last meal, while so many diet-crazed Americans talk more about what they didn't eat."

In 1982, Gilmore headed for Los Angeles to open Camelions as executive chef, then helped to launch Tumbleweeds (featuring Texas-style barbecue and Mexican-style fish cookery) in Beverly Hills. With managing partner John Banta, Gilmore opened her own namesake restaurant, Elka, in San Francisco in 1991.

Her creativity and her personality have made her a standout, even on the highly competitive San Francisco restaurant scene.

Kasu-marinated Sturgeon with Grilled Rice Cakes, Umaboshi Plum Vinaigrette, and Beet Oil

Elka Gilmore
Elka
San Francisco, California

This brilliant example of Pacific Rim cuisine combines sturgeon fillets, a marinade of sake lees, a sweet-sour plum vinaigrette, and warm sautéed cakes of short-grain rice.

Serves 4

Sturgeon and Marinade
¼ cup kasu (sake lees)
1 teaspoon grated fresh ginger
½ cup coarsely chopped fresh cilantro
1 teaspoon freshly ground black pepper
¼ cup mirin (sweet sake) or
  sweet sherry
Four 6-ounce sturgeon or salmon fillets

Plum Vinaigrette and Puree
5- to 6-ounce jar of Japanese umaboshi
  pickled plums, pitted
½ cup rice wine vinegar
¾ cup ginger oil (recipe follows)
3 tablespoons minced shallots

Rice Cakes
1 cup short-grain rice
2½ cups water
1 teaspoon salt
3 tablespoons clarified unsalted butter
  (see page 223)
¼ cup reserved Plum Puree, above
Four ¾-inch-wide nori strips
  (Japanese seaweed)

¼ cup clarified unsalted butter

Garnish
3 ounces daikon sprouts
3 ounces enoki mushrooms
Beet oil (recipe follows)

To prepare the sturgeon and marinade:
Combine the kasu, ginger, cilantro, black pepper, and mirin or sherry in a blender or food processor, then process to a paste. Spread this on both sides of the sturgeon fillets, place them in a nonaluminum container, cover, and refrigerate overnight or up to 2 days.

To make the vinaigrette and puree: Puree the plums in a blender. Reserve ¼ cup of the plum puree. Place the remaining puree in a medium bowl and whisk in the rice wine, vinegar, ginger oil, and shallots. Set the vinaigrette aside.

To make the rice cakes: In a medium saucepan over medium-high heat, combine the rice, water, and salt. Cover and cook until the liquid is absorbed, about 15 to 20 minutes.

Divide the rice among four 3-inch-diameter stainless-steel rings to make ¾-inch-thick rice cakes. Press the rice firmly into the rings, then remove the rings. In a medium sauté pan or skillet over medium heat, heat the 3 tablespoons clarified butter and cook the rice cakes until golden and thoroughly heated, about 3 to 5 minutes on each side. Spread the reserved plum puree on the rice cakes and wrap a strip of nori around the sides of each cake.

Scrape most of the paste marinade from the sturgeon fillets. In a large sauté pan or skillet over medium-high heat, heat the ¼ cup clarified butter and sauté the sturgeon fillets until they are nicely brown and starting to caramelize, about 3 to 5 minutes on each side. (It is important that the fish be thoroughly cooked, to retain the moisture.) Set aside and keep warm.

To prepare the garnish: Remove the root ends from the enoki mushrooms. Combine the sprouts and mushrooms and toss with ½ cup of the plum vinaigrette.

To serve: Pool some of the remaining vinaigrette in the center of each plate. Place 1 rice cake on top of the vinaigrette and arrange 1 sturgeon fillet alongside each cake. Garnish each plate with the enoki mushrooms and daikon sprout garnish. Drizzle the plates with beet oil.

Ginger Oil: In a small saucepan, combine ¼ cup minced fresh ginger with ¾ cup canola oil. Bring the mixture to a boil, remove from heat, and let sit for 2 hours. Strain through a fine-meshed sieve. Cover and store in the refrigerator. Makes ¾ cup.

Beet Oil: In a heavy, medium nonaluminum saucepan over medium heat, cook 2 cups of beet juice to reduce it to ¼ cup, about 20 minutes. Whisk in ½ cup canola oil to make an emulsion. Cover and store in the refrigerator. Makes ¾ cup.

Kasu-marinated Sturgeon with Grilled Rice Cakes, Umaboshi Plum Vinaigrette, and Beet Oil; *Elka Gilmore, Elka*

Pesto-crusted Salmon Skewers with Wild Mushroom Risotto and Arugula-Basil Vinaigrette

■▪■▪■▪■▪■▪■▪■▪■▪■▪■

Kevin Rathbun
Nava
Atlanta, Georgia

What a satisfying combination of colors, tastes, and textures: skewers of crisp sautéed salmon with a coating of pesto, a bright-green vinaigrette that echoes the basil flavor, and risotto made with mushrooms, mushroom soy sauce, and reduced veal stock.

Serves 4

Pesto Sauce
1 cup dried white bread crumbs, preferably Panko (available in Asian markets)
1/3 cup (1 1/2 ounces) finely grated Asiago cheese
2/3 cup unbleached all-purpose flour, plus up to 4 tablespoons more if needed
3 tablespoons pine nuts
1 tablespoon minced shallots
1 tablespoon minced garlic
1/4 cup tightly packed chopped spinach
1/4 cup tightly packed chopped fresh basil
Salt and freshly ground black pepper to taste

Salmon
1/3 cup buttermilk
1 egg
One 18-ounce salmon fillet, skinned
Salt to taste
3/4 cup unbleached all-purpose flour
Pesto Sauce, above

Wild Mushroom Risotto
2 tablespoons olive oil
1/4 cup minced red onion
2 teaspoons minced garlic
3/4 cup Arborio rice
1 cup diced stemmed shiitake mushrooms
1 cup finely diced cremini or morel mushrooms
1/4 cup dry red wine
3 cups chicken stock (see page 228)
1/3 cup mushroom soy sauce
1/4 cup rich veal stock (see page 228, 231)
Salt and freshly ground black pepper to taste
1 tablespoon minced fresh basil
2 teaspoons minced fresh thyme

Arugula-Basil Vinaigrette
1 tablespoon minced shallot
Puree from 1 roasted garlic head (see page 234)
2 tablespoons minced fresh basil
1/4 cup chopped arugula
2 tablespoons champagne vinegar
2 tablespoons honey
1 tablespoon chicken stock (see page 228)
1/4 cup olive oil
1/4 cup safflower oil
Salt and freshly ground black pepper to taste
2 tablespoons butter
2 tablespoons olive oil

Garnish
1 large red onion, cut into eight 1/4-inch-thick slices
Olive oil for brushing
4 triangles *each* roasted and peeled red and yellow peppers (see page 235)

To make the pesto: Combine the bread crumbs, cheese, 2/3 cup flour, and pine nuts in a blender or food processor and grind to a powder. Add the shallots, garlic, spinach, and basil and blend again, then season with salt and pepper. If the mixture is too wet, add up to 4 tablespoons more flour. Set aside.

To coat the salmon: Whisk together the buttermilk and egg. Cut the salmon fillet into 12 portions about 1 1/2 inches wide and 2 inches long. Season both sides lightly with salt. Pour the flour into a shallow dish. Dust each piece of fish with flour, dip in the egg wash, then coat with pesto. Lay the coated pieces of fish flat on a nonaluminum tray and refrigerate until ready to cook.

Pesto-crusted Salmon Skewers with Wild Mushroom Risotto and Arugula-Basil Vinaigrette; *Kevin Rathbun, Nava*

To make the risotto: In a large, heavy saucepan over medium heat, heat the olive oil and sauté the onion and garlic until translucent, 2 to 3 minutes. Add the rice and stir to coat all the grains. Add the mushrooms and sauté for 2 to 3 minutes, then add the wine and stir constantly until it is absorbed. Add half the chicken stock, lower the heat to medium or medium low, depending on the heaviness of the pan, and cook, stirring constantly, until almost all the liquid is absorbed. Add the remaining chicken stock and continue to cook, stirring constantly, until the liquid is again absorbed. The total cooking time will be 30 to 40 minutes. Add the mushroom soy sauce and the rich veal stock. Season with salt and pepper, then add the herbs. Set aside and keep warm.

To make the arugula-basil vinaigrette: In a blender or food processor, combine the shallot, roasted garlic puree (there will be about 1 tablespoon), basil, arugula, vinegar, and honey, and blend until smooth. Add the chicken stock. While the motor is running, gradually add the oils to make an emulsion. Season with salt and pepper.

In a large sauté pan or skillet over medium-high heat, melt the butter with the oil until the butter foams. Add the salmon pieces and sauté, turning once, until crusty and browned, 7 to 8 minutes. Transfer the salmon to a plate and thread 4 wooden skewers with 3 pieces of salmon each. Meanwhile, preheat the broiler. Brush the onion slices with olive oil. Broil for 5 to 8 minutes, turning once. The onions can also be pan-fried over high heat.

To serve: Place a 3-inch stainless steel ring in the center of each plate and fill each with some of the risotto, pressing down on the surface with the back of a spoon to compact it into the rings. Remove the rings, place 1 triangle of each colored pepper on each portion, and top with 2 grilled onion slices. Place 1 skewer standing against each portion of risotto and drizzle vinaigrette around the plate.

KEVIN RATHBUN
Nava, Atlanta, Georgia

Exciting food that is beyond the expected: This is how critics describe Kavin Rathbun's cooking at Nava. It's the kind of food he has spent his career learning how to create. His previous position as executive chef at Baby Routh in Dallas let Rathbun bring to Nava a grounding in popular Southwest flavors and a well-rounded understanding of regional American food.

You could say that his Missouri birth placed him at the very center of it all, able to gaze out in all directions with a certain amount of perspective. One of Rathbun's first jobs was in the kitchen at Kansas City's Au Bonne Auberge, where his mother served as maître d' for seven years. Rathbun's major apprenticeship was under chef Bradley Ogden, at the American Restaurant in the same city. Within a year, he was promoted to sous-chef.

"I learned a lot from Bradley," Rathbun recalls. "And I especially admired his ability to work with, challenge, and nurture his staff. That trait, together with my mother's example of hospitality and rapport with dining guests, I will always carry with me from my early training."

Completing his apprenticeship in 1984, Rathbun headed south to Texas to serve as sous-chef at Brennan's of Houston. Three years later, remaining within the Brennan family, he moved to New Orleans as sous-chef at Commander's Palace. By 1988, it was back to Texas, to serve as sous-chef and eventually executive chef at Baby Routh.

Before the restaurant closed its doors and Rathbun took on the brave new world of Atlanta, Baby Routh had a highly praised run. While Rathbun was at the helm, it drew praise from Mimi Sheraton in *Travel & Leisure* as "one of America's 25 best restaurants." In 1993, it received the DiRona Award for Dining Excellence.

MONIQUE ANDRÉE BARBEAU
Fullers, Sheraton Seattle Hotel & Towers, Seattle, Washington

When she stepped on board as chef at Fullers in Seattle, Monique Andrée Barbeau had more than her share of cynics to win over.

For starters, there were those who figured no one could replace Caprial Pence, who had taken the restaurant so far before departing for Portland. And there were those who dismissed her as a Pence clone: just another woman chef under thirty, in a kitchen that had seen a series of such chefs in the past few years.

In one way or another, Barbeau has won the cynics over. She even won back Fullers fourth star from *Seattle Best Places*, a publication that had fretted in print over the establishment's Pence-less future. No fretting was called for, as things turned out.

The Vancouver-born Barbeau was named chef at Fullers at the Sheraton Seattle Hotel & Towers in January 1992, after the property had conducted a month-long search and interviewed more than two hundred candidates from all over the country. Her local roots proved a culinary boon, placing her at the heart of the movement to celebrate foods of the Pacific Northwest.

As a 1987 graduate of the Culinary Institute of America, Barbeau cooked at a trio of four-star restaurants in New York: the Quilted Giraffe, Le Bernardin, and Chanterelle. She also picked up a bachelor of science degree in hospitality management from Florida International University in 1991.

Since taking over the kitchen at Fullers, Barbeau has continued in her predecessor's award-winning ways. Two of her proudest honors include a nomination as Rising Star Chef for the 1993 James Beard Awards, and an award as Beard's Best Chef of the Pacific Northwest the following year.

Other special recognitions have rolled in as well, including the chance to cook with three other Americans for the Women Chefs for Peace event held in Israel in 1994. Barbeau was the only West Coast chef invited, joining Rozanne Gold of the Rainbow Room and Anne Rozenzweig of Arcadia, both in New York, and Susan Spicer of Bayona in New Orleans.

Salmon Salad with Avocado Vinaigrette and Corn Salsa

▰▰▰▰▰▰▰▰▰▰▰▰

Monique Andrée Barbeau
Fullers
Sheraton Seattle Hotel & Towers
Seattle, Washington

A Pacific Northwest salad with Southwest flavors makes a fine summer lunch or supper entrée. Crisp fried shallots add a surprise crunch. For a first course, cut the recipe in half.

Serves 6

Avocado Vinaigrette
2 large avocados, peeled, pitted, and
    quartered (1 pit reserved)
Juice of 3 limes
½ cup rice wine vinegar
1 teaspoon minced garlic
¾ cup olive oil
Salt and freshly ground black pepper
    to taste

Salmon
2 tablespoons cumin seed
2 tablespoons coriander seed
1 tablespoon kosher salt
Six 5-ounce salmon fillets, skin on
3 tablespoons olive oil

Fried Shallots
⅓ cup all-purpose flour
6 large shallots, cut into thin slices and
    separated into rings
Vegetable oil for frying
Salt to taste

6 cups mesclun (mixed baby greens)
Salt and freshly ground pepper to taste
Fresh chives, snipped into 1-inch pieces

To make the vinaigrette: Coarsely chop the avocados and place them in a blender or food processor. Add the lime juice, rice vinegar, and garlic. With the motor running, slowly add the oil to make a thick sauce. Season with the salt and pepper. If necessary, adjust the tartness with more lime juice or rice vinegar, according to taste. Place in a bowl, add the avocado pit, cover, and refrigerate. (The pit will help to keep the vinaigrette green.)

To prepare the salmon: Grind the dry spices in a mortar with a pestle, or grind for a few seconds in a spice grinder or a well-washed coffee grinder, until they have the texture of the kosher salt. Mix the spices with the salt and generously coat the flesh side of each fillet with some of the spice mixture.

In a large nonstick pan or seasoned cast-iron skillet over medium-high heat, heat the olive oil and add the salmon, spice-coated side down. Cook for 3 to 5 minutes, or until golden brown, then turn and cook on the skin side for 2 to 3 minutes. Remove from the pan and set aside.

To make the fried shallots: Place the flour in a shallow container and lightly dredge the shallot rings. In a medium sauté pan or skillet over medium-high heat, heat the oil. Shake the excess flour from the shallots and fry them for about 30 seconds, or until golden brown. Using a slotted spoon, remove them from the pan and drain on paper towels. Season to taste.

To serve: Toss the greens with half the vinaigrette, then add half the shallot rings and season with salt and pepper. Divide this mixture among the serving plates. Place 3 tablespoons of corn salsa on top of each serving, then top with a portion of fish. Sprinkle the remaining shallot rings over the dish and garnish with the chives. Serve the remaining vinaigrette and salsa on the side.

Corn Salsa
(Makes about 2 cups)

2 to 3 ears of corn, husked
$\frac{1}{2}$ cup $\frac{1}{4}$-inch-diced red onion
$1\frac{1}{2}$ tablespoons minced seeded jalapeño chili
3 tablespoons coarsely chopped fresh cilantro
$\frac{1}{4}$ cup rice wine vinegar
$\frac{1}{4}$ cup olive oil
Salt and freshly ground black pepper to taste
$\frac{1}{2}$ avocado, peeled, pitted, and diced

Bring a large pot of lightly salted water to a boil, add the corn, and cook for 3 minutes. Drain and cut the kernels from the cobs. You should have about 1 cup kernels. In a large bowl, combine the corn, onion, jalapeño, cilantro, vinegar, and oil. Season the mixture with salt and pepper, cover, and let sit at room temperature for up to 2 hours. Just before serving, gently stir in the avocado.

Salmon Salad with Avocado Vinaigrette and Corn Salsa;
Monique Andrée Barbeau, Fullers

Shrimp Enchiladas on Black Bean Sauce

Stephan Pyles
Star Canyon
Dallas, Texas

A new take on a Southwestern standard, this recipe combines shrimp and papaya, avocados and tomatillos, and serves up the enchiladas on a bed of black bean sauce, garnished with mango puree.

Serves 6

Ancho Puree
5 to 6 ancho chilies
1 cup warm water

Avocado-Tomatillo Salsa
2 large avocados, peeled, pitted, and
    cut into 1/2-inch dice
1 tablespoon minced green onion,
    white part only
1 teaspoon 1/4-inch-diced red bell pepper
1 teaspoon 1/4-inch-diced green
    bell pepper
4 tomatillos, husked and diced
1 garlic clove, minced
2 tablespoons fresh cilantro leaves,
    chopped
2 serrano chilies, seeded and minced
2 teaspoons fresh lime juice
3 tablespoons olive oil
Salt to taste

Black Bean Sauce
1 cup chicken stock (see page 228)
1/2 cup cooked black beans
3 serrano chilies, seeded
2 garlic cloves, chopped
1 1/2 tablespoons chopped fresh tomatillo
1 tablespoon chopped fresh cilantro
2 teaspoons chopped onion
2 teaspoons chopped green bell pepper
1 teaspoon fresh lime juice
Salt to taste

Shrimp Filling
2 tablespoons olive oil
2 large onions, minced (2 cups)
2 tablespoons minced garlic
2 pounds medium shrimp, peeled,
    deveined, and cut into 1/2-inch pieces
1/2 teaspoon salt
4 poblano chilies, roasted, peeled,
    seeded, and diced (see page 235)
3 tablespoons minced fresh cilantro
1 papaya, peeled, seeded, and diced
1/4 cup Ancho Puree, above
1 3/4 cups (7 ounces) grated Chihuahua
    or Monterey jack cheese

1 cup canola oil for frying tortillas
18 corn tortillas
1 3/4 cups (7 ounces) grated Chihuahua
    or Monterey Jack cheese

Mango Puree
2 ripe mangos, peeled, pitted, and diced
1/2 Scotch bonnet (habanero) chili,
    seeded and deveined

Garnish
1 large tomato, peeled, seeded, and
    diced (see page 234)
3 green onions, thinly sliced
    on the diagonal

To make the ancho puree: Preheat the oven to 250°F. Place the chilies on a baking sheet and roast until they are crisp, 20 minutes. Remove the stem and seeds from the chilies, cover with the

Shrimp Enchiladas on Black Bean Sauce; *Stephan Pyles, Star Canyon*

warm water, and allow to soak until they are soft, 30 minutes. Strain the liquid through cheesecloth and set aside. Place the peppers in a blender and puree, adding a small amount of the strained liquid to form a thick puree. Set the puree aside and reserve the remaining strained liquid.

To make the salsa: In a large bowl, combine the avocado, green onions, bell peppers, and half of the diced tomatillos. Set aside. In a blender, combine the garlic, cilantro, serranos, lime juice, and remaining tomatillos and puree until smooth. Slowly drizzle in the oil. Pour the puree over the avocado mixture, toss to combine, and season with salt. Let sit for 30 minutes before serving.

To make the black bean sauce: In a medium saucepan over medium heat, combine the stock, beans, serranos, garlic, tomatillo, cilantro, onion, and bell pepper. Reduce heat to low and simmer for 5 minutes. Drain, reserving the cooking liquid. Place the bean mixture in a blender and puree for 1 minute, adding just enough of the reserved cooking liquid to make a smooth sauce. Season the sauce with lime juice and salt and set aside. Keep warm or reheat gently before serving.

To make the filling: In a medium sauté pan or skillet over high heat, heat the oil and sauté the onion and garlic for 30 seconds. Add the shrimp and salt, and cook until the shrimp turn pink, 2 to 3 minutes. Add the poblanos, cilantro, papaya, and ancho puree. Stir gently, remove from heat, and add the cheese. Stir lightly to melt the cheese. Set aside.

To make the enchiladas: Preheat the oven to 350°F. In a large sauté pan or skillet over medium-high heat, heat the oil until it reaches 375°F, or until almost smoking. Dip the tortillas in the hot oil one at a time, turning once, just until they are softened, for about 15 seconds. Drain on paper towels.

Place a tortilla on a work surface, spoon ¼ cup filling down the center, and roll the tortilla tightly. Place the rolled tortilla in a baking pan or dish, seam-side down. Repeat with the remaining tortillas. Thin the remaining ancho puree with 2 tablespoons of the reserved liquid and brush the tortillas with it. Sprinkle the top with the remaining grated cheese, cover the baking pan with aluminum foil, and bake until heated through and the cheese has melted, about 15 minutes.

To make the mango puree: In a blender, blend the mango with the chili until smooth. Place in a squeeze bottle.

To serve: Pool some black bean sauce on each serving plate. Place 3 enchiladas on each plate and sprinkle with some of the diced tomatoes and green onions. Spoon some avocado salsa over the enchiladas and squeeze some of the mango puree over the plate. Garnish with a little more diced tomato and green onion.

Roasted Marinated Long Island Duck with Duck Liver Crostini and Braised Escarole; *Jody Adams, Michela's*

Hearty Courses: Poultry and Meats

▀▜▀▜▀▜▀▜▀▜▀▜▀▜▀▜▀

Despite the occasional prediction to the contrary, America's love affair with meat continues, epitomized by what can be called a new golden age of steakhouses. Meat is still one of the most popular choices in fine restaurants. People want only the best when they decide to splurge.

The kinds of dishes presented in this chapter reflect the trend: smaller portions of meat, showcased with vegetables and dazzling sauces. You will find exotic, ethnic, and down-home dishes here, all based on the ingenuity of our chefs and the high quality of their ingredients.

This chapter also includes some unusual treatments of duck, quail, chicken, sweetbreads, and rabbit. Like the meat recipes, they draw their inspiration from regions as far away as India, and as close to home as the local diner.

While America remains generally skeptical of liver, brain, tongue and other so-called specialty meats, it seems willing and able to eat the meat of almost anything that flies, walks or lumbers along. Beef and chicken remain the basics, followed by pork and lamb, then by duck, venison and a host of game.

For those who like to eat hearty, in other words, there's no shortage of opportunities in our nation's restaurants.

Seattle, Washington

Tandoori Quail with Sesame-Sage Vinaigrette; *Raji Jallepalli, Raji*

Tandoori Quail with Sesame-Sage Vinaigrette

Raji Jallepalli
Raji
Memphis, Tennessee

Quail goes to India by way of Santa Fe here, with a rub of tandoori spices, a vinaigrette of fresh sage, and a compote that combines corn kernels, turmeric, cumin, and cilantro.

Serves 4

Quail
8 semi-boned quail
3 tablespoons extra-virgin olive oil
Salt and freshly ground black pepper
  to taste
8 teaspoons tandoori spice mix (available in Indian markets and specialty foods stores)

Sesame-Sage Vinaigrette
6 tablespoons extra-virgin olive oil
1/2 cup fresh sage leaves
2 tablespoons balsamic vinegar
1 teaspoon minced fresh ginger
1/2 teaspoon salt
1 tablespoon white sesame seeds

Corn-Cilantro Compote
3 tablespoons butter
3 cups fresh or frozen corn kernels
1 tablespoon white sesame seeds
2 teaspoons ground turmeric
2 teaspoons ground cumin
6 tablespoons chopped fresh cilantro
1 teaspoon salt

To prepare the quail: Rub the quail with 2 tablespoons of the oil. Sprinkle each inside and out with salt and pepper and 1 teaspoon of the spice mix. Rub the seasonings into the meat and under the skin. In a large sauté pan or skillet over high heat, brown the quail on all sides, then cook each breast-side down for 2 to 3 minutes. Remove and set aside. The quail should be nicely browned on the outside but rare inside.

To make the vinaigrette: In a blender or food processor, combine all the ingredients and puree for 1 minute. Strain the vinaigrette through a fine-meshed sieve and set aside.

To make the corn-cilantro compote: In a small sauté pan or skillet over medium-high heat, melt the butter. Add the corn, sesame seeds, turmeric, and cumin, and sauté for 2 to 3 minutes. Add the cilantro and salt, and cook for 1 minute.

To serve: Preheat the oven to 375°F. Place the quail in the oven to warm for 5 minutes. Mound some of the corn compote in the center of each serving plate, center 2 quail on top of the corn, and drizzle the vinaigrette around the edges of the plate and over the quail.

RAJI JALLEPALLI
Raji, Memphis, Tennessee

Several chefs in this book thank their mothers for inspiring their culinary careers, but Raji Jallepalli tells a different tale. Her mother doesn't understand that Raji is a chef – and, according to the Memphis sensation, wouldn't like it one bit if she did.

"I come from a wealthy Indian family, and my mother is a diplomat in India," reports the founder of Raji. "When I was growing up, chefs were cooks, not celebrities. Her idea of me is not sweating behind a hot stove. She thinks of me in fine linen dresses, walking around the restaurant to see if everything is all right."

Jallepalli does her share of sweating behind the hot stove at Raji, which has earned an enthusiastic following in Memphis and beyond for its fusion of Indian and French cuisines.

Yet Jallepalli is something of a celebrity as well (though usually in chef's whites rather than linen dresses); she was invited to join Jean-Louis Palladin, Michel Richard, and a handful of other luminaries cooking at President Bill Clinton's inauguration.

Jallepalli has an unusual background for a chef, starting out as a medical technologist. Since she also managed her husband's medical practice, she was familiar with one of the things that most chefs know little about: handling finances.

This has helped her immensely in the business running her restaurant, originally known as the East India Company and serving strictly Indian cuisine from 1989 to 1992. In 1992, with the change of the name to Raji, Jallepalli's cooking began to evolve in a more personal direction.

"I got into cooking because it's an art form, and I enjoy expressing myself," Jallepalli explains. "Cooking to me is an emotional experience. The way food tastes is an extension of myself. As a child in India, I was into theater, music and all kinds of art forms.

"There's something special about owning a restaurant and seeing people happy when lingering over a meal, and it's a fun way to make a living."

In her own creative pilgrimage, Jallepalli found Jean-Louis Palladin of Jean-Louis at the Watergate an especially inspiring role model. It was he who helped her learn the sophisticated French techniques that resulted in some of best-known dishes, such as a *croustillade* of crab with Arkansas razorback caviar and blackberry chutney.

SUSAN SPICER
Bayona, New Orleans, Louisiana

Throughout most of her dazzling career as a chef, Susan Spicer has opened her eyes to a new world every day. So it only follows that when she was asked to label her style of cooking, New World cuisine made the most sense.

Inspired by chef Daniel Bonnot, Spicer started out with a three-year apprenticeship at his Louis XVI in New Orleans – about as close to an Old World apprenticeship as could be found in the New. Spicer spent the summer of 1982 cooking with Roland Durand in Paris.

Those came to her quickly, in the form of the executive chef's job at a place called Savoir Faire. That restaurant quickly became, in a phrase, the talk of New Orleans. For one thing, it typified the new bistro movement, combining robust cuisine with a casually elegant ambiance. For another thing, the chef was a woman, the first New Orleans had ever encountered in a classical French kitchen.

Spicer does not see herself as the leader of a movement, but she does expect to have the freedom to ply her trade and to be judged by her work alone. In time, other young women around New Orleans caught her fire, often working in her kitchen for a time as part of their apprenticeships.

After cooking for local and national celebrities at Savoir Faire for three years, Spicer took a year off to travel through Europe and California. Her influences became even more diverse as she traveled, picking up Greek flavorings in this journey, North African in that one. Truth is, each mile she traveled would eventually make her customers vicarious adventurers.

A major breakthrough occurred in 1986, when Spicer opened the Bistro at the Maison de Ville, a tiny dining room with a tiny kitchen in a small French Quarter hotel. Tables soon became hard to get at the Bistro, as local foodies and national media jockeyed for a chance to taste Spicer's food.

In 1990, such fame allowed her to open her own restaurant near the Bistro. She dubbed the new place Bayona, after a town on the French-Spanish border. Yet she insisted Bayona was not a town or cuisine she wished to promote – just a sound she liked, an image that seemed to capture her kind of cooking.

Based on the success of Bayona since the day it opened, and the awards from all over the world lining its walls, Susan Spicer has also captured the hearts of her diners.

Smoked Duck Hash
▼▲▼▲▼▲▼▲▼▲▼▲▼▲▼▲▼

Susan Spicer
Bayona
New Orleans, Louisiana

Purchase a whole smoked duck for this dish and use the carcass to make a rich duck stock for the apple-perfumed sauce. Add salt cautiously to the hash to achieve a good balance of savory, sweet and smoky in the hash-filled pastries.

Serves 6

Smoked Duck Hash
1 tablespoon clarified unsalted butter
  (see page 223)
½ cup finely chopped onion
½ cup finely chopped celery
4 ounces andouille sausage, cut into
  ½-inch dice
1 apple, peeled, cored, and cut into
  1-inch cubes
½ smoked duck, cut into 1-inch cubes
1 sweet potato, baked, peeled, and cut
  into 1-inch cubes
2 tablespoons dry sherry
1 tablespoon flour
1 teaspoon minced fresh sage
1 teaspoon minced fresh thyme
Salt to taste
½ cup duck or chicken stock
  (see page 228, 231)

Crust
1½ cups unbleached all-purpose flour
1 teaspoon salt
½ cup (1 stick) cold unsalted butter,
  cut into bits
8 to 10 tablespoons cold water
1 egg
¼ cup milk

Sauce
1 tablespoon clarified unsalted butter
  (see page 223)
1 shallot, minced
1 cup apple juice
1 cup duck or chicken stock
  (see page 228, 231)
2 tablespoons apple cider vinegar
2 tablespoons apple jelly
2 tablespoons Calvados brandy
1 tablespoon cold unsalted butter
Salt to taste

Garnish

Crème fraîche (see page 220)

3 tablespoons mixed fresh parsley and celery leaves

6 celery leaf sprigs

To make the hash: In a large sauté pan or skillet, heat the clarified butter over medium-high heat and sauté the onion and celery until they begin to color, about 2 minutes. Add the andouille sausage to the pan and stir, then add the apple and continue to cook and stir until the apple begins to color, 2 to 3 minutes. Add the duck and sweet potato and cook for another 2 minutes. Add the sherry, then sprinkle the mixture with the flour to lightly coat the vegetables. Add the herbs and salt, then add the stock, stirring to scrape up the browned bits on the bottom of the pan. Remove from the heat, let cool, and refrigerate for 30 to 40 minutes.

To make the crust: In a large bowl, combine the flour and salt. Using a pastry blender or 2 knives, cut in the butter until the mixture resembles coarse meal. Stir in the water 1 tablespoon at a time until the dough begins to hold together. Form the dough into a disc, wrap in plastic wrap, and refrigerate for 30 minutes.

Preheat the oven to 375°F. Roll the pastry dough to a 1/8-inch thickness on a lightly floured surface. Cut the dough into six 5-inch squares. Spoon approximately 1/2 cup of the hash into the center of each square. Whisk together the egg and milk to make an egg wash and brush the edges of a square of dough. Pull two opposite corners of the dough together in the center and pinch them together, then bring the remaining corners to the center. Crimp the seams to seal the dough completely. Repeat to fill all the squares. Brush the pastries with the egg wash and place on a lightly buttered baking sheet. Bake until golden brown, 20 to 25 minutes.

To make the sauce: In a medium sauté pan or skillet over medium heat, melt the butter and sauté the shallot for 1 minute. Add the apple juice, stock, and cider vinegar and cook over high heat to reduce to 1 1/2 cups, 15 to 20 minutes. Add the apple jelly and stir until it is melted, then remove the pan from heat and add the Calvados. Strain the sauce through a fine-meshed sieve and return it to the pan. Just before serving, place the pan over medium heat, quickly whisk in the cold butter, and add salt.

To serve: Place the crème fraîche in a squeeze bottle and squeeze some of it into the center of each serving plate. Place 1 duck hash pastry on each plate and spoon some of the sauce over and around each serving. Garnish each plate with the chopped parsley and celery and insert a sprig of celery leaves in the crust of each pastry.

Smoked Duck Hash; *Susan Spicer, Bayona*

Ballottine of Braised Duck, Chicken, Veal, and Foie Gras

Jeremiah Tower
Stars
San Francisco, California

The ultimate version of cabbage rolls: a stuffing of mixed meats and foie gras, topped with a ragout of tomatoes and olives and drizzled with basil oil. The rolls may also be filled with a mixture of all chicken and veal.

Serves 6

Mirepoix

3 carrots, peeled and cut into ¹/₂-inch dice
1 yellow onion, cut into ¹/₂-inch dice
6 celery stalks, cut into ¹/₂-inch dice
3 garlic cloves, minced
Leaves from 3 fresh thyme sprigs, minced

1 pound duck leg meat
4 cups duck stock (see page 231)
1 cup white wine
8 ounces chicken thigh meat
4 cups chicken stock (see page 228)
8 ounces stewing veal
4 cups veal stock (see page 228)
8 ounces fresh foie gras, cut into 6 cubes
1 head Savoy cabbage
¹/₄ cup minced fresh tarragon leaves
1 pinch ground cardamom
Salt and freshly ground black pepper to taste
6 fresh tarragon sprigs

Ragout

¹/₂ cup blended duck, chicken, and veal stock
3 cups cherry tomatoes, halved
¹/₂ cup Kalamata olives, pitted and chopped
1 teaspoon grated orange zest
Salt and freshly ground black pepper to taste
¹/₄ cup fresh tarragon leaves, minced

Basil Oil (see page 223)
2 tablespoons minced parsley for garnish

Combine all the ingredients for the mirepoix. Place the duck meat in a medium stockpot and add the duck stock. Add ¹/₃ cup of the white wine, then one third of the mirepoix. Cover and cook over low heat for 2 hours, or until the duck is very tender. Using a slotted spoon, remove the duck; let cool in the refrigerator. Reserve the stock.

Repeat the same procedure with the chicken meat, chicken stock, ¹/₃ cup of the white wine, and one third of the mirepoix. Cover and cook over low heat for 1 hour. Using a slotted spoon, remove the chicken; let cool in the refrigerator. Add the chicken stock to the duck stock.

Ballottine of Braised Duck, Chicken, Veal, and Foie Gras; *Jeremiah Tower, Stars*

Repeat the same procedure with the veal meat, using veal stock, the remaining 1/3 cup white wine, and the remaining mirepoix. Cover and cook for 1 1/2 hours. Using a slotted spoon, remove the veal; let cool in the refrigerator. Add the veal stock to the combined duck and chicken stock and set aside.

Remove the cabbage leaves from the core. Bring a large pot of salted water to a boil. Place the cabbage leaves, 2 to 3 at a time, in the boiling water. Cook for 2 to 3 minutes, then remove with a slotted spoon and place in an ice-water bath until cold. Remove from the bath and cut out any thick ribs from the leaves. Place the leaves on paper towels and set aside.

Preheat the oven to 350°F. Chop the cooked duck, chicken, and veal meat into 1/2-inch cubes. Combine and season with the tarragon and cardamom. Mix well, adding salt and pepper.

Lay out one or more cabbage leaves, overlapping them to make an 8-inch surface; you may need 2 or 3 leaves per roll. Place one sixth of the seasoned meat mixture in the center and add 1 cube of foie gras. Carefully fold the cabbage leaves over until the filling is wrapped. Turn the packet over, making sure the edges are tucked under, and shape into a ball with your hands. Repeat to make 6 balls. Place the balls in a shallow baking dish, lay the sprigs of tarragon on top, and add 1/2 inch of the mixed stocks. Cover with aluminum foil and bake for 20 minutes.

To make the ragout: Place the remaining 1/2 cup mixed stock in a medium sauté pan or skillet. Add the tomatoes and olives and heat over medium heat until just warm. Add the orange zest and tarragon, and season with salt and pepper.

To serve: Place the cabbage balls on a platter and surround with the ragout. Drizzle the cabbage with basil oil and sprinkle with the chopped parsley.

JEREMIAH TOWER
Stars, San Francisco, California

American-born Jeremiah Tower has a strong academic background, with his early schooling in England and his master of architecture degree from the Harvard Graduate School of Design. Yet biographically speaking, the phrase that best describes Tower might be "present at the creation."

Tower was one of a handful of chefs whose passion and discipline helped to make American cuisine worthy of global attention. Now, as chef-owner of Stars and Stars Cafe in San Francisco, as well as of Stars Oakville Cafe in Napa Valley, Tower can look back over the terrain he helped to discover in the early 1970s.

Tower became chef and co-owner of Chez Panisse, Alice Waters's groundbreaking eatery in Berkeley. Borrowing from the robust traditions of the French bistro, this restaurant more than any other gave birth to California cuisine, thereby launching a revolution in American regional cookery.

In 1976, Tower conceived and prepared a California regional dinner at Chez Panisse that brought the restaurant and its chef almost overnight fame. Tower moved on eventually, opening a place called Santa Fe Bar and Grill in Berkeley and, in 1984, Stars Restaurant in San Francisco's Civic Center area.

Today, Stars and its spinoff cafe serve a changing menu of innovative dishes in the style Tower helped create: new American cuisine. In 1986, that label became part of the title on the cover of his cookbook, *Jeremiah Tower's New American Classics*, (HarperCollins).

In addition to its success and longevity, Stars has helped to set the standard for innumerable restaurants around the country. Such places, Tower realized from the start, had to be known for superior food of a creative character, service bordering on religious zeal, and an extensive wine selection with a preference for California.

Part of doing what he does has made Tower a public figure indeed. Fame pretty much goes with having a culinary gospel to preach, and Tower has preached it often and audibly.

The highlights of his career to date include preparing a luncheon to honor Julia Child and Robert Mondavi, founders of the American Institute of Wine and Food; and launching the television series "Cooking With Master Chefs" with a sellout dinner at Stars benefitting KQED/PBS. Tower has also donated his time to Citymeals on Wheels in New York, 7th on Sale, and both local and national AIDS organizations.

JODY ADAMS
Michela's, Cambridge, Massachusetts

Jody Adams began her first cooking apprenticeship early, spending time in the kitchen while other kids her age were watching television. But in her case, TV was out of sight and out of mind.

"We were a family without television," she recalls. "I think that left a lot of room and time to do things that were creative, and one of them was cooking." Pondering why she loves it so, Adams sets forth a series of descriptions. "It's physical. It's creative. It's immediate. It makes people happy."

Adams went on to study anthropology at Brown University in Rhode Island, helping to pay her way by washing dishes for Nancy Verde Barr's cooking classes. Soon, Adams was also helping to prep for and assist in the classes. This arrangement lasted until Adams' graduation from college.

In 1983, it was time to find a restaurant job, and Adams found two of the best ones in New England. Cooking first with Lydia Shire at Seasons and then as sous chef under Gordon Hamersley at Hamersley's Bistro, Adams developed her taste and techniques for the day she'd run a kitchen of her own.

That day came in 1990, with the opening of Michela's in East Cambridge, directly across the Charles River from Boston. Cooking regional Italian cuisine at Michela's, she says, was the only job in the Boston area that attracted her.

The restaurant's appeal had something to do with the similarities Adams finds between the cooking of Italy and that of her native New England. Both are rustic, hearty, and unaffected.

"I think the best food is simple, honest food," she offers, "where tradition, seasonal changes and individual ingredients are respected. People say that the choices on Michela's menu range from really rich to downright heart-healthy. My first concern is taste, and happily, Italian cuisine offers people the best of both worlds."

Michela's is thriving these days, gaining strength from Adams' growing reputation. One of the restaurant's first chefs, by the way, was Todd English (who went on to greater fame starting Olives across town). There was a slump when he departed, which was more than corrected by Adams' arrival on the scene.

Boston Magazine named Adams the best chef of 1991. But the *Boston Globe* stated the news about her even more directly. "This woman," wrote its restaurant critic, "can really cook."

Roasted Marinated Long Island Duck with Duck Liver Crostini and Braised Escarole

Jody Adams
Michela's
Cambridge, Massachusetts

This earthy dish uses an intense marinade for the duck, which is sauced with a flavorful reduction of duck stock and red wine with green olives. The escarole and crostini are the perfect final touches for this savory entree.

Serves 2

One 5-pound Long Island duck

Marinade
1 cup balsamic vinegar
½ cup soy sauce
2 tablespoons Dijon mustard
3 tablespoons chopped onion
1 tablespoon minced garlic
2 tablespoons cracked mustard seeds
1 tablespoon dried rosemary
Salt and freshly cracked black pepper
  to taste

Rich Duck Stock
Heart from duck, above
2 tablespoons olive oil
Wing tips and neck from duck, above
½ cup ¼-inch-diced celery
½ cup ¼-inch-diced carrot
½ cup ¼-inch-diced onion
4 cups chicken stock (see page 228)

Sauce
1 cup rich duck stock, above
2 cups dry red wine
1 fresh rosemary sprig
1 teaspoon balsamic vinegar
2 bay leaves
½ cup pitted Italian green olives, rinsed
Salt and freshly ground black pepper
  to taste

Braised Escarole
2 tablespoons olive oil
1 bunch escarole, cut lengthwise into
  quarters
1 cup thinly sliced white onion

1 teaspoon minced fresh rosemary
1 teaspoon minced garlic
½ cup rich duck stock, above

Duck Liver Crostini

1 liver from duck, above
2 tablespoons olive oil
½ cup thinly sliced red onion
4 small slices coarse brown bread or
    olive bread
Salt and freshly ground black pepper
    to taste

Salt and freshly ground black pepper
    to taste
1 tablespoon balsamic vinegar
1 tablespoon olive oil

Preheat the oven to 350°F. Cut off and discard the neck flap of the duck. Remove and reserve the neck and giblets. Remove and discard the membrane from the liver and gizzard. Pour off any blood. Remove and discard the flaps of skin and fat between the legs; cut off and reserve the last two joints of the wings. Puncture the duck well with a sharp-tined fork or an ice pick, piercing the skin and flesh all over and paying particular attention to the fatty area between the wings and the body. Set aside.

To make the marinade: Combine all the ingredients in a large bowl. Roll the pierced duck in the marinade, making sure that the duck is completely coated inside and out.

Place the duck on a rack over a deep baking pan. Add 1 inch of water to the pan to prevent the fat from smoking as it drips during the baking process. Pour the remaining marinade over the duck and bake for 3½ hours. Remove the duck from the oven and let cool slightly, then cut down one side of the breastbone and one side of the backbone, splitting the duck in half. Using your hands, remove the rib cage, thigh bone, and neck bone from the duck half. Leave the drumstick intact. Cut out the backbone and remove the rib cage and thigh bone from the second half. Discard all the bones. Remove and discard any pockets of fat near the legs. Set the duck aside.

To make the duck stock: Cut the duck heart into 6 pieces. Over medium-high heat, heat the olive oil and brown the wing tips, neck, and heart for 3 to 4 minutes. Add the celery, carrot, and onion, and brown for 2 to 3 minutes, then add the chicken stock. Simmer to reduce to 1½ cups, about 30 minutes, then strain the stock.

To make the sauce: In a medium saucepan, combine the rich duck stock with the wine and cook over medium heat to reduce to 1 cup. Add the rosemary and balsamic vinegar, and heat for 5 minutes. Remove the rosemary and add the olives. Season with salt and pepper, and keep warm.

To make the escarole: Preheat the oven to 325°F. In a large ovenproof skillet or sauté pan over medium-high heat, heat the olive oil and sauté the escarole, onion, rosemary, and garlic for 2 to 3 minutes. Add the duck stock. Bake for 45 minutes.

To make the crostini: Preheat the broiler. Cut the liver into 4 slices. In a medium skillet over medium-high heat, heat 1 tablespoon of the olive oil and sauté the liver with the red onion for 2 to 3 minutes. The liver should remain medium rare. Drizzle the bread with the remaining 1 tablespoon olive oil and toast under the broiler until light golden brown. Place 1 piece of liver on each piece of toast with some of the onions, and season with salt and freshly ground black pepper to taste.

To serve: Season the cavity of the duck with salt and pepper and sprinkle with the balsamic vinegar. In a large skillet or sauté pan over medium-high heat, heat the olive oil and add the duck halves, skin-side down. Place 1 piece of braised escarole in each cavity, cover the pan, and cook for 2 to 4 minutes, or until hot. Place some of the remaining escarole on each serving plate with a duck half alongside and ladle sauce around the duck. Garnish with the crostini and serve.

Roasted Marinated Long Island Duck with Duck Liver Crostini and Braised Escarole;
Jody Adams, Michela's

Veal Chops Two Ways, with Mushroom Sauce

▼▼▼▼▼▼▼▼▼▼▼▼▼▼▼▼▼▼

Gerard Crozier
Crozier's
New Orleans, Louisiana

The sauce for the two grilled chops is a heady blend of mushrooms and glace de viande, that luxurious and intensely flavored reduction of meat stock. You may buy the glace in a specialty foods store, or use demi-glace. The other two veal chops are pan-fried and served with a mushroom sauce without glace de viande.

Serves 4

Four 10-ounce veal chops
Olive oil for brushing, plus 1 tablespoon
Flour for dredging
Salt and freshly ground black pepper to taste
3 tablespoons butter
2 pounds white mushrooms, coarsely chopped
1 tablespoon glace de viande or demiglace (see page 232)
1 cup French white wine or chicken stock (see page 228)
Gratin Dauphinois (recipe follows)

To prepare the grilled chops: Prepare a medium-hot fire in an outdoor or indoor grill. Lightly brush 2 of the veal chops with a little olive oil and grill them, turning twice, for a total of about 10 minutes for medium, or until cooked to the desired doneness. Set aside and keep warm.

To prepare the pan-fried chops: Lightly dust the remaining 2 chops with flour, salt, and pepper. In a large sauté pan or skillet over medium-high heat, heat the 1 tablespoon olive oil with 1 tablespoon of the butter. Add the chops to the pan and cook, turning every 2 minutes, for a total of 8 to 10 minutes. Cover the pan and cook an additional 5 minutes for medium, or until the chops are cooked to the desired doneness. Remove the chops from the pan, set aside, and keep warm.

Veal Chops Two Ways, with Mushroom Sauce; *Gerard Crozier, Crozier's*

To make the mushroom sauce for the grilled chops: In a large sauté pan or skillet over medium-high heat, melt 1 tablespoon of the butter and sauté half of the mushrooms until they have released their juices and most of the liquid has evaporated, about 5 minutes. Add the glace de viande and ½ cup of the wine or stock, cooking and stirring for 2 minutes. Season with salt and pepper, set aside, and keep warm.

To make the mushroom sauce for the pan-fried chops: Place the pan in which the chops were sautéed over medium-high heat, add the remaining 1 tablespoon butter and the remaining mushrooms, and sauté until they have released their juices and most of the liquid has evaporated, about 5 minutes. Season the mushrooms with salt and pepper. Add the remaining ½ cup wine or stock to the pan, stir to scrape up any browned bits from the bottom of the pan, and continue to cook for 2 minutes. Set aside and keep warm.

To serve: Arrange the grilled chops on one end of a large serving platter and spoon their accompanying sauce over them. Place the pan-fried chops on the other end, along with their sauce. Serve with gratin dauphinois.

Gratin Dauphinois
Serves 4

3 large baking potatoes, peeled and
  thinly sliced
2 tablespoons minced garlic
Salt and freshly ground black pepper
  to taste
2 cups heavy (whipping) cream or milk
2 cups half-and-half

Preheat the oven to 450°F. Generously butter a 12-inch baking dish. Place some of the potatoes in a layer in the bottom of the pan and sprinkle with some of the garlic, then season with salt and pepper. Continue in this fashion to make 3 layers of potatoes, garlic, salt, and pepper. Pour the cream or milk and half-and-half over the dish, stir, and smooth the top of the gratin with the back of a spoon. Bake until the potatoes are tender when pierced with a knife and the top is browned and bubbly, 35 to 40 minutes.

GERARD CROZIER
Crozier's, New Orleans, Louisiana

Although Gerard Crozier is a chef of few words, his low-key approach doesn't diminish the success of his small but excellent classical French restaurant.

"I keep it small because my customers like to see me walking through the dining room," Crozier says. "They know me, and I know what they like to eat."

In his native Lyons, Crozier embarked upon the traditional apprenticeship at age fourteen, then put in two years in Lausanne as assistant to the chef of a seafood restaurant.

Two more years took him to St. Tropez on the French Riviera, followed by a series of jobs in restaurants around France. Crozier and his wife Eveline moved to the United States in 1970, becoming the sous-chef at a fancy private club in Milwaukee. As no one in that kitchen spoke French, and he spoke nary a word of English, that job required some adjustment.

Later, Crozier headed for New Orleans by way of Key Biscayne. For eight years he stepped out of the kitchen to concentrate on administrative work for Sonesta hotels. That took him to south Florida and then to New Orleans. As have so many before and since, the Croziers decided to put down roots.

They opened the first Crozier's in a small shopping center in the city's eastern section, then moved to bigger quarters — seventeeen tables — not too far away. Eventually, the Croziers moved the whole operation to suburban Metairie. Happily, their best customers went with them, and soon many more customers discovered them.

Eveline has become the restaurant's savvy wine buyer. "I spend a great deal of time carefully shopping for the wines we serve, which are primarily French with a few from California," she reports. "I'm very proud that we not only have one of the city's best French wine lists but that our prices are very affordable."

Her search for fine, reasonably priced wines is conducted with an undisguised love of her task — much like her husband's love of cooking wonderful food.

LARRY FORGIONE
An American Place, New York, New York

Larry Forgione hopes no one gets the wrong idea when insiders call him the "Godfather of American Cuisine." The reference is not to anything in Mario Puzo's best-selling book or to that trio of famous movies but to his profound influence on fellow chefs, restaurateurs and the nation's dining public.

For two decades, Forgione has been a leader (in some cases, *the* leader) of the movement to upgrade American food products and to celebrate them in creative dishes. Today, in addition to cooking appearances all over America and in many corners of the world, Forgione expresses himself and his philosophy at An American Place on Park Avenue in Manhattan and at the Beekman 1776 Tavern in the historic village of Rhinebeck, New York.

Born on Long Island in 1952, Forgione graduated from the Culinary Institute of America in 1974 and began his career at London's Connaught Hotel under chef Michel Bourdin. In 1976, he was a silver medalist in the British Culinary Olympics before becoming the first American chef to win a Mention of Honor in the Prix Pierre Taittinger in Paris. He returned to his homeland in 1977 to hold executive chef positions at New York's El Morocco, Regine's and the River Cafe in Brooklyn, where he enjoyed his first taste of culinary stardom.

Forgione opened An American Place on Manhattan's Upper East Side in 1983, enchanting customers in his fifty-seat dining room with a fixed-price menu of dishes made solely with American ingredients. In 1989, he relocated An American Place to an Art Deco landmark with 125 seats at Park Avenue and Thirty-second Street. He developed an a la carte menu this time, but stuck to his insistence on American products.

Other ventures have expanded Forgione's vision and influence. He opened the Beekman 1776 Tavern with business partner Michael Weinstein of Ark Restaurants and began serving as culinary advisor to the Morgan Hotel Group. He also founded a specialty foods company along the way, American Spoon Foods of Petoskey, Michigan.

Always at the head of culinary causes, Forgione is a founding trustee of the James Beard Foundation and sits on the educational policy committee of the Culinary Institute of America. In addition to his work for New York's Meals on Wheels program, he is one of the founders of Fresh Start at Rikers Island Prison.

Veal Steak Sauté with Jerky Sauce

Larry Forgione
An American Place
New York, New York

Veal gets an unusual treatment with a very American sauce of julienned beef jerky, cream, and chili powder. Cornstarch is used to thicken the sauce, and the veal is garnished with chick-peas.

Serves 4

2 ounces unprocessed beef jerky
1½ cups veal stock (see page 228)
Four 5-ounce 1-inch-thick veal loin
  steaks
Salt and freshly ground black pepper
  to taste
3 tablespoons olive or vegetable oil
1 onion, sliced
1 tablespoon coarsely ground
  black pepper
¼ cup white wine vinegar
¼ cup dry white wine
1 garlic clove, crushed
1 cup cooked chick-peas (rinsed and
  drained, if using canned)
1 teaspoon chili powder
1 teaspoon cornstarch
½ cup heavy (whipping) cream
½ cup finely chopped red bell pepper
½ cup finely chopped poblano or green
  bell pepper
1 teaspoon fresh lemon juice
1 tablespoon cold butter

To prepare the jerky: Cut the jerky into fine julienne and soak it in 1 cup of the veal stock for 1 hour at room temperature. Strain the stock and reserve both the sauce and the jerky.

To prepare the veal: Preheat the oven to 375°F. Trim the veal steaks and season with salt and pepper. In a large sauté pan or skillet over high heat, heat 2 tablespoons of the oil and sauté the steaks, turning them to sear them completely on both sides and all of the edges, a total of about 2 minutes. Transfer the meat to a plate and keep it warm.

To make the sauce: In the same pan, over high heat, place half of the onion with the black pepper and sauté until the onion is wilted, 1 to 2 minutes. Add the wine vinegar and stir for 30 seconds, then add the wine, the reserved stock used to soak the jerky, and the remaining ½ cup stock. Bring the mixture to a boil and skim off any fat or foam that rises to the surface. Continue to cook until the liquid has reduced by two-thirds and is thick and syrupy, 7 to 8 minutes.

Finely chop the remaining sliced onion. In a medium sauté pan or skillet over medium-high heat, add the remaining 1 tablespoon olive oil and sauté the onion and garlic until they are wilted, about 2 minutes. Add the chick-peas and chili powder and cook over low heat until the chili powder has mellowed in flavor, 3 to 4 minutes.

In a small bowl, stir the cornstarch into the cream, then add the cream to the pan with the reduced stock, reduce heat to low, and simmer until the liquid is reduced slightly, 2 to 3 minutes. Strain the mixture into the pan containing the chick-peas and simmer for 1 to 2 more minutes.

Place the veal steaks in the oven for 3 minutes. In a large sauté pan or skillet, combine the chopped peppers and the jerky. Strain the veal and cream sauce from the chick-peas into the pan and return to medium heat for 2 to 3 minutes. Off heat, add the lemon juice and stir in the cold butter until the sauce is smooth.

To serve: Place a veal chop on each serving plate and spoon the sauce over and around the chop. Spoon some of the chick-peas in 5 small mounds around the outside of the plate.

Veal Steak Sauté with Jerky Sauce; *Larry Forgione, An American Place*

Sweetbreads with Camomile and Morels; *Daniel Boulud, Restaurant Daniel*

Sweetbreads with Camomile and Morels

Daniel Boulud
Restaurant Daniel
New York, New York

The flowery flavor of camomile is a good match for the delicate taste of sweetbreads, which are braised with morels and finished with peas and fava beans.

Serves 4

2 lobes of sweetbreads, about 1 pound
    each
12 fresh camomile sprigs, plus more
    for garnish
Salt and freshly ground black pepper
    to taste
3 tablespoons flour
¼ cup olive oil
1 Vidalia onion, quartered and sliced
    ¼-inch thick
2 celery stalks, cut on the diagonal into
    1-inch pieces

2 tablespoons minced garlic
16 baby carrots
24 morel mushrooms, split lengthwise
    if large
¼ cup dry white vermouth
1 cup vegetable or chicken stock
    (see page 228, 231)
½ cup water
1 cup peas, blanched
1 cup fava beans, blanched and peeled
2 tablespoons butter

Rinse the sweetbreads in cold water, then soak in several changes of cold water for 2 hours. Carefully pull off the filament and soak the sweetbreads again for 2 hours in several changes of cold water with 1 tablespoon vinegar added. Peel off any more filament. Separate the two lobes. Cut off and discard the connecting tube.

Using the rod of a knife-sharpening steel or the blade of a thin-bladed knife, make 1 hole lengthwise on either side of each sweetbread lobe. Stuff the holes with 10 camomile sprigs, reserving the remaining 2 sprigs. Season the sweetbreads with salt and pepper on both sides. Lightly dust the sweetbreads with flour.

In a large, heavy pan over medium-high heat, heat the olive oil. Add the sweetbreads and brown on both sides for a total of 4 to 6 minutes. Add the onion, celery, garlic, carrots, and the 2 reserved camomile sprigs.

Lightly salt and pepper the vegetables, then add the morels. Add the vermouth and cook over high heat until the liquid evaporates, about 4 to 6 minutes. Add the stock and water, then cover the pan tightly. Reduce the heat to low and cook for 15 minutes.

Remove the sweetbreads from the pan. Remove the camomile sprigs from the pan and from the sweetbreads. Increase the heat to medium and add the peas and fava beans to the juice and vegetables. Cook for 10 to 15 minutes, then swirl in the butter.

To serve: Slice the sweetbreads and arrange the slices down the center of the plates. Spoon the warm vegetables and juice over sweetbreads. Garnish with camomile sprigs.

Country-Style Pork Ribs in Green Chili Sauce

Robert Del Grande
Rio Ranch
Houston, Texas

Though pork ribs and steamed cabbage could turn up on any table in America, the addition of chilies and pureed tortillas to the sauce and the garnish of pico de gallo and Mexican cheese make this a Southwest dish all the way.

Serves 4

8 double-cut country-style pork ribs
  (4 pounds)
5 cups water
1 large white onion, cut into eighths
4 garlic cloves, slightly smashed
2 teaspoons salt
2 poblano or Anaheim chilies
1 teaspoon vegetable oil
2 corn tortillas, preferably white
1 cup minced fresh cilantro

Steamed Cabbage
1 head green cabbage, cut into
  2-by-2-inch pieces
1/2 cup water
2 tablespoons virgin olive oil
1/2 teaspoon salt
Freshly ground black pepper to taste

Garnish
Pico de Gallo (recipe follows)
1/4 cup crumbled queso fresco (optional)

To prepare the ribs: In a deep 5-quart Dutch oven, place the pork, water, onion, garlic, and salt. Bring the mixture to a boil, then lower the heat to a simmer. Partially cover and cook for 1 1/2 hours.

Lightly rub the chilies with the oil and char the skin over an open flame or under a preheated broiler for about 10 minutes, turning frequently. Cover the chilies with a damp towel and let cool. When cool enough to handle, peel all of the skin from the chilies and remove the stems, seeds, and ribs.

In a large dry skillet over medium heat, lightly toast the tortillas. Tear them into small pieces and set aside.

When the ribs are tender, remove them from the pot and bring the liquid back to a boil. Cook the liquid over high heat until it is reduced to about 3 cups, 10 minutes. Remove 1/2 cup of the liquid and reserve. Transfer the rest of the liquid, along with the onions and garlic, to a blender or food processor. Add the chilies and the tortilla pieces and blend to a coarse puree.

Return the sauce to the pot, taste and adjust the seasoning as needed, and bring the sauce to a boil. Reduce heat to a simmer and return the pork to the sauce. Add the cilantro and continue to cook over low heat for 15 to 30 minutes, adding some of the reserved liquid if necessary to thin the sauce slightly. (If the dish is made ahead of time, do not add the cilantro until just before reheating.)

To make the cabbage: In a large sauté pan or skillet, combine the cabbage, water, olive oil, and salt. Cover and cook over high heat until the water boils and the cabbage wilts, 3 to 5 minutes. Add pepper.

To serve: Place some of the steamed cabbage in the center of each serving plate, top with 1 or 2 pork ribs, and spoon the sauce over the chops and cabbage. Garnish with pico de gallo and crumbled queso fresco, if desired.

Pico de Gallo
Makes about 2 cups

1 tomato, seeded and cut into 1/4-inch
  dice
1/2 cup 1/4-inch-diced onion
2 garlic cloves, minced
1 jalapeño, minced (with or without its
  seeds)
2 tablespoons minced fresh cilantro
1 tablespoon fresh lime juice
1 tablespoon olive oil
Salt to taste

In a small bowl, combine all of the ingredients, mix, and let sit for about 30 minutes before serving.

Country-Style Pork Ribs in Green Chili Sauce; *Robert Del Grande, Rio Ranch*

Pork Tenderloin with Apple-Onion Confit

▪▪▪▪▪▪▪▪▪▪▪▪▪▪▪

Victor Gielisse
CFT/Culinary Fast-Trac & Associates
Zale Lipshy University Hospital
Dallas, Texas

It's the garnishes that set this dish of sautéed pork tenderloin medallions apart, especially the delightful apple-onion confit, which can also be served with fish and chicken. The cranberry-tomato sauce adds flavor and color, and the fried mushroom slices, sautéed potatoes, and blanched asparagus tips are a perfect mix of textures.

Serves 4

One 16-ounce pork tenderloin, cut into
  8 medallions
Salt and freshly ground black pepper
2 teaspoons olive oil

Sauce
3 tablespoons dry sherry
1 tablespoon balsamic vinegar
1 cup veal stock (see page 228)
2 tablespoons finely diced seeded
  tomato
2 tablespoons dried cranberries,
  chopped

Apple-Onion Confit
1 tablespoon canola or olive oil
1/3 cup finely sliced red onion
2 tablespoons balsamic vinegar
3 tablespoons dry red wine
1 small green apple, peeled, cored, and
  cut into fine julienne
Salt and freshly ground white pepper
  to taste
1 tablespoon butter

Garnish
4 fresh shiitake mushrooms, stemmed
  and sliced
2 tablespoons canola oil
8 potatoes, peeled, trimmed into
  1-inch-by-2-inch ovals, and blanched
8 asparagus tips
1 cup chicken stock (see page 228)
4 fresh basil sprigs

Season the pork with salt and pepper and let sit for 5 to 10 minutes. Spray a large nonstick sauté pan or seasoned cast-iron skillet with vegetable-oil spray and wipe the pan with a paper towel. Place the pan over medium heat, add the medallions of pork, and cook until they are nicely browned on the bottom, 2 minutes. Drizzle the medallions with the olive oil and turn them. Cook until browned on the second side, 2 minutes. Remove the medallions from the pan and place them on a baking pan. Preheat the oven to 350°F.

To prepare the sauce: Add the sherry and vinegar to the same pan in which the pork was cooked, place the pan over high heat for 2 to 3 minutes, and stir

Pork Tenderloin with Apple-Onion Confit;
Victor Gielisse, CFT/Culinary Fast-Trac & Associates,
Zale Lipshy University Hospital

to scrape up the browned bits from the bottom of the pan. Add the veal stock and cook over high heat until the liquid thickens and is reduced by one half, 15 minutes. Add the tomato and cranberries and set aside in a warm place until ready to serve.

To make the confit: In a medium saucepan over medium heat, combine the oil and onion and cook, stirring occasionally, until the onion is caramelized, 8 to 10 minutes. Add the vinegar and wine, raise the heat to high, and continue to cook until the liquid is reduced and the pan is almost dry, 3 to 5 minutes. Add the apple, lower the heat, and simmer gently for 20 minutes, stirring occasionally. Season the confit with salt and white pepper, whisk in the butter, and set aside and keep warm until ready to serve.

To make the garnish: Preheat the oven to 375°F. Toss the shiitake slices in the canola oil, spread them out on a baking sheet, and bake for 15 to 20 minutes, or until crisp. Spray a medium nonstick pan or a seasoned cast-iron pan with vegetable oil spray and place it over medium-high heat. Sauté the potatoes, shaking the pan frequently, until they are golden brown, 20 to 30 minutes. In a small saucepan over high heat, bring the chicken stock to a simmer. Add the asparagus tips and cook just until they are tender, about 3 to 4 minutes.

To serve: On each serving plate, place a mound of the apple-onion confit and arrange 2 asparagus tips and 2 potatoes on one side. Place 2 of the pork medallions on the other side and spoon some of the sauce, including the cranberries, over and around the pork. Sprinkle the dish with some mushroom chips and garnish each plate with a basil sprig.

VICTOR GIELISSE
CFT/Culinary Fast-Trac & Associates,
Zale Lipshy University Hospital, Dallas, Texas

When Victor Gielisse opened his restaurant in Dallas in 1985, everybody around him was labeling his food "new Southwestern." Although Gielisse did cook his own versions of regional dishes, he had his own label in mind: He dubbed his restaurant Actuelle, after the French *cuisine actuelle*, or "today's cuisine."

After eight years of fame as chef-owner at Actuelle, earning a cover feature in *Bon Appétit*, Gielisse left to become principal partner at Culinary Fast-Trac & Associates, a company that advises some of America's largest corporations.

Gielisse's work at CFT is anchored in his solid background in Europe. Born into a restaurant family, Gielisse graduated from culinary college in the Netherlands and completed his apprenticeship there.

Before coming to the United States, he worked in kitchens in Germany, Switzerland, and South Africa. Gielisse is one of only forty-four certified master chefs in America; the CMC degree requires a 140-hour, ten-day exam that few attempt and as many as half fail.

Gielisse arrived in Texas in 1979, to serve as executive sous-chef and then executive chef at the Westin Oaks Hotel. Westin moved him to Dallas, where he transferred to the even more posh Adolphus Hotel in 1984. The Adolphus provided the springboard to opening Actuelle, which caused Mimi Sheraton to add its name to her list of fifty American restaurants labled "Worth the Journey."

JOSE GUTIERREZ
Chez Philippe, The Peabody, Memphis, Tennessee

Convincing diners that some of America's finest French cuisine is served in the city of Elvis' Graceland and barbecue has never been an easy task. But in a grande dame southern hotel most famous for its daily parade of ducks, anything is possible.

Cooking at Chez Philippe, the small and elegant dining room of The Peabody, Gutierrez has made a happy alliance between his own French heritage and the South's traditional tastes. Guests at the Peabody love the pairing, and so do the people of Memphis.

In recent years, the cross-cultural borrowing has become more complex. Now more and more dishes are showing the Pacific Rim influence that fascinates so many chefs in this country these days.

At the same time, this fine French restaurant has been updated for the nineties. The dress code has been relaxed, and prices have been lowered. As a result, this cuisine has become more accessible to more people.

"We can do very nice things with produce grown locally and people are more familiar with them," observes Gutierrez. "It helps bring the cost of food down." Such considerations are basic to traditional French cuisine, which seeks to use regional foods at their best. And Gutierrez learned his art from some of the finest masters of this tradition.

Starting his career at the Professional Culinary School in Manosque, France, he followed up with two years at the Hôtel de France at Jura under the direction of chef Roger Petit, who in turn had studied under the legendary Fernand Point. Gutierrez then put in an instructive year with chef Francis Trocelier, followed by another year at La Réserve de Beaulieu on the French Riviera.

After working in several other restaurants, Gutierrez spent a year cooking with the celebrated Paul Bocuse at his namesake restaurant near Lyons, then headed for the Restaurant de France at the Meridien Hotel in Houston. From there, Chez Philippe at the Peabody seemed a logical step.

Lightly Smoked Pork Tenderloin with Grits Pilaf

▼▟▼▟▼▟▼▟▼▟▼▟▼

Jose Gutierrez
Chez Philippe
The Peabody
Memphis, Tennessee

Pork, grits, and green tomatoes, those favorite southern foods, are combined here in surprising ways in this prime example of new American regional cuisine.

Serves 4

1 teaspoon juniper berries, ground in a
   spice grinder
1 teaspoon ground coriander
⅛ teaspoon red pepper flakes
Salt and freshly ground black pepper
   to taste
2 pork tenderloins (about 8 ounces
   each)
1 tablespoon olive oil
½ cup chopped fresh lemongrass
1 teaspoon grated fresh ginger
½ cup dry white wine
½ cup rich veal stock (see page 231)

Grits Pilaf
2 tablespoons olive oil
1 cup ¼-inch-diced smoked pig jowl
1 cup finely diced yellow onion
2 tablespoons minced garlic
1 cup stone-ground grits
2 fresh thyme sprigs
2 bay leaves
1 cup dry red wine
1 cup chicken or vegetable stock
   (see page 228, 231)

Green Tomato Garnish

4 fresh basil leaves, cut into fine shreds
½ cup cornmeal
3 green tomatoes, halved and seeded
Salt and freshly ground black pepper
    to taste

1 plum (Roma) tomato, diced
2 tablespoons snipped fresh chives or
    finely chopped green onion tips
Salt and freshly ground black pepper
    to taste

Preheat the oven to 450°F. Combine the ground juniper berries, coriander, red pepper flakes, salt, and pepper. Rub this mixture into the pork. On a well-ventilated stove-top smoker with mesquite wood chips, or in a covered charcoal grill, lightly smoke for 5 minutes. In a medium ovenproof skillet or sauté pan over medium-high heat, heat the olive oil and sauté the pork on all sides until brown, about 4 minutes, then bake for 8 to 10 minutes. Remove the pork tenderloin and keep warm.

Add the lemongrass, ginger, and wine to the same pan in which the pork was roasted. Simmer on medium heat for 4 minutes, stirring to scrape up the browned bits from the bottom of the pan. Add the veal stock and cook to reduce for 2 more minutes. Strain the sauce and set aside.

To make the grits: Preheat the oven to 350°F. In a medium pot over medium-high heat, heat the olive oil and sauté the smoked jowl for 3 to 4 minutes, or until the meat is brown and the fat has been rendered. Pour off most of the rendered fat, add the onion and garlic, and sauté until the vegetables are translucent, about 3 minutes. Add the grits,

thyme, bay leaves, red wine, and stock. Bring to a boil, then cover and bake for 15 minutes. Set aside.

To make the garnish: Mix the basil with the cornmeal. Cut the tomatoes into ¼-inch lengthwise strips. Toss the tomato strips in the cornmeal mixture to coat them. In a medium sauté pan or skillet over medium-high heat, quickly fry the tomatoes until they are golden brown, about 2 to 3 minutes. Using a slotted spoon, remove the tomatoes and drain on paper towels. Season with salt and pepper.

To serve: Remove the herbs from the grits and stir in the tomato and chives or green onion. Season with salt and pepper. Pack the finished grits tightly in a 3-inch-diameter ring in the center of each serving plate. Slice the tenderloin into 8 slices per tenderloin. Remove the ring from the grits and arrange overlapping slices of the pork in a circle on top of the unmolded grits. Surround each circle of grits with 3 tablespoons of sauce. Divide the fried tomatoes among the plates.

Lightly Smoked Pork Tenderloin with Grits Pilaf;
Jose Gutierrez, Chez Philippe, The Peabody

Braised Rabbit with Black Olives; *Klaus Helmin, Tivoli*

Braised Rabbit with Black Olives

Klaus Helmin
Tivoli
Rosslyn, Virginia

The Italian countryside springs to life
in this rustic dish of braised rabbit,
complete with Barolo wine and olives
from Liguria.

Serves 4

Two 2½-pound rabbits
Salt and freshly ground black pepper
　to taste
About 6 tablespoons canola oil
1 cup coarsely chopped onions
About 2¼ cups Barolo or other dry red
　wine
4 large tomatoes, coarsely chopped
2 garlic cloves, chopped
3 tablespoons olive oil
8 ounces Ligurian or other black salt-
　cured olives, pitted and chopped
6 fresh rosemary sprigs

To prepare the rabbit: Remove the legs
from the rabbits and remove the thigh
bone, leaving the leg bone intact. Cut
down the spine of each rabbit and cut
and pull the loin from each side of the
back. Coarsely chop the remainder of
the carcasses and set them aside. Season
meat with salt and pepper.

In a large sauté pan over high heat,
heat 3 tablespoons of the canola oil and
sauté the legs and loins until browned
on all sides, about 8 minutes. Add the
chopped carcass pieces to the pan

and sauté until well browned, about 10 minutes, adding more oil as necessary. Remove the legs and loins, and continue to brown the carcass pieces for another 10 minutes. Add the onions to the pan and cook until they are also well browned, about 15 minutes. This thorough browning will create a rich, deep flavor for the sauce. After each phase of the browning process, add a small amount of the wine to the pan and stir to scrape up the browned bits on the bottom of the pan. Cook over high heat to reduce the liquid.

Add the tomatoes and garlic to the pan, along with about 1/2 cup of the wine, and cook over medium heat for 15 minutes. Return the legs and loins to the pan and add enough of the wine to half-cover the meat with liquid. Cover, lower the heat, and simmer for 40 minutes. Remove the legs and loin from the pan and keep warm, then strain the sauce, with the bones, in a fine-meshed sieve. Add more wine or reduce the sauce as necessary to make 1 cup sauce.

In another large sauté pan or skillet over high heat, combine the olive oil, meat, olives, and 2 of the rosemary sprigs. Add 1/4 cup of the wine and cook until the mixture is warmed through and the flavors are blended.

To serve: Place 1 rabbit leg on each serving plate and spoon some of the sauce over it. Slice 1 loin piece diagonally into 1/2-inch-thick slices and fan them around the edge of the plate. Garnish each serving with a rosemary sprig.

KLAUS HELMIN
Tivoli, Rosslyn, Virginia

Those who know that Klaus Helmin hails from Berlin may wonder how he came to cook for a restaurant that specializes in northern Italian cuisine. However, anyone who tastes his terrine of squab breast and wild mushrooms or his braised rabbit with black olives knows that he has found a true home at Tivoli.

Helmin says that his affinity for fine Italian food is partly a response to the time and place in which he was raised. In the days following World War II, there was little to eat in Germany, so his mother could prepare only the most basic dishes. When young Helmin tasted his first northern Italian cuisine, it was a revelation.

The chef has been running the kitchen at Tivoli in the northern Virginia business enclave of Rosslyn since 1983. His cooking evolved into a founding partnership in the American Restaurant Corporation, which now operates not only the restaurant but a pair of Tivoli Gourmet shops and the wonder-filled Watergate Pastry Shop.

Helmin graduated from Berlin's Hotel and Restaurant School in 1957, moving to Hamburg to practice his trade. A contract brought him from there to The Broadview Hotel in Wichita, Kansas, the first in a series of American kitchens: the Brown Palace in Denver, the Del Coronado in San Diego, and the Rice in Houston.

The opportunity to work in the nation's capital came in 1965, when a sous-chef's position opened at the Washington Hilton. Later, Helmin became a partner in the Restaurant Corporation of America, which operated the Watergate Restaurant, Les Champs Restaurant, and the Watergate Pastry Shop.

It was after selling his interest in that company in the mid 1970s that Helmin and partners started the operation that would create the Tivoli.

LYNNE ARONSON
Lola, New York, New York

Lynne Aronson wanted to be an artist, but she finally found her perfect medium not in an artist's studio but in the kitchen.

In the beginning, her love of cooking was born of necessity. Having decided at age thirteen that she wanted to be a vegetarian, she began to learn to cook for herself. Aronson kept on cooking for herself, first at the Fashion Institute of Technology, then at the School of Visual Arts in New York and in the fine arts graduate program at Carnegie Mellon in Pittsburgh.

After several years working as a graphic artist, Aronson gave in to her love of cooking and enrolled in the New York Restaurant School. After graduation, Aronson went to see Ali Barker, chef at the fledgling Union Square Cafe, who immediately put her to work on the lunch line. Though she had spent most of her life seeking the peace to create visual art, she found herself thriving amid the chaos of the busy kitchen.

After a stint as a sous-chef at The Frog, a whimsical seafood restaurant in Philadelphia where she was the only woman in the kitchen, Aronson returned to New York to become executive chef at John Clancy's East. It was here that she really hit her stride, experimenting with unique combinations of ingredients and gaining a following among savvy New York diners.

Next, Aronson catapulted the restaurant called Lola beyond its previous incarnation as an island-themed hot spot into a place where the excitement centers around the food. The *New York Times*, in granting Lola two stars, approved of Aronson's new direction: "With its able new chef, the restaurant's culinary octane level has moved a notch higher, making Lola an overall delight."

Since 1990, Aronson has been part-owner and executive chef at Lola, being named one of *Esquire's* best young American chefs in 1992. It was her food, in fact, that helped to lift Caribbean cuisine from its "street food" roots to its current level of sophistication.

Her influences include foods from far beyond the islands: Thai, Southwestern, modern Creole and Cajun, all flavors find their way into such dishes as fried Louisiana shrimp with Asian barbecue sauce and peanut sauce, and Szechwan peppercorn-seared monkfish with ancho chili sauce. Lola's 100-spice Caribbean fried chicken is also a signature dish.

Grilled Rack of Lamb with Risotto, Fava Beans, and Cardamom Sauce

Lynne Aronson
Lola
New York, New York

Beets take an intriguing turn in this creative entrée, producing a dramatic red risotto. The cardamom pods are roasted to add maximum perfume to the intense red wine sauce. You can use more than the 10 called for in this recipe, but only if you like strong flavors.

Serves 4

Cardamom Sauce
10 whole cardamom pods, or more
   to taste
3 cups lamb or beef stock
   (see page 228, 231)
1 cup dry red wine
1/2 cup chopped peeled carrots
1/2 cup chopped onion
1/2 cup chopped celery
2 whole bay leaves
Salt and freshly ground black pepper
   to taste

Lamb
Two 8-bone racks of lamb, Frenched
1 tablespoon olive oil
Salt and freshly ground black pepper
   to taste

Garnish
8 ounces fava beans, shelled
2 tablespoons butter
1 tablespoon olive oil
8 ounces beet greens or spinach,
   stemmed
1/2 cup (2 ounces) freshly grated
   Parmesan cheese

To make the sauce: In a small, heavy sauté pan or skillet over medium heat, toast the cardamom seeds until they are very aromatic; set aside. In a medium saucepan, combine the stock, wine, carrots, onion, celery, bay leaves, and toasted cardamom pods and place over medium-high heat. Bring the mixture to a boil. Lower the heat and simmer until the liquid has reduced by half, about 30 minutes.

Strain the sauce through a fine-meshed sieve and test it for consistency; it should hold its shape when spooned onto a plate. If the sauce is too thin, return it to the pan and continue to cook until it thickens. Season the sauce with salt and pepper and set aside in a warm place. There should be about 1 cup of sauce.

To prepare the lamb: Cut the racks of lamb into 4 servings of 4 ribs each, then remove the first bone from each portion. Wrap the exposed bone ends with foil, rub the meat with olive oil, and season with salt and pepper.

Prepare a charcoal or wood fire in a grill and grill the lamb racks over hot coals, turning once, just until the outside is crisp, about 3 minutes. The lamb should remain rare. Set the lamb aside for 15 to 20 minutes, then slice each rack into 3 chops. Season the chops with salt and pepper, return them to the grill, and cook for 1 to 2 minutes on each side, or until medium rare.

To prepare the garnish: Cook the fava beans in lightly salted water in a small saucepan over high heat just until they turn bright green, about 2 minutes. Drain the beans and plunge them into cold water, then drain again and peel. Just before serving, melt the butter in a small sauté pan or skillet over high heat and sauté the beans until they are hot, 2 minutes.

Wash the beet greens or spinach very well and pat dry with a towel. Heat the oil in a large sauté pan or skillet over high heat; add the greens and cook, stirring, until they are wilted, about 30 seconds.

To serve: Place a mound of the greens in the center of each serving plate. Spoon some of the beet risotto over the greens. Sprinkle each plate with some Parmesan cheese. Place 3 lamb chops against each serving of risotto with the bones pointing upward and ladle about 1/4 cup of the cardamom sauce over the lamb. Garnish the plate with some of the fava beans and serve.

Beet Risotto
Serves 4

3 beets
2 cups dry white wine
2 cups chicken stock (see page 228)
2 tablespoons olive oil
6 tablespoons minced onion
2 tablespoons minced garlic
1 1/2 cups Arborio rice
1/4 cup freshly grated Parmesan cheese

Preheat the oven to 450°F. Place the beets on a baking sheet and roast them until they can be easily pierced with a knife, 30 to 40 minutes. Let cool, then peel and dice the beets. Place the diced beets in a small bowl, add 1/4 cup of the wine, and set aside.

In a medium saucepan over medium heat, bring the stock to a simmer. Lower the heat and maintain the stock at a bare simmer. In a large, heavy saucepan over medium heat, heat the olive oil and sauté the onion and garlic until they are translucent, 5 to 7 minutes. Add the rice and stir until the rice grains are coated with oil. Add half of the remaining 1 3/4 cups wine and cook, stirring constantly, until the wine is absorbed. Repeat with the remaining wine, then begin adding the chicken stock 1/2 cup at a time in the same manner. The entire process will take about 30 minutes. The rice should be tender with a creamy texture.

Add the beets and all of their juice to the rice and stir until the beets are warmed through. Stir in the Parmesan cheese and serve hot.

Grilled Rack of Lamb with Risotto, Fava Beans, and Cardamom Sauce;
Lynne Aronson, Lola

Roasted Rack of Lamb with Ratatouille Polenta and Black Olive Lamb Juice

■▪■▪■▪■▪■▪■▪■▪■▪■▪■▪■▪

Patrick Clark
Hay-Adams Restaurant
The Hay-Adams Hotel
Washington, D.C.

This roasted lamb is complemented by a flavorful sauce of lamb stock, wine, and niçoise olives. The polenta is combined with a fennel-scented ratatouille that you can make yourself (see page xx), or you can buy prepared ratatouille in a specialty foods shop.

Serves 4

2 racks of lamb (16 ribs)
½ cup plus 2 tablespoons olive oil
2 garlic cloves, thinly sliced
1 fresh thyme sprig, coarsely chopped
1 fresh rosemary sprig, coarsely chopped
1 tablespoon cracked black pepper

Black Olive Lamb Juice
½ cup Cabernet red wine
Roasted lamb juices, above
1 cup lamb stock (see page 231)
1 fresh thyme sprig
½ cup pitted niçoise olives, chopped
2 tablespoons unsalted butter

Ratatouille Polenta
¾ cup milk
¾ cup chicken stock (see page 228)
½ cup polenta (coarse yellow cornmeal)
Salt and freshly ground black pepper to taste
½ teaspoon fennel seed, crushed
½ cup ratatouille (see Note)

Fresh rosemary sprigs for garnish

Combine the ½ cup olive oil, the garlic, thyme, rosemary, and pepper in a baking pan. Add the lamb, and turn to coat it. Cover and refrigerate. Before cooking, scrape most of the marinade herbs and garlic from the meat to prevent burning and bitter flavor.

Roasted Rack of Lamb with Ratatouille Polenta and Black Olive Lamb Juice;
Patrick Clark, Hay-Adams Restaurant, The Hay-Adams Hotel

Preheat the oven to 450°F. In a large sauté pan or skillet over medium-high heat, heat the 2 tablespoons olive oil and sear the lamb for 2 to 3 minutes. Place the lamb in the oven and roast for 15 minutes, turning the lamb halfway through the cooking time. Remove from the oven and let rest, bone-side down, for 5 to 7 minutes before carving.

To make the lamb juice: Place the roasting pan over high heat, add the wine, and stir, scraping up any browned bits from the bottom of the pan. Pour in any juices that have drained from the resting lamb. Cook the pan liquid over medium heat to reduce it until almost dry. Add the stock and thyme, and cook to reduce to ³⁄₄ cup, about 8 to 10 minutes. Strain the liquid through a fine-meshed strainer, add the olives, and swirl in the butter. Set aside in a warm place.

To make the polenta: Combine the milk and chicken stock in a medium saucepan over medium-high heat and bring to a boil. Whisk in the cornmeal, and continue to whisk while bringing the mixture back to a boil. Stirring constantly, cook for 2 to 3 more minutes over medium-high heat, or until the polenta has thickened and is of a creamy consistency. Add the salt and pepper, cover, and set aside in a warm place. Just before serving, add the fennel seeds to the ratatouille and stir the ratatouille into the polenta.

To serve: Carve the racks into chops. Place 1 scoop of polenta on each serving plate and nap with a portion of the sauce. Stand the chops around the polenta and garnish with fresh rosemary sprigs.

Note: *A ratatouille recipe of your choice may be used, keeping in mind that the vegetables should be finely diced. Jean Martin–Ratatouille Provençal is a superb prepared product that can be purchased in most specialty foods stores. A recipe for ratatouille is given in this book on page 142.*

PATRICK CLARK
Hay-Adams Restaurant, The Hay-Adams Hotel, Washington, D.C.

In the opinion of food critics, Patrick Clark succeeded in his personal goal: making the restaurant in Washington's Hay-Adams Hotel as famous as the hotel that surrounds it.

He did so by blending lessons learned from his parents with tips picked up from some of the most sophisticated chefs on earth. As a chef of contemporary American cuisine, he was free to draw upon any of the myriad influences in the nation's multicultural capital.

Clark was President Bill Clinton's first choice as chef for the White House, which is right across Lafayette Square from the hotel. Clark felt honored, of course, but had to say no; the salary simply wasn't enough to support his large family. To the delight of the Hay-Adams crowd, Clark felt compelled to stay put. It wasn't until 1995 that he moved on to New York's Tavern on the Green.

Clark was introduced to the kitchen early on, since his father served as a chef with Restaurant Associates when that company operated the Four Seasons and La Fonda del Sol in New York. Following in his father's footsteps, Clark trained at the same school, New York City Technical College. Later, he traveled to England and France to add to his professional training.

On that pilgrimage, Clark studied at the Bournemouth Technical College of Great Britain and apprenticed at Braganza Restaurant in London and with the famed Michel Guerard at Les Prés d'Eugénie in Eugénie-les-Bains. Then it was time to return to his native land, which in Clark's Brooklyn vocabulary meant New York City.

Although anyone seeking him out could have sampled his cooking at Regine's, Le Coup de Fusil, La Boîte, and the Pear Tree, it was his work at three other Manhattan restaurants that made his reputation. Clark proved instrumental in improving the culinary fortunes of the Odeon and Cafe Luxembourg, as well as of his own place called Metro.

Clark's personal blend of French and American cuisines earned two stars for each place from the *New York Times*. It was such accolades that propelled him to Bice Ristorante in New York and onward to Bice in Beverly Hills, serving as executive chef there for two years.

After his applauded term at the Hay-Adams Restaurant, Clark has followed his star to New York. In a city filled with outstanding restaurants and chefs, he is certain to become a standout.

Pork Confit with Apple, Date, and Onion Marmalade

▼■▼■▼■▼■▼■▼■▼■▼■▼■▼■

Gerald Hirigoyen
Fringale
San Francisco, California

Pork confit, made with pork tenderloin, is combined with sautéed cabbage and served with a fruit-and-vegetable marmalade for an elegant version of a rustic dish.

Serves 4

Pork Confit
2 pork tenderloins, 12 ounces each
1 tablespoon coarse salt
1 tablespoon whole black peppercorns, crushed
4 cloves garlic, thickly sliced
2 fresh thyme sprigs
2 bay leaves
2 pounds lard

Apple, Date, and Onion Marmalade
3 tablespoons olive oil
1 white onion, thinly sliced
Salt and freshly ground black pepper to taste
¹/₃ cup balsamic vinegar
¹/₃ cup sherry vinegar
1 cup water
2 tablespoons unsalted butter
1 small apple, peeled, cored, and cut into ¹/₂-inch dice
3 dates, thinly sliced
1 cup veal stock (see page 228)

Cabbage
1 gallon water
2 tablespoons salt
3 cups shredded green cabbage
4 tablespoons unsalted butter

2 tablespoons minced fresh parsley for garnish

To make the pork confit: Sprinkle the tenderloins with the salt and pepper, then combine with the garlic, thyme, and bay leaves. Wrap tightly in plastic wrap and refrigerate for 24 hours.

In a large sauté pan or skillet over medium-high heat, melt the lard and bring it to a boil. Add the tenderloins and lower the heat, then cover and simmer for 30 to 40 minutes. Transfer the tenderloins to a storage container and pour the lard over them to completely cover the meat. Let cool at room temperature, then refrigerate for a minimum of 24 hours and/or up to 1 week.

To make the marmalade: In a small, heavy saucepan over medium heat, heat the oil and sauté the onion until it is golden brown, about 20 minutes. Add the salt and pepper, then add the vinegars and water. Lower the heat to a simmer and cook until the liquid has evaporated and the onions are very soft, about 45 minutes. Set aside.

In a small sauté pan or skillet over high heat, melt the butter and sauté the apple and dates for 2 minutes. Add the onion mixture and sauté for another 2 minutes. Add the veal stock and bring it to a boil, then remove from heat and set aside.

To make the cabbage and finish the dish: Preheat the oven to 450°F. Bring the tenderloins to room temperature, remove them from the container, and scrape off the lard. Bake the tenderloins until warmed throughout, about 10 minutes.

Bring the water to a boil in a large pan over high heat. Add the salt and the cabbage and cook for 2 minutes. Remove the cabbage from the water and rinse it under cold water to stop the cooking process. In a large sauté pan or skillet over high heat, melt the butter and sauté the cabbage until tender, about 2 minutes. Season the cabbage with salt and pepper.

To serve: Mound the cabbage in the center of a large serving platter. Slice the tenderloin into ¹/₂-inch slices and arrange them around the cabbage. Spoon the marmalade around the pork and garnish the platter with the parsley.

Pork Confit with Apple, Date, and Onion Marmalade; *Gerald Hirigoyen, Fringale*

Lamb Chops with Goat Cheese-Macaroni Soufflé

▼■▼■▼■▼■▼■▼■▼■▼■

William C. Greenwood
The Jefferson
Washington, D.C.

You haven't had macaroni and cheese till you've had this soufflé of macaroni and goat cheese, served with sautéed lamb chops and garnished with peas and tiny onions.

Serves 6

Lamb Chops
1 cup olive oil
3 tablespoons chopped fresh rosemary
3 tablespoons finely sliced garlic
Salt and freshly ground black pepper
   to taste
18 rib lamb chops, Frenched

Vegetables
1 cup fresh or frozen peas
1 cup small pearl onions
2 tablespoons unsalted butter

Goat Cheese-Macaroni Soufflés
10 ounces dried macaroni
1 cup heavy (whipping) cream
11 ounces fresh white goat cheese,
   crumbled (2 cups)
2 tablespoons cornstarch
2 tablespoons cold water
8 egg whites
Pinch of salt

6 cups unsalted beef stock (see page 228)
3 tablespoons minced fresh tarragon
   leaves
3 tablespoons minced fresh mint leaves
Salt and freshly ground black pepper
   to taste

To prepare the lamb chops: Combine the olive oil, rosemary, garlic, salt, and pepper. Rub the chops well with the mixture, cover, and refrigerate overnight.

To prepare the vegetables: In a medium saucepan of lightly salted boiling water, blanch the fresh peas until they are bright green, about 2 minutes. Remove them from the water with a slotted spoon, drain, then plunge them into ice water. Drain the vegetables again and set aside. If using frozen peas, omit the blanching.

In the same saucepan of boiling water, blanch the pearl onions for 2 minutes, then drain and slip off their skins. In a medium sauté pan or skillet over low heat, melt the butter, add the onions, cover, and cook until tender, about 10 minutes. Set aside.

To make the soufflés: Preheat the oven to 375°F. Butter six 8-ounce ovenproof ramekins and set aside. In a large pot of lightly salted boiling water, cook the macaroni for 6 to 8 minutes, or until al dente. Rinse the pasta in cool water, drain well, and set aside.

In a small, heavy saucepan over low heat, simmer the cream, add the cheese, and stir until smooth. In a small bowl, combine the cornstarch and water, and add this to the cheese mixture, stirring until thickened, about 1 minute. Transfer to a larger bowl, add salt and pepper, and set aside to cool.

In a large bowl, using an electric mixer, beat the egg whites with the salt until they are foamy. Increase the speed to high and continue to beat until stiff peaks form. Stir about one fourth of the egg whites into the cheese mixture in order to lighten it, then fold in the remaining egg whites. Gently fold in the macaroni. Spoon the mixture into the prepared ramekins and bake for 20 to 25 minutes, or until firm to the touch.

To serve: In a medium saucepan over medium heat, cook the stock until reduced to 3/4 cup, about 1 hour. Add the tarragon, mint, salt, pepper, and the mixed peas and onions; set aside. In a large sauté pan or skillet over high heat, sauté the lamb chops until they are medium rare, 3 minutes per side. The lamb chops can also be grilled over a hot charcoal or wood fire.

Unmold a soufflé into the center of each serving plate and position 3 of the lamb chops upright around the soufflé with the bone tips touching. Spoon some of the vegetables and stock reduction around the rim of the plate.

Lamb Chops with Goat Cheese–Macaroni Soufflé;
William C. Greenwood, The Jefferson

GEORGE BUMBARIS
The Dining Room, The Ritz-Carlton Chicago, Chicago, Illinois

George Bumbaris came of age in the kitchens of The Ritz-Carlton Chicago. Now he runs those kitchens.

Bumbaris joined the hotel in 1983, immediately after graduation from Cooking School Dumas Père in Glenview, Illinois. Clearly, the young man was recognized as a promising talent – for he was moved by Ritz-Carlton management through a series of jobs aimed at giving him the whole kitchen picture.

After six years of moving through the culinary chain of command, Bumbaris was named executive sous chef. In a large hotel operation, this is a position with the dizzying responsibility of handling the food and beverage operation while the executive chef is meeting with the guys in the suits.

Bumbaris handled the job so well that eventually he was named executive chef. Unlike many other chefs, who have hopped from one restaurant to another seeking experience and further challenge, this chef found what he needed in one place – although the dining options at the Ritz include the posh Dining Room, the more casual Cafe, and the Greenhouse, plus of course banquets and room service.

Happily, the high quality of Bumbaris' work has provided him both a creative outlet and a chance to travel. He won first place for the United States in the 26th Prix Culinaire International in 1992 in Paris.

Bumbaris was chosen to represent the United States in 1991 at the International Bocuse d'Or competition, which was staged in Lyons during the Salon des Metiers de Bouche, a leading French gastronomic show. At that competition, he bested chefs from twenty-two countries around the world, capturing a top prize for his dish, Sole of the Four Seasons.

Saddle of Lamb with Pesto and Fingerling Potato, Baby Artichoke, and Oven-dried Tomato Ragout

George Bumbaris
The Dining Room
The Ritz-Carlton, Chicago
Chicago, Illinois

In this elegant preparation, a pesto mixture is used to stuff the lamb loins, which are served with a sauce of white wine and veal stock, and a marvelous quick vegetable ragout.

Serves 4

Pesto
4 cups packed fresh basil leaves with some stems
2 garlic cloves, minced
1/2 cup pine nuts
3/4 cup olive oil
1/2 cup (2 ounces) freshly grated Parmesan cheese
Salt and freshly ground black pepper to taste
1 cup dried bread crumbs

One 4-pound saddle of lamb
Salt and freshly ground black pepper to taste

Sauce
3/4 cup reserved trimmings from lamb, above
Salt and freshly ground black pepper to taste
1/2 cup minced shallots
3/4 cup dry white wine
2 cups veal stock (see page 228)
2 teaspoons chopped fresh parsley
2 teaspoons chopped fresh thyme
4 to 6 tablespoons unsalted butter
Salt and freshly ground black pepper to taste

1/4 cup olive oil

Ragout
12 fingerling potatoes or small yellow potatoes
2 baby artichokes, trimmed (see page 234)

Three ¼-inch-thick lemon slices
4 tablespoons clarified unsalted butter
 (see page 223)
1 tablespoon minced fresh parsley
2 tablespoons minced fresh thyme
6 oven-dried plum (Roma) tomatoes
 (see page 225)
Salt and freshly ground black pepper
 to taste

To make the pesto: Place the basil, garlic, and pine nuts in a blender or food processor. Puree the mixture, stopping to scrape down the sides. With the motor running, slowly add the olive oil in a thin stream. Transfer the mixture to a medium bowl and stir in the cheese and bread crumbs. (The bread crumbs help firm the pesto for easier stuffing.) Set aside.

Have your butcher remove the loins from the saddle, reserving the trimmings and the bones, and trim the fat on the loins to an ⅛-inch thickness. Loosen the fat from the meat of each loin, leaving the sheet of fat attached at one end, and rewrap the loin with it.

Using a sharpening steel wrapped in plastic wrap, force the steel lengthwise through the center of each loin, applying pressure to widen the opening. Using a pastry bag fitted with a large tip, firmly stuff the loins with the mixture. Season the loins with salt and black pepper. Wrap each loin in its own fat, being sure not to overlap the edges, and tie the fat with white cotton string to hold it in place. Set aside while making the sauce.

To make the sauce: Using the same pan, pour off the excess fat and add the lamb trimmings. Brown the trimmings over high heat, stirring to scrape up the browned bits from the bottom of the pan. Turn heat down to medium. Season with salt and pepper and continue to cook for 10 to 15 minutes. Add the shallots and continue stirring until the shallots start to brown. Add the white wine to the pan, stir to scrape up the browned bits from the bottom of the pan, and cook to reduce by about two-thirds, about 10 minutes. Add the veal stock and cook to reduce by half, about

20 minutes depending on the size of the pan. Add the fresh herbs and cook 3 to 4 more minutes. Strain, then finish the sauce by swirling in the butter 1 tablespoon at a time until it is all incorporated. Season with salt and pepper. Set aside and keep warm.

In a large cast-iron skillet over medium heat, heat the olive oil and cook the loins, turning frequently, until medium-rare and browned, 10 to 12 minutes. Most of the fat will render out during the process. Let the lamb rest for 5 to 7 minutes before slicing.

Meanwhile, to make the ragout: Boil the potatoes in their skins until tender but still firm, about 10 to 15 minutes, depending on the size of the potatoes. Drain, let cool, and peel. Leave the potatoes whole if very small, otherwise slice about ¼ inch thick. Set aside.

Place the lemon slices in the bottom of a small saucepan. Stand the artichokes, stem down, on the lemons. Add water to cover. Weight

the artichokes with a small plate and simmer for 15 minutes. Drain and cut each artichoke in half. Set aside.

In a medium sauté pan or skillet over medium-high heat, heat 2 tablespoons of the clarified butter and sauté the potatoes until golden, about 5 minutes. Sprinkle with the parsley and 1 tablespoon of the minced thyme. Using a slotted spoon, remove from the pan and set aside.

Melt the remaining 2 tablespoons clarified butter in the same pan over medium heat, add the artichokes and tomatoes, and sauté for about 3 minutes. Sprinkle with salt and pepper.

To serve: Slice each lamb loin into 6 slices. Combine the potatoes, artichokes, and tomatoes. Mound one quarter of the vegetable mixture in the center of each serving plate. Place 3 slices of lamb around the vegetables on each plate. Spoon sauce around edge of plate and garnish with the remaining 1 tablespoon minced thyme.

Saddle of Lamb with Pesto and Fingerling Potato, Baby Artichoke, and Oven-dried Tomato Ragout; *George Bumbaris, The Dining Room, The Ritz-Carlton, Chicago*

Braised Lamb Shanks with Carrots, Leeks, and Coriander Sauce

Gordon Hamersley
Hamersley's Bistro
Boston, Massachusetts

Lamb shanks are given a Moroccan treatment in this dish, with a sauce that combines coriander, marjoram, and blood orange slices, and uses a little couscous as a thickener.

Serves 4

Four 8-inch leeks
4 lamb shanks
Salt and freshly ground black pepper
2 tablespoons vegetable oil
3 carrots, peeled and cut into large
  chunks
3 small garlic cloves, sliced
1 tablespoon finely julienned peeled
  fresh ginger
2 cups dry red wine
1 cup chicken stock (see page 228)
1 tablespoon coriander seeds
1 tablespoon tomato paste
1 tablespoon minced fresh marjoram
1 unpeeled blood orange, thinly sliced
2 tablespoons steamed couscous

Braised Lamb Shanks with Carrots, Leeks, and Coriander Sauce;
Gordon Hamersley, Hamersley's Bistro

Garnish
2 tablespoons minced fresh parsley
Fresh marjoram sprigs

To prepare the lamb: Preheat the oven to 350°F. Trim the root ends and cut the tops off the leeks, leaving an 8-inch length. Split the leeks in half through the root end, cutting 6 inches toward the top. Rinse well to remove any dirt from between the leaves.

Trim the shanks of all excess fat and season liberally with salt and pepper. In a large sauté pan or skillet over high heat, heat the oil and sauté the shanks until they are evenly browned all over, 15 to 20 minutes. Pour off any excess fat from the pan. Add the carrots, leeks, garlic, and ginger to the pan and continue to cook for 5 minutes. Add the wine, stock, coriander seeds, tomato paste, marjoram, and orange, and bring the liquid to a boil. Cover and bake for 2 to 2½ hours, or until the meat is very tender and falling off the bone.

Remove the pan from the oven, arrange the lamb and vegetables on a warm serving platter, and place the pan over medium heat. Add the couscous to the juices and stir until the couscous slightly thickens the sauce. Ladle some of the sauce over the meat and vegetables, and garnish the platter with the parsley and marjoram sprigs.

GORDON HAMERSLEY
Hamersley's Bistro, Boston, Massachusetts

Wolfgang Puck was one of the first chefs to wear a baseball cap instead of the French *toque blanche*. Gordon Hamersley adopted that style during his three years of cooking for Puck at Ma Maison in Los Angeles. But Hamersley also wears a baseball cap because he really likes baseball—and because he is usually on his way to Fenway Park whenever he can steal a few moments away from his kitchen.

Hamersley's choice of headgear is also apt, for he has reinvented the French bistro as the perfect showcase for New England-inspired American food.

"Glorified peasant cooking": That's how one writer described Hamersley's Bistro, which the chef opened in 1987 with his wife Fiona. "Rustic as a Breughel wedding scene and as comforting as hot chocolate on a winter's night." Not bad for a breezy little storefront in Boston's eclectic South End. And not bad for a guy who started out washing dishes to subsidize his career in rock and roll.

Hamersley picked up a degree in education from Boston University. The famous blizzard of 1978 convinced him to seek warmer climes, so off to California he trundled, taking a kitchen job at the Bel Air Sands Hotel and meeting his wife-to-be in the process.

Having switched from dishwashing to cooking because it paid better, Hamersley trained under a series of European chefs, then put himself at Puck's service at Ma Maison. Puck's version of California's creativity opened his eyes to a new world, and inspired him to spend virtually all of 1983 eating and drinking his way through France.

Back in Boston, Hamersley was fortunate enough to meet Lydia Shire. He worked as executive sous-chef at Seasons in the Bostonian Hotel until the summer of 1986, when he started scouting locations for a place of his own. He and Fiona settled on their fifty-seat storefront the following year, Hamersley as a purveyor of New England's culinary renaissance.

Awards and honors have beaten a path to his door ever since, including Best New Restaurant from *Esquire* and Best New Chef from *Food & Wine* the year Hamersley's opened.

The local media love the place as well, especially *Boston Magazine*, which always remembers Hamersley's and its cap-topped proprietor around restaurant-ranking time. Now, if only the Red Sox would win the pennant, life would be sweet indeed.

GEORGES PERRIER
Le Bec-Fin, Philadelphia, Pennsylvania

When casting about for a name to hang on his restaurant more than a quarter-century ago, Georges Perrier thought of a French idiom that means simply "the good taste." All these years later, Le Bec-Fin to many means not simply good taste but arguably the best.

Though Philadelphia is not a city that most people think of as offering the top French dining in the country, many believe they've found it at Le Bec-Fin. William Rice, for example, wrote about Le Bec-Fin in an article the editors at *Connoisseur* magazine head-lined "The Best French Food in the U.S.? Try Philadelphia." Craig Claiborne also wrote about the restaurant's glories in the *New York Times*.

Like many in the older school of French chefs, Perrier believes that success in the kitchen is based on hard work, not media hype. His attention to detail is legendary; one employee describes Perrier this way: "He has a thousand eyes."

Perrier created his first entrée when he was only twelve, by whip-ping up an order of sweetbreads with mushrooms and Madeira. Relishing the attention this dish earned him, he decided to become a professional chef.

Training in the great restaurants of France was essential to achiev-ing Perrier's vision, so he made the circuit with enthusiasm. Among his mentors were Jacques Picard at Oustàu de Baumanière in Provence, Michel Lorrain at Casino de Chabonnières in Lyons, and Guy Thivard at La Pyramide in Vienne.

Perrier came to the United States in 1967 to cook for the late Peter von Starck, who had opened La Panatière, Philadelphia's first French restaurant. Three years later Perrier became the chef-owner of Le Bec-Fin. In 1983, the acclaimed restaurant moved to larger quarters.

Enjoying five-star status in the *Mobil Guide* since 1979, Perrier has also received accolades from many of the top gastronomical orga-nizations: the Chaîne de Rôtisseurs, Les Amis du Vin, Le Circle des Vingt, the Commanderie de Bordeaux, the Wine and Food Society, Les Bon Vivants, the Bacchus Society and Les Chevaliers du Taste Vin.

In 1981, Perrier was admitted to the elite Maîtres Cuisiniers de France, an order of French master chefs numbering only two hundred worldwide. Later, he was inducted into the exclusive Academie de France, founded more than a century ago by Joseph Favre.

Spring Lamb with Vegetables

Georges Perrier
Le Bec-Fin
Philadelphia, Pennsylvania

Young spring lamb should be used in this dish, which consists of layers of sliced lamb loin, caramelized turnips, and a mixture of braised vegetables. A sauce of rich flavored lamb stock is the final touch.

Serves 4

Two 1-pound lamb loins, trimmed of fat
 and silverskin
1 tablespoon olive oil
Salt and freshly ground black pepper
 to taste

Lamb Jus
2 pounds lamb bones
Salt and freshly ground black pepper
 to taste
½ teaspoon dried thyme
4 tablespoons olive oil
½ cup chopped peeled carrot
1 cup chopped celery
½ cup chopped onion
5 garlic cloves, minced
2 fresh thyme sprigs
2 bay leaves
6 tablespoons dry white wine
1 teaspoon white peppercorns
3 cups lamb stock (see page 231)

Caramelized Turnips
2 turnips
1 tablespoon unsalted butter
Salt and freshly ground black pepper
 to taste
1 tablespoon sugar

1 tablespoon olive oil
3 tablespoons butter
3 tablespoons dry white wine
¼ teaspoon minced fresh rosemary

Vegetables
2 tablespoons unsalted butter
1 carrot, peeled and cut into ¼-inch dice
1 cup fava beans, blanched and peeled

1 large tomato, peeled, seeded, and cut into ¼-inch dice (see page 234)
Salt and freshly ground black pepper to taste

Rub each loin with the olive oil and season with salt and pepper. Set aside, or cover and refrigerate.

To make the jus: Preheat the oven to 450°F. Place the bones on a roasting tray and season with thyme, salt, and pepper. Drizzle with 2 tablespoons of the olive oil. Place in the oven and roast, turning occasionally, until well browned, about 30 minutes.

Meanwhile, heat the remaining 2 tablespoons oil in a medium, heavy pot over medium-high heat and sauté the carrot, celery, onion, garlic, thyme, and bay leaves until the vegetables begin to soften, 10 to 15 minutes. Be careful not to let the vegetables get too brown. Add the wine and stir, scraping up the browned bits from the bottom of the pan. Add the bones, white peppercorns, and lamb stock. Cover and cook over medium heat for at least 1 hour. Strain the juice and set aside. You should have about 2 cups.

To make the turnips: Peel and slice the turnips into ¼-inch discs. Set aside 8 of the largest discs. In a medium sauté pan or skillet over medium-high heat, melt the butter and sauté the 8 turnip discs, turning frequently, for 8 to 10 minutes. The slices will begin to lightly brown. Season with salt and pepper and continue to sauté for another 2 to 3 minutes. Once the turnips are lightly golden and tender, sprinkle the sugar over them and continue to turn and brown them for another 1 to 2 minutes. Remove and keep warm.

To finish the lamb and juice: Preheat the oven to 450°F. In a 10-inch sauté pan or skillet, heat the oil and 2 tablespoons of the butter over medium-high heat and sauté the lamb loins, turning frequently, until browned, about 5 to 7 minutes. Place the lamb in the oven for about 5 minutes to finish cooking to medium

rare. Remove the loins from the pan and set aside in a warm place. Add the wine and stir, scraping up the browned bits from the bottom of the pan. Add the reserved juice and cook over high heat to reduce slightly. Add the rosemary and swirl in the remaining 1 tablespoon butter.

To make the vegetables: In a medium sauté pan or skillet over high heat, melt the butter in the water. Reduce heat to medium, add the carrots, and cook for

2 to 3 minutes. Add the beans and tomatoes and cook for 2 to 3 minutes. Season with salt and pepper.

To serve: Slice the lamb loins about ¼ inch thick. For each serving, arrange 1 turnip disc in the center of the plate, place 3 slices of lamb overlapping a circle on the turnip, and top with some of the vegetable mixture. Repeat with another turnip disc and 3 lamb slices, and end with vegetables on top. Ladle some of the juice over and around the edge of each plate.

Spring Lamb with Vegetables; *Georges Perrier, Le Bec-Fin*

Roasted Baby Rack of Lamb with Stuffed Sweet Mini-Peppers and Eggplant Cake

■▼■▼■▼■▼■▼■▼■▼■▼■▼■▼■▼■

Gabino Sotelino
Ambria
Chicago, Illinois

This very Mediterranean dish draws its flavors from both shores of that inland sea, and tops everything off with a brilliant sauce of reduced carrot juice, lamb stock, and rosemary.

Serves 4

Lamb
Two 8-bone baby racks of lamb
1/4 cup olive oil
Salt and freshly ground black pepper
  to taste

Stuffed Sweet Mini-Peppers
8 baby red bell peppers
2 tablespoons olive oil
Salt and freshly ground black pepper
  to taste

Ratatouille
6 tablespoons olive oil
1 cup 1-inch-cubed eggplant
1/2 cup finely chopped onion
Salt and freshly ground black pepper
  to taste
1 cup finely diced red and yellow
  bell peppers
1 cup finely diced zucchini
1/2 cup finely diced yellow squash
4 to 5 garlic cloves, minced

1 tablespoon minced fresh basil
1 tablespoon minced fresh thyme
1 tomato, peeled, seeded, and diced
  (see page 234)

Tapenade
3/4 cup niçoise olives, pitted and
  chopped
2 teaspoons roasted garlic puree
  (see page 234)
1 1/2 tablespoons chopped mixed fresh
  herbs such as parsley, chervil,
  tarragon, and chives
1 tablespoon minced sun-dried tomatoes
Salt and freshly ground black pepper
  to taste

Eggplant Cake
1 large eggplant, peeled
4 tablespoons olive oil
1/2 cup diced fresh fennel bulb (not
  feathery tops)
1 cup boiling lightly salted water
2 tablespoons diced red and yellow
  bell pepper
1 cup chicken stock (see page 228)
1/2 tablespoon curry powder
2 cups instant couscous
Salt and freshly ground black pepper
  to taste

Rosemary-Carrot Sauce
1 cup freshly extracted carrot juice
  (about 4 to 6 carrots)
1 cup lamb stock (see page 231)
Salt and freshly ground black pepper
  to taste
1 tablespoon minced shallot
1 garlic clove, minced
One 3-inch fresh rosemary sprig
1/2 teaspoon curry powder
1 tablespoon butter

To prepare the lamb: Preheat oven to 500°F. Place the racks back-to-back and tie together with white cotton string. In a large sauté pan or skillet over high heat, heat the olive oil. Season the lamb with salt and pepper and place it in the hot skillet with the bones standing upright. Brown on the bottom for about 3 minutes, then turn the racks over, and place the pan in the oven for 5 to 7 minutes, or until the lamb is medium-rare.

To prepare the mini peppers: Preheat the broiler. Rub the peppers with the oil, place them under the broiler 2 inches from the heat, and broil them until the skin is charred and loosened but not burned, 1 to 2 minutes per side. Place the peppers in a paper or plastic bag, close it, and let them cool until they can be handled. Split the peppers in half lengthwise through the stem. Remove the seeds, veins, and skin. Season the peppers with salt and pepper and set aside.

To make the ratatouille: In a large sauté pan or skillet over high heat, heat 2 tablespoons of the oil and sauté the eggplant until it begins to brown, 5 to 7 minutes. Add the onion and another 2 tablespoons of oil, season with salt and pepper, and cook until the vegetables are a light golden brown, about 3 minutes.

Meanwhile, in another large sauté pan or skillet over high heat, heat the remaining 2 tablespoons olive oil. Add the peppers, zucchini, squash, garlic, salt, pepper, and herbs, and sauté for 5 minutes, or until vegetables are just tender. Transfer the mixture to a bowl and let cool, then add the diced tomato and sautéed eggplant.

To make the tapenade: Combine all of the ingredients in a blender or food processor and briefly process until mixture forms a coarse puree.

To make the eggplant cakes: Cut the eggplant lengthwise into 1/4-inch-thick slices. In a large sauté pan or skillet over high heat, heat 1 tablespoon of the olive oil and sauté some of the eggplant slices until lightly colored on each side,

Roasted Baby Rack of Lamb with Stuffed Sweet Mini-Peppers and Eggplant Cake;
Gabino Sotelino, Ambria

about 4 minutes. Drain on paper towels. Repeat to cook all eggplant slices, adding the remaining olive oil 1 tablespoon at a time as necessary.

Poach the diced fennel in the boiling salted water for about 10 minutes, or until tender. Add the bell pepper, chicken stock, and curry powder. Stir in the couscous, cover, and remove from heat. Add the salt and pepper, and let sit for 10 minutes.

Place four 2½-inch stainless-steel rings or similar molds on an oiled baking sheet. Line the bottom of each mold with eggplant slices, overlapping them and allowing the ends to extend over the sides. Fill the molds with the couscous mixture, packing lightly, and fold the ends of the eggplant over the top. Set aside until ready to serve.

To finish the peppers: Fill half the roasted pepper halves with the ratatouille and the other half of the pepper halves with the tapenade. Let sit at room temperature until ready to serve.

To make the sauce: In a small saucepan over medium-high heat, cook the carrot juice until it is reduced by half. Add the lamb stock, salt, and pepper. Add the shallot, garlic, rosemary, and curry, and simmer over medium-low heat for at least 10 minutes, or until the flavors have mingled. Strain the sauce into a small saucepan and swirl in the butter over low heat.

To serve: When the lamb has been roasted to the desired doneness, let it sit in a warm place for 10 to 15 minutes. Reheat the eggplant cakes in the hot oven for 5 to 7 minutes. Warm the serving plates.

Place a warmed eggplant cake, smooth-side up, in the center of each warmed serving plate, and carefully remove the ring. Remove the strings from the lamb and slice between the bones to cut it into chops. Place 2 of each of the filled red peppers at opposite positions on the plate and place 4 lamb chops in between the peppers. Ladle some of the strained sauce over the chops and around the edges of the plates. Serve hot.

GABINO SOTELINO
Ambria, Chicago, Illinois

The decor of Gabino Sotelino's restaurant reminds him of his youth. Though his cooking has grown lighter and more innovative over the years, Ambria's elegant Art Nouveau trappings remain the stuff of grand hotels in Europe. And Sotelino loves it that way.

A co-creator of Ambria in 1978 (and a partner with Richard Melman of Lettuce Entertain You in that and several other restaurant ventures), Sotelino can trace his path back to his native Spain in the early fifties.

"I was a bellboy at the Ritz Hotel in Madrid when I was not even thirteen," Sotelino recalls. "After that I started working in the kitchen as an apprenticeship."

For a boy who had lived in a monastery for part of his early childhood, the world of the grand hotel was a revelation. The world came and went through the Ritz's elegant doors, and Sotelino couldn't get enough of it.

Without leaving his Spanish heritage behind, he embarked on a process of transforming himself into a fully qualified European chef. Cooking took him to the Plaza Athénée in Paris and the Koons in Switzerland, plus a string of Hiltons in Hong Kong, Istanbul, Tokyo, and Montreal. With the addition of resort areas as different as the Canary Islands and the French Riviera, Sotelino was building quite a résumé.

Washington was his first stop in the United States. Between 1968 and 1974, Sotelino worked as sous chef at the Madison Hotel, launched several other hotels as executive chef, opened the Kennedy Center, and even worked with Henry Naller on special functions at the White House. Then the call came from Chicago.

Sotelino's two positions before hooking up with Melman couldn't have been higher in profile. He served as executive chef at Le Perroquet from 1975 to 1977, and at the Pump Room from 1977 to 1978.

Melman, who spins off successful restaurant concepts the way some minds entertain summer fantasies, convinced Sotelino to join him on a three-week dining trip through Europe. Melman had an idea for a restaurant called Ambria, one that was based on the classical cuisines of the Continental while also reflecting some of the newest trends.

The trip was designed to create the outlines of Ambria-to-be. After tasting food at no fewer than twenty-eight restaurants, the pair knew exactly what kind of cuisine their new restaurant off Lincoln Park would have.

BRUCE COST
Ginger Island, Berkeley, California

Bruce Cost, a devoted student of Asian foods for more than twenty years, is also a popular teacher of Eastern cuisine.

For six years, Cost conducted comprehensive courses in Chinese and Southeast Asian cuisine in San Francisco, while also lecturing at the California Culinary Academy, the DeGustibus culinary section at Macy's and at *Food & Wine* magazine's annual festival in Aspen. As though that wasn't enough, he has lectured on Asian food at the Smithsonian Institute and the San Francisco Academy of Sciences, as well as on various panels across the United States and Canada.

For Cost, writing has always been a natural extension of teaching. He began by writing food features in the *San Francisco Chronicle* and a weekly column that ran concurrently in the *Washington Post*. Articles have also appeared in the *New York Times*, the *Chicago Tribune* and the *Los Angeles Times*, plus hundreds of other papers large and small by way of the Los Angeles Times Syndicate.

He has also written two books on his chosen subject: *Bruce Cost's Asian Ingredients* (William Morrow) and *Ginger East to West* (Addison-Wesley).

On top of teaching and writing, Cost has opened not one but two restaurants of his own in recent years. A place called Monsoon was launched in November 1989 in San Francisco, wowing not only local diners and critics but propelling Cost to the James Beard Awards in New York two years in a row with nominations as the best chef in California.

In May 1993, he opened Ginger Island on the former site of Mark Miller's Fourth Street Grill in Berkeley. Like his predecessor, Cost is a kind of cooking anthopologist exploring exotic terrain. Thanks to him, the East is even more intriguing, and much closer to home.

Thai Yellow Curry Noodles with Beef

▀▄▀▄▀▄▀▄▀▄▀▄▀▄▀▄▀▄▀▄

Bruce Cost
Ginger Island
Berkeley, California

The typical sauces used to flavor Thai foods take their names from the color of the main ingredient. In this yellow curry paste, the fresh turmeric, a member of the ginger family, turns the paste a bright yellow. The small dried red chilies give this dish its heat; you may wish to start with 8 to 12, using as many as 15 to 18 if you enjoy an extremely spicy dish.

Serves 4 to 6

1 cup peanut oil
1/2 cup raw blanched peanuts
8 ounces fresh Chinese egg noodles

12 ounces flank steak
1 tablespoon dark soy sauce
2 teaspoons cornstarch
1 tablespoon toasted sesame oil
2 tablespoons peanut oil
1/4 cup Yellow Curry Paste
   (recipe follows)
1 cup fresh Chinese chives, cut into
   1-inch lengths
1/3 cup chicken stock (see page 228)
1 tablespoon fresh lemon juice
1 tablespoon Thai fish sauce
1 teaspoon half-and-half

To prepare the peanuts: Heat a wok over high heat for 3 minutes. Add the peanut oil and heat to 375°F, or until smoking. Add the peanuts, turn off the heat, and let the peanuts sit in the oil until it cools. Using a slotted spoon, transfer the peanuts to paper towels to drain. Chop the peanuts coarsely and set aside. Remove all but 2 tablespoons of the oil from the wok and set the wok aside.

To prepare the noodles: Place a large pot of lightly salted water over high heat and bring to a boil. Add the noodles and cook for 3 1/2 minutes, or until just tender. Drain them and rinse under cold water to stop the cooking process. Place the noodles in a large bowl, add 1 tablespoon of the peanut oil, and toss the noodles to coat them. Set aside.

To prepare the meat: Slice the flank steak thinly across the grain into 1/8-inch-thick slices, then cut the slices in half. In a small bowl, combine the soy sauce, cornstarch, and sesame oil and add the flank steak slices. Mix with a fork and set aside for 15 to 20 minutes.

Place the wok with the 2 tablespoons oil over high heat until the oil is smoking. Add the beef, lower the heat to medium, and toss the beef in the oil using a fork or chopstick to separate the pieces, for about 30 seconds, until the beef begins to lose its pink color but is not completely cooked. Using a slotted spoon, transfer the beef to a colander.

Add the curry paste to the wok and stir quickly, then add the chives. Stir for 20 seconds, then add the stock. Add the noodles, lemon juice, and fish sauce, and stir and cook for 30 seconds. Add the beef with the half-and-half and stir until the meat is reheated and well combined with the noodles. Spoon the noodles and beef onto a large serving platter, sprinkle with the peanuts, and serve.

Yellow Curry Paste
Makes 1 cup

12 to 15 small dried red Thai chilies*
1 1/2 tablespoons coriander seeds
1/2 tablespoon cumin seeds, or
   2 teaspoons ground cumin
3/4 teaspoon black peppercorns
1 tablespoon minced fresh turmeric*, or
   2 teaspoons ground turmeric
1 tablespoon chopped fresh galangal*
Roots and 1 inch of stems from 1/2
   bunch fresh cilantro, or 1 1/2 cups
   cilantro leaves
6 garlic cloves
1/4 cup chopped shallots
Bulb of 1/2 large fresh lemongrass stalk,
   chopped
4 tablespoons peanut oil
1 teaspoon salt
1 tablespoon ground fish sauce
   (anchovy cream) or shrimp sauce*
1 tablespoon fresh lime juice

In a large dry sauté pan or skillet over medium heat, toast the chilies, coriander seeds, cumin seeds or cumin, and peppercorns until they are fragrant, 3 to 4 minutes. In a spice grinder or coffee mill, grind the spices to a coarse powder.

In a blender or food processor, combine the turmeric, galangal, cilantro roots and stems, garlic, shallots, lemon grass, and 2 tablespoons of the oil, and grind to a coarse paste. Add the spices, salt, fish sauce or shrimp sauce, and lime juice to the machine and continue to blend for 20 seconds. Transfer the sauce to a bowl and stir in the remaining 2 tablespoons oil. Store leftover curry paste in an airtight container in the refrigerator for several weeks.

*Available in Asian markets.

Thai Yellow Curry Noodles with Beef; *Bruce Cost, Ginger Island*

Venison with Rhubarb and Spelt-Corn Relish; *Jack McDavid, Jack's Firehouse*

Venison with Rhubarb and Spelt-Corn Relish

Jack McDavid
Jack's Firehouse
Philadelphia, Pennsylvania

This venison dish combines some surprising ingredients: raisins, Cognac, and rhubarb for a tangy-sweet sauce, and corn, bell pepper, and spelt, an ancient grain, for a colorful relish.

Serves 4

Spelt-Corn Relish
1 cup spelt (available in natural foods stores)
4 cups vegetable or chicken stock (see page 228, 231), or more as needed
½ teaspoon saffron
½ teaspoon dried thyme
1 bay leaf
2 tablespoons unsalted butter
1 cup fresh corn kernels
1 cup ¼-inch-diced yellow bell pepper
½ teaspoon ground cumin
Salt and freshly ground black pepper to taste

One 2¼-pound venison loin
Salt and freshly ground black pepper to taste
1 cup stock reserved from spelt (see recipe)
½ cup dark raisins
½ cup Cognac
4 tablespoons olive oil
2 cups very thinly sliced rhubarb stalks (3 to 4 stalks)
24 to 36 asparagus spears, peeled, blanched, and trimmed to 4-inch lengths
3 tablespoons olive oil
Salt and freshly ground black pepper to taste

To make the spelt-corn relish: Combine the spelt, stock, saffron, thyme, and bay leaf in a medium, heavy saucepan and bring to a boil. Cover the pan tightly, reduce heat to medium, and cook for 45 minutes, or until the spelt is tender. Add more stock as needed to keep the mixture moist. Pour off the remaining stock and reserve. You should have at least 1 cup.

In a medium sauté pan or skillet over medium-high heat, melt the butter, add the corn and bell pepper, and toss together for 2 to 3 minutes. Add the cumin, salt, and pepper and cook 1 minute, then add this mixture to the spelt. Taste and adjust seasoning as necessary. Set aside and keep warm.

Preheat the oven to 450°F. Remove the excess fat and silverskin from the loin, then cut the meat into medallions. Use the flat side of a chef's knife or a cleaver to slightly flatten each medallion. Season both sides with salt and pepper and set aside.

Place the reserved stock in a small saucepan; add the raisins, and heat until raisins are plump, about 5 minutes. Add the Cognac, heat until warm, and ignite the Cognac with a match. Shake the pan until the flames subside. Set aside.

Heat a large cast-iron skillet over high heat until very hot. Add 2 tablespoons of the oil and as many venison medallions as will fit. Sear on one side for 1 to 2 minutes, then turn and sear the opposite side; the venison should be rare and not too browned. Remove the meat from the skillet and set aside. Repeat to cook the remaining medallions, adding additional oil as needed.

Once all the medallions are seared, pour off any excess oil, then add the rhubarb. Sauté the rhubarb for 2 to 3 minutes, then add the raisins and liquid, return the medallions to the skillet, and cook for 2 to 3 minutes.

Meanwhile, roll the asparagus spears in the olive oil and spread them out on a sided baking sheet. Season with salt and pepper and bake for 5 minutes.

To serve: Place 3 medallions on each serving plate and spoon some rhubarb sauce over the venison and around the edge of the plate. Place a portion of spelt-corn relish at the top of each plate and arrange the spears of asparagus on either side.

JACK McDAVID
Jack's Firehouse, Philadelphia, Pennsylvania

Jack McDavid was in a frenzy. There he was, invited to cook something for the 25th anniversary of Georges Perrier's Le Bec-Fin in Philadelphia. And he knew it had to be good.

"I wanted to do something special," the chef recalls in his signature Virginia drawl. "I beat my brains out. This was going to be all the chefs that ever worked for him. And all of them were French except me, and I'm an American. I didn't want to be embarrassed. I beat my head up against the wall. What am I going to serve?"

In the the end, McDavid settled on a simple dish of roast baby lanb, so tender that it wasn't even served with knives.

"Everybody thought I was a genius," McDavid says, touching a hand to the baseball cap he wears instead of a *toque*. "But it wasn't that I was a genius. It was that I had the best food in the world to serve. So that's what we try to do in all three places."

The "three places" in McDavid's life are all in Philadelphia: the Down Home Diner opened in 1987, Jack's Firehouse opened in 1989, and the Down Home Grill opened in 1993. Though each eatery plays a different theme within American cuisine, each shows the steady hand of the man who knocked the smocks off Georges Perrier and a roomful of French chefs.

At first, it wasn't about cooking at all. McDavid was working his way through the University of Virginia in accounting. The big plan included law school.

Somehow, though, he found himself handling the books for a sandwich shop, then handling the kitchen too. When nearby Monticello needed a chef, the owners decided it needed McDavid. The rest is history, including cooking for Camp David peacemakers Jimmy Carter, Anwar Sadat and Menachim Begin.

Once he decided on a career as a chef, McDavid sought and found education in some of the strangest places. From a Greek short-order cook, he learned how to sauté. From Chiang Kai-Shek's former chef Charlie Yu, he learned about knives and presentation. From Marriott's top chef Dietmar Salat, he picked up the rudiments of French technique, while from Jean Pierre Goyenvalle of Washington's Lion d'Or he took on discipline.

Finally, he opened Jack's Firehouse. Philadelphians were delighted by such presentations as black-eyed pea and hog jowl soup, crawdads and macaroni with spicy tomato sauce, and Indian Ridge buffalo with moonshine sauce and pickled turnips.

Beef with Portobello Mushrooms and Pennsylvania Dutch Pepper Hash

▼▼▼▼▼▼▼▼▼▼

Jack McDavid
Jack's Firehouse
Philadelphia, Pennsylvania

Both the rib-eye steaks and the hash are made without oil, but this entrée is full of flavor, thanks to the meaty mushrooms and the wilted cabbage hash sparked with chipotle chilies and black pepper.

Serves 4

Four 10- to 12-ounce beef rib-eye steaks, preferably from organically grown lean beef
Salt and freshly ground black pepper to taste
2 to 4 very large portobello mushrooms
8 sun-dried tomato halves, diced
2 cups beef stock (see page 228)

Pennsylvania Dutch Pepper Hash
2 cups shredded cabbage
1/4 cup rock salt
1/2 cup 1/4-inch diagonal-cut sliced whole green onions
1/2 cup diced seeded red bell pepper
3 canned chipotle chilies, drained and finely diced
1 tablespoon sugar
1/2 tablespoon freshly ground black pepper

Season the steaks with salt and pepper. Place a very heavy large sauté pan or skillet, preferably of seasoned cast iron, over high heat. When very hot, add the steaks and cook them for 4 minutes on each side, turning once.

Meanwhile, remove the stems from the mushrooms and reserve them for another use. Slice the caps into 1/2-inch-thick slices. When the beef is golden brown, remove the steaks and keep warm. Add the mushrooms to the pan, flat-sides down, and sauté until they are browned, 2 to 3 minutes. Add the tomatoes and sauté for 3 to 5 minutes. Add the stock to the pan and cook for 15 to 20 minutes, or until it is reduced to about 1 cup of liquid. Adjust the seasoning.

To make the hash: Place the cabbage in a large bowl. Add the salt, toss, and let stand for 2 hours. Rinse the cabbage, then add the green onions, bell pepper, chipotle, and sugar. Toss the mixture together, place a piece of plastic wrap on top of the cabbage, and weight it down with a pan. Let the cabbage stand for 12 hours. Just before serving, season the cabbage with the pepper.

To serve: Place 1 steak on each serving plate and arrange slices of mushrooms around the steak. Spoon the tomatoes and sauce over and around the steaks, and add some of the pepper hash along one side of each plate.

Beef with Portobello Mushrooms and Pennsylvania Dutch Pepper Hash;
Jack McDavid, Jack's Firehouse

Medallions of Venison with Caramelized Green Apples

▀▄▀▄▀▄▀▄▀▄▀▄▀▄▀▄▀▄▀▄▀▄▀

Julian Serrano
Masa's
San Francisco, California

When venison loins are cut from the saddle, the bones can be used to make a rich brown stock and sauce, and the marrow can be poached and sliced as a garnish. Sweet-tart green apples complement the rich-tasting but low-fat venison.

Serves 6

1 saddle of venison
Salt and freshly ground black pepper
  to taste
4 celery sprigs
3 fresh thyme sprigs
2 bay leaves
1 tablespoon extra-virgin olive oil
1/2 cup 1/4-inch-diced peeled carrot
1/2 cup 1/4-inch-diced celery
1/2 cup 1/4-inch-diced onion
1 tablespoon tomato paste
2 1/2 quarts water
1/4 cup chopped shallots
2 cups dry red wine
1/2 cup port

Caramelized Green Apples

5 Granny Smith apples
1/4 cup clarified unsalted butter
  (see page 223)
2 tablespoons confectioners' sugar, sifted

Reserved marrow, above
1 tablespoon snipped fresh chives
1 tablespoon olive oil

Garnish

36 asparagus tips, blanched
18 baby carrots, blanched

Have your butcher remove the loins from the saddle and split the large bones, reserving all bones and scraps. Remove the marrow from the backbone and reserve it. Remove all the fat and silverskin from the loins with your fingers and a very sharp knife. Cut the loins into eighteen 3/4-inch-thick medallions, sprinkle them with salt and pepper, and set aside.

Place the celery sprigs, thyme sprigs, and bay leaves on a square of cheese-cloth and tie into a bouquet garni with white cotton string. In a 6-quart Dutch oven over high heat, heat the oil and brown the bones. Drain any excess oil from the pan and add the carrot, diced celery, onion, tomato paste, and bouquet garni. Add the water, lower the heat, and simmer for 1 hour.

Place the shallots, wine, and port in a small, heavy saucepan over medium-high heat and cook to reduce to 1 tablespoon. Strain the stock from the bones into a medium saucepan, add the wine reduction, and cook over medium heat to reduce for 40 minutes, or until it has reached a syrupy thickness. Strain the sauce and adjust the seasoning. Set aside and keep warm.

To make the caramelized apples: Cut each apple into 8 to 10 wedges (you will need 6 wedges per person). Peel, core, and evenly trim the slices. Place the butter and the apples in a large, heavy sauté pan or skillet over medium-high heat. Sprinkle the apples with the confectioners' sugar and cook for 1 minute, then turn and cook on the second side for about 40 seconds, or until the apples are nicely browned and tender when pierced with a knife. Remove the pan from heat and set it aside with the apples inside it. They will continue to cook slightly.

To prepare the marrow: Slice the reserved marrow into thirty-six 1/3-inch-thick slices. In a medium saucepan of lightly salted water, poach the marrow pieces for 1 minute, drain, then sprinkle with chives.

To cook the venison medallions: In a large sauté pan or skillet over high heat, heat the olive oil and sauté the medallions, turning once, for a total of 1 to 2 minutes. Remove the medallions, drain them on paper towels, and keep warm until all the venison is cooked.

To serve: On each serving plate, arrange each of 3 pairs of the apple wedges back to back to resemble a butterfly shape. Place 2 asparagus spears between the apples and center 1 baby carrot between the asparagus spears. Between the apple garnishes, place 3 medallions of venison and nap lightly with the sauce. Place a slice of marrow on each medallion and serve.

Medallions of Venison with Caramelized Green Apples; *Julian Serrano, Masa's*

Feuillant of Fresh Berries with Mango-Raspberry Coulis, *Christian Gille, Le Jardin, The Westin Canal Place*

Sweet Finales: Desserts

It is one of the sublime ironies of the New American Diet: the generation that spent more effort than any other insisting that their appetizer and entrée be light and healthy is also the generation of the extravagant dessert. Seldom has such emphasis been placed on the meal's sweet finale, a simple sweet treat no more. And seldom have pastry chefs done so much to send out swirls of delicious form, color and taste to bring a meal to a sensational close.

These dessert recipes run the national gamut and reflect the national imagination, with a few slots remaining for traditions like bread pudding, angel food and apple tart but most now taken by such brave new worlds as sun-dried cherry charlotte with tea ice cream or dusty road plum soup with roasted plums and plum tart. A few of the recipes, we admit, present technical challenges—yet we've worked with our chefs and pastry chefs to reach their destinations by the clearest, most direct routes possible.

Finally, as this book in its own way is a celebration of American bounty, you mustn't fail to notice the rich array of fresh fruits showcased in these desserts. Of course, chocolate is well represented in these pages; but we think you'll be impressed by how much flavor (and especially how much bursting color) is derived from things that do, for the most part, just grow on trees. Whether native or foreign born, every chef in this section pays tribute to this bounty each time he serves dessert.

San Francisco, California

EMILY LUCHETTI
Stars, San Francisco, California

"I believe if you're going to do something you love, you might as well do it all the time. And if you're going to do it all the time, then you might as well get paid for it."

That's how Emily Luchetti, the pastry chef at Stars, describes the process by which she decided on a career in cooking. Though she had always loved working in kitchens, it took her a while to see such labors as a career, and even longer for her to settle on desserts. It was Stars owner Jeremiah Tower who offered her the chance to specialize.

"When Jeremiah said, 'Do you want to give it a try'," she remembers, "there was no going back. While I enjoy cooking and have been doing it for years, desserts are my real love."

Luchetti remains largely unintimidated by the number of celebrities finishing meals with her pastries in the Stars dining room. She is also unintimidated by the sheer volume of the work she and her assistants turn out. On a daily basis, they use 200 pounds of butter, 40 gallons of cream, 80 pounds of chocolate, 450 pounds each of sugar and flour, and more than 1,500 eggs.

For all of her finesse, Luchetti sometimes looks out across the dining room and wonders: Why all the fuss? After all, there are few secrets in what she does—few, at least, that any careful home cook using her 1991 cookbook *Stars Desserts* (HarperCollins) couldn't replicate with satisfaction.

"I try to take the nervousness out of baking," she states. "There's really nothing difficult about any of my recipes." Luchetti sees sweets as a special form of comfort food, one that, when not used to excess, makes for a well-balanced diet and a well-balanced mind. "I recommend moderation, but not abstinence. If you're going to order dessert, order the best."

Luchetti attended the New York Restaurant School and cooked for a year with French chef Gerard Pangard before accepting a position as line cook at Stars. Tower recognizes a talent when he sees one, and he rapidly promoted her upward to sous-chef and finally day chef. The time came when he needed someone to do desserts, and Luchetti proved to be the one.

No shortage of honors have come Luchetti's way, even in addition to the verbal praise her pastries pick up at Stars and Stars Cafe in San Francisco, as well as at Stars Oakville Cafe in the Napa Valley.

Mascarpone Caramel Cream with Berries and White Chocolate–Raspberry Brittle

Emily Luchetti
Stars
San Francisco, California

This caramel cream is not a rich custard, but a mixture of caramel, Mascarpone cheese, and cream that is chilled, then dolloped onto plates and served with berries, two sauces, and an elegant "brittle" of raspberry-flavored white chocolate.

Serves 8

Mascarpone Caramel Cream
1/2 cup sugar
1/4 cup water
1/2 plus 3/4 cup heavy (whipping) cream
8 ounces Mascarpone cheese at room temperature

Raspberry Sauce
2 cups fresh raspberries
2 tablespoons sugar, or to taste
1/4 teaspoon fresh lemon juice
Pinch of salt

Blackberry Sauce
2 cups fresh blackberries
2 tablespoons sugar, or to taste
1/4 teaspoon fresh lemon juice
Pinch of salt

White Chocolate–Raspberry Brittle
7 ounces white chocolate, chopped
2 tablespoons raspberry sauce (above)

Garnish
2 cups fresh raspberries
2 cups fresh blackberries

   To make the Mascarpone caramel cream: In a small, heavy saucepan, combine the sugar and water. Place over low heat and stir to melt the sugar until the mixture starts to boil. Stop stirring and allow the mixture to boil until the sugar is golden; occasionally brush the inside of the pot with a wet pastry brush to prevent the sugar from crystallizing. Remove from heat and slowly stir in the ½ cup cream; be careful, as the caramel will bubble and spatter. Chill the caramel for 30 minutes.

Place the Mascarpone in a medium bowl and fold the caramel into it. Blend in the remaining cream and chill the mixture for at least 1 hour, or until ready to serve.

To make the berry sauces: Puree the raspberries in a blender or food processor. Strain the puree through a fine-meshed sieve. Stir in the sugar, lemon juice, and salt. Adjust the amount of sugar if necessary, and refrigerate until needed. Prepare the blackberry sauce in the same manner. Set aside.

To make the brittle: Line a baking sheet with parchment paper or waxed paper. In a double boiler over simmering water, melt the chocolate. Whisk the chocolate until smooth and pour it out onto the prepared pan. With an icing spatula or a rubber spatula, spread the chocolate in a rectangle about 10 by 14 inches. Place the raspberry sauce in a squeeze bottle and drizzle the sauce over the chocolate. With a skewer or a toothpick, swirl the raspberry sauce into the chocolate. Let the chocolate harden. Using a thin metal spatula or palette knife, loosen the brittle from the paper and carefully break it into 16 pieces.

To serve: Place a large dollop of the cream in the center of each dessert plate. Arrange some berries around the cream, and lace the plates with drizzles of the 2 sauces. Stand 2 pieces of the brittle in the caramel cream.

Mascarpone Caramel Cream with Berries and White Chocolate-Raspberry Brittle; *Emily Luchetti, Stars*

Maple Sugar Crème Caramel; *Melanie Coiro, Jasper's*

Maple Sugar Crème Caramel

Melanie Coiro
Jasper's
Boston, Massachusetts

Crème caramel takes on a New England flavor when both the caramel and custard are made with maple sugar. Lightly whipped cream and bittersweet chocolate shavings top it all off.

Serves 6

Maple Sugar Caramel
1 cup maple sugar (see Note)
½ cup water
1 tablespoon unsalted butter

Maple Sugar Custards
4 eggs
2 egg yolks
1 cup maple sugar (see Note)
2½ cups milk

Garnish
1 cup heavy (whipping) cream
Sugar to taste
Bittersweet chocolate shavings

To make the caramel: In a small saucepan, combine the sugar and water and bring to a boil over high heat. Reduce heat to medium and continue to cook for 5 to 10 minutes, or until the mixture coats a spoon. Remove from heat and stir in the butter until it is melted.

Ladle 3 tablespoons of caramel into the bottom of each of six 6-ounce ramekins or custard cups. Let cool and thicken.

To make the custards: Preheat the oven to 325°F. Line the bottom of a baking pan with a napkin. Place the ramekins or cups in the baking pan. (This will prevent the ramekins or cups from sliding.)

In a large bowl, combine all the custard ingredients and whisk together until the sugar is dissolved. Fill each ramekin or cup with custard. Pour hot water in the baking pan to come halfway up the sides of the custards. Cover the custards loosely with aluminum foil. Bake the custards for about 35 minutes, or until a toothpick inserted in the center of a custard comes out clean. Remove to a tray and chill thoroughly before serving.

To serve: In a deep bowl, beat the cream until slightly thickened and sweeten it lightly with sugar. Run a thin-bladed knife around the inside edge of each custard and invert and unmold it onto a dessert plate. Be sure to serve all the sauce from the bottom of the containers. Garnish each custard with a spoonful of cream and sprinkle with chocolate shavings.

Note: *If maple sugar is unavailable, place 2 cups granulated sugar and 1 tablespoon maple extract in a blender or food processor and blend together.*

MELANIE COIRO
Jasper's, Boston, Massachusetts

Pastry chef Melanie Coiro attributes her love of cooking to growing up in an Italian family. But she credits her sensible approach to desserts to a career that emphasized quality ingredients.

"I've greatly enhanced my understanding of classical cooking," Coiro says of her work at Jasper's in Boston. "The opportunity to use the freshest ingredients available from local producers has been especially rewarding. The high standards I've always set for myself are matched by the standards Jasper has set for the restaurant."

Coiro sets the start of her professional career in 1978, when she went to work at a collectively run vegetarian restaurant called Greenfield Street in Buffalo, New York. That evolved after a time into a job at a small-scale bakery called Yeast-West.

In 1984, she moved to Manhattan, but not to one of the big, high-profile restaurants. Coiro found employ in Soho, continuing her interest in natural foods by working at an alternative place called Arnold's Turtle. Three years later she moved to Boston, pursuing an expanded interest in classical cuisine.

Her first home was a bistro called Rebecca's, but the lure of fine dining wouldn't let her rest. When she settled into the kitchen with Jasper White as his sous-chef, she knew she had a lot to learn—and a lot to offer as well.

THOMAS WORHACH
The Ocean Grand, Palm Beach, Florida

Tom Worhach's position as executive pastry chef at the Ocean Grand in Palm Beach is his fourth job with the friend and colleague he admires most: executive chef Hubert Des Marais.

"When Hubert called me to discuss my joining him, it really didn't take very long for me to make my decision," Worhach remembers. "Not only would I again have the pleasure and inspiration of working with him, his description of the hotel and its owners' philosophy made the offer irresistible. Hubert's cuisine and mine complement each other very well—and I'm given carte blanche to be as imaginative as I wish."

That carte blanche has led Worhach to such creations as a ginger buttermilk wrap, which was featured in *Chocolatier* magazine, as well as a chocolate praline pecan tart, a passion fruit cheesecake, and a Key lime crème brûlée. These and other desserts, along with a diverse selection of gourmet breads, are featured daily at both of the Ocean Grand's food outlets: the Restaurant and the less formal Ocean Bistro.

Worhach started cooking at age ten, when he took up the task of feeding his brothers and sisters lunch after his mother returned to the business world. While studying at the Culinary Institute of America, Worhach so impressed Albert Kumin, a master of the pastry art and former pastry chef at the White House, he was invited to start teaching—even before he graduated.

On-the-job training consisted of pastry work at some of America's finest hotels, including Innisbrook in Tarpon Springs, Florida, the Hotel Bel-Air in Los Angeles, and the Mansion on Turtle Creek in Dallas, where he met his wife Malgorzata, then a new immigrant from Poland.

Prior to joining the Ocean Grand, Worhach was executive pastry chef for the Ritz-Carlton in Philadelphia. He had held the same post under Des Marais at the Ritz-Carlton in Houston from 1987 to 1989. The two had begun their professional association at Kiawah Island in South Carolina and teamed up again at Hawk's Cay Resort in the Florida Keys.

Though Worhach loves his work enough to justify twelve-hour days, he does indulge in a pair of what he dubs "calming hobbies." One is golf, and the other is playing the stock market, both presumably less demanding than the job of being a top-flight pastry chef.

Chocolate–Macadamia Nut Meringue with Tropical Fruit Cream

Thomas Worhach
The Ocean Grand
Palm Beach, Florida

This elaborate Caribbean dessert fantasy layers a chewy chocolate meringue with mango and guava creams, toffee crunch, ganache, and chocolate glaze. The garnish gilds the lily by adding a variety of sauces, sorbets, and fresh fruit.

Serves 12

Chocolate–Macadamia Nut Meringue
2 cups egg whites (about 8 to 10)
2 cups sugar
1 pound macadamia nuts, toasted (see page 236)
1 pound semisweet chocolate, chopped

Mango Cream
2 cups heavy (whipping) cream
2 mangos
3 tablespoons sugar
1 1/2 tablespoons (1 1/2 envelopes) plain gelatin
2 tablespoons water

Guava Cream
2 cups heavy (whipping) cream
3 guavas
3 tablespoons sugar
1 1/2 tablespoons (1 1/2 envelopes) plain gelatin
2 tablespoons water

Chocolate Ganache
2 pounds semisweet chocolate, chopped
4 cups heavy (whipping) cream
1/4 cup sugar

Chocolate Glaze
1 1/2 pounds semisweet chocolate, chopped
1 pound (4 sticks) unsalted butter
1/2 cup dark rum
1/4 cup light Karo syrup

Toffee Crunch

2 Heath candy bars

Chocolate Finish

6 ounces white chocolate, chopped
6 ounces milk chocolate, chopped

Garnish

Mango, blackberry, guava, and raspberry sauces (see Basics)
1 cup crème fraîche (see page 220)
1 quart passion fruit sorbet
1 quart raspberry sorbet
24 fresh raspberries
12 fresh strawberries, hulled
12 fresh plum wedges

To make the meringue: Heat the oven to 325°F. Lightly spray a 13-by-17-inch sided baking sheet with vegetable-oil spray and line it with parchment paper or waxed paper. In a large bowl, beat the egg whites until foamy, then gradually beat in 1 cup of the sugar until stiff peaks form. In a blender or food processor, grind the nuts with the remaining 1 cup sugar. Fold the two mixtures together and spread evenly in the prepared pan.

Bake for 25 to 30 minutes, or until golden brown. Let cool and remove from pan. In a double boiler over simmering water, melt the chocolate and spread evenly over the top of the meringue. Let the chocolate set, then cut the meringue into 3 lengthwise strips. Set aside.

To make the mango cream: Peel, pit, and coarsely chop 1 of the mangos and puree in a blender or food processor until smooth. Strain through a fine-meshed sieve and add 1 tablespoon of the sugar. In a deep bowl, whip the cream until stiff peaks form. Fold in the mango puree.

Peel, pit, and cut the remaining mango into ¼-inch dice. Toss the diced mango with the remaining 2 tablespoons sugar and let stand for 2 to 3 minutes until the sugar is dissolved. Fold into the cream. In a small saucepan, dissolve

Chocolate-Macadamia Nut Meringue with Tropical Fruit Cream;
Thomas Worhach, The Ocean Grand

the gelatin in the water, then heat just until dissolved. Let cool and fold into the cream. Refrigerate.

To make the guava cream: Peel, seed, and coarsely chop one of the guavas and puree in a blender or food processor until smooth. Strain through a fine-meshed sieve and add 1 tablespoon of the sugar. Follow the instructions for the mango cream, above, substituting guava puree and fresh guava.

To make the chocolate ganache: Combine all the ingredients in a medium saucepan. Bring to a boil over medium heat and cook, stirring constantly, until the chocolate is melted and the mixture is smooth. Let cool.

To make the chocolate glaze: In a double boiler over simmering water, combine all the ingredients and heat until the chocolate is melted. Stir to combine. Let cool.

To make the toffee crunch: Using a heavy chef's knife, coarsely chop the candy bars. Set aside.

To assemble the meringue: Place 1 strip of meringue on a baking sheet lined with parchment paper or waxed paper. Spread the mango cream over the layer and sprinkle with half the toffee crunch. Place a second layer of meringue on top, spread with the guava cream, and sprinkle the remaining toffee crunch on top. Place the third layer on top and cover with the ganache. Place in the refrigerator to chill until set, about 2 hours. Pour the glaze over the top. Don't worry if some runs down the sides, as the edges will be trimmed.

To make the chocolate finish: In a medium saucepan over simmering water, melt the white chocolate. In another medium saucepan over simmering water, melt the milk chocolate. Make alternate lines down the length of the meringue with the white chocolate and milk chocolate. Pull a knife through the chocolate across the width of the meringue in opposite directions, making a decorative design. Refrigerate for at least 1 hour.

To serve: Trim the edges, using a sharp thin-bladed knife. The piece will measure approximately 4 by 17 inches. Cut across the width into 12 alternating wedges about 1½ inches wide at the widest point. Place the sauces and crème fraîche in squeeze bottles.

For each dessert plate, make concentric circles of the sauces in the order in which they are listed. Highlight the sauces with a few circles of crème fraîche. Tilt and shake the plates, twirling to make a swirled design of the sauces. Stand 1 meringue wedge upright on the wide end on each plate. Place small scoops of the sorbets to one side and garnish with the fresh fruits.

White Pepper Ice Cream with Bananas

▪▪▪▪▪▪▪▪▪▪▪▪▪▪▪

Gene Bjorklund
Aubergine
Memphis, Tennessee

A lovely surprise: an ice cream seasoned with ground white pepper and served on a bed of orange-glazed bananas.

Serves 4 to 6

White Pepper Ice Cream
1 tablespoon freshly ground
    white pepper
1 cup milk
10 eggs
1½ cups sugar
¼ cup heavy (whipping) cream

Bananas
½ cup (1 stick) unsalted butter
1 cup sugar
1 cup fresh orange juice
4 to 6 small bananas

Garnish
4 to 6 fresh mint sprigs
Freshly cracked white pepper
    for sprinkling

To make the ice cream: Combine the pepper and milk in a small saucepan and bring to a boil over medium heat. In a large bowl, beat the eggs and sugar together until the mixture is thick, pale in color, and forms a slowly dissolving ribbon on its surface when dropped from a spoon. Slowly add the hot milk, being careful not to cook the eggs. Strain the mixture through a fine-meshed sieve to remove the pepper. Chill for 30 minutes, then add the cream

and freeze in an ice cream maker according to the manufacturer's directions.

To cook the bananas: In a large sauté pan or skillet over medium heat, melt the butter with the sugar and cook until the mixture turns a rich golden brown. Carefully pour in the orange juice (the caramel will bubble and spatter) and whisk until smooth. Peel and cut the bananas into ¼-inch-thick diagonal slices. Add the bananas to the boiling mixture, reduce heat, and cook for just 2 to 3 minutes, or until the bananas are coated and cooked.

To serve: Arrange the banana slices in a sunburst pattern in the bottom of 4 to 6 shallow soup bowls. Divide the sauce over the bananas, using all of it. Place a small scoop of the ice cream in the center of each. Decorate with mint sprigs and lightly sprinkle pepper over each serving.

White Pepper Ice Cream with Bananas; *Gene Bjorklund, Aubergine*

Chocolate Parfait

▪▪▪▪▪▪▪▪▪▪▪▪▪▪▪

Bruce Molzan
Ruggles Grill
Houston, Texas

Chocolate cake, layered with chocolate mousse and fresh berries, is drizzled with one or more sauces and garnished with additional berries in this elegant dessert.

Serves 8

Chocolate Cake

2 tablespoons unsalted butter at room temperature
1³/₄ cups plus 2 tablespoons unbleached all-purpose flour
2 cups granulated sugar
³/₄ cup unsweetened cocoa powder
2 teaspoons baking soda
1 teaspoon baking powder
1 teaspoon salt
1 cup brewed coffee
1 cup buttermilk
¹/₂ cup vegetable oil
2 eggs
1 teaspoon vanilla extract

Chocolate Mousse

11 ounces semisweet chocolate, chopped
6 tablespoons unsalted butter, melted
4 eggs, separated, at room temperature
2 cups heavy (whipping) cream)
2 tablespoons confectioners' sugar, sifted
1 teaspoon vanilla extract

For Assembly

³/₄ cup Chambord liqueur
2 cups fresh berries
1 cup each white and dark chocolate shavings (do not pack down)

Garnish

¹/₂ cup one or more sauces such as crème anglaise, raspberry, chocolate, or strawberry (see Basics)
8 Chocolate Triangles (recipe follows)
¹/₄ cup confectioners' sugar, sifted
Additional fresh berries

To make the chocolate cake: Preheat the oven to 350°F. Butter a 10-inch round springform pan and lightly dust

Chocolate Parfait; *Bruce Molzan, Ruggles Grill*

it with flour. Sift all the dry ingredients together into a large bowl. Add the coffee, buttermilk, and oil, and beat until combined. Continuing to beat, add the eggs, then the vanilla. Pour the batter into the prepared pan and bake for 25 to 30 minutes, or until a toothpick inserted in the center comes out clean. Remove from the pan and let cool.

To make the chocolate mousse: In a double boiler over simmering water, melt the chocolate. Stir in the melted butter. Mix in the egg yolks, stirring constantly to incorporate the yolks and to prevent them from scrambling. Remove from heat and let cool for 10 to 15 minutes. In a large bowl, beat the egg whites until stiff, glossy peaks form. Fold the whites into the chocolate while it is still warm. In a deep bowl, whip the cream to soft peaks, then blend in the sugar and vanilla. It is important not to overwhip this mixture. Fold the cream into the chocolate mixture and set aside.

To assemble the parfaits: Place eight 3-by-1¹/₂-inch pastry rings on a sided baking sheet lined with waxed paper or parchment paper. Cut additional paper into eight 12-by-4¹/₂-inch strips. Fold the strips into thirds lengthwise and place inside the molds to make collars extending 1¹/₂ inches above the rings. Using another 3-by-1¹/₂-inch pastry ring, cut 4 circles from the cake, then cut

each circle into 2 layers. Place 1 layer in the bottom of each ring. Drizzle each with 1 tablespoon of the Chambord. Arrange 1 layer of berries on top of each cake layer. Dice the remaining cake and place in a bowl. Drizzle with the remaining Chambord and let stand for a few minutes.

Scoop the mousse into the rings over the berries. Top each with some of the diced cake pieces. Sprinkle 1 heaping tablespoonful white chocolate shavings over each parfait. Repeat with the dark chocolate shavings. Refrigerate for at least 3 hours.

To serve: Remove the rings and paper from the parfaits. Drizzle the sauce(s) over and around the plates. Garnish each parfait with 1 chocolate triangle or a purchased wafer. Dust the plates with confectioners' sugar and garnish with the berries.

Chocolate Triangles: In a double boiler over simmering water, melt 6 ounces chopped bittersweet chocolate. Separately melt 2 ounces chopped white chocolate. Pour the bittersweet chocolate out on a baking sheet lined with waxed paper and spread thinly with a spatula. Drizzle with the white chocolate, using a toothpick to swirl the white chocolate into the dark. Let cool to harden, then break into triangles by hand.

Brioche Pain Perdu with Orange-Balsamic Syrup; *Allen Susser, Chef Allen's*

Brioche Pain Perdu with Orange-Balsamic Syrup
▼■▼■▼■▼■▼■▼■▼■▼■▼

Allen Susser
Chef Allen's
Miami Beach, Florida

Pain perdu is "lost," or stale, bread that has been saved by using it to make what Americans know as French toast. In this sublime dessert, which the chef adapted from his mother's recipe, the custard mixture is enlivened with fresh ginger, the syrup is a reduction of balsamic vinegar and orange juice, and the dish is garnished with mango and chocolate sorbets.

Serves 8

Orange-Balsamic Syrup
One 28-ounce (1¾ cups) bottle balsamic vinegar
4 cups fresh orange juice

Pain Perdu
Eight ¾-inch slices orange-flavored
   brioche loaf or challah
2 large eggs
1 cup milk
¼ cup vanilla extract
½ teaspoon ground cinnamon
½ teaspoon minced fresh ginger
Pinch of salt
6 tablespoons unsalted butter

Garnish
Candied orange zest (recipe follows)
Mango and chocolate sorbets (optional)

To make the syrup: In a medium saucepan over medium heat, combine the vinegar and juice and cook to reduce to 1½ cups, about 30 to 40 minutes. This can be made up to 2 weeks in advance and stored in an airtight jar in the refrigerator.

To make the pain perdu: Trim the crusts from the loaf, cut each slice in half on a diagonal, and let the slices set for 10 to 15 minutes. In a large shallow bowl, whisk together the eggs, milk, vanilla, cinnamon, fresh ginger, and salt. Place the bread slices in the milk mixture, turn to coat both sides, and allow them to absorb the liquid for 2 to 3 minutes.

In a large skillet, over medium heat, melt 2 tablespoons of the butter. When it foams, add as many bread slices as will fit comfortably in the pan. Brown until golden, turning once, a total of about 2 to 3 minutes per side. Remove with a slotted metal spatula, drain on a paper towel, and repeat with remaining butter and bread. Serve warm.

To serve: Place 2 pieces of pain perdu on each serving plate, overlapping them slightly. Sprinkle a little candied orange zest over each plate and add a small scoop of each sorbet. Drizzle the syrup over and around the bread toast.

Candied Orange Zest: Using a vegetable peeler, remove the zest from 8 scrubbed navel oranges; you should have about 1 cup. Trim the edges of each piece of zest and cut each piece into fine julienne. In a medium sauté pan or skillet over medium to high heat, combine ⅓ cup sugar and the zest, toss the mixture, shaking the pan constantly, until the sugar caramelizes onto the zest, about 5 to 7 minutes. Transfer to a tray to dry for about 3 to 4 hours. Store in an airtight jar. Makes 1 cup.

ALLEN SUSSER
Chef Allen's, Miami Beach, Florida

Allen Susser remembers the Brooklyn of his childhood as a place that loved "the celebration and warmth of food." Knowing his destiny when he saw it, Susser embraced a culinary career early on and has never wavered.

By 1976, he had cooked his way through the New York City Technical College Restaurant Management School at the top of his class, receiving the Ward Arbury Award. The years immediately after were spent absorbing classic French cooking and discipline, both at the Bristol Hotel in Paris and at Le Cirque in New York. This, he says, gave him "balance and respect for foods."

For all the wonders of these two great cities, Susser felt himself drawn to the warmth of Miami and what was then undiscovered culinary territory. As a chef at the elegant Turnberry Isle Resort, he began to explore the native foods of south Florida, combining fresh local fish with tropical fruits.

In 1986, Susser opened his own place, Chef Allen's. *Crisp, satisfying* and *refreshing* are some of the adjectives Susser uses to describe what he's about in the kitchen, where his cooking is defined as New World cuisine.

The Caribbean, Latin America, and the United States are all sources for Susser's pantry, which includes fruits such as mango, and star fruit, fish such as cobia, wahoo and pompano, Scotch bonnet chilies, saffron, vanilla, and rum.

In his spare time, Susser picked up another degree, with honors, at the Florida International University School of Hospitality Management, and stayed on to teach classes.

As first Miami and then the rest of the world began to appreciate this new cuisine, Susser built up his press scrapbook. Laudatory pieces came in from *Food & Wine*, which named him best new chef in America in 1991, and from *Time* magazine, which proclaimed his Florida cuisine "a New World marvel." In the *New York Times*, Bryan Miller called Susser "the Ponce de Leon of New Floridian Cooking."

Joining chefs around the country, Susser takes time to help feed the homeless and the homebound elderly. He chairs both SOS Taste of the Nation and the Miami branch of Meals on Wheels. As he puts it: "I love to cook. I make food my hobby, my profession, and my charity." For Allen Susser, all three begin at home.

KASPAR DONIER
Kaspar's, Seattle, Washington

Swiss-born and Swiss-trained chef Kaspar Donier first saw the city that would be the home of his future restaurant while he was living just across the border in Canada. After his arrival in North America in 1976, Donier worked at a series of jobs in Vancouver. When the timing felt right to open his own place, he knew he wanted to go to Seattle.

Donier and his wife Nancy have operated Kaspar's since May 1989, moving along the way from their original location to a spot at the heart of Seattle Center, near the opera, the symphony and the Coliseum. The chef has developed what he calls contemporary Pacific Northwest cuisine, blending the region's passion for the freshest seafood and produce with flavors from France, Asia, and the Southwest.

The chef-owner has received considerable recognition for his cooking, and is considered a standout among Pacific Northwest chefs. In addition to a scrapbook of "bests" from local media, Donier's handiwork has been featured in such diverse publications as *Gourmet*, *USA Today*, *Money* and the *New York Times*. National radio and television has also discovered him, including TV's Frugal Gourmet, Jeff Smith.

Born in Davos, Donier began his training at age sixteen as a chef apprentice at the Hilton Hotel in Zurich. In short order, he was pressed onward by his teachers to serve as *commis rôtisseur* at the five-star Suvretta House in St. Moritz and then as *commis garde manger* at the equally starred Beau Rivage in Lausanne.

Hilton brought Donier to Vancouver in 1976, launching him on a New World journey that took him to the Four Seasons in Vancouver and a sister property in Houston, the Inn on the Park, where he was promoted to his first executive chef's job in 1986. It was this position, in which he was responsible for all the hotel's outlets – including the four-star La Reserve – that turned his thoughts to owning his own restaurant.

When it came to choosing the location, Donier couldn't help remembering the Pacific Northwest. There was, in the end, little doubt as to where his heart belonged.

Earl Grey Sorbet with Fresh Berries

Kaspar Donier
Kaspar's
Seattle, Washington

Earl Grey tea, scented with oil of bergamot, makes a subtle and refreshing sorbet to serve with sugar-dusted fresh berries.

Serves 8

3³/₄ cups water
1¹/₂ cups granulated sugar
6 Earl Grey tea bags
Juice of 1 lemon

Garnish
4 cups fresh strawberries
4 cups fresh blackberries
4 cups fresh blueberries
8 fresh grape leaves
Sifted confectioners' sugar for dusting

In a large saucepan, combine the water and sugar and heat over high heat until the sugar has dissolved. Remove from heat and add the tea bags. Let steep at room temperature for 30 minutes, then remove the tea bags and refrigerate the syrup until it is well chilled, 1 hour or more. Add the lemon juice and freeze in an ice cream maker according to the manufacturer's directions. When the ice cream is frozen, remove it from the ice cream maker and place in an airtight container in the freezer to ripen for at least 1 hour or up to 24 hours before serving.

To prepare the garnish: Cut the strawberries into flowers by cutting off the stem end of each to form a flat surface. Stand the berries up on the cut end and use a paring knife to cut petals by cutting around the berry from the tip toward the stem end. Or, the berries may be cut in parallel slices from the tip toward the stem end and fanned out.

To serve: Place a row of strawberries down the center of each dessert plate. Arrange a row of blackberries and blueberries on either side of the strawberries. Place 1 grape leaf on the edge of the plate and add 2 small scoops of the sorbet. Dust confectioners' sugar over the berries and the plate and serve immediately.

Earl Grey Sorbet with Fresh Berries; *Kaspar Donier, Kaspar's*

Rum Banana and Maple Ice Cream Sandwich; *Michael Lomonaco, The '21' Club*

Rum Banana and Maple Ice Cream Sandwich

▼▲▼▲▼▲▼▲▼▲▼▲▼▲▼▲▼▲▼▲

Michael Lomonaco
The '21' Club
New York, New York

This interpretation of the ice cream sandwich is made with crisp butter cookies, maple ice cream, and bananas cooked in butter, brown sugar, and rum.

Serves 6 to 8

Maple Ice Cream
4 cups milk
1 vanilla bean, split lengthwise
12 egg yolks
1 cup sugar
1 cup maple syrup
1 cup (4 ounces) black or English
  walnuts, chopped

Cookies
1½ cups (3 sticks) unsalted butter
½ cup honey
¼ cup water
2¼ cups sugar
1 teaspoon ground cinnamon
Pinch of salt
¾ cup unbleached all-purpose flour

Rum Bananas
4 to 6 bananas
3 tablespoons unsalted butter
½ teaspoon ground cinnamon
½ cup packed brown sugar
¼ cup dark rum
1 cup (4 ounces) sliced almonds

Garnish
Chocolate sauce (see page 223)
Raspberry sauce (see page 224)

To make the ice cream: In a heavy, large pan, heat the milk and vanilla bean over low heat. In a large bowl, whisk together the egg yolks, sugar, and maple syrup. When the milk is hot, remove about ½ cup and whisk it into the egg mixture. Return this mixture to the hot milk and whisk until the mixture thick ens enough to coat a spoon; do not let the mixture boil. Remove from heat and cool over an ice water bath, or cover and refrigerate until chilled. Add the walnuts and freeze in an ice cream maker according to the manufacturer's instructions.

To make the cookies: In a medium saucepan, combine the butter, honey, water, sugar, cinnamon, and salt. Bring to a boil and simmer for 5 minutes. Whisk in the flour slowly, then reduce heat and cook for 5 more minutes to remove the raw flour taste. Let cool for 20 minutes, or until cool enough to handle but not too stiff. If the dough becomes too stiff, warm in a bowl placed over a warm water bath until it reaches spreading consistency.

Preheat the oven to 375°F. Line 2 baking sheets with parchment paper or aluminum foil and butter the paper or foil. Spoon 12 to 16 dollops of batter (2 tablespoons of batter per dollop) 4 inches apart on the prepared pans. Bake for 10 minutes. Use a metal spatula to remove the cookies from the sheet pans and let cool on a metal rack.

To make the bananas: Peel and cut the bananas into ¼-inch-thick diagonal slices. In a large sauté pan or skillet over medium heat, melt the butter and cook the bananas until they begin to soften. Add the cinnamon and brown sugar and continue cooking until the sugar melts. Remove the pan from the heat. Add the rum and warm it. Light the rum with a match and shake the pan until the flames subside. Add the almonds, lower heat, and cook for 1 minute.

To serve: Place the sauces in separate squeeze bottles. Place a small amount of syrup from the bananas on each dessert plate to hold the cookie. Place 1 cookie on top, add a scoop of ice cream, and cover with some of the rum bananas. Place another cookie on top and add an additional banana slice to the top. Drizzle the chocolate and raspberry sauces over the top of each cookie.

MICHAEL LOMONACO
The '21' Club, New York, New York

With his roots deep in Brooklyn, Michael Lomonaco began his career in a different field: He was a trained actor for eight full years. So for anyone who wonders if cooking isn't partly theater, Lomonaco is more qualified than most to answer. In the end, the kitchen became his stage, and the '21 Club' became his theater.

Lomonaco's entire training and career have taken place in New York City, where just about every cuisine can be accounted for on one street corner or another. After training at New York City Technical College's Department of Hotel and Restaurant Management, Lomonaco spent time in many of the kitchens that set the culinary pace throughout the 1980s. French and Swiss chefs proved to be the most formative, particularly Alain Sailhac and Daniel Boulud, under whom he worked at Le Cirque.

It was at the urging of Sailhac that Lomonaco moved with his mentor to the newly renovated '21' Club in 1987. After about a year, opportunity knocked and drew him away to work as executive sous-chef at Werner LeRoy's legendary Maxwell's Plum. But he couldn't stay away from '21' for long.

He credits the mystique of that former speakeasy, with its enduring ambience and loyal clientele, for luring him back. Being asked to serve as executive chef may have had something to do with it as well.

It wasn't long before Lomonaco's multi-ethnic cooking was being given credit for reviving '21,' by updating its grand tradition. The chef believes in what he's doing, whether he's creating new recipes, supervising his kitchen staff of thirty-four or checking out one of the eight hundred meals the restaurant serves each day. Michael Lomonaco may have started out as an actor, but his food is the real thing.

CAPRIAL PENCE
Westmoreland Bistro & Wines, Portland, Oregon

Working side by side with her husband John, Caprial Pence has enjoyed the national and even international limelight for several years now, first at Fullers in Seattle and now at their own place in Portland, the twenty-three-seat bistro called Westmoreland Bistro & Wines. As a woman chef and an eloquent spokesman for foods of the Pacific Northwest, Pence has come a long way since her days at the Culinary Institute of America.

It was at Fullers that Pence's talent found not only its true voice but its major recognition. Some of it was the good fortune of timing: Pacific Northwest cuisine was just coming into its own. Some of it was the good work of promotion: The Sheraton Seattle Hotel & Towers decided that publicizing its gourmet restaurant was a good way to toot its own horn. A lot of it, though, was simply Pence's personal charisma – and a confidence that expressed itself on each plate.

Pence was chef at Fullers from 1985 until the end of 1991, in the final years serving as co-chef with her husband. In 1988, she and two of her Fullers kitchen staff were flown to cook in the Soviet Union, the first Americans to take part in an exchange of chefs with that country. The word of mouth from that trip was so extraordinary that she was invited to Washington late in the same year to prepare a gala meal at the Soviet Embassy.

In 1989, Pence was off to Malaysia. This time, she and her staff flew in with Pacific Northwest ingredients to prepare a birthday dinner for seventy-five people for one of the leaders of that country.

All the attention and the chance for the couple to work on their own lured them to Portland in 1992. Together, they've parlayed their twenty-three bistro seats into an average of 105 meals served per day. And they get to sing the praises of their three hundred or so vintage wines.

Pence's fame has kept her in the media spotlight as well, drawing glowing reviews in the national media and being selected in 1990 as the James Beard Awards' Best Chef in the Northwest.

Two cookbooks have resulted from her work in the kitchen: *Caprial's Seasonal Kitchen* (Alaska Northwest Books) and *Caprial's Cafe Favorites* (Ten Speed Press). Along the way, she has acquired her own weekly cooking show on the Learning Channel.

Poached Pear and Plum Flan with Mango-Ginger Coulis

Caprial Pence
Westmoreland Bistro & Wines
Portland, Oregon

A shortbread crust and an almond paste filling are the base for this elegant flan of pears and plums, which is served with a sauce of fresh mango, rum, and ginger.

Serves 6

Shortbread Dough
2 cups unbleached all-purpose flour
½ cup confectioners' sugar, sifted
Pinch of salt
1 teaspoon vanilla extract
1 cup (2 sticks) unsalted butter at room temperature, divided into 4 pieces

Poached Pears
1 bottle Pinot Noir wine
2 cups granulated sugar
One 3-inch cinnamon stick
6 to 8 whole cloves
1 teaspoon ground nutmeg
8 Bosc pears, peeled but not cored

Almond Paste Filling
¼ cup slivered almonds
1 egg
1½ tablespoons unsalted butter
¼ cup almond paste
1 teaspoon almond extract

1 egg
1 egg yolk
¼ cup half-and-half
1 tablespoon granulated sugar
3 or 4 plums, depending on size

Mango-Ginger Coulis
3 ripe mangos
2 tablespoons dark rum
¼ cup granulated sugar
1 teaspoon minced peeled fresh ginger

Garnish
Sifted confectioners' sugar for dusting
12 fresh flowering borage sprigs or other edible flowers

To make the shortbread dough: Place the flour, confectioners' sugar, salt, and vanilla in a food processor and pulse 3 times. Add the butter one piece at a time and process just until a ball forms. Or, to make by hand, in a medium bowl, combine the flour, confectioners' sugar, and salt. Add the butter one piece at a time and, using a pastry cutter or 2 knives, cut the butter into the dry ingredients until the mixture resembles coarse cornmeal. Be careful not to overblend. (This dough freezes well; return to room temperature before using.)

Preheat the oven to 350°F. Spray a 6-by-12-inch rectangular tart pan with a removable bottom with vegetable-oil spray. Make 1-inch-thick ropes of the dough and press them around the sides of the tart pan. If the dough is too sticky to work with, chill it for a few minutes or dust some flour on your fingers. Press the remaining dough into the bottom of the pan, being careful to press it evenly, starting from the middle and working out to the edges. The dough should be about ¼-inch thick. Run your finger across the top edge of the tart pan to remove the excess dough. (Any trimmings can be baked into cookies.) Bake for 8 to 10 minutes, then let cool on a rack.

To poach the pears: In a medium saucepan, bring the wine, sugar, and spices to a boil. Add the pears and reduce heat to a simmer. Cook, turning occasionally, until tender when pierced with a knife, about 10 to 15 minutes. Let the pears cool in the liquid, then transfer to a nonaluminum container. Pour the liquid over, cover, and refrigerate overnight.

To make the almond paste filling: Place the almonds in a blender or food processor and grind into a fine meal. Add the egg and butter and process until incorporated. Add the almond paste and almond extract and process until combined.

To assemble the flan: In a small bowl, whisk together the egg, egg yolk, half-and-half, and sugar. Set aside. Remove the pears from the liquid and cut them in half lengthwise. Remove the core from each. Cut the halves into quarters, then cut each quarter into 3 or 4 lengthwise slices. The pears will be red on the outside and white on the inside. Cut the plums in half lengthwise and remove the pit.

Place the almond paste in the center of the cooled tart shell and spread it out toward the edges, being careful not to break the shell. Place the plums, cut-side up, randomly over the almond paste filling, slightly pressing them into the paste. Beginning on the outside edge, fill the tart with the poached pear slices, fitting the slices around the plums. It does not matter if gaps exist, as the egg mixture will fill in the spaces. Pour the egg mixture into the tart, being careful not to coat the fruit. Bake for 25 to 30 minutes, or until the custard is set. Let cool.

To make the mango-ginger coulis: Cut a slice from both ends of the mangos. Cut the flesh away from the pit in 4 lengthwise slices. Place each slice cut-side up and cut a ½-inch dice into the flesh down to the skin. Using a knife, scrape the flesh from the peel and place it in a blender or food processor. Add the rum, sugar, and ginger and puree until very smooth, scraping down the sides of the bowl once or twice while processing.

To serve: Using a serrated knife, cut the flan into three 6-inch squares. Cut each square diagonally into a triangle. Serve 1 wedge on each plate, and spoon 2 or 3 tablespoons of the mango-ginger coulis along one side. Dust the flan and each plate with confectioners' sugar and garnish with a flower.

Poached Pear and Plum Flan with Mango-Ginger Coulis; *Caprial Pence, Westmoreland Bistro & Wines*

Dusty Road Plum Soup with Roasted Plums and Plum Tart

Sanford D'Amato
Sanford
Milwaukee, Wisconsin

This American take on Scandinavian fruit soup takes its name and its inspiration from a Milwaukee ice cream dish, the dusty road sundae, which is topped with malt sugar.

Serves 6

Plum Ice Cream
Ice Cream Base (see page 220)
1½ pounds fresh plums, pitted and
 coarsely chopped
½ cup dry white wine
¾ cup granulated sugar

Plum Soup
¼ cup sliced fresh ginger
1 bay leaf
2 teaspoons whole peppercorns
1 teaspoon whole allspice
1 whole clove
One 3-inch piece cinnamon stick
⅛ teaspoon ground nutmeg

2 star anise pods
2 pounds plums, pitted and coarsely
 chopped
2½ cups dry white wine
½ cup granulated sugar

Roasted Plums
6 plums halved, pitted, and quartered
1 teaspoon ground cinnamon
1 tablespoon granulated sugar

Plum Tarts
½ cup (2½ ounces) hazelnuts, toasted
 and peeled (see page 236)
½ cup plus 1½ tablespoons unbleached
 all-purpose flour
4 tablespoons unsalted butter at room
 temperature
⅓ cup confectioners' sugar, sifted
1 egg yolk at room temperature
Pinch of ground cinnamon
Pinch of kosher salt
3 plums, pitted and cut into very
 thin slices

Garnish
½ cup heavy (whipping) cream
2 tablespoons confectioners' sugar, sifted
1 pint Plum Ice Cream, above
Malt sugar for dusting
Fresh mint leaves

To make the ice cream: Prepare the ice cream base. In a medium saucepan, combine the plums, wine, and sugar and bring to a boil. Reduce heat to medium and cook until plums are tender and most of the liquid has evaporated, 10 to 15 minutes. Puree the mixture and strain through a fine-meshed sieve. Let cool for 30 minutes. Add the plum puree to the chilled ice cream base and freeze in an ice cream maker according to the manufacturer's instructions.

To make the spice sachet: Cut a 6-inch square of cheesecloth and place the ginger, bay leaf, peppercorns, allspice, clove, cinnamon, nutmeg, and star anise in the center. Tie into a bag with white cotton string and leave one string about 12 inches long.

To make the soup: In a medium nonaluminum saucepan, combine the plums, wine, sugar, and spice sachet and bring to a boil. Lower the heat as much as possible and simmer, stirring occasionally, until the mixture is reduced to a soft sauce, about 2 hours. You will have about 4 cups of soup. Puree the mixture in a blender, press through a fine-meshed strainer, cover, and chill until ready to use.

Dusty Road Plum Soup with Roasted Plums and Plum Tart; *Sanford D'Amato, Sanford*

To make the roasted plums: Preheat the oven to 275°F. Line a baking sheet with parchment paper or aluminum foil and place the plums on the sheet skin-side up. Combine the cinnamon and sugar and reserve 2 tablespoons. Sprinkle the remainder over the plums and bake them for about 2 hours, or until the pieces are tender and caramelized but still hold their shape.

To make the plum tarts: Preheat the oven to 400°F. Line a baking sheet with parchment paper or butter it. In a blender or food processor, grind the hazelnuts with the 1½ tablespoons flour for about 15 seconds. Blend in the ½ cup and 1½ tablespoons flour and remove the mixture to a small bowl. Process the butter and sugar until smooth, 5 to 10 seconds. Add the egg yolk and blend again for 5 seconds. Add the hazelnut mixture and pulse 4 times, just until mixed; do not overprocess the dough.

Remove the dough to a lightly floured work surface and gather it together with your fingers. Press it into a log shape and divide it into six 2-inch balls. Place each ball between 2 sheets of plastic wrap and roll into a ¼-inch thick circle. Remove one of the sheets of plastic and cut the dough into six 3½-inch circles. Invert each circle onto the prepared pan. Using ½ plum for each, spiral slices of the plum on top of each tart, then sprinkle lightly with 1 teaspoon of the reserved cinnamon sugar. Bake the tarts until the bottoms are lightly browned, 6 to 8 minutes.

To serve: In a deep bowl, whip the cream with the confectioners' sugar until stiff peaks form. Spoon the whipped cream into a pastry bag fitted with a large star tip. Ladle about ⅔ cup of soup into each of 6 shallow soup bowls. Arrange some of the roasted plums, skin-side down, around the edges. Pipe a rosette of whipped cream into the center of each serving and top with one of the plum tarts. Place scoops of ice cream between the roasted plums, dust with malt sugar, and garnish with a mint leaf.

SANFORD D'AMATO
Sanford, Milwaukee, Wisconsin

Sanford D'Amato traveled from his hometown of Milwaukee to attend the Culinary Institute of America. And throughout the 1970s, it looked as though the East Coast had claimed him as one of its own.

Finally, his ties to the Midwest grew stronger, and he dared return to a city that had named its baseball team after beermakers, that considered sausage and cheese its finest food products, and that knew little about the wonders of New York restaurants.

More than fifteen years of growth, plus a lot of hard work by D'Amato, have changed Milwaukee's definition of fine dining. And the chef, who started his mission at John Byron's Restaurant before opening his own place called Sanford in late 1989, is glad he decided to come home.

"Being in Milwaukee affects the restaurant a lot," says D'Amato, who runs the kitchen while his wife Angie manages the dining room. "Even though we're in the city, we have a top end for what we can charge. We're always looking at value. Nobody considers us cheap, but people consider us good value." D'Amato smiles. "I saw a listing of the Top 30 check averages around the country. Our checks are thirty-five dollars below No. 30."

The financial dynamics of running a fine restaurant in Milwaukee requires the chef and the manager to stay close to their business. The revenues generated just don't justify layers of managers, or a chef to do the cooking while D'Amato tours the dining room in clean, crisp whites.

This is all right with D'Amato, who considers the restaurant, on the site of his father's and his grandfather's grocery store, too special to be left to hired hands.

"I have the utmost confidence in the people I have in the kitchen and Angie's people in the front of the house," he says. "But if you're not there, all of a sudden it becomes somebody else's restaurant. People have different ideas of how it should be. No one is going to handle a situation the same way you do."

Since his stint at John Byron's (during which *Food & Wine* magazine named him one of 1985's Hot New Chefs), D'Amato has witnessed considerable growth in Milwaukee's dining sophistication. Whereas in the beginning diners were impressed by strange ingredients, now they're more likely to assess what he does with those ingredients.

Apple and Pecan Gratin with Macerated Fruits in Citrus-Honey Consommé

▮▮▮▮▮▮▮▮▮▮▮▮▮▮▮▮

Hubert Keller
Fleur de Lys
San Francisco, California

Dessert-lovers who delight in the combination of flavors, textures, and temperatures will adore these warm little apple-nut cakes served with chilled fruits.

Serves 4

Citrus-Honey Consommé
2 cups fresh orange juice
1 1/2 cups fresh grapefruit juice
1/4 cup fresh lemon juice
2 tablespoons minced fresh ginger
1/3 cup honey
1/4 cup rum

Macerated Fruits
1 cup green grapes
1/2 cup sliced kumquats
1 cup blueberries
1/2 cup orange segments
1 banana, cut into 1/2-inch-thick diagonal slices
1 star fruit, cut into thin slices
Citrus-Honey Consommé, above

Apple and Pecan Gratin
4 tablespoons unsalted butter at room temperature
1/4 cup sugar
1/4 cup pecans, ground
1 egg white
2 Granny Smith apples
1 tablespoon lemon juice

Topping
1/4 cup heavy (whipping) cream
1 1/2 teaspoons ground cinnamon
1 egg yolk, beaten
4 fresh raspberries

8 large fresh mint leaves, cut into fine julienne, for garnish

To make the citrus and honey consommé: Combine all the ingredients in a medium nonaluminum saucepan and bring the mixture to a rapid boil. Turn off the heat.

To make macerated fruits: Combine all the fruits in a large bowl and pour the hot consommé over. Refrigerate for at least 1 hour.

To make the apple and pecan gratin: Place the butter in a small bowl and stir until it is creamy. Add the sugar and pecans and stir together, then mix in the egg white. Refrigerate this mixture for about 30 minutes, or until it firms up.

Preheat the oven to 375°F. Line a baking sheet with parchment paper or aluminum foil. Peel and core the apples. Using a mandoline or a V-slicer, cut the apples into fine julienne. If the apples have a lot of moisture, squeeze them with your hands to remove some of it. Toss the apples with the lemon juice, then mix the pecan mixture into the apples. Place four 2-inch ring molds on the prepared pan. Fill the rings with the apple mixture, pressing the mixture in tightly. (It is not necessary to butter the rings because of the amount of butter in the mixture.) Carefully lift off the rings.

In a deep bowl, whip the cream until soft peaks form. Fold in the cinnamon and egg yolk. Dollop a spoonful of this mixture on top of each cake. Place 1 raspberry in the center of each. Bake for 10 minutes, or until the glaze turns a golden brown.

To serve: Ladle some of the chilled macerated fruits and consommé into each of 4 shallow soup bowls. Be careful to equally distribute the fruits around the edge, leaving space in the center. Place a warm gratin in the center of each dish and sprinkle the julienned mint around it.

Apple and Pecan Gratin with Macerated Fruits in Citrus-Honey Consommé;
Hubert Keller, Fleur de Lys

Mascarpone-Fig Tart

▼▪▼▪▼▪▼▪▼▪▼▪▼▪▼▪▼▪

Jody Adams
Michela's
Cambridge, Massachusetts

This dessert is redolent with Mediterranean flavors: The hazelnut crust is filled with a mixture of figs, orange juice, and Mascarpone cheese, and toasted hazelnuts.

Makes one 9-inch tart; serves 6 to 8

Hazelnut Crust

1 cup unbleached all-purpose flour
1/2 cup (2 1/2 ounces) hazelnuts, toasted, peeled, and finely chopped (see page 236)
2 tablespoons sugar
1/4 teaspoon salt
1/2 cup (1 stick) cold unsalted butter, cut into small pieces

Fig Filling

8 ounces Kalamata figs, stemmed and cut into quarters
Grated or minced zest of 1 blood orange or regular orange
3 large eggs
1 egg yolk
1 tablespoon flour
3/4 cup Mascarpone cheese at room temperature
Juice of 1 lemon

1/2 cup granulated sugar
Pinch of salt
1/2 cup (2 1/2 ounces) hazelnuts, toasted, peeled, and coarsely chopped (see page 236)

Optional Garnishes

Sifted confectioners' sugar
1/3 cup apricot jam
1/4 cup water

To make the crust: Preheat the oven to 350°F. In a food processor, combine the flour, hazelnuts, sugar, and salt. Process the dry mixture to combine, then add the butter and again process until the mixture comes together. Or, to make the dough by hand, in a medium bowl, combine the flour, hazelnuts, sugar and salt, add the butter and, using a pastry cutter or 2 knives, cut the butter into the dry ingredients until the mixture resembles coarse cornmeal. (Because there is no water added to this crust, it takes longer to blend the ingredients.) Remove the dough from the processor or bowl and pull it together by hand. (Wear plastic gloves to keep the dough from sticking to your hands.)

Press the dough into a 9-inch springform pan. The dough should cover the bottom of the pan and come up about 1 inch on the sides. Place the pan in the freezer for 30 minutes to firm up the dough. Bake the dough for 10 minutes, then remove from the oven and push the

dough down again. Reduce the oven temperature to 325°F and return the crust to the oven for another 10 minutes, or until crisp. Let cool.

To make the filling: Place the figs in a small saucepan and add the orange zest and juice. Cover, place over medium heat, and cook for 8 to 12 minutes, or until the figs have absorbed the juice. Let cool.

Preheat the oven to 400°F. In a medium bowl, combine the eggs, egg yolk, flour, Mascarpone cheese, lemon juice, sugar, and salt and whisk the mixture together until the sugar dissolves. Arrange the cooled figs over the top of the crust. Sprinkle the chopped hazelnuts over the figs, then pour in the cheese mixture. Bake for 10 minutes, then reduce the oven temperature to 350°F and continue to bake for 20 to 30 minutes, or until the custard is set. Let cool.

To serve: Dust the tart with confectioners' sugar. Or, place the apricot jam in a saucepan with the water and melt over low heat. Strain through a fine-meshed sieve and brush the glaze over the tart.

Note: *Dried figs may be substituted for the fresh figs. Increase the amount of orange juice to 1/2 cup.*

Mascarpone-Fig Tart; *Jody Adams, Michela's*

PATRICK O'CONNELL

The Inn at Little Washington, Washington, Virginia

Patrick O'Connell entered the restaurant world through one of its many back doors. As a student of speech and drama at Catholic University in Washington, O'Connell dreamed of being an actor. Through his subsistence work as a waiter, however, he discovered that the stage had nothing on the emotional frenzy of feeding people for a living.

To O'Connell, who now performs at the Inn at Little Washington sixty-seven miles from the the nation's capital, the business is nothing short of living theater.

O'Connell likes to call himself a self-taught cook and compared to most of his peers, he is. There was, however, a high-school stint as a short-order cook in his hometown of Clinton, Maryland, plus those college years of waiting on tables. Mostly, though, it's a case of an artist creating magic.

As proof of O'Connell's magic touch, the Inn has only sixty-five tables but has received upwards of three thousand requests for reservations on a single Saturday night.

"This is a team of the artist and the businessman," says partner Reinhardt Lynch. "You can ask Patrick what somebody ate a year ago, and he'll be able to tell you in great detail. Ask him how much business we did a year ago and he doesn't have a clue."

The partners met in "big" Washington, where O'Connell was studying drama and Lynch had come as a conscientious objector to work in a hospital after graduating from Indiana University. Two years after meeting, O'Connell and Lynch bought a 100-acre farm bordering Virginia's Shenandoah National Park, supporting themselves by running a catering business.

A six-year search led them to a building that had served as a gas station, dance hall, stage, and basketball court. They opened the Inn there on a fast track indeed. That first weekend in January 1978, they served seventy diners with only one part-time kitchen helper. The second weekend, a Washington restaurant critic came calling – and proclaimed the place the best eatery within 150 miles of the city.

Since that strange and wondrous opening, the Inn at Little Washington has grown to fifty-five employees, and the net worth of its owners has jumped from their five-thousand-dollar investment to something over $3 million.

Rhubarb Pizza

■▼■▼■▼■▼■▼■▼■▼■▼■▼■

Patrick O'Connell
The Inn at Little Washington
Washington, Virginia

A free-wheeling American version of the humble Neapolitan pizza tops the crust with two forms of cooked rhubarb and a reduced rhubarb syrup, then finishes the hot dessert off with a scoop of ginger ice cream.

Serves 6

Ginger Ice Cream
Ice Cream Base (see page 220)
1/2 cup minced peeled ginger
1/4 cup granulated sugar
1 tablespoon minced lemon zest (optional)

Rhubarb Mush
Six 3/4-inch-thick rhubarb stalks, coarsely chopped
1/2 cup sugar
1 cup water

Blanched Rhubarb
2 cups water
1 cup sugar
Six 3/4-inch-thick rhubarb stalks, cut into 1/8-inch-thick diagonal slices

8 ounces pizza dough

Garnish
3 tablespoons sugar
1 tablespoon ground cinnamon
6 scoops Ginger Ice Cream, above

To make the ice cream: Prepare the ice cream base. In a small sauté pan or skillet over medium heat, cook the ginger and sugar until the sugar has melted and the mixture has caramelized slightly, 8 to 10 minutes. Watch carefully, as the mixture can burn easily. Remove from the stove and let cool for 30 minutes. Add the caramelized ginger to the chilled ice cream base. If desired, add lemon zest. Freeze in an ice cream maker according to the manufacturer's instructions.

To make the rhubarb mush: Place the rhubarb in a heavy, medium sauté pan or skillet. Add the sugar and water and cook over medium-low heat until the rhubarb disintegrates and the mixture is a thick saucelike consistency, 12 to 15 minutes. Let cool.

To make the blanched rhubarb and syrup: In a medium saucepan, combine the water and sugar and bring to a boil. Add the sliced rhubarb and immediately remove from heat. Let the rhubarb cool in the liquid. Using a slotted spoon, remove the rhubarb to a bowl. Place the liquid over high heat and cook to reduce to a syrupy consistency, 10 to 15 minutes. Set aside and keep warm.

Preheat the oven to 425°F. Grease 2 baking sheets. Divide the pizza dough into 6 balls and roll each one into a 6-inch-diameter round. Place them on the prepared pan. Spread the rhubarb "mush" over the dough, leaving a 1/2-inch margin. Arrange the sliced rhubarb over the sauce to create a flower design, leaving the 1/2-inch margin. The pizzas can be assembled several hours ahead of time and refrigerated; allow to come to room temperature for 30 minutes before baking. Bake on the floor or bottom shelf of the oven for 6 to 7 minutes, or until the crust is golden. Remove from the oven and brush the rhubarb syrup over the pizzas, including the crust.

To serve: Combine the sugar and cinnamon and dust the plates with the mixture. Place a pizza in the center of each and place a scoop of ice cream in the center of each.

Rhubarb Pizza; *Patrick O'Connell, The Inn at Little Washington*

Sweet Dim Sum Box

▼▪▼▪▼▪▼▪▼▪▼▪▼▪▼▪▼

Gale E. O'Malley
Hilton Hawaiian Village
Honolulu, Hawaii

This elaborate South Seas dessert sampler was created for President and Mrs. George Bush during one of their visits to Hawaii, where it was spectacularly presented in a bamboo steamer over dry ice.

Serves 4

Marzipan and Azuki Bean Paste Egg Rolls
8 ounces marzipan
1/2 cup azuki bean paste
   (available in Asian markets)

Candied Kumquat Pot Stickers
Four 2-inch circles puff pastry
4 candied kumquats (available in
   Asian markets)

Prune Wontons
Oil for deep-frying
4 wonton skins
4 tablespoons prune puree

Papaya and Mango Beggar's Purses
1/2 cup 1/4-inch-diced papaya
1/4 cup mango puree
2 tablespoons cake or cookie crumbs
Four 6-inch egg roll skins

Cream Puffs with Orange Filling
Four 2-inch cream puffs (see page 225)
1/2 cup heavy (whipping) cream
1 tablespoon orange concentrate
1/2 tablespoon (1/2 envelope)
   plain gelatin
1 tablespoon water
3/4 cup plain fondant
Red paste food coloring

Phyllo Tartlets
3 phyllo dough sheets
1/2 cup fresh bread crumbs
6 tablespoons unsalted butter, melted

Pistachio Sauce
1 cup crème anglaise (see page 220)
3 tablespoons pistachio paste

Garnish
1 1/2 tablespoons confectioners' sugar,
   sifted
1/2 cup blackberry sauce (see page 224)
1/2 cup chocolate sauce (see page 223)

4 small scoops Green Tea Ice Cream
   (see page 192)
Pastillage fans or wafer triangles
   (optional)
2 cups dry ice chips (optional)

To make the marzipan and azuki bean paste egg rolls: Preheat the broiler. Divide the marzipan in half and roll between 2 sheets of waxed paper into 2 strips, each 1 1/2 inches wide and 8 inches long. Fill a pastry bag fitted with a plain 1/2-inch tip with the azuki bean paste. Pipe a 1/2-inch strip of paste lengthwise along each strip. Roll up lengthwise into a long slender strip and cut into 3-inch-long pieces. Decoratively score the tops of each on the diagonal, making a ropelike effect. Place on a baking pan close under the broiler for a few seconds, or until lightly browned.

To make the candied kumquat pot stickers: Preheat the oven to 375°F. Gently roll the puff pastry rounds on a lightly floured board. Place a kumquat on each, centered on one half of the circle. Fold the dough over, press together, and use a 2-inch round cutter to trim the excess dough. Bake for 10 to 15 minutes, or until puffed and golden brown.

To make the prune wontons: Pour oil to a depth of 2 inches in a heavy pot or skillet. Heat to 375°F, or until almost smoking. Meanwhile, lay out the wonton skins and place 1 tablespoon prune puree in the center of each. Fold up 2 opposing corners toward each other, but do not press them together. Grasp the other 2 opposing corners in your fingers and twist them, clockwise, around the 2 standing corners. Twist until the filling is enclosed and the packet holds its shape, and then turn back the points of each corner like a petal.

Fry the wontons, turning frequently, until golden and crisp, 4 to 5 minutes. Using a slotted spoon, remove from the oil and drain on paper towels. Reserve the oil.

To make the papaya and mango beggar's purses: In a small bowl, combine the diced papaya, mango puree, and cake or

Sweet Dim Sum Box; *Gale E. O'Malley, Hilton Hawaiian Village*

cookie crumbs. Lay out the egg roll skins and place about 2 tablespoons of the papaya mixture in the center of each. Pull up the edges, gathering at the top, and tie each gently with an 8-inch piece of white string. Reheat the wonton oil to 375°F, or until almost smoking. Fry the purses in the hot oil, turning frequently, until golden and crisp, 4 to 5 minutes. Using a slotted spoon, remove from the oil and drain on paper towels.

To make the cream puffs: In a deep bowl, whip the cream until stiff peaks form. Fold in the orange concentrate. In a small saucepan, combine the gelatin and water. Heat over low heat until the gelatin is dissolved. Let cool, then fold into the cream mixture. Place the mixture in a pastry bag fitted with a small tip. Make a small X in the bottom of each cream puff and fill the puffs with the cream mixture. Refrigerate until chilled.

In a double boiler over simmering water, heat the fondant until it is liquid enough to coat. Insert a skewer in the bottom of a cream puff and dip the puff into the fondant to coat it. Remove and place on a baking sheet lined with parchment paper or waxed paper to dry. Repeat with the remaining cream puffs. Place 1 dot of paste food coloring on top of each, in the center. Refrigerate.

To make the phyllo tartlets: Preheat the oven to 375°F. Place 1 sheet of the phyllo dough on a sheet of parchment paper or waxed paper. Sprinkle lightly with some of the bread crumbs and drizzle 2 tablespoons of the butter over using a pastry brush. Repeat with another sheet, then place the final sheet on top. Brush the top with the final 2 tablespoons of butter. Using a 3-inch round cutter, cut out 8 circles. Press the circles into eight 2-inch fluted shell tins. Bake 10 to 12 minutes, or until golden and crisp. Let cool.

To make pistachio sauce: In a small bowl, whisk together the crème anglaise and pistachio paste. Set aside.

To serve: Preheat the oven to 350°F and reheat the pot stickers, beggar's purses, and wontons for 6 to 8 minutes.

GALE E. O'MALLEY
Hilton Hawaiian Village, Honolulu, Hawaii

For nearly ten years, Gale O'Malley enjoyed one of the best seats in the house. He looked out on Central Park – and got to serve his creations to luminaries from the farflung corners of the globe – as executive pastry chef at the Plaza Hotel in New York.

Like the artist Gauguin and thousands of others before him, however, O'Malley heard the song of the South Seas; and like many a diner faced with his dessert collection, he simply couldn't resist.

Not the shrinking violet that some in the pastry kitchen can be, O'Malley has spent the past decade not just making dessert at the Hilton Hawaiian Village and seeing that his staff adheres to the highest standards; he has also gone a long way toward winning a leadership position among the chefs born on the islands.

In 1995, he was nominated by the Honolulu chapter of the Chefs de Cuisine Association of Hawaii as the American Culinary Federation's Western Regional Chef of the Year. Success within the ACF is no small matter to O'Malley, as he's been active in the professional organization since long before he left the winters of New York City for the eternal summer of Hawaii.

O'Malley has picked up many honors during his career. The most important came when he became the youngest, and indeed the first American-born, pastry chef to receive the Medal of the French Government Grand Prize for Pastry in 1981. This is considered to be the most prestigious award given to a chef in the United States.

Dust the beggar's purses with confectioners' sugar. Place the sauces in squeeze bottles. Divide the serving plates down the center with an elongated S of chocolate sauce. Fill one side with blackberry sauce and the other with pistachio sauce. Place 1 beggar's purse in the center of each plate, then alternate the pot stickers and wontons around the plate. Place the green tea ice cream in the phyllo shells at the last moment.

To duplicate the chef's presentation, top the ice cream with a pastillage fan or wafer. Place 1/2 cup of the dry ice chips in the bottom of each of 4 lacquer boxes (handle the dry ice chips with small tongs; do not touch them with your fingers). Add a small amount of hot water. Place a small bamboo steamer on top of each box and place the plated dessert in the steamer. The hot water will activate the dry ice and steam will pour out.

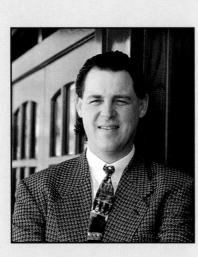

RICHARD CHAMBERLAIN
Chamberlain's Prime Chop House, Dallas, Texas

Richard Chamberlain's career has been a journey through some of the finest gourmet restaurants in north Texas, and along the way he has achieved an expertise in cooking steak than can only be described as rare.

Chamberlain's Prime Chop House, in Addison just outside Dallas, was named one of the country's Top 10 new restaurants by *Bon Appétit* magazine in 1993. The place was the first venture for Prime Steak Ltd., a company for which Chamberlain serves as vice-president and corporate chef.

After high school, Chamberlain embarked on his culinary career by picking up formal training at El Centro College in Dallas while serving an apprenticeship at the renowned Mansion on Turtle Creek.

Unlike those chefs who travel far and wide, Chamberlain has stuck pretty much to the west. He put in three years as executive chef at the Little Nell Hotel in Aspen, where he attracted wide attention for pioneering something dubbed American alpine cooking as well as a Regional Best Chef nomination from the James Beard Foundation. Writeups on his mountain-inspired food appeared in such high-profile publications as *Connoisseur*, *Ski*, *Destinations*, *Food & Wine*, and *Esquire*.

From 1986 to 1989, Chamberlain served as executive chef for San Simeon Restaurant in Dallas, where his refinements on American regional cuisine earned him a spot as one of *Food & Wine's* Rising Stars to Watch. In addition, Chamberlain worked as executive chef at Ratcliff's in Dallas, as executive sous-chef at the Hotel Bel-Air in Los Angeles and as executive sous-chef under Dean Fearing at his critically acclaimed Agnew's.

Bread Pudding

Richard Chamberlain
Chamberlain's Prime Chop House
Dallas, Texas

This old-fashioned bread pudding with Jack Daniel's whiskey has an up-to-date garnish of edible flowers, confectioners' sugar, and vanilla ice cream.

Serves 6

3 tablespoons unsalted butter at room temperature
4 eggs
³/₄ cup granulated sugar
1 cup half-and-half
¼ teaspoon ground cinnamon
½ cup raisins
½ cup (2½ ounces) pecans, chopped
1 teaspoon vanilla extract
¼ cup Jack Daniel's whiskey
3 cups ½-inch-cubed day-old bread trimmed of crusts

Garnish
Fresh mint sprigs
Edible flowers such as pansies
Sifted confectioners' sugar for dusting
6 small scoops vanilla ice cream

Preheat the oven to 350°F. Select six 3-inch ramekins or similar baking dishes. Generously butter the ramekins or dishes. In a large bowl, combine all the ingredients except the bread cubes and garnish and whisk until the sugar is dissolved. Add the bread cubes and let them soak for about 5 minutes, then ladle the mixture into the prepared rame-kins or dishes, mounding the tops. Bake for 20 to 30 minutes, or until golden, puffed, and firm to the touch. Let cool slightly.

To serve: Set each ramekin on a serving plate. Garnish around the ramekins or dishes with mint sprigs and flowers. Dust confectioners' sugar over the top of each pudding and place 1 scoop of ice cream on top of each.

Brutti Ma Buoni

▼■▼■▼■▼■▼■▼■▼■

Lidia Bastianich
Felidia
New York, New York

Brutti ma buoni—"ugly but good"—describes these unevenly shaped but marvelously chewy hazelnut cookies.

Makes 18 to 20 cookies

4 egg whites
1 cup (5 ounces) hazelnuts, toasted, peeled, and finely chopped (see page 236)
1 cup confectioners' sugar, sifted, plus confectioners' sugar for dusting
¹/₄ teaspoon ground cinnamon

Preheat the oven to 400°F. Line 2 baking sheets with parchment paper or heavy brown paper. In a large bowl, beat the egg whites until stiff peaks form. In a heavy, medium saucepan, combine the hazelnuts, 1 cup confectioners' sugar, and cinnamon. Mix in the egg whites. Place the mixture over medium heat and cook, stirring constantly, until the mixture pulls away from the sides of the pan and is a light golden brown, about 15 minutes.

Using 2 teaspoons, scoop out the mixture and place rough mounds 3 inches apart on the prepared pans. Bake for 10 to 15 minutes, then transfer the cookies and the paper to wire racks and let cool. The cookies will harden during cooling.

To serve: Dust the cookies with confectioners' sugar.

Bread Pudding; *Richard Chamberlain, Chamberlain's Prime Chop House*

Brutti Ma Buoni; *Lidia Bastianich, Felidia*

Dentelle Croustillante;
Daniel Bonnot, Chez Daniel

Dentelle Croustillante

▼■▼■▼■▼■▼■▼■▼■▼■▼■▼■▼■

Daniel Bonnot
Chez Daniel
New Orleans, Louisiana

The name means "lacy cookie," but it only partly describes these chocolate wafers, which are filled with pistachio cream and served in a sea of chocolate sauce.

Serves 6

Chocolate Cookies

¹/₂ cup granulated sugar
¹/₂ cup firmly packed brown sugar
1 cup unsweetened cocoa powder
6 tablespoons unsalted butter at room temperature
1 cup plus 1¹/₂ tablespoons unbleached all-purpose flour
¹/₂ cup fresh orange juice
2 tablespoons dark rum

Pistachio Cream

2 cups heavy (whipping) cream
1 tablespoon confectioners' sugar, sifted
3 rounded tablespoons pistachio paste

Chocolate ganache (see page 200)

Garnish

8 fresh strawberries, cut into fans
3 tablespoons pistachio nuts, chopped
18 fresh mint leaves, cut into shreds
4 fresh mint sprigs
Sifted confectioners' sugar for dusting

To make the chocolate cookies: Preheat the oven to 375°F. In a large bowl, combine the granulated and brown sugars. Add the cocoa and butter and beat together vigorously with a wooden spoon for 1 to 2 minutes. Add the 1 cup flour and stir in. The batter will be stiff. Add the orange juice and rum and mix until smooth.

Dust a baking sheet with the 1¹/₂ tablespoons flour. Alternating the dollops of batter so that 12 will fit on the pan with at least 3 inches of space between them, spoon about 2 tablespoons of batter per dollop onto the pan. Using a rubber spatula, spread each dollop out to a 3¹/₂-inch circle. Bake for 10 minutes. Let cool completely, then cut a circle out of each cookie with a 3-inch ring mold or cookie cutter.

To make the pistachio cream: In a deep bowl, whip the cream with the sugar until soft peaks begin to form. Add the pistachio paste and beat for 1 or 2 minutes, or until stiff peaks form. Transfer the cream to a pastry bag fitted with a ¹/₂-inch star tip and refrigerate.

To serve: Spoon chocolate ganache in the center of each of 6 dessert plates and place a chocolate cookie in the center of each. Pipe rosettes of the pistachio cream over the cookie. Top with another cookie and pipe cream on top. Garnish each plate with 2 fanned strawberries. Sprinkle the pistachios and shredded mint around each plate. Garnish with mint sprigs and dust the plates with confectioners' sugar.

Alsatian Sour Cream Coffee Cake; *Jean-Luc Albin, Maurice French Pastries*

Alsatian Sour Cream Coffee Cake

▪▪▪▪▪▪▪▪▪▪▪▪▪▪

Jean-Luc Albin
Maurice French Pastries
New Orleans, Louisiana

The recipe for this traditional sour cream coffee cake, made with blueberries and almonds, can be varied by chocolate chips, raisins, dried fruit, or cranberries and grated orange zest.

Serves 8 to 10

³/₄ cup (1¹/₂ sticks) plus 2 tablespoons
   unsalted butter at room temperature
2¹/₂ cups granulated sugar
3 eggs
1 teaspoon vanilla extract
Pinch of salt
1 teaspoon baking powder
2 cups cake flour
1 cup (8 ounces) sour cream
2 tablespoons kirsch
1 cup fresh blueberries
³/₄ cup (3 ounces) sliced blanched
   almonds, lightly toasted
   (see page 236)
¹/₂ cup packed brown sugar
Sifted confectioners' sugar for dusting

   Preheat the oven to 325°F. Spray a 10-inch bundt pan or angel food cake pan with vegetable-oil spray. Using an electric mixer, cream together the butter and granulated sugar. When the mixture is smooth, beat in the eggs, one at a time. Add the vanilla and salt. Mix the baking powder and flour together, then add this mixture to the bowl. Stop the mixer and scrape down the sides. Continue to mix, adding the sour cream and kirsch.

   Remove the bowl from the mixer and fold in the blueberries. Spoon the batter into the pan and smooth the top. Sprinkle the almonds over the top and press the brown sugar through a sieve with the back of a spoon to cover the top of the cake evenly. Bake for 1¹/₂ hours, or until a toothpick inserted in the center comes out dry.

   To serve: Unmold the cake onto a serving platter and generously dust the top with confectioners' sugar. Cut into wedges.

JEAN-LUC ALBIN
Maurice French Pastries, New Orleans, Louisiana

   The world of food has carried Jean-Luc Albin from France to America by way of Bermuda and through a series of jobs in large operations and small. Some might be surprised to find the former hotel food and beverage director now running a bakery in a suburb of New Orleans—but not Albin himself.

   To be the owner, not just the employee: That was burned into his heart as a goal since his youth in Briançon in the French Alps. Albin's father was a talented chef, and the boy was barely fifteen when he decided to follow in his dad's footsteps. He worked in small resort hotels in the south of France, signed on as a three-year apprentice in Marseilles as soon as he was old enough, then got a job in a classical kitchen.

   Albin credits the legendary chef Alexandre Chabert, and the time spent with him at Tain L'Hermitage, with helping him turn a youthful experience into career commitment. A mere six months later, Albin was ready to head for Paris, and not just to the City of Light but to the Georges V Hotel, where he remained for five years.

   Those years at one of the world's most famous properties served as the resumé that would make possible much of what happened next. Albin made it as far west as Bermuda to serve as chef at the Southampton Princess, then on to Atlanta to take a job at the Omni International. He was only twenty-six when Fairmont brought him to New Orleans as executive chef, eventually promoting him to director of food and beverage.

   Albin later moved on to the Fairmont in Dallas, also as food and beverage director, then on to Los Angeles as executive assistant to the chairman of Filmland Corporate Center, headquarters for MGM/UA Studios. Before long, he was that company's chief of operations and building manager, as well as overseeing Five-Star Catering Company as general manager and vice-president.

   What lured Albin back to New Orleans was the chance to serve as food and beverage director at the Windsor Court Hotel, the city's most highly rated property. But what kept him in town, with his wife Marlene, his son Jean-Henri and his daughter Lilli Margaux, was the chance to buy Maurice French Pastries.

   Not only could he now excel at producing the best pastries he knew how to make; he could have the satisfaction of being the master of his own destiny. And for Jean-Luc Albin, that was a sweet treat indeed.

JOHN CALUDA
Coffee Cottage, New Orleans, Louisiana

John Caluda's life has always been a quest for excellence, as his sixth-degree black belt in karate proves. In his culinary life, that quest has led him not far away but into the heart of the place he knows best.

"I always liked this little spot on Metairie Road," he says of his chosen location in a quiet residential section just outside New Orleans. "I'd looked at it before. So when it became available, I decided to take it and open the Coffee Cottage.

"This is what I always wanted to do: open a pastry shop in my old neighborhood—one that would make fresh pastries daily for people who appreciate quality pastries."

In opening his shop, Caluda created one of the New Orleans area's most popular coffee stops as well as a business that supplies fine pastries to some of the best hotels and restaurants in town.

The Culinary Institute of America struck Caluda as a good place to start on the road to his own business. He graduated from the Hyde Park, New York, program in 1983. The next year he was back home in New Orleans, running the Beignet Cafe at the World's Fair.

A series of chef jobs followed the fair, with an increasing specialization in pastry. Caluda worked under pastry chef Jeffrey Brooks at the Royal Sonesta in the French Quarter, followed Brooks to the Hotel Iberville (now the Westin Canal Place), then signed on at the Royal Orleans. It was there that Chef Kevin Graham promoted Caluda to running the pastry kitchen.

A two-year adventure in owning and operating a Sweet Basil's Italian outlet took Caluda and his wife to Panama City, Florida, but when their first child was born the urge to go home got the better of them. The dream of Coffee Cottage and the little location Caluda remembered so well came into focus, and Caluda shifted into full speed ahead.

This former hotel chef has many skills that go unused while cooking breakfast, lunch, and dinner at his coffeehouse. But all his haute cusine talents have been steps along the way to serving simple foods at his very own counter.

Tiramisù

John Caluda
Coffee Cottage
New Orleans, Louisiana

Tiramisù ("pick me up") is so named because of the caffeine in the espresso and cocoa in this popular Italian dessert. This version is rolled like a bûche de Noël and coated with Mascarpone cream.

Serves 6 to 8

Cake
2 tablespoons unsalted butter, melted
10 large egg yolks
1½ cups sugar, plus sugar for sprinkling
¾ cup unbleached all-purpose flour, sifted
1 tablespoon vanilla extract
8 large egg whites
⅛ teaspoon salt
⅛ teaspoon cream of tartar

Mascarpone Cream
2 cups heavy (whipping) cream
3 egg yolks
½ cup sugar
8 ounces Mascarpone cheese at room temperature

Coffee Syrup
1½ cups brewed espresso or dark French roast coffee
1 cup sugar
2 tablespoons Myers's rum
3 tablespoons Kahlúa liqueur

Garnish
½ cup unsweetened cocoa powder
1 cup chocolate sauce (see page 223)

To make the cake: Preheat the oven to 400°F. Line a 13-by-17-inch sided baking sheet with parchment paper or waxed paper and brush it with the melted butter. In a large bowl, combine the egg yolks with 1 cup of the sugar. Place over simmering water and beat until the mixture is pale in color and doubled in volume, 5 to 6 minutes. Add the flour to the yolks and mix in quickly, then add the vanilla and set aside.

In a large bowl, beat the egg whites until foamy. Gradually beat in the remaining 1/2 cup sugar, then the salt and cream of tartar, until stiff, glossy peaks form. Fold the egg whites into the yolk mixture and spread the batter in the prepared pan. Bake for 8 to 10 minutes, or until a toothpick inserted in the center comes out clean. Let cool.

Sprinkle the top of the cake with sugar, then invert onto a sheet of parchment paper or waxed paper.

To make the Mascarpone cream: In a deep large bowl, whip the cream until stiff peaks form. In a double boiler over simmering water, whisk the egg yolks and sugar until pale in color and thick, 3 to 4 minutes. Add the cheese and continue to whisk until the mixture is smooth. Let cool, then fold the egg yolk mixture into the whipped cream. Refrigerate until chilled.

To make the coffee syrup: In a small saucepan, combine the coffee and sugar and heat over low heat until the sugar dissolves. Let cool to room temperature, then add the rum and Kahlúa.

To assemble the tiramisù: Soak the sponge with about 1 1/2 cups of the coffee syrup. Reserve the remaining coffee syrup. Reserve about 3/4 cup of the Mascarpone cream and spread the remaining cream on the soaked sponge. Smooth the surface, going all the way to the edges. Using the parchment or waxed paper to lift and roll the cake, roll the cake tightly lengthwise into a log. Transfer the log, seam-side down, to a pan and refrigerate for 6 to 8 hours.

To serve: Unwrap the chilled log and brush it with the remaining coffee syrup. Spread the outside with the remaining Mascarpone cream and dust well with the cocoa. Cut into 2-inch-thick slices. Place the chocolate sauce in a squeeze bottle. Place 1 slice of tiramisù on each dessert plate and drizzle the plates with chocolate sauce.

Tiramisù; *John Caluda, Coffee Cottage*

Key Lime Pie; *John Caluda, Coffee Cottage*

Key Lime Pie

John Caluda
Coffee Cottage
New Orleans, Louisiana

Authentic Key lime pie is made with the juice of the mellow Key lime, which is now available in bottles. This classic recipe can be garnished two ways.

Makes one 10-inch pie; serves 8 to 10

Crust
4 tablespoons unsalted butter, melted
2 cups crushed graham crackers or
   chocolate cookie crumbs
½ teaspoon ground cinnamon

Filling
3 eggs
2 egg yolks
1 cup Key lime juice, preferably Nellie
   and Joe's brand
6 tablespoons hot water
2 envelopes unflavored gelatin
Two 14-ounce cans sweetened
   condensed milk

Garnish
1 cup heavy (whipping) cream
2 tablespoons confectioners' sugar,
   sifted
1 tablespoon Grand Marnier
Graham or chocolate crumbs
   for sprinkling
Thin lime wedges

To make the crust: Preheat the oven to 350°F. Brush the sides and bottom of a 10-inch springform pan with some of the melted butter. Place the crumbs and cinnamon in a blender or food processor and, with the machine running, drizzle in the remaining butter until the mixture begins to hold together. Press the crumb crust into the bottom of the springform pan. Bake for about 10 minutes, or until set. Set aside to cool. Leave the oven on.

To make the filling: In a small bowl, dissolve the gelatin in the hot water and stir. Combine the eggs and egg yolks in the bowl of an electric mixer. Whisk the eggs in the bowl over simmering water until they are lukewarm, then continue to beat with an electric mixer at high speed until they are thick, pale, and doubled in volume, about 3 to 4 minutes.

In a small saucepan, warm half of the lime juice. Add 2 tablespoons of the warm lime juice to the gelatin and stir until the gelatin is completely dissolved. Combine the gelatin mixture with the remaining juice. Add the condensed milk to the beaten eggs, then add the gelatin mixture. Pour into the cooled shell and bake for 15 minutes. Refrigerate overnight.

To garnish: In a deep bowl, whip the cream with the confectioners' sugar until stiff peaks form. Fold in the Grand Marnier. Pipe rosettes of cream around the edge of the pie and garnish with crumbs and lime wedges.

Tequila Pie: To garnish the pie, substitute tequila for the Grand Marnier in the whipped cream. Set aside. In a small saucepan, melt ½ cup apricot or apple jelly and brush on top of pie. Sprinkle the pie with crystallized sugar. Garnish with thin lime wedges and serve the whipped cream on the side.

Frozen Soufflés Under a Chocolate Dome

John Caluda
Coffee Cottage
New Orleans, Louisiana

In this spectacular presentation, scoops of frozen soufflés in three different flavors with three different sauces are hidden under chocolate domes that have been dusted with real gold. For a simpler dessert, forego the domes and just garnish the soufflés with fresh berries.

Serves 8

Basic Frozen Soufflé Mixture
(Makes 1 soufflé with one of the
   following flavors; repeat 3 times to
   make 3 soufflés.)

2 cups heavy (whipping) cream
3 eggs, separated
¾ cup sugar

Flavorings
¼ cup green crème de menthe with
   2 ounces white chocolate, melted
¼ cup Grand Marnier and Orange Zest
   Powder (see page 80)
¼ cup grated dried coconut, ½ cup
   praline paste, and 1/4 cup dark rum

Chocolate Domes
2 pounds good-quality semisweet
   coating chocolate, chopped
8 Mexican balloons (see Note)
2 ounces milk chocolate, chopped
1 ounce white chocolate, chopped

Garnish
8 fresh strawberries
Gold dust (see Note), optional
Caramel, mango, and chocolate sauces
   (see Basics)

To make the soufflés: In a deep bowl, whisk the cream until firm but not stiff peaks form. Place the egg yolks and sugar in the bowl of an electric mixer. Place the bowl over simmering water and whisk until the mixture is lukewarm. Beat the mixture at high speed until doubled in volume. Blend the crème de menthe and melted white chocolate into the whipped cream. Gently fold whipped cream into the egg yolk mixture. Pour into a 6-cup bowl and freeze. Repeat to make and freeze a second soufflé, flavoring it with Grand Marnier and orange zest powder. Repeat again to make and freeze a third soufflé, flavoring it with coconut, praline paste, and rum.

To make the domes: In a double boiler over simmering water, melt the 2 pounds chocolate and stir until cool to the touch but still liquid. Blow up the balloons until they are the proper size to make a dome that will cover the soufflés and sit on the serving plates to be used. Tie a knot in the top to hold the air.

Dip a balloon into the chocolate to a depth necessary to achieve the diameter needed. Tip it to evenly coat up the sides if necessary. The coating should reach about 3 to 4 inches up the sides of the balloon. Lift the coated balloon from the chocolate and let the chocolate drain for a second, then turn it right-side up and let the excess chocolate run down toward the base. Turn the balloon constantly to build up the thickness around the base of the dome. Your goal is to make chocolate shells thin enough to break with a spoon, but thick and firm enough to hold up while the dessert is being served. When the chocolate is thick enough, place the balloon knot-end down in a container that will hold it without touching the dome. Chill or freeze for about 5 minutes, or until the chocolate is completely firm.

Remove the balloons when the chocolate is hardened and place them on a piece of waxed paper. Hold the knot between 2 fingers, pierce a balloon with a knife, and slowly release the air. The balloon may stick at the base, but it can be easily pulled loose. If a small hole develops in the dome, repair it with additional melted chocolate. If the dome crumples as the balloon deflates, the side wall may not have been coated thickly enough. Repeat to make the remaining domes.

In a separate small saucepan, melt the milk and white chocolates over simmering water. Place each melted chocolate in a small pastry bag with a fine writing tip. Turn the domes over and drizzle lines of both chocolates over them. Lightly dust each dome with the gold dust. Place the domes in the freezer until ready to serve.

To serve: Place about 2 tablespoons of each sauce on each dessert plate, spreading the pools out slightly. Place 1 scoop of the crème de menthe soufflé on each pool of chocolate sauce, 1 scoop of Grand Marnier soufflé on each pool of caramel sauce, and 1 scoop of coconut-rum soufflé on each pool of mango sauce. Garnish the center of each soufflé with a strawberry and place a dome over each plate.

Variations: Substitute one or both of the following flavorings for one or two of the above flavorings: 2 tablespoons white crème de menthe mixed with 2 tablespoons crème de cacao, or ½ cup chocolate chips.

Note: *Mexican balloons seem to hold up best to the heat of the chocolate in this process, and are used by many chefs. Check party supply stores and departments, looking for balloon packages that say "made in Mexico." Gold dust for decorating food may be obtained from Albert Uster Imports, 1-800-231-8154.*

Frozen Soufflés Under a Chocolate Dome; *John Caluda, Coffee Cottage*

Chocolate Tart;
Maurice Delechelle, Croissant d'Or

Chocolate Tart

Maurice Delechelle
Croissant d'Or
New Orleans, Louisiana

Chocolate-lovers will rejoice in this rich
tart, which is gilded with caramelized
confectioners' sugar and topped with
a luxurious chocolate sauce.

Makes one 9-inch tart; serves 6 to 8

Tart Shell
1 cup (2 sticks) unsalted butter at room
  temperature
$\frac{1}{2}$ cup confectioners' sugar, sifted
1 egg
1 egg yolk
$\frac{1}{2}$ cup ($2\frac{1}{2}$ ounces) pecans, finely
  chopped
1 cup unbleached all-purpose flour

Chocolate Filling
2 cups milk
1 tablespoon plus 1 teaspoon unsalted
  butter
8 ounces semisweet chocolate, chopped
1 egg

Chocolate Sauce
1 cup heavy (whipping) cream
$\frac{1}{4}$ cup hazelnut paste
2 ounces semisweet chocolate, chopped
6 tablespoons confectioners' sugar,
  sifted, for dusting

To make the tart shell: Combine
the butter and confectioners' sugar in
the bowl of an electric mixer. Cream
together, then add the egg and egg yolk
and beat until mixed. Add the pecans
and flour and beat to mix. Form the
dough into 2 equal balls. Wrap and chill
1 ball of dough for 2 hours. Freeze the
second ball of dough for later use.

Preheat the oven to 375°F. Divide the
chilled dough in half and roll it out on
a well-floured board. Roll up the circle
of dough onto the rolling pin and transfer it to a 9-inch tart pan with a removable bottom. Press the dough into the
pan carefully, then roll the pin across
the top of the pan to remove excess
dough. Press the dough into the pan
around the edges. Bake for 15 minutes
or until very lightly browned and crisp.
Let cool. Leave the oven on.

To make the chocolate filling: In a medium saucepan, combine the milk, butter,
and chocolate and cook over medium
heat, stirring constantly, just until the
chocolate is melted. Let cool slightly,
then whisk in the egg. Ladle the mixture
into the cooled shell. Bake in the 375°F
oven for 12 to 15 minutes, or until set.

To make the chocolate sauce: In
a medium saucepan, combine all the
ingredients. Place over medium heat,
bring the mixture to a boil, and whisk
until smooth and somewhat thick, about
10 minutes. Let cool, then transfer to
a paper cone or a squeeze bottle
for piping.

To serve: Preheat the broiler. Dust the
top of the tart with the confectioners'
sugar and place 2 inches from the heat
for about 10 seconds, or until the sugar
is melted and lightly browned. Cut the
tart in 6 or 8 pieces. Place 1 slice on
each serving plate and pipe or drizzle
the chocolate sauce over and around.

Lemon Chess Pie

Jeffrey Buben
Vidalia
Washington, D.C.

Here's a down-home southern favorite
dressed up in its Sunday best, complete
with strawberry puree, fanned strawberries, and whipped cream.

Lemon Chess Pie; *Jeffrey Buben, Vidalia*

2 cups granulated sugar

6 eggs

2 tablespoons fine cornmeal

1 teaspoon vanilla extract

1 tablespoon distilled white vinegar

¼ cup fresh lemon juice

⅔ cup (1⅓ sticks) unsalted butter, melted

1 baked 9-inch pie shell (see page 226), cooled

Strawberry Puree

2 cups fresh strawberries, hulled and sliced

½ cup simple syrup (see page 227)

Garnish

2 cups heavy (whipping) cream

¼ cup confectioners' sugar, sifted

8 fresh strawberries

8 fresh mint sprigs

Preheat the oven to 350°F. In a large bowl, combine the sugar, eggs, and cornmeal and whisk until the sugar dissolves. Add the vanilla, vinegar, and lemon juice and whisk the mixture while gradually adding the butter. Pour the mixture into the pie shell, filling it as full as possible. Bake for 25 minutes, or until golden and set. Let cool.

To make the strawberry puree: In a medium bowl, combine the strawberries and simple syrup and let sit at room temperature for 1 hour. Puree the mixture in a blender or food processor and strain through a fine-meshed sieve.

To serve: In a deep bowl, whip the cream with 1 tablespoon of the confectioners' sugar, then transfer the mixture to a pastry bag fitted with a star tip. Make lengthwise slices through the strawberries not quite all way to the stem end, and fan them out. Cut the pie into 8 wedges. Place a wedge on each dessert plate. Ladle some strawberry puree onto each plate, decorate each with some of the whipped cream, and garnish with the fresh mint and a dusting of the remaining 3 tablespoons confectioners' sugar.

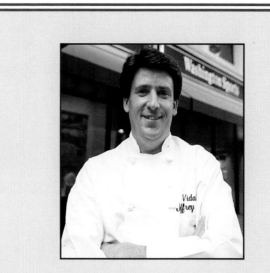

JEFFREY BUBEN
Vidalia, Washington, D.C.

When Jeffrey Buben and his wife Sallie opened their restaurant in Washington's chic West End, they called it Vidalia because they liked the sound of the word. Yet Buben's "provincial American" cuisine is also as many-layered as the sweet Georgia onion.

Since opening at Dupont Circle in 1993, amid a rejuvenated swirl of shops, galleries and street life, Vidalia has been providing uncomplicated, enjoyable, and moderately priced food.

Buben tries to celebrate all of America in his cooking, but admits to a special emphasis on the Mid-Atlantic region, especially when it comes to the freshest local seafood and vegetables. Oysters, crabs, and rockfish from nearby Chesapeake Bay are special picks from Buben's menu, right along with farm-raised lamb, veal and turkey from Virginia.

A graduate of the Culinary Institute of America, the chef has worked in some of New York City's finest kitchens, including Sign of the Dove, Le Cygne, Le Chantilly, and the Hotel Pierre. The French influence remained for a time after Buben relocated to Washington, cooking in Aux Beaux Champs in the Four Seasons Hotel and at La Bagatelle.

Slowly, however, for the chef as for the nation, the lure of American cuisine took over. Buben developed the award-winning concept for Nicholas, the restaurant in the Mayflower Hotel, and spent six years as executive chef for the critically acclaimed Occidental Restaurant and Grill.

When Buben opened Vidalia, he realized that his wife was good at everything most chefs are not; so he invited her to join him at the office. Sallie Buben has a degree in business administration, plus experience in personnel recruitment and computer software marketing. Between them, they cover all the bases and keep peeling away layers of the great American onion

MAURICE DELECHELLE
Croissant d'Or, New Orleans, Louisiana

Maurice Delechelle is hardly the best-known chef in New Orleans. Yet his pastries have delighted thousands of diners since he came to New Orleans in 1972, and inspired dozens of chefs from around the world to take the meal's sweet course more seriously. A practitioner of the French art of *pâtisserie*, Delechelle has taught his skills to a new generation of bakers.

Delechelle grew up in a farming family in the Loire Valley. His father died when he was very young, forcing the family to give up the farm and seek a livelihood in the food business.

Delechelle's three-year apprenticeship, from age fourteen to seventeen, took place in the city of Tours. He spent years on the Riviera, in Paris, and in the Atlantic resort of Biarritz before being lured to the New World. He spent a season on British Antigua and five years on French Guadaloupe, then headed for New Orleans.

For most of this work history, Delechelle's specialty was pastry — an interest sparked by a neighborhood baker and also by his own sweet tooth. In New Orleans, he applied his skills first at the ritzy Plimsoll Club, then in Cincinnati as executive chef at the Pierre, before returning to New Orleans for good.

Finding his spiritual home, not surprisingly, in the villagelike French Quarter, Delechelle over the years successfully launched not one but two *pâtisseries*. The first was La Marquise in 1972, the second Croissant d'Or in 1983. Together, they are dedicated to producing one of the highest forms of cooking art.

Like all the best *pâtissiers*, Delechelle uses only the freshest and highest-quality ingredients. Of course, he is a master of technique as well. French pastry is a demanding art; only a true zealot can make it a lifelong pursuit. In Delechelle's case, every exquisite taste of his pastries proves that his zeal was not misplaced.

Charlotte aux Fruits

Maurice Delechelle
Croissant d'Or
New Orleans, Louisiana

This traditional French dessert draws its fresh flavor from strawberries, peaches, and kiwi fruits, all coated with an apricot glaze.

Serves 8 to 10

Sponge Cake and Ladyfingers
8 egg whites
1 1/2 cups granulated sugar
10 egg yolks
2 teaspoons vanilla extract
3/4 cup unbleached all-purpose flour, sifted
Sifted confectioners' sugar for dusting

Filling
4 egg yolks
1/2 cup granulated sugar
2 cups milk
1 1/2 tablespoons (1 1/2 envelopes) plain gelatin
1 tablespoon vanilla extract
2 cups heavy (whipping) cream
8 ounces cream cheese at room temperature
Juice of 1/2 lemon

1 cup simple syrup (see page 227)
24 to 30 fresh strawberries
2 fresh peaches, peeled, pitted, and cut into thin slices
4 fresh kiwi fruits, peeled and cut into thin slices
1 cup apricot jam, melted and strained

To make the sponge cake and ladyfingers: Preheat the oven to 375°F. Line 2 baking sheets with parchment paper or grease them. In a large bowl, beat the egg whites until foamy. Gradually beat in 1/2 cup of the sugar until stiff, glossy peaks form. In a medium bowl, beat the egg yolks with the remaining 1 cup sugar until pale in color and fluffy. Fold the egg yolk mixture into the beaten whites. Fold in the vanilla and mix into the batter, then gradually fold in the flour.

Charlotte aux Fruits; *Maurice Delechelle, Croissant d'Or*

Place a 10-inch stainless-steel ring mold on one of the prepared baking sheets and fill it with half the batter. Bake for 20 minutes, or until a toothpick inserted in the center comes out clean. Let cool in the pan for 10 minutes, then unmold and let cool completely on a wire rack. Place the remaining batter in a pastry bag fitted with a 1-inch tip. Pipe 3-inch-long lady fingers on the other prepared pan. Generously dust confectioners' sugar over the tops of the ladyfingers and bake for 12 to 15 minutes, or until golden brown. Let cool on the pan.

To make the filling: In a medium bowl, beat the egg yolks and sugar until the mixture forms a slowly dissolving ribbon on its surface when dropped from a beater or whisk. In a medium saucepan, bring the milk to a boil. Whisk a small amount of the hot milk into the egg yolks, then add the yolk mixture to the milk and whisk until the mixture thickens enough to coat a spoon, 7 to 8 minutes. Remove from heat and whisk in the gelatin until it is completely dissolved. Mix in the vanilla. Pour the mixture into a large bowl, cover, and refrigerate for at least 1 hour.

In a deep bowl, whip the cream until stiff peaks form. Fold the cream cheese into the cream, blending well. Blend in the lemon juice. Fold the whipped mixture into the chilled custard, cover, and refrigerate until needed.

To assemble the cake: Cut the cooled sponge cake into 3 layers. Place 1 layer on a 12-inch cardboard round on a baking sheet. Brush the layer with simple syrup, then spread with a layer of the cream filling. Place a second layer on top and again brush with syrup and spread with filling. Place the third layer on top and brush with syrup, then cover the entire charlotte with cream. With the back of a knife, score the cream to divide the cake into 12 sections.

Hull and halve all but 1 of the strawberries. Arrange the strawberries in overlapping rows in 4 opposing sections to form a spoke pattern. Arrange 4 rows of overlapping kiwi slices next to each section of strawberries. Fan the peach slices between the strawberries and kiwi. Place 1 whole strawberry in the center. Glaze the fruits with the warm apricot glaze. Stand the cooled ladyfingers around the cake, pressing them in gently so they stick to the sides. They will extend over the top, creating a border. Chill the charlotte for at least 2 hours, or until set.

Apple Tart

Pat Coston
Aqua
San Francisco, California

Three kinds of caramel–the syrup from the cooked apple wedges used for a filling, and light and dark caramels for garnish–glorify this tart, which is further fancified with vanilla ice cream and julienned raw apple.

Serves 4

Tart Dough
2 cups unbleached all-purpose flour
3/4 cup sugar
Pinch of salt
3/4 cup (1 1/2 sticks) plus 2 tablespoons cold unsalted butter, cut into pieces
1 egg

Apple Filling
4 cups sugar
Juice of 1 lemon
3 tablespoons unsalted butter
One 3-inch piece cinnamon stick
1 vanilla bean, split lengthwise
4 Granny Smith apples, peeled, cored, and cut into 10 wedges each

Light Caramel
1 cup sugar
2 tablespoons plus 1/4 cup water
1/2 teaspoon fresh lemon juice

Dark Caramel
1 cup sugar
2 tablespoon water
1/2 teaspoon fresh lemon juice
1/2 cup heavy (whipping) cream

Garnish
Four 2-inch slices of sponge cake or pound cake
Vanilla ice cream
Twelve 3-inch pieces of julienned apple
4 spun sugar spirals (see page 228), optional
4 fresh mint sprigs

To make the tart dough: Preheat the oven to 350°F. In the bowl of a food processor or a heavy-duty electric mixer fitted with a paddle, combine the flour, sugar, and salt. Mix on low speed, adding the butter in 3 parts, until the mixture resembles coarse meal. Add the egg and mix for 30 seconds. Or, to make the dough by hand, cut the butter into the dry ingredients with a pastry cutter or 2 knives, then mix in the egg. On a lightly floured board, knead the dough for 2 to 3 minutes, or until smooth. Cover with plastic wrap and let sit for 30 minutes.

Preheat the oven to 375°F. On a lightly floured board roll the dough out and cut four 7-inch circles. Press the circles into four 5-inch tart pans (preferably with removable bottoms), and run the rolling pin over the top of each to remove the excess dough. Place a circle of aluminum foil in each pan and fill with dried beans or pie weights. Bake for 10 minutes. Remove the beans or weights and foil, reduce the oven temperature to 350°F, and bake for another 3 to 5 minutes, or until golden brown. Set aside and let cool.

To make the filling: In a heavy, medium saucepan, combine the sugar, lemon juice, butter, cinnamon stick, and pulp

Apple Tart; *Pat Coston, Aqua*

from the vanilla bean. Cook over high heat, stirring frequently, until the mixture turns a light golden brown. Constantly stir the caramel until it is smoking, then add the apples and cook for 2 to 3 minutes. The apple wedges will puff up. Remove from the heat and drain. Cover and refrigerate the apples, reserving the caramel. Remove the cinnamon stick. Chill the apples and caramel.

To make the light caramel: In a small, heavy saucepan, combine the sugar, 2 tablespoons of the water, and lemon juice. Cook over high heat, stirring frequently, until the sugar turns amber in color. Add the ¼ cup water (the mixture will sizzle). Let cool. Return to a boil and cook for 1 or 2 minutes, or until the sugar is dissolved.

To make the dark caramel: In a small, heavy saucepan, combine the sugar, water, and lemon juice. Cook over medium-high heat, stirring frequently, until the mixture turns a deep golden brown. Add the cream, return to a boil, and cook for 1 to 2 minutes. Let cool.

To assemble the tarts: Preheat the oven to 375°F. Arrange 10 apple wedges in each tart shell. Spoon 3 to 4 tablespoons of the sauce from the cooked apples over each tart. Bake for 2 to 3 minutes, or until warmed throughout.

To serve: Remove the tarts from the pans. Place 1 tart in the center of each serving plate. Spoon alternate pools of the light and dark caramel sauces around each tart. Place a thin circle of cake on top of each tart to absorb the melting ice cream, and place 1 scoop of ice cream on top. Stand the apple stick in the ice cream and place a sugar spiral on top, if you like. Garnish each serving with a mint sprig.

PAT COSTON
Aqua, San Francisco, California

San Francisco's much-praised Aqua is well-known for its elegant seafood dishes, but sometimes they have to compete with the desserts for the spotlight, thanks to pastry chef Pat Coston.

Coston sees his job as providing a fitting finale to the exotic and innovative creations on which Aqua has built its dizzying reputation. Although this is an unceasing challenge, Coston never wanted to spend his life doing anything else.

Growing up in Oklahoma City, he was intrigued by the wedding cake business owned and operated by his mother. Right after graduating from high school, young Coston grabbed a job in a local restaurant. Still, he knew there was a big world beyond Oklahoma City, so he took his first steps into it by moving to Vail.

There, at a classic French restaurant called Left Bank, Coston learned the basics. After two years, he took his show on the road to San Francisco, working under Alain Rondelli at Ernie's. Having acquired a healthy set of general kitchen skills, Coston felt prepared to make great desserts for the rest of his life.

He signed on with Aqua as assistant pastry chef, rising to the job of pastry chef only six months later. Coston has come a long way from Oklahoma City, and diners at Aqua are glad he made the trip.

Apple and Almond Tart; *Reed Hearon with Shari O'Brien, LuLu*

Apple and Almond Tart

Reed Hearon with Shari O'Brien
LuLu
San Francisco, California

In this cunning variation on the caramelized apple tart, the pastry crust is
layered with almond cream and topped
with apple pieces cooked in a creamy
caramel sauce.

Serves 8 to 10

Caramelized Apples
8 Fuji or black Jonathan apples
2 tablespoons unsalted butter
1 cup granulated sugar
1 cup heavy (whipping) cream
$^1/_4$ cup Cognac

Pâte Brisée
2 cups unbleached all-purpose flour
$^1/_2$ teaspoon salt
$^3/_4$ cup ($1^1/_2$ sticks) cold unsalted butter,
   cut into $^1/_2$-inch cubes
About $^1/_2$ cup ice water

Frangipane (Almond Cream)
$^1/_3$ cup (3 ounces) almond paste
1 tablespoon confectioners' sugar, sifted

$^1/_2$ teaspoon grated lemon zest
3 tablespoons unsalted butter at
   room temperature
1 egg, beaten
$1^1/_2$ tablespoons flour

2 tablespoons granulated sugar

To make the caramelized apples: Peel and
core the apples and cut them in halves
or quarters, depending on the size. Place
a large sauté pan or skillet at least 3
inches deep over medium-high heat.
Add the apples, butter, and sugar and
cook, stirring frequently, until the sugar
and butter mixture begins to smoke and
turns a reddish-golden color. Remove
the pan from the heat and add the
cream, then the Cognac. Return to the
heat and continue to cook until the
caramel is thick and syrupy and the
apples are tender. If the caramel reduces
before the apples are tender, add a small
amount of water.

To make the pâte brisée: Preheat the
oven to 425°F. Line a 10- to 12-inch
deep-sided pizza pan or tart pan with
parchment paper or aluminum foil. In
a food processor, combine the flour and
salt. Add the butter and process until
only small bits of butter remain. (It
should not look like cornmeal.) With the

machine running, gradually add enough
water to make a soft but not wet dough.
Or, to make the dough by hand, combine the flour and salt in a medium
bowl. With a pastry cutter or 2 knives,
cut in the butter until only small bits
remain. Stir in enough water to make a
soft but not wet dough.

Transfer the dough to a floured pastry board and roll out $^1/_4$-inch thick.
Place the dough in the prepared pan and
fold the excess dough over to build up
the sides. Crimp the edges, then bake in
the oven until browned, 15 to 20 minutes.

Meanwhile, to make the frangipane: In a
medium bowl, blend together the
almond paste, confectioners' sugar, and
lemon zest. Add the butter and continue
to stir until light and creamy. Mix the
egg into the paste, then stir in the flour.

To assemble the tart: Spread the frangipane over the bottom of the baked crust.
Sprinkle the crust edge with granulated
sugar and return to the oven for 10 minutes. Remove from the oven and attrac-
tively arrange the apple halves or quarters, cut-side down, on top. Spoon the
caramel sauce over the apples and serve.

Lemon Angel Food Chiffon

▼▼▼▼▼▼▼▼▼▼▼▼▼▼▼

Larry Forgione
An American Place
New York, New York

Cubed angel food cake and lemon chiffon are combined in an all-American loaf cake that is sliced, drizzled with raspberry sauce, and garnished with fresh berries.

Serves 8

Angel Food Cake

1 cup cake or all-purpose flour
1 cup confectioners' sugar, sifted
2 cups egg whites (about 8 to 10 eggs)
    at room temperature
1 1/2 teaspoons cream of tartar
2 teaspoons vanilla extract
1 cup granulated sugar

Lemon Chiffon

2 1/4 teaspoons plain gelatin
3 tablespoons water
1/2 cup fresh lemon juice
Grated zest of 1 lemon
1/3 cup plus 1/2 cup granulated sugar
4 large eggs, separated, at room
    temperature
1/2 teaspoon cream of tartar
1/2 teaspoon vanilla extract
1/2 cup heavy (whipping) cream

Garnish

1 cup raspberry sauce (see page 224)
Fresh raspberries

To make the cake: Preheat the oven to 350°F. Sift together the flour and confectioners' sugar and set aside. In a large bowl, beat the egg whites at high speed with the cream of tartar and vanilla until they are foamy. Gradually beat in the sugar, 1 tablespoon at a time, until all is incorporated and the egg whites form stiff peaks. Using a rubber spatula, gently fold in one-third of the sifted dry ingredients at a time. Pour the batter into an ungreased 10-inch angel food cake pan, and tap the pan on the counter and cut through the batter vertically with a spatula to eliminate large bubbles.

Bake for 40 minutes, or until browned and springy to the touch. Remove the cake from the oven and invert it to cool for about 1 1/2 hours. With a thin-bladed knife, run around the edges of the pan and unmold the cake. With a finely serrated knife, cut the cake into 3/4-inch cubes (the crust can be removed if you like).

To make the lemon chiffon: In a small bowl, mix the gelatin and water and set aside. In a medium bowl, combine the lemon juice, 1/3 cup sugar, and zest. Place the second bowl over a pan of boiling water and whisk to warm the mixture and dissolve the sugar. Place the egg yolks in a medium bowl, stir, then add one-third of the lemon mixture to the yolks to warm them. Stir the remaining lemon mixture into the yolks and place the bowl over the boiling water. Cook, stirring constantly, for about 5 to 7 minutes, or until the mixture is thick enough to coat a spoon. Remove from heat and warm the gelatin mixture over the same water. Stir the gelatin into the lemon mixture. Let cool, or place over an ice water bath and stir until cooled to room temperature.

In a large bowl, beat the egg whites at high speed with the 1/2 cup sugar and the cream of tartar. Add the vanilla. Gently fold the lemon curd into the whites. In a deep bowl, beat the cream to soft peaks. Fold the whipped cream gently into the mixture, then add the cake cubes. Spoon the mixture into a 9-by-5-inch loaf pan. Tap down on the counter to remove any large bubbles and smooth the top. Cover and chill for 4 to 6 hours.

To serve: Dip the loaf pan in warm water to loosen the chiffon, then unmold. Cut the cake into 8 slices. Place 1 slice of cake in the center of each dessert plate and top with fresh berries. Drizzle raspberry sauce around the cake in a pleasing design.

Lemon Angel Food Chiffon; *Larry Forgione, An American Place*

WILLIAM C. GREENWOOD
The Jefferson, Washington, D.C.

Will Greenwood sees himself as a man with a mission. "The food industry is changing," he observes. "Expensive fine dining is declining. Trendy, experimental entrées priced under $20 are appearing in many new city restaurants. We can all create memorable meals with foie gras and truffles. The less expensive entrée is a special challenge."

A native of Oklahoma, Greenwood is a graduate of the Culinary Institute of America and studied with Madeleine Kamman at the Beringer Vineyards New School for American Chefs. Apart from that specific culinary education, he drew inspiration and direction from such kitchen standouts as George Blanc and Jean-Louis Palladin.

Greenwood served as executive chef for the Maryland Inn in Annapolis and cooked in other acclaimed hotel restaurants, including La Brasserie in the Peabody Court Hotel in Baltimore, before launching Gaspard's, on what he calls the "culinary frontier" in Winchester, Virginia. In 1989, Greenwood joined the Jefferson Hotel, where he developed his own version of the region's cuisine. Recently, Greenwood moved to the Sunset Inn in Nashville to bring his style of cooking to "Music City, USA."

Greenwood's success has eased his parents' earlier concerns about his choice of career.

"Culinary school was placed in the same category as any trade school," Greenwood recalls, "an education discussed within the family in whispered tones. What a change a decade can make! I never thought that my parents would brag to others about my accomplishments as a chef – any more than I thought they would tell me I have my hair cut too short."

Sun-dried Cherry Charlotte with Green Tea Ice Cream
▞▞▞▞▞▞▞▞▞▞▞▞

William C. Greenwood
The Jefferson
Washington, D.C.

A dessert in homage to Thomas Jefferson, who sun-dried his own cherries, loved ice cream, was fond of tea, and was a connoisseur of fine food and unusual inventions.

Serves 4

Green Tea Ice Cream
2 1/2 cups heavy (whipping) cream
1/2 cup half-and-half
1/4 cup Chinese green tea leaves
6 egg yolks
1 cup sugar

Sun-dried Cherry Charlottes
2 cups dried cherries
2 cups fresh orange juice
1/4 cup sugar
16 to 20 slices good-quality white bread, crusts removed
4 cups (1 pound) clarified unsalted butter, warmed (see page 223)

Garnish
1/4 cup crème anglaise (see page 220)
1/4 cup raspberry sauce (see page 224)
1/4 cup chocolate sauce (see page 223)
Fresh mint sprigs or leaves

To make the ice cream: In a medium saucepan, combine the cream, half-and-half, and tea. Bring to a boil over high heat, then immediately remove from heat and let steep for 30 minutes. Strain through a fine-meshed sieve.

Meanwhile, in a small bowl, whisk together the egg yolks and sugar. Add some of the hot cream mixture to the yolk mixture to warm the yolks. Add this mixture to the cream mixture in the pan and cook over medium heat, stirring constantly, until the custard coats a spoon, about 5 to 7 minutes. Chill the mixture for 30 minutes, then freeze in an ice cream maker according to the manufacturer's instructions.

To make the charlottes: Preheat the oven to 350°F. In a medium saucepan over medium heat, combine the cherries, orange juice, and sugar and bring to a simmer. Let cook for 10 minutes, or until the sugar is dissolved. Remove from heat, cover, and let stand for about 15 minutes, or until the cherries are plump and all liquid has been absorbed.

Cut 4 of the bread slices into rounds to fit the bottom of each of four 4-inch tart pans. Cut the remaining bread into 1½-by-2½-inch rectangles. Pour the butter into a shallow bowl and dip the bread circles in the butter to saturate them. Place 1 circle in each pan. Dip the rectangles in the butter to saturate them and arrange the strips, slightly overlapping, around the sides of the pans. The strips will extend over the tops, but should be arranged evenly. Press the slices together around the edges so that they stick together. Bake until browned and crusty, about 10 minutes. Let cool. Reheat just before serving.

To serve: Heat the cherries and divide them among the tart pans. Place a dessert plate over each charlotte, then invert, turning the charlotte out onto the plate. Garnish around the charlottes with drizzles of the sauces and, using the tip of a knife, pull through the sauces to make a design. Place a scoop of tea ice cream alongside each charlotte and garnish with a mint sprig.

Sun-dried Cherry Charlotte with Green Tea Ice Cream;
William C. Greenwood, The Jefferson

Passion Fruit Cheesecake; *Janet Rikala, Postrio*

Passion Fruit Cheesecake

Janet Rikala
Postrio
San Francisco, California

A cheesecake-lover's idea of heaven could well be this creamy cake flavored with passion fruit puree, topped with crème fraîche, and garnished with passion fruit sauce.

Serves 6

1¹/₃ cups unbleached all-purpose flour
5 tablespoons granulated sugar
1 cup (2 sticks) unsalted butter, melted

Passion Fruit Puree
8 passion fruits

Cheesecake Filling
1 pound cream cheese at room
   temperature
1¹/₃ cups granulated sugar
2 tablespoons plus 2 teaspoons
   cornstarch
2 eggs
1 teaspoon vanilla extract
¹/₂ cup sour cream
¹/₂ cup passion fruit puree, above

Topping and Garnish
³/₄ cup crème fraîche (see page 220)
1 tablespoon confectioners' sugar, sifted
1 cup passion fruit puree, above
2 tablespoons granulated sugar
1 tablespoon rum
Reserved passion fruit seeds from puree,
   above
6 spun sugar swirls (see page 228),
   optional

   To make the crust: Preheat the oven to 350°F. Combine the flour and sugar in a large bowl. Add the melted butter and mix with a wide spatula until a firm dough is formed. Lightly butter six 3-inch ring molds or one 9-inch springform pan. If using ring molds, place them on a baking sheet lined with parchment paper or aluminum foil. Using your fingers, press the dough into the bottom only of the ring molds or pan. Bake the crust until golden brown, 8 to 10 minutes. Let cool completely.

To make the puree: Cut the passion fruits in half and scrape the pulp and seeds into a fine-meshed strainer. Press against the sides of the strainer with the back of a large spoon to extract as much of the fruit as possible. Remove some of the seeds from the strainer, wash, and reserve them for the garnish.

To make the cheesecake filling: Preheat the oven to 275°F. Using an electric mixer fitted with a paddle attachment or beaters, whip the cream cheese until it is fluffy. Add the sugar and cornstarch, and blend. Gradually add the eggs, vanilla, and finally the sour cream. Scrape down the sides of the bowl and add the passion fruit puree. Strain the mixture through a fine-meshed sieve and carefully ladle it into the prepared rings or pan. Bake the cheesecakes until set, 30 to 40 minutes if using the ring molds or about 1 hour if using a pan. Chill for at least 2 hours.

To serve: Combine the crème fraîche and confectioners' sugar and spread it on top of the cheesecake(s). Smooth the top with a spatula. Carefully remove the ring molds and place a cheesecake in the center of each dessert plate. Or, remove the springform pan, cut the cheesecake into 6 wedges, and place a wedge in the center of each dessert plate. Combine the remaining puree with the granulated sugar and rum, and mix until blended. Spoon some of the mixture around each of the cheesecakes or wedges, garnish the plates with a sprinkling of passion fruit seeds, and top each serving with a spun sugar swirl, if you like.

JANET RIKALA
Postrio, San Francisco, California

Pastries, ice creams, and confections are a menu highlight at San Francisco's acclaimed Postrio, where they are created in the pastry kitchen by the sure hands of fourteen staffers and one executive pastry chef, Janet Rikala.

Though desserts usually get a bad rap in the world of dieting, Rikala became fascinated by them while studying food and nutrition. After graduating from the University of Minnesota, she took a summer job baking pies and muffins at a small country inn in Maine. Without abandoning her interest in good health, Rikala discovered that baking was her true love.

In 1987, she moved to the Bay Area to open a tea and pastry cafe with a close friend. One year of this convinced her the restaurant business was her calling, so she moved on to a position as assistant pastry chef at San Francisco's popular Kuleto restaurant. Here she picked up valuable lessons in high-volume baking – something she would never have learned in her own small cafe.

Moving south to San Diego in 1989, Rikala won the coveted position of executive pastry chef at the elegant Rancho Valencia Resort. Still, within a year, she was dreaming about returning to San Francisco. She could make terrific pastries anywhere, but her heart was in that city in Northern California.

Postrio gave Rikala a warm welcome back to her adopted home. The pastry kitchen gets to show off each day with twelve to fourteen creations featuring the finest available fresh fruits, imported chocolates, and nuts.

Recently, Rikala's talents earned her desserts the equivalent of a people's choice award; Postrio was selected for the Best Desserts in the Bay Area award in a survey taken by *Focus* magazine, proving that Rikala's true love is loved by her favorite city as well.

GERALD HIRIGOYEN
Fringale, San Francisco, California

When he named his San Francisco restaurant Fringale (French slang for "the urge to eat"), Basque-born chef Gerald Hirigoyen knew what he was doing. Once people are introduced to his unusual marriage of French and Spanish flavors, they find themselves compelled to return.

"America has only just begun to discover southern French cuisines," says Hirigoyen, referring not only to his own Basque heritage from the Pyrénées but to the cooking of Bordeaux, Gascony and the Périgord. "Food from the Mediterranean has become tremendously popular here, and rightfully so. But there's a lot of wonderful cooking in these other regions too that deserves to be much better known."

Fringale (in a section of San Francisco known as South of Market) is the result of a collaboration between Hirigoyen, who was chef at the popular Le St-Tropez, and that restaurant's owner, Jean Baptiste Lorda. Both men hail from Biarritz, near the Spanish border in the Basque region of southwest France. Bounded by both coastline and mountains, the area offers a wealth of raw ingredients, plus a worldview that's decidedly multicultural.

Joining forces with Lorda, Hirigoyen turned a former Mexican restaurant into a quietly elegant dining space. Muted sand and earth tones, a verdigris column and bar top, subtly sponged eggshell-hued walls, and blond wooden chairs, banquettes and wainscotting add a sense of both space and sophistication.

Signature dishes at Fringale include Roquefort ravioli with basil and nuts, artichoke and sea scallop ragout with balsamic vinaigrette, and braised sweetbreads served with white bean purée and baby leeks.

Hirigoyen uses olive oil instead of butter, and very little cream. Everything – right down to the mayonnaise on the Basque Fisherman Sandwich – is made right on the premises. And everything that comes out of the kitchen is characterized by what the *San Francisco Chronicle* called the "vibrant, refined flavors" of Hirigoyen's food.

Hazelnut and Roasted-Almond Mousse Cake

Gerald Hirigoyen
Fringale
San Francisco, California

This French confection is made with a genoise cut into layers, filled with a mousse made of hazelnut paste, and topped with toasted glazed almonds and a dusting of cocoa and confectioners' sugar.

Makes one 10-inch layer cake; serves 8 to 10

Genoise
1 tablespoon unsalted butter, melted
1/2 cup granulated sugar
4 large eggs
3/4 cup cake flour

Hazelnut Mousse
1 cup (2 sticks) unsalted butter at room temperature
1/2 cup (4 ounces) hazelnut paste
4 eggs, separated, at room temperature
1 cup granulated sugar
1/3 cup water

Garnish
Glazed almonds (recipe follows)
2 tablespoons unsweetened cocoa powder
2 tablespoons confectioners' sugar

To make the genoise: Preheat the oven to 400°F. Brush a 10-by-3-inch round cake pan with the melted butter and lightly dust it with flour. Combine the sugar and eggs in the bowl of an electric mixer. Place the bowl over simmering water and whisk the mixture until it is lukewarm. Transfer the bowl to the mixer stand and beat with a wire whip attachment until the mixture is cool, light, and fluffy. This will take about 15 minutes. Gradually sift the flour over the mixture and fold in gently. Pour the batter into the prepared pan and bake for about 20 minutes, or until a toothpick inserted in the center comes out clean.

To make the mousse: In a medium bowl, combine the butter and hazelnut paste and mix together until smooth. Mix in the egg yolks and set the mixture aside. In a small saucepan over medium heat, combine the sugar and water, bring to a boil, and cook for about 5 to 7 minutes, or until it reaches 240°F on a candy thermometer, or a small amount of the mixture dropped into a glass of cool water forms a soft ball.

Meanwhile, in a large bowl, beat the egg whites on high until they form soft peaks. Pour the sugar syrup in a thin stream into the beating egg whites. Spread the meringue onto a sided baking sheet and refrigerate for at least 30 minutes. Once cooled, use a whisk or spatula to fold the meringue into the egg yolk mixture.

To assemble the cake: Using a serrated knife, trim off the outer edges of the cake, then slice the cake into 4 layers. Place a 10-inch ring mold on a baking sheet covered with plastic wrap or waxed paper. Place 1 layer of genoise in the mold and spread it with one-fourth of the mousse. Continue to layer, ending with mousse on the top. Smooth the top and refrigerate for several hours.

To serve: Transfer the cake to a cake board or serving plate. Dip the ring mold into hot water, then remove the ring. Sprinkle the top of the cake with the glazed almonds. Press the cocoa and confectioners' sugar through a fine-meshed sieve. Mix to combine and sift the mixture over the entire top of the cake. Cut into wedges with a hot knife.

Glazed Almonds

Makes 1 cup

1 cup (4-1/2 ounces) sliced blanched
  almonds
1/4 cup granulated sugar
1/4 cup water

Preheat the oven to 325°F. In a medium bowl, dissolve the sugar in the water and add the almonds, stirring to coat the almonds completely. With a slotted spoon, transfer the almonds to a sided baking sheet covered with aluminum foil or parchment paper. Place the almonds in the oven and bake until glazed and golden, 6 to 8 minutes. Let cool.

Hazelnut and Roasted-Almond Mousse Cake; *Gerald Hirigoyen, Fringale*

Almond Heart; *Antoine Bouterin, Le Périgord*

Almond Heart

Antoine Bouterin
Le Périgord
New York, New York

Heart shaped and very light in texture, these flourless little cakes are flavored with almond and orange, and garnished with grated bittersweet chocolate and edible flowers.

Serves 6

3 tablespoons unsalted butter at room
 temperature
5 tablespoons plus ³/₄ cup granulated
 sugar
1¹/₂ cups almond flour
³/₄ cup dried white bread crumbs made
 from crust-trimmed bread
3 eggs
1 egg yolk
1 tablespoon almond extract
1 tablespoon orange flower water
1 tablespoon grated orange zest
1 tablespoon peanut oil
5 egg whites at room temperature
¹/₂ cup (2¹/₂ ounces) pine nuts, toasted
 (see page 236)

Garnish
6 ounces bittersweet chocolate, grated
Confectioners' sugar for dusting

6 to 12 small edible flowers
6 fresh mint sprigs
3 tablespoons pine nuts, toasted
  (see page 236)
Chocolate sauce (see page 223),
  optional

Preheat the oven to 400°F. Butter six 8-ounce heart molds with the butter and dust with 4 tablespoons of the sugar. In a large bowl, combine the almond flour, bread crumbs, and the 3/4 cup sugar and stir together. Lightly beat the eggs and egg yolk and mix with the flour mixture. Add the almond extract, orange flower water, zest, and oil and stir together.

In a large bowl, beat the egg whites with the remaining 1 tablespoon sugar until very firm glossy peaks form. Mix about one-fourth of the whites into the almond mixture, then fold in the rest. Divide the pine nuts among the heart molds. Spoon the batter on top. Bake for 25 minutes, or until a toothpick inserted in the center of a cake comes out clean.

To serve: Unmold the hearts onto dessert plates. Sprinkle the grated chocolate over and around the cakes and dust them with confectioners' sugar. Garnish with the flowers, mint, and pine nuts. Serve chocolate sauce alongside, if you like.

ANTOINE BOUTERIN
Le Périgord, New York, New York

"I was four years old when I first made my very own culinary creations: pâtés of sand mixed with leaves and flowers from the garden. A year and a half later, I made a chocolate cake for my sister's seventh birthday. It was very good and I received many compliments."

A lot has changed since those quiet childhood days at Saint-Rémy in the south of France. But Antoine Bouterin is still creating, and still receiving many compliments.

As executive chef at the esteemed Le Périgord in New York City, Bouterin has the most food-savvy clientele on earth, and his setting is among the most luxurious. For more than a decade, Bouterin has collected raves for the kind of cooking that he sees as a rather simple and direct art.

It all goes back to his roots in Provence, and to his grandmother. "The cooking of Provence is scented with thyme, basil, and rosemary, all mixed with the sublime perfume of garlic and parsley," he remembers. "These sweet smells of my childhood drew me into the kitchen, and because of them I knew I wanted to be a cook.

"My grandmother Marguerite lived near us, and she is the person whose cooking influenced me the most. Like an alchemist, she knew the magic to transform practically nothing into a sublime and succulent dish. Every Sunday I watched her bustle about her wood stove and admired her preparations for the weekly family dinner."

The inspiration may have come from Bouterin's grandmother, but the "great style" came from a tough apprenticeship followed by the traditional trip through French kitchens. He started not too far from his family's farm, at the two-star La Riboto de Taven in Les Baux-de-Provence. For a decade, Bouterin worked at a series of restaurants, including several belonging to the Relais Chateaux and Relais Gourmands Association.

According to Bouterin, the chef who inspired him the most along the way was Charles Berot. At L'Escale, Berot's restaurant on the Mediterranean near Marseilles, Bouterin learned lessons in fish cookery no academy could have taught him.

Bouterin came to the United States in 1980, as a chef on tour with Paris' La Varenne cooking school through New York, Ohio, Texas, and California. By the end of that trip, the chef's course was set. He'd fallen in love with America.

Chocolate-Rum Truffle Cake; *Richard Rivera, Ambrosia Euro-American Pâtisserie*

Chocolate-Rum Truffle Cake

■▼■▼■▼■▼■▼■▼■▼■

Richard Rivera
Ambrosia Euro-American Pâtisserie
Barrington, Illinois

A host of popular flavors—almond,
vanilla, and raspberry, along with
chocolate and rum—take on a variety
of roles in this big production number.
This dessert is almost a course in the art
of pastry making. The bisquit décor is
similar to a roulade; meringue is folded
into the batter so that it is flexible after
baking.

Serves 10

Bisquit Décor Sheet
6 egg yolks
1 whole egg
1 cup granulated sugar plus 2 tablespoons
3/4 cup egg whites (about 6 whites)
2 teaspoons almond extract or vanilla
  extract
1 cup cake flour, sifted
3 tablespoons unsweetened
  cocoa powder

Genoise
3 large eggs
6 tablespoons granulated sugar
1/2 cup cake flour
1/2 teaspoon baking powder
2 teaspoons vanilla extract
1 tablespoon unsalted butter, melted

Rum Syrup
2 cups water
1 cup granulated sugar
1/4 cup Myers's dark rum, or to taste

Chocolate Bavarian Cream
12 ounces semisweet chocolate,
  chopped
2 envelopes plain gelatin
1/4 cup water
1 cup crème anglaise (see page 220)
3 cups heavy (whipping) cream

Chocolate Ganache
12 ounces semisweet chocolate,
  chopped
1 cup heavy (whipping) cream

Chocolate-Rum Truffles

15 ounces semisweet chocolate, chopped
$1/2$ cup heavy (whipping) cream
$1^1/2$ tablespoons unsalted butter
3 tablespoons granulated sugar
3 tablespoons Myers's dark rum, to taste
1 cup unsweetened cocoa powder

Mocha Butter Cream

3 tablespoons water
1 cup granulated sugar
6 large egg yolks
2 cups (4 sticks) unsalted butter at room temperature, cut into small pieces
2 tablespoons coffee extract or double-strength brewed espresso

Garnish

$1^1/4$ cups apricot jam
$1^1/2$ cups crème anglaise (see page 220)
6 tablespoons raspberry sauce (see page 224)
Unhulled fresh strawberries, halved
Fresh raspberries

To make bisquit décor: Preheat the oven to 400°F. Line a 13-by-17-inch sided baking pan with parchment paper or waxed paper.

Combine the egg yolks, egg, and 1 cup sugar in the bowl of an electric mixer. Beat at high speed until mixture is pale in color and thick, about 10 minutes. Add the extract. Fold the flour into the egg mixture.

In a large bowl, beat the egg whites with the 2 tablespoons sugar until stiff, glossy peaks form. Remove one-third of the batter to a separate bowl and fold the cocoa into it. Refrigerate the remaining batter. Place the chocolate batter in a pastry bag fitted with a plain tip and pipe diagonal stripes onto the prepared pan. The stripes should be $1/2$ to $3/4$ inches thick and spaced 1 inch apart. Place in the freezer until firm to the touch.

Carefully spread the reserved batter over the chocolate. Smooth lightly, so the darker lines are not disturbed. Place in the oven and bake until golden, about 10 minutes. Let cool slightly, then remove from the pan. Trim the edges to square them off, then cut into 1-inch-wide lengthwise strips. Set aside.

To make the genoise: Preheat the oven to 350°F. Butter an 8-inch round cake pan and line it with parchment paper or waxed paper. Combine the eggs and sugar in the bowl of an electric mixer. Whisk together over simmering water until warm to the touch. Remove and beat with the machine until the mixture cools, about 10 minutes. The mixture will double in volume. Sift together the flour and baking powder. Gently fold the dry ingredients into the egg mixture, then add the vanilla. Fold the butter into the batter and pour into the prepared pan.

Bake for 10 to 15 minutes, or until a toothpick inserted in the center comes out clean. Let the cake cool for a few minutes, then remove from the pan. Let the cake cool completely. Using a sharp serrated knife, cut the browned outside surface from the top, bottom, and sides of the cake. Carefully split the cake into 3 layers. Set aside.

To make the chocolate Bavarian cream: In a double boiler over simmering water, melt the chocolate. Place the water in a cup and sprinkle the gelatin over. Let sit for 2 minutes. In a small saucepan, combine the crème anglaise and gelatin mixture and heat over low heat until the gelatin dissolves. Stir the crème mixture into the melted chocolate. Let cool to lukewarm. In a deep bowl, whip the cream until stiff peaks form, then fold it into the chocolate. Let sit until ready to use.

To make the chocolate ganache: In a double boiler over simmering water, melt the chocolate. In a small saucepan, bring the cream to a boil over medium heat. Stir the warm cream into the chocolate, being careful not to beat air into the mixture. Reserve 1 cup for the top of the torte and keep warm. Refrigerate the remaining ganache.

To make the chocolate-rum truffles: In a double boiler over simmering water, melt 9 ounces of the chocolate. In a small saucepan, combine the cream, butter, and sugar and heat over low heat until the butter and sugar are melted. Pour the cream mixture into the chocolate and stir until mixed. Let cool slightly, then stir in the rum. Refrigerate until firm.

In a double boiler over simmering water, melt the remaining 6 ounces of the chocolate. Place the cocoa in a pie tin. Roll the chilled truffle mixture into 1-inch balls and place them on the prepared pan. You will have 24 to 30 truffles. Refrigerate again for a few minutes. Dip each ball into the melted chocolate to coat, then drop the ball into the cocoa and coat it by shaking the container. Transfer to the prepared pan and repeat until all balls are coated. Refrigerate until needed.

To prepare the mocha butter cream: In a small saucepan, combine the water and sugar and cook over medium heat until the syrup is light golden and registers 242°F on a candy thermometer or reaches the soft ball stage: A small amount of the syrup dropped into cold water will form a soft and pliable ball. Let cool slightly.

Place the egg yolks in the bowl of an electric mixer and begin to beat at high speed. Gradually add the sugar syrup and continue to beat until the mixture cools. Gradually add the butter, beating after each addition and stopping occasionally to scrape down the sides of the bowl. Add the coffee extract or espresso.

To assemble the torte: Line a baking sheet with parchment paper or waxed paper. Place an 8-inch stainless-steel ring that is 3 inches deep on the prepared pan. Place 1 layer of the genoise in the bottom of the ring. Line the sides with the bisquit décor, placing it in the ring with the chocolate-striped side facing the sides. Be sure to press the sections together tightly. Brush the sides and bottom generously with the rum syrup.

Whip the chilled ganache in an electric mixer until creamy, then place it in a pastry bag with a plain tip. Spread a layer of chocolate Bavarian cream over the genoise. Pipe a layer of the ganache on top of the cream. Add a second layer of genoise and gently press down on it to bond. Brush the genoise with rum syrup, then repeat the layers of chocolate Bavarian cream and ganache. Place the last layer of genoise on top and

continued

RICHARD RIVERA
Ambrosia Euro-American Pâtisserie, Barrington, Illinois

Richard Rivera, who runs Ambrosia Euro-American Pâtisserie in a suburb of Chicago, trained under French, German and Swiss pastry masters during a trip through hotel kitchens in Illinois, Tennessee, and Texas, an experience best described as "mixed."

"European chefs are generals," he recalls. "They think that to brutalize is the best way to learn." He ponders a moment. "But they're the best."

Rivera glances about his kitchen at the pastry cooks working for him, and explains his own teaching method, which is clearly derived from the European. "These guys are really maturing as chefs," he offers. "But I like to keep them on their toes. Each time they think they've perfected the last thing they learned and gotten really confident, I like to throw them something else they don't know."

Rivera came to pastry making by way of several other art forms. After growing up with a baker for a father, he attended Elgin Community College for a couple of years studying sculpture and ceramics. When his efforts earned him acceptance to the Art Institute of Chicago, reality quickly set in. Student loans and day-to-day expenses had to be met, somehow.

"I really found a happy medium," he says. "I can be creative on a daily basis, working with food as my medium."

That is just what Rivera did, through a string of hotel jobs over about ten years: the Hyatt Regency in Schaumberg, Illinois; the Westin in Chicago and at that city's O'Hare International Airport; the Vanderbilt Plaza in Nashville; the Remington in Houston; and the Charles in Cambridge, Massachusetts.

Finally, though, he yielded to his desire to go back to Chicago. With his wife Debbie working the front of the shop and himself overseeing the kitchen, Rivera opened Ambrosia in 1989. The place has been going strong ever since.

again press down gently. Brush the top with rum syrup and place the cake in the freezer until firm.

Remove the cake from the freezer and wrap a hot towel around the ring for a few seconds to help unmold it. Invert the cake onto the center of a cardboard cake round (preferably gold). Remove the ring. Spread a thin layer of buttercream over the top to seal the porous pastry. Smooth with a wet knife, removing excess. Chill again until the buttercream is firm.

In a small heavy pan, warm the jam over low heat. Push the jam through a fine-meshed sieve with the back of a large spoon. Using a pastry brush, coat the sides of the torte with the apricot glaze to seal the sponge. This will retain moisture and give a beautiful sheen. Remove any excess glaze from around the edge of the torte.

The reserved unrefrigerated ganache should now be warm enough to spread, but not so hot that it will melt the buttercream. Ladle the ganache onto the center of the top of the cake and smooth it outward without going over the edge onto the sides. It should just cover the top. Wipe off any drips from the sides. While the ganache is still warm, space 10 truffles around the outer edge. Refrigerate the cake.

To serve: Use a warmed knife to cut the cake. Be sure to clean off the knife after each cut to assure attractive servings. Place 1 wedge on each dessert plate. Ladle 2 tablespoons of crème anglaise alongside each portion. Dot the cream in 5 or 6 places with the raspberry sauce and use the point of a knife to pull downwards through each dot, making hearts. Brush the strawberries with some of the apricot glaze and garnish the plates with the strawberries and raspberries.

Lemon Custard Gratiné with Fresh Berries and Candied Lemon

▪▪▪▪▪▪▪▪▪▪▪▪▪▪

Jose Gutierrez
Chez Philippe
The Peabody
Memphis, Tennessee

These chilled lemon and berry mousses are unmolded onto dessert plates and garnished with candied lemon slices, lemon and berry sauces, and fresh berries.

Serves 8

Lemon Custards

1/2 cup fresh lemon juice
2 tablespoons heavy (whipping) cream
Grated zest of 1 lemon
2 egg yolks
1/2 cup plus 2 tablespoons sugar
1 tablespoon flour
1 1/2 tablespoons (1 1/2 envelopes) plain gelatin
1/4 cup cold water
3 egg whites at room temperature
2 cups fresh raspberries or other fresh berries

Lemon Sauce

1 cup heavy (whipping) cream
1/2 cup chilled reserved cooking liquid from cooked lemons, above

Garnish

1 cup raspberry sauce (see page 224)
1/2 cup confectioners' sugar, sifted
4 cups fresh raspberries, blueberries, strawberries, or blackberries
1/4 cup julienned fresh mint leaves

To make the lemon custards: In a small bowl, combine the gelatin and cold water and set aside. In a small saucepan, combine the lemon juice, cream, and zest, and bring the mixture to a boil. Meanwhile, in a medium bowl, whisk the egg yolks and the 1/2 cup sugar together until the mixture is light and creamy. Add the flour and whisk together again, then slowly whisk in the hot cream mixture. Return the mixture to the saucepan, place over low heat, and cook, whisking constantly, for 2 to 3 minutes, or until the mixture

is thickened. Remove from heat.

Pour 2 tablespoons of the lemon mixture into the softened gelatin and stir until the mixture is smooth. Pour the gelatin mixture back into the saucepan with the lemon mixture and stir until smooth. Let cool.

Arrange eight 4-ounce ring molds on a tray lined with plastic wrap or waxed paper. In a large bowl, beat the egg whites with the 2 tablespoons sugar until firm and glossy peaks form. Mix a small amount of the beaten egg whites into the cooled lemon mixture with a whisk. Gently fold the lemon mixture into the remaining whites. Fill the molds halfway with the custard, add a layer of raspberries, then fill with the remaining custard. Smooth the top of each with a straight-edged spatula or dinner knife and chill for at least 2 hours.

To make the lemon sauce: In a deep bowl, softly whip the cream. Fold in the lemon liquid until blended.

To serve: Preheat the broiler. Spoon some of the lemon sauce into each of 8 shallow soup bowls. Drizzle raspberry sauce around the outer edge and arrange some berries on top. Run a thin-bladed

knife around the inside edge of the molds, invert, and unmold a custard onto the center of each dessert plate. Dust the top of each custard with confectioners' sugar. Place the bowls 2 inches from the broiler for 10 seconds to caramelize the confectioners' sugar, remove from the broiler, dust again, and caramelize again. Garnish between the berries with candied lemon slices, using 3 to 4 per serving. Sprinkle some julienned mint over each dish.

Candied Lemons
Makes about 3/4 cup

2 lemons
2 cups sugar, plus more for dipping
2 cups water

Cut the lemons in half lengthwise, then cut each half into thin 1/8-inch slices. In a medium saucepan, combine the sugar, water, and lemon slices and bring to a boil. Reduce heat to low and cook for 15 to 20 minutes, or until the lemons are translucent and tender. Drain, reserving the liquid. Chill the liquid. Dip the warm lemon slices in additional sugar, coating both sides generously. Lay out on a tray lined with waxed paper to dry for 4 hours.

Lemon Custard Gratiné with Fresh Berries and Candied Lemon;
Jose Gutierrez, Chez Philippe, The Peabody

Gâteau Chocolat Fondant; *Jacques Torres, Le Cirque*

Gâteau Chocolat Fondant

Jacques Torres
Le Cirque
New York, New York

This flourless cake, meltingly soft on the inside, is served hot from the oven with freshly whipped cream, chocolate sauce, and a garnish of candied orange peel.

Serves 8

Flourless Chocolate Cakes

1/2 cup (1 stick) unsalted butter, cut into
   pieces
Pinch of salt
15 ounces bittersweet chocolate,
   preferably Valrhona, chopped
4 egg whites
1/2 cup granulated sugar

Garnish

1 1/2 cups heavy (whipping) cream
1 tablespoon confectioners' sugar, sifted
Candied orange peel (optional)
2 cups chocolate sauce (see page 223)

To make the cakes: Preheat the oven to 400°F. Lightly butter and sugar eight 3-inch disposable aluminum tins,

2 inches deep. In a heavy, large saucepan, melt the butter with the salt over low heat. Add the chocolate and stir over low heat until the chocolate is melted and the mixture is smooth. Be careful not to burn the chocolate. Let cool to room temperature.

In a large bowl, beat the egg whites until foamy, then gradually beat in the sugar until stiff, glossy peaks form. Fold the egg whites into the cooled chocolate. Do not overmix or the batter will lose volume. Fill a pastry bag with batter and pipe into the tins, filling each just over half full. Bake for 4 to 5 minutes. (It is important that the cakes are baked just before serving so the texture is correct. However, they can be made ahead and frozen before baking. Remove from freezer at least 1 hour before baking.)

To serve: In a deep bowl, whip the cream with the confectioners' sugar until stiff peaks form. Fill a pastry bag fitted with a star tip and pipe rosettes of the cream around the outer circle of the plates. Cut the orange peel into 1-inch strips and place 2 pieces criss-crossed between the rosettes, if you like. Turn the warm cakes out into the center of the plates and pour chocolate sauce over the top and around the sides.

JACQUES TORRES
Le Cirque, New York, New York

For eight years, Jacques Torres enjoyed the challenge of one of the most sought-after cooking jobs in Europe: serving as pastry chef to Jacques Maximin at the Hotel Negresco in Nice. After such a supreme showcase, deciding how to move on wasn't easy.

Obviously, he couldn't accept just anything. After all, his labors at the Negresco had earned him the Meilleur Ouvrier de France at the tender age of twenty-six, the youngest chef to receive the award at that time.

Torres had accomplished a lot in a few short years. A native of Bandol, a small village on the French Riviera, he began his apprenticeship in pastry at age fifteen. Shortly after his French military service, he settled in as a pastry worker at the Negresco in 1980, rising to the pastry chef's job the very next year.

Just as Torres was thinking of leaving that grand hotel, another top-line hotel company stepped in. Ritz-Carlton invited Torres to ply his trade in America, shunting him through the pastry departments (with an emphasis on training personnel) in Laguna Niguel in California, Naples in Florida, and Atlanta. It was in that Georgia city that Torres got the call from Sirio Maccioni of Le Cirque in New York.

Accepting the advice of colleagues and embracing the chance to work with the legendary restaurateur, Torres packed up his belongings and headed for Manhattan. In an amazingly short time, his creations at Le Cirque were being praised as some of the most innovative desserts around.

In addition to his employment credits, Torres has participated in numerous competitions and demonstrations worldwide. In Tokyo, he received the medal of honor of the Confederation of Japan; in the United States he cooked for the gala dinner for the 1986 rededication of the Statue of Liberty. During that event, Torres' desserts were served to President Ronald Reagan and French President Francois Mitterand.

Torres has also done work for Cointreau, the French-owned liqueur company. Two of his desserts were the focus of a series of advertisements, giving his work a visibility that few pastry chefs on earth have enjoyed.

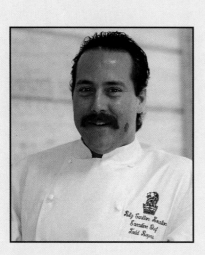

TODD ROGERS

The Dining Room, The Ritz-Carlton Houston, Houston, Texas

If you have to be an executive chef in a hotel, where you must worry incessantly about things like food costs and profit margins, a Ritz-Carlton is a pretty good choice. Todd Rogers learned that after joining the company in Naples, Florida, then moving with it to Houston during the takeover and upgrade of a four-diamond hotel with an eight million-dollar food and beverage operation.

As a chef, Rogers has a difficult task: to achieve all sorts of numerical management goals while maintaining impeccable culinary standards. But his training prepared him to be one of the best in his demanding position.

A 1982 graduate of the Culinary Institute of America, Rogers did his externship at the Sun Valley Resort in the mountains of Idaho. In short order, he worked his way through positions as chef-proprietor of Gourmet Caterers in Huntington, West Virginia, and as *saucier* at the Hotel Europe in Chapel Hill, North Carolina. The big-hotel world called in 1983, in the form of the thirteen-hundred-room Hyatt Regency in Atlanta.

For almost three years, Rogers moved through progressive stations at the busy convention property, even assisting in the renovation of kitchen facilities. In addition to learning to excel in ice carving and personnel training, Rogers considers a highlight of this period a party he and his staff put on for Coca-Cola – and four-thousand of the company's guests.

Joining Ritz-Carlton at Naples meant starting on the road to executive sous-chef, a job that put him in charge of twelve sous-chefs and ninety-five line employees. Rogers transferred to Houston in 1990. In addition to his work at that property, he has been a member of the opening teams for Ritz-Carltons in Pasadena and Cancun.

Double-Chocolate Torte with Mascarpone Mousse and Wild Berry–Chocolate Sauce

Todd Rogers
The Dining Room
The Ritz-Carlton, Houston
Houston, Texas

This could be the ultimate Texas dessert: a slice of chocolate torte with a heart of white chocolate terrine and a coating of chocolate ganache, topped with a chocolate oil rig filled with Mascarpone mousse and spouting a "Texas tea" of berry and chocolate sauce.

Serves 12 to 16

Chocolate Torte
20 egg yolks
3^1/4 cups sugar
2^1/4 cups (4^1/2 sticks) unsalted butter
18 ounces semisweet chocolate, chopped
12 egg whites

White Chocolate Mousse
8 ounces white chocolate, chopped
^{1}/2 cup sugar
6 tablespoons water
3 envelopes plain gelatin
3 cups heavy (whipping) cream
^{1}/4 cup pistachio nuts, chopped

Mascarpone Mousse
1 pound Mascarpone cheese at room temperature
^{3}/4 cup sugar
4 cups heavy (whipping) cream

Chocolate Oil Rigs and Spouts
2 pounds semisweet chocolate, chopped

Wild Berry–Chocolate Sauce
4 cups water
3^1/2 cups sugar
5 tablespoons cornstarch
^{1}/2 cup dark rum
1^1/2 cups unsweetened cocoa powder
6 ounces semisweet chocolate, finely chopped
1 cup *each* fresh raspberries, blueberries, and blackberries

Ganache

12 ounces semisweet chocolate, chopped
1 cup heavy (whipping) cream

Garnish

2 cups *each* fresh raspberries, blueberries, and blackberries
12 to 16 fresh mint sprigs

To make the chocolate torte: Preheat the oven to 350°F. Line a 13-by-17-inch sided baking pan with parchment paper or waxed paper. In a large bowl, beat the egg yolks until they are pale yellow and a slowly dissolving ribbon is formed on the surface of the yolks when the beater or whisk is lifted. In a double boiler over simmering water, melt the butter and chocolate. Stir until smooth, then blend the chocolate mixture into the egg mixture.

In a large bowl, beat the egg whites until stiff, glossy peaks form, then fold them into the chocolate mixture. Spread the batter onto the prepared pan and bake for about 30 minutes, or until a toothpick inserted in the center comes out clean. Let cool for 10 minutes, then invert and unmold onto a sheet of parchment paper or waxed paper. Scrape the top of the cake to remove the crust. Set aside.

To make the white chocolate mousse: Line a 6-cup semi-circular terrine, no deeper than 2 inches, with plastic wrap. In a double boiler over simmering water, melt the chocolate and sugar, stirring to dissolve the sugar. Place the water in a cup and sprinkle the gelatin over. Let it dissolve for about 3 minutes. Add the gelatin mixture to the chocolate and stir until smooth. Let cool slightly.

In a deep bowl, whip the cream until stiff peaks form, then fold in the pistachio nuts. Fold the chocolate mixture into the whipped cream. Pour the mousse into the prepared terrine. Cover and freeze overnight, or at least 4 to 5 hours.

To make the Mascarpone mousse: In a large bowl, whisk the cheese and sugar together until the sugar is dissolved. In a deep bowl, whip the heavy cream until stiff peaks form, then fold into the Mas-

Double-Chocolate Torte with Mascarpone Mousse and Wild Berry–Chocolate Sauce;
Todd Rogers, The Dining Room, The Ritz-Carlton, Houston

carpone mixture. Place in a pastry bag with a plain tip and refrigerate until needed.

To make the oil rigs and spouts: In a double boiler over simmering water, melt the chocolate until smooth. Draw 4 equal sides of an oil rig on paper. Cover each with an acetone plastic sheet and pipe the chocolate outline of the oil rig. Let cool to harden. The oil spout can also be drawn free hand in a fountain or feather-like shape and piped as above on an acetone sheet. Make 12 to 16 rigs (4 sides each) and spouts.

To assemble the oil rigs, place 2 sides at right angles with long edges together, and "glue" them with additional melted chocolate piped on the inside edges. Hold in place to let the chocolate cool and firm. Repeat with the remaining 2 sides, then "glue" the 4 sides together into a tower. Repeat with the remaining sides to form all rigs.

To make the wild berry-chocolate sauce: In a medium saucepan, combine 3 cups of the water and the sugar and bring to a boil over medium heat. In a small bowl, dissolve the cornstarch in the remaining water and add the rum. Whisk the cornstarch mixture into the boiling sugar syrup. Add the cocoa and stir until the mixture is thickened.

Meanwhile, in a double boiler over simmering water, melt the chocolate. Remove the rum mixture from the heat and stir in the melted chocolate. Strain the berries through a fine-meshed sieve, pushing them through with the back of a large spoon. Add the berry puree to the chocolate mixture. Let cool, then strain the sauce through a fine-meshed sieve.

To make the ganache: In a double boiler over simmering water, melt the chocolate with the cream, whisking gently to a smooth consistency. Let cool slightly to a pourable consistency.

To assemble the cake roll: Remove the white chocolate terrine from the freezer and unmold onto parchment paper or waxed paper. Remove the plastic wrap and cut the cake to the proper length to encircle the terrine. Place the terrine at one edge of the cake and, with the aid of the parchment or waxed paper, roll the cake around the terrine to encase it, placing the seam on the flat side of the terrine. Trim the ends of the cake flush with the terrine. Place the cake roll flat-side down. Coat the top and sides of the cake roll with the ganache and return it to the freezer to firm up.

To serve: Remove the cake roll from the freezer and cut it into ³/4-inch-thick slices. Place one slice on each dessert plate and stand an oil rig alongside. Fill the rigs with the Mascarpone mousse, piping it in from the top. Place the fresh berries around the edge of the plates. Ladle the sauce down the sides of the rigs and around the plate over the berries. Garnish with fresh mint and stand a chocolate spout in the mousse at the top of each rig.

Strawberry Crème Fouette; *Jean-Louis Palladin, Jean-Louis at the Watergate*

Strawberry Crème Fouette

Jean-Louis Palladin
Jean-Louis at the Watergate
Washington, D.C.

Wedges of feuilles de Brigue, a thin round dough found in Middle Eastern markets, are a crisp contrast to strawberry mousse and fresh berries in this dessert, which is brightened with a raspberry coulis.

Serves 4

Pastry
4 feuilles de Brigue, or 12 sheets phyllo
  dough, ¹/₂ cup (1 stick) unsalted butter,
  melted, and granulated sugar for
  sprinkling

Strawberry Mousse
6 tablespoons water
1 envelope plain gelatin
1 cup heavy (whipping) cream
2¹/₂ cups fresh strawberries, hulled
2¹/₂ cups red and yellow fresh wild
  strawberries, hulled
¹/₄ cup confectioners' sugar, sifted

Raspberry Coulis
2 cups fresh raspberries
¹/₄ cup confectioners' sugar, sifted
2 tablespoons water

Garnish
3 to 4 cups red and yellow fresh
  wild strawberries, hulled
Sifted confectioners' sugar for dusting

   To make the pastry: Preheat the oven to 350°F. Line a baking sheet with parchment paper or aluminum foil. Cut each feuille into 8 equal pie shapes and place the triangles on the parchment paper. Bake for 10 to 15 minutes, or until golden brown. Let cool. Or, substitute phyllo dough: Preheat the oven to 375°F. Lay 4 sheets of phyllo on the prepared pan. Lightly brush the phyllo with 1 tablespoon melted butter. Repeat 2 more times, lightly sprinkling the top layer with sugar, and cut each stack into 8 triangles. Cover the pastry with another sheet of parchment or aluminum foil and set a second pan on top. Bake the triangles for 8 to 10 minutes, or until golden brown. Remove the top pan and paper or foil and let the pastries cool completely.

To make the strawberry mousse: Place 2 tablespoons of the water in a cup and sprinkle the gelatin over it. Let dissolve for 3 minutes. Stir the gelatin mixture into the cream and refrigerate until it begins to firm, about 10 minutes. Meanwhile, puree the berries in a blender with the confectioners' sugar and the remaining 4 tablespoons water. Strain the puree through a fine-meshed sieve. Whip the firmed cream in an electric mixer until stiff peaks form, gradually adding the strawberry puree. Refrigerate if the mousse is not used immediately.

To make the raspberry coulis: Puree all the ingredients in a blender. Strain through a fine-meshed sieve.

To serve: Transfer the mousse to a pastry bag fitted with a star tip. Pipe a strip of mousse down the center of the plates. Place 5 wedges of pastry standing in a line in the mousse with the narrow point up. Alternate some of the berries between each pastry. Pour some of the raspberry coulis on each side of the mousse and place additional berries in the sauce. Dust confectioners' sugar on top of the dessert and around the plate.

Alternatively, for a simplified presentation, form the feuille or phyllo into circles instead of triangles before baking. To assemble, place one pastry circle on the plate, and pipe mousse into the center of the pastry. Surround the mousse with strawberries. Place another pastry circle on top of the mousse and press down gently. Dust the pastry and plate with confectioners' sugar. Pool raspberry coulis on the plate (crème anglais, page 220, can also be added) and garnish with berries.

JEAN-LOUIS PALLADIN
Jean-Louis at the Watergate, Washington, D.C.

Many chefs welcome the challenge of creating a special "tasting" menu, selecting a many-splendored *dégustation* that gives samples of the kitchen at its best. One of the first chefs to do this in the United States, and still one of the best at it, is Jean-Louis Palladin.

Since arriving in this country in 1979, Palladin has maintained his presence at his own restaurant, Jean-Louis at the Watergate, while racking up an impressive array of guest appearances and consultations everywhere.

At the same time, he has managed to establish several new ventures: He founded a seafood market and trattoria called Pesce with Robert Donna, and helped launch The Frog and the Redneck with Jimmy Sneed in Richmond, Virginia. He even installed a brasserie called Palladin right above his own Jean-Louis. Clearly, we're dealing with a restlessly creative soul here, who has learned the French art of staying the course while indulging in the American zeal for following several different courses at once.

Palladin learned the basics of what he calls "instinctive cuisine" quite early. He went to work in a restaurant kitchen in his native Gascony at age twelve, then moved on to hotel school in Toulouse, a *saucier's* job at the Hotel de Paris in Monte Carlo, and a stint at the Plaza Athénée in Paris.

Feeling the urge for home, Palladin returned to Gascony and turned a fourteenth-century monastery into his own restaurant, La Table des Cordeliers. Michelin gave La Table two stars, making its twenty-eight-year-old visionary the youngest chef to be so honored. It was on these wings that Palladin flew to America.

In addition to his version of French cuisine and his tireless expansion into new ventures, Palladin has been an inspiration to his American peers in at least two other ways. He has aggressively explored the wine world for specific combinations that suit his food, turning out a stellar list that serves both Jean-Louis and Palladin.

He also pioneered the mystique of chef as a zealot for fine ingredients. Long before it was stylish to do so, Palladin spent his early mornings strolling through the seafood and produce markets of Washington.

This combination of inspiration and early rising has helped Palladin take his place among the chefs who've changed the way America dines. He started out to make his own menu, and ended up making a lot of other people's as well.

SHELLEY LANCE
Dahlia Lounge, Seattle, Washington

It was English literature that drew Shelley Lance to the Pacific Northwest, but it was pastry that inspired her to stay. After earning her BA, she quickly embarked on a course that would place her at the forefront of Seattle's culinary renaissance.

Born in Chicago, Lance studied her new subject as fervently as she'd studied Chaucer, Shakespeare, or Hardy. She earned a degree from the California Culinary Academy and went on to Madeleine Kamman's School for American Chefs at Beringer Vineyards in St. Helena, California.

All the rest was on-the-job training, mostly at Seattle restaurants run by Tom Douglas. Her eight years of cooking for Douglas included a stint at Cafe Sport before her move to the Dahlia Lounge. At the Dahlia, Lance handles all the pastries but is willing and able to work any part of the cooking line. This being a typical smallish restaurant, she is called to do so on occasions.

She has also helped with recipe development for the Dahlia Lounge, something for which Douglas is grateful. Now he has invited Lance to work with him on a cookbook evoking their version of Pacific Northwest cuisine.

Apple Dumpling with Cinnamon-Rum Sauce

Shelley Lance
Dahlia Lounge
Seattle, Washington

The apple is filled with date butter and served with vanilla ice cream and cinnamon-rum sauce in this version of a beloved dessert.

Serves 8

Dough
2^1/$_2$ cups unbleached all-purpose flour
1 teaspoon salt
1 tablespoon granulated sugar
1 cup (2 sticks) cold unsalted butter, cut into small pieces
^{1}/$_2$ cup ice water

Date Butter
6 ounces Medjool dates, pitted and finely chopped
^{1}/$_2$ cup (1 stick) unsalted butter at room temperature
^{1}/$_4$ cup packed brown sugar
1 teaspoon ground cinnamon

Juice of 1 lemon
4 Granny Smith or Gala apples, halved lengthwise, cored, and peeled
2 egg yolks
2 tablespoons heavy (whipping) cream
^{1}/$_2$ cup granulated sugar
1 tablespoon ground cinnamon

Cinnamon-Rum Sauce
1 cup packed brown sugar
1 tablespoon cornstarch
1 cup water
2 cinnamon sticks
1 tablespoon unsalted butter
2 tablespoons rum

Garnish
Eight 3-inch cinnamon stick pieces
^{1}/$_2$ cup confectioners' sugar, sifted
8 scoops vanilla ice cream

To make the dough: Combine the flour, salt, and sugar in a food processor. Add the butter and pulse to incorporate, mixing to a crumb texture. Or, to make by hand, in a medium bowl, combine the flour, salt, and sugar. Cut in the butter with a pastry cutter or 2 knives until the mixture resembles coarse cornmeal. Slowly stir in the water until the dough comes together. Cover and refrigerate for at least 1 hour.

To make the date butter: Place the dates in a blender or food processor and pulse 2 or 3 times. Add the butter, sugar, and cinnamon and puree, scraping down the sides of the container several times.

Preheat the oven to 375°F. Line a baking sheet with parchment paper or grease it. Add the lemon juice to a bowl of cold water and add the apples to prevent any discoloration.

Divide the chilled dough in half and roll each out on a lightly floured board. Roll it into a 1/8-inch-thick square. Trim the edges to square the pastry off, then cut each square into fourths, each about 7 inches square. Reserve the trimmings for decoration. From each corner, cut into the dough about 1 1/2 inches toward the center, so the dough can be folded up pinwheel style.

Drain the apple halves and pat them dry with paper towels. Place an apple half, cut-side up, on each square. Fill the center of each apple with 1 1/2 tablespoons date butter. Pull up alternate corners, pinwheel style, and seal at the top. From the trimmings of the dough, cut a triangular piece and pinch one end to form a leaf shape.

In a small bowl, whisk the egg yolks and cream together. Combine the sugar and cinnamon. Brush the entire surface of the dumplings with the egg mixture and place a dough leaf on top of each. Brush each leaf with the egg wash. Sprinkle the dumplings with the cinnamon sugar.

Transfer the dumplings to the prepared pan and bake for 20 to 25 minutes, or until the pastry is golden and the apple is tender when pierced with a knife. The dumplings can be made ahead and reheated in a preheated 350°F oven for 10 to 12 minutes.

To make the cinnamon-rum sauce: In a small saucepan, whisk together the brown sugar, cornstarch, and water. Add the cinnamon sticks and place over medium heat. Bring the mixture to a boil, then lower heat and simmer for 5 minutes, or until thickened. Remove from heat and stir in butter and rum. Set aside and keep warm.

To serve: Place a dumpling on one side of each dessert plate. Stand the cinnamon stick pieces against the dumplings. Ladle the sauce over the top of the dumplings and around the plates. Dust each plate with confectioners' sugar and garnish with a scoop of ice cream.

Apple Dumpling with Cinnamon-Rum Sauce; *Shelley Lance, Dahlia Lounge*

No-Cholesterol Raspberry Soufflé

▼▼▼▼▼▼▼▼▼▼▼▼▼

Gary Danko
The Dining Room
The Ritz-Carlton, San Francisco
San Francisco, California

Because they are made without a cream-sauce base, these soufflés are delicate and must be served immediately. They are also light and intensely flavored, with a spoonful of sweetened raspberries nestled in the center of each one.

Serves 6

Soufflés

6 tablespoons sugar
1¼ cups raspberry jam, sieved
1 tablespoon Grand Marnier liqueur
6 egg whites

Raspberry Sauce

2 cups fresh raspberries
2 to 4 tablespoons sugar
2 tablespoons Grand Marnier liqueur

To prepare the soufflés: Preheat the oven to 350°F. Spray six 6-ounce soufflé dishes with vegetable-oil spray and coat lightly with the sugar. Stir together the jam and liqueur. Using a fat-free copper or other large bowl (clean the bowl with lemon juice before using), beat the egg whites by hand with a balloon whisk until a topknot of beaten whites clings to the end of the whisk when you lift it. (Whisking by hand makes the egg whites more creamy and less dry.) Add the jam and fold it in with the whisk until thoroughly blended.

Fill the dishes generously, mounding the tops, then use a palette knife or dinner knife to smooth the tops flat. Use your thumb and finger to clean around the rim of each dish. Bake on the middle rack of the oven for 10 to 15 minutes, or until golden.

To make the sauce: In a small saucepan, combine all the ingredients and place over low heat until the sugar is melted and the berries are just warmed through.

To serve: Quickly place each soufflé on a doily- or napkin-lined dessert plate. Cut into the center of each soufflé and spoon in some of the berries and juice. Serve immediately.

No-Cholesterol Raspberry Soufflé; *Gary Danko, The Dining Room, The Ritz-Carlton, San Francisco*

GARY DANKO
The Dining Room, The Ritz-Carlton San Francisco,
San Francisco, California

If you ask Gary Danko how he became a chef, he can't tell the story without dropping two famous women's names: Betty Crocker and Madeleine Kamman.

That first, if fictional, matriarch was his earliest inspiration, setting him to baking cakes and cookies at age six in his mother's kitchen in Massena, New York. The second woman was one of those figures who turn up rather mysteriously whenever a guiding word or a fresh direction is needed.

On the strength of Ms. Crocker, Danko aimed his life toward restaurants from his first job at age fourteen: bussing tables and washing dishes at Massena's Village Inn. By the time he had completed high school, he had also completed what he calls an "American apprenticeship," working through all facets of the Inn's kitchen and dining room.

The only natural "university" for Danko seemed the Culinary Institute of America, which he completed in 1977. He attracted attention in his first real outing after graduation, cooking at Vanity Fair, a small bistro and bookstore in San Francisco's Embarcadero Center. A new mission soon presented itself, however, taking Danko back east.

He spent a full year working restaurant jobs in New York and Vermont while petitioning the legendary Madeleine Kamman for the chance to cook with her.

Danko spent six months under Kamman's skilled direction, then moved on with her help to an externship with Beringer Vineyard's food and wine program. After that, he managed the kitchen for the St. Helena-based Beringer while consulting with San Francisco's Washington Square Bar and Grill.

In 1986, Danko headed east again, answering a call from Kamman to assist at her New Hampshire cooking school, then traveling with her through France in a flourish of cooking and teaching. With this experience in his portfolio, Danko spent the next five years with the Chateau Souverain Winery's restaurant in Geyserville, California, slowly transforming the place into a culinary destination.

Danko, named a Best New Chef by *Food & Wine* in 1989, joined Ritz-Carlton two years after that. He helped open the Nob Hill property in April 1991 and rose to the job of chef in the Dining Room in May 1992. In 1995, he was named the best chef in California by the James Beard Awards Committee.

PATRICE SERENNE
Mark's Place, Miami, Florida

Some kids grow up selling chocolate to raise money for the Boy or Girl Scouts, for the YMCA, or for their church. Patrice Serenne grew up eating Valrhôna chocolate, which was made just down the street, so to speak, in his hometown of Tain-l'Hermitage. To this day, he uses no other brand in his pastry kitchen at Mark's Place in Miami.

For all his memories of home, Serenne is sold on America and its entire culinary scene. "I love Florida," he enthuses. "The fruits are great and so is the weather." Then he explains his preference for the American professional cooking style. "Chefs in France have a bad attitude. They shout a lot, and they're more old-fashioned. Americans are more relaxed and give you plenty of artistic freedom."

At age sixteen, Serenne began his apprenticeship at the Poussin Bleu pastry shop in Tain-l'Hermitage in 1983. From there, the road led to the prestigious Pignol pastry shop and catering company in Lyons, then across the Atlantic to a place called Chillingsworth on Cape Cod.

Life turned delightfully seasonal for the next few years, as Serenne divided his cooking between the ski resorts of the French Alps in winter and Chillingsworth in summer. He also squeezed in a season in St. Martin and Aruba, picking up a passion for tropical fruits along the way.

That passion has served him well in the kitchen of Mark Militello's Mark's Place. Serenne's colorful desserts close a meal there with the Caribbean flourish the south Florida visionary's food deserves.

Napoleon of Tropical Fruit

▛▀▜▛▀▜▛▀▜▛▀▜▛▀▜▛▀▜

Patrice Serenne
Mark's Place
Miami, Florida

This tropical interpretation of the napoleon consists of passion fruit and Key lime curds, white chocolate mousse, and phyllo dough triangles, served with a sauce of passion fruit seeds and raspberries. Both the curds and the mousse must be made the day before assembling and serving the dessert.

Serves 8

Passion Fruit Curd
10 to 12 passion fruits
³/4 cup granulated sugar
5 eggs
4 egg yolks
1/2 cup (1 stick) unsalted butter, cut into small pieces
4 ounces white chocolate, chopped

Key Lime Curd
³/4 cup Key lime juice
³/4 cup granulated sugar
5 eggs
4 egg yolks
1/2 cup (1 stick) unsalted butter, cut into small pieces
4 ounces white chocolate, chopped

White Chocolate Mousse
1/2 cup light corn syrup
13 ounces white chocolate, chopped
⁷/8 cup sweetened condensed milk
1/2 cup light rum
1 envelope plain gelatin
3 cups heavy (whipping) cream

Pastry Triangles
6 sheets phyllo dough
2 cups (4 sticks) unsalted butter, melted
1 cup granulated sugar

Passion Fruit–Raspberry Sauce
1 cup reserved passion fruit seeds from Passion Fruit Curd, above
1 vanilla bean, halved lengthwise
1 cup raspberry sauce (see page 224)

Garnish
1 large block white chocolate at room temperature
Sifted confectioners' sugar for dusting
1 fresh mango, peeled and diced
8 fresh mint sprigs

To make the passion fruit curd: Squeeze the passion fruits to make ³/4 cup juice. Reserve the seeds. In a double boiler over simmering water, whisk the juice, sugar, egg, and egg yolks until the mixture becomes very thick, 5 to 10 minutes. Remove from heat and stir in the butter, then the white chocolate. Cover and refrigerate the mixture overnight.

To make the Key lime curd: Make the Key lime curd in the same manner as the passion fruit curd, substituting the lime juice for the passion fruit juice. Cover and refrigerate overnight.

To make the white chocolate mousse: In a medium, heavy saucepan, bring the corn syrup to a boil over medium heat. Remove the pan from the heat and add the chocolate. Whisk until the chocolate is melted, then add the milk and continue whisking until the mixture is blended. Set aside. In a small saucepan, stir the rum and gelatin over low heat until the gelatin is completely dissolved. Stir the gelatin mixture into the chocolate mixture. Add the heavy cream and whisk all together. Strain the mixture into a bowl, cover, and refrigerate overnight. The next day, place the mousse in the bowl of an electric mixer and beat until the mixture is light and fluffy, 2 to 3 minutes. Take care not to overmix.

To make the pastry triangles: Preheat the oven to 375°F. Line a baking sheet with parchment paper or aluminum foil. Place 1 sheet of phyllo dough on a large cutting board. Keep the remaining dough covered with a towel to keep it moist. Lightly brush the phyllo with melted butter and sprinkle with some of the sugar. Repeat to make 6 layers of the phyllo. Cut the dough in half lengthwise, then divide each half into 8 equal squares. Cut each square in half diagonally, making 32 triangles. Transfer the triangles to the prepared pan. Cover the pastry with another sheet of parchment or foil and set a second pan on top. (The additional pan helps the triangles keep their shape and helps to caramelize the phyllo dough.)

Bake the triangles for 8 to 10 minutes, or until golden brown. The pastry burns easily, so watch carefully. Remove the top pan and paper or foil and let the pastries cool completely.

To make the passion fruit-raspberry sauce: In a small saucepan, combine the passion fruit seeds and vanilla bean and cook over low heat for 8 to 10 minutes. Add the raspberry sauce and let cool. Remove the vanilla bean.

To make the chocolate curls: Place the white chocolate on a piece of parchment paper or waxed paper. Using a small ring mold or cookie cutter, pull the mold or cutter across the chocolate, making curls. Set aside in a cool place.

To serve: Place the passion fruit curd, Key lime curd, and mousse in 3 separate pastry bags fitted with fluted tips. Place 1 pastry triangle on a large dessert plate with the wide end towards the center. Pipe a rosette of passion fruit curd on the wide end. Place another triangle on top at an angle from the first, so the points are fanned. Press down lightly to secure the triangle, and pipe a rosette of white chocolate mousse on the wide end of this triangle. Add a third triangle, again at an angle, and pipe a rosette of Key lime curd on it. Repeat with the remaining plates.

Dust the 8 remaining triangles with confectioners' sugar and place one on top of each dessert. Garnish the plates with the diced mango. Spoon the sauce around the plates and garnish with a mint sprig and 4 chocolate curls.

Napoleon of Tropical Fruit; *Patrice Serenne, Mark's Place*

Feuillant of Fresh Berries with Mango-Raspberry Coulis

▰▱▰▱▰▱▰▱▰▱▰▱▰

Christian Gille
Le Jardin
The Westin Canal Place
New Orleans, Louisiana

Imagine a well of puff pastry, filled with crème Chantilly and fresh berries, and you will understand the appeal of this dessert. Wedges of nectarine and three different sauces garnish each plate.

Serves 6

Puff Pastry Squares
One 6-by-9-inch sheet puff pastry dough
3 tablespoons flour

Chantilly Cream
2 cups milk
1 tablespoon unsalted butter
¼ cup sugar
2 eggs
¼ cup cornstarch
1 cup heavy (whipping) cream
1 teaspoon confectioners' sugar, sifted

Sauces and Berries
1 cup mango sauce (see page 224)
1 cup raspberry sauce (see page 224)
1 cup crème anglaise (see page 220)

2 cups fresh raspberries
2 cups fresh blueberries
2 cups fresh blackberries

Garnish
2 fresh nectarines
Sifted confectioners' sugar for dusting
6 fresh mint sprigs

To make the pastry: Preheat the oven to 375°F. Line a baking sheet with parchment paper or grease it. Flour a pastry board and lightly roll out the dough. Trim the edges to make a square, then cut the dough into 3-inch squares. Place the squares on the prepared pan and let sit for 30 minutes. Bake for 15 minutes, or until puffed and golden brown. Let

Feuillant of Fresh Berries with Mango-Raspberry Coulis, *Christian Gille, Le Jardin, The Westin Canal Place*

cool, then split in half. Press down on the center of half of each square making a well. Set aside.

To make the Chantilly cream: In a medium saucepan, combine 1½ cups of the milk, the butter, and sugar and bring the mixture to a boil. Meanwhile, combine the remaining ½ cup milk, eggs, and cornstarch in a medium bowl and whisk until smooth. When the milk is boiling, whisk some of the hot milk into the egg mixture, then return the egg mixture to the milk in the pan and whisk while cooking over medium heat until the cream is thick, about 3 to 5 minutes. Pour into a shallow pan, cover the top with plastic wrap, and chill in the refrigerator for 4 hours.

In a deep bowl, whip the cream until stiff peaks form. Fold the whipped cream and confectioners' sugar into the cooled pastry cream and transfer to a pastry bag fitted with a star tip.

To serve: Select large dessert plates. Place the mango sauce, raspberry sauce, and crème anglaise in individual squeeze bottles. Beginning on one side of each plate, make a 1-inch band of the raspberry sauce from the center to the outer edge. Repeat with the mango coulis, then the crème anglaise, then the raspberry coulis, and finally the mango. Using a toothpick, pull through the sauces in 2 directions, making a design. Repeat with the remaining plates. Place a puff pastry bottom in the center of each plate. Pipe some of the Chantilly cream into the bottom of each.

Arrange the berries on top of the cream, beginning with the raspberries, then the blueberries, and finally the blackberries. Cut the nectarines into 18 wedges and place 3 wedges on each dessert at one corner. Pipe rosettes of Chantilly cream on the 4 corners of each pastry. Dust the top pastry halves with confectioners' sugar and set on top of the filled pastry bottoms, allowing the rosettes of cream to hold them in place. Place a sprig of mint on the top of each and serve.

CHRISTIAN GILLE
Le Jardin, The Westin Canal Place, New Orleans, Louisiana

Perched twelve stories high above a luxury retail and office complex, French-born Christian Gille has no need for any Big Apple-style "windows on the world." A Big Easy-style "windows on the Mississippi" is all the panorama he needs.

In fact, returning to New Orleans as executive chef at the Westin Canal Place meant coming back to the scene of some of his greatest professional triumphs as well as some of his greatest personal satisfactions. His primary showcase, Le Jardin, is a restaurant for which his ambitions are every bit as lofty as its location.

"Eating is one of the great measures of a culture and its people," says Gille, who fell in love with New Orleans during five years as executive chef at Arnaud's in the French Quarter. "Fine dining should foster an artistic response, not just nourishment. My goal is to refresh our guests with a complete experience that inspires as well as satisfies."

Inspiring others is easy for Gille, after his years of experience. A native of Poitiers, Gille began his apprenticeship (and his almost-legendary globe-trotting) in Morocco at the age of thirteeen. Next, his European training kept him on the move both by sea and rail, working aboard the *S.S. France* (now the *S.S. Norway*) and the famed overnight trains of Wagon Lits.

After running his own hotel and restaurant in France for eight years, Gille served as chef for Sofitel Hotels in that country, in the Middle East, and finally in the West Indies. In 1982 he accepted a position opening a Sofitel property in Houston. The following year brought him to New Orleans.

Gille took special pleasure in running the kitchen at Arnaud's, a Creole landmark established in 1918. In some ways, it resembled the grand family proprietorships of his native France, while in others it resembled a grand hotel, with banquet business almost around the clock in private rooms. Gille helped to revise many classic Creole recipes, and during his tenure *Arnaud's Creole Cookbook* was published by Simon and Schuster.

In 1988, Gille grew restless again, relocating to Orlando as executive recruiter in a hospitality search company and later as owner of his own restaurant. In 1991, he signed on with Westin as executive chef at the famed Las Hadas Resort in Mexico; this opened the door for his return to New Orleans in late 1993.

Redfish with Shrimp and Crab Roasted-Pepper Butter and Pumpkin Seeds; *Bruce Molzan, Ruggles Grill*

Basic Recipes and Techniques

The professional kitchen can be overwhelming for a home cook, filled as it is with almost frenetic activity. The professional kitchen staff's goal is not just to create delicious and beautifully presented foods, but to do so in a relatively short amount of time. Patrons are willing to wait for a splendid meal, but they won't wait all evening.

To accomplish their alchemy, chefs must prepare their ingredients ahead of time, a technique known as mise en place. It is a key secret of great kitchens. Not only are basics such as stocks prepared in advance, but ingredients such as vegetables and fruits are peeled and chopped and in place, ready to be assembled and cooked at the last minute. This chapter includes basic recipes and basic preparation techniques and cooking techniques so that you can create your own version of mise en place.

Chicago, Illinois

Basic

Crème Anglaise
Makes 2 cups

4 egg yolks
⅓ cup sugar
1½ cups milk, heated
2 teaspoons vanilla extract
1 tablespoon butter at room temperature (optional)

Place the egg yolks in a medium, heavy saucepan and whisk them over low heat until they are pale in color. Add the sugar 1 tablespoon at a time, beating well between each addition. Beat until the mixture reaches the consistency of cake batter.

Whisk in the milk, then stir continuously with a wooden spoon until the custard coats the spoon and a line drawn down the back of the spoon remains visible. Remove from heat and stir in the vanilla.

If the custard is to be chilled, press a sheet of plastic wrap directly onto the surface to prevent a skin from forming, or dot the top with bits of the optional butter. Chill the custard for up to 2 days.

Note: If the custard begins to overheat and the egg yolks are forming lumps, remove it immediately from the heat and whisk briskly to cool the mixture. Push the custard through a fine-meshed sieve with the back of a spoon to remove the lumps. If it has not sufficiently thickened, return it to heat to complete cooking.

Crème Fraîche
Crème fraîche is now widely available in specialty foods stores; however, it is also easy to make by combining 1 cup of heavy (whipping) cream (preferably not ultra-pasteurized) with 1 tablespoon of buttermilk in a small saucepan. Slowly heat the cream to warm, 105° to 115°F. Pour the mixture into a clean glass container and cover it loosely. Set in warm place (70° to 80°F) until thickened, about 24 to 36 hours. Cover tightly and refrigerate for 1 more day to develop the tangy flavor.

Ice Cream Base
Makes 3 cups

2 cups heavy (whipping) cream
½ cup half-and-half
8 egg yolks
1 cup sugar

In a medium saucepan over medium-high heat, bring the cream and half-and-half to a boil. Meanwhile, beat the egg yolks with the sugar in a medium bowl until light and fluffy, 6 to 8 minutes. Stir some of the hot cream mixture into the egg yolks, then add the egg yolks to the hot cream mixture and cook over medium heat for 8 minutes, or until the mixture begins to boil and is thick enough to coat a spoon. Remove from heat. Cover and chill in the refrigerator.

Vanilla Ice Cream Split 1 vanilla bean lengthwise and add it to the cream mixture before cooking. Remove the bean pieces before adding the eggs. Or, stir 1 tablespoon vanilla extract into the chilled ice cream base and freeze in an ice cream maker according to the manufacturer's directions.

Fruit Ice Cream Stir 1 cup pureed fruit into the chilled ice cream base and freeze in an ice cream machine according to the manufacturer's directions. Makes 1 quart.

Liqueur-flavored Ice Cream Stir up to ¼ cup liqueur into the chilled ice cream base and freeze in an ice cream maker according to the manufacturer's directions.

To freeze ice cream without using an ice cream machine, see page 237.

Rabbit Ravioli in a Potato Crust with Red Pepper Oil;
Jean-Georges Vongerichten, JoJo's/Vong

Caramel Sauce
Makes 2 cups

This thick caramel sauce is enriched with butter and cream.

1½ cups sugar
½ cup water
3 tablespoons butter
1 cup heavy (whipping) cream, heated
½ teaspoon vanilla extract

Place the sugar and water in a medium, heavy saucepan. Bring to a simmer over medium heat, swirling occasionally. Cover the pan, raise heat to medium high, and cook for 2 minutes, or until the liquid gives off large, thick bubbles. Remove the cover and cook, swirling the syrup, until it turns golden brown.

Remove the pan from heat and stir in the butter with a wooden spoon. Add the cream, stirring constantly, then add the vanilla. Return the pan to low heat and stir constantly until any lumps have melted and the syrup is smooth. Serve warm over ice cream or cake, or pour into a jar, cover, and refrigerate for up to 1 week.

Butterscotch Sauce Substitute light brown sugar for the granulated sugar, and add 2 teaspoons of cider vinegar to the syrup along with the vanilla.

Iron Skillet roasted Mussels; *Reed Hearon, LuLu*

White Chocolate Sauce
Makes about 1½ cups

8 ounces white chocolate, chopped
½ cup heavy (whipping) cream
1 tablespoon Grand Marnier or other liqueur (optional)

In a double boiler over barely simmering water, melt the chocolate, stirring until smooth. Remove from heat and mix in the heavy cream and liqueur. Serve warm, or pour into a jar, cover, and refrigerate for up to 1 week.

Chocolate Sauce
Makes about 4 cups

1 cup sugar
2 cups half-and-half
8 ounces bittersweet or semisweet chocolate, chopped
8 ounces unsweetened chocolate, chopped

In a large, heavy saucepan, heat the sugar and half-and-half over medium-low heat until hot but not boiling. Add the chocolate and stir until the chocolate is melted and the mixture is smooth. Serve warm, or pour into a jar, cover, and refrigerate for up to 1 week.

Clarified Butter Melt butter over low heat, then cover and refrigerate it. Once the fat has hardened, scoop it off, being careful to leave the bottom layer of milk solids. Store the clarified butter covered in the refrigerator for up to 2 weeks.

If you don't have time to let the butter chill, melt the butter gently so that the milk solids settle on the bottom of the pan, forming a creamy white sediment. Carefully and slowly pour off the clear yellow butter and discard the milk solids or add them to soup or sauce.

Basil Oil In a medium bowl, combine ¾ cup minced fresh basil leaves with 1 cup of canola oil. Cover and let sit for a minimum of 48 hours. Pour through a fine-meshed sieve into a glass jar or bottle and cover. Makes 1 cup.

Mint Oil Replace the basil in the above recipe with ¾ cup minced fresh mint leaves and proceed as directed.

Variations The same procedure can be used to make tarragon, thyme, chive, and other herb oils.

Cooked Berry Puree or Sauce
Makes about 2 cups

4 cups fresh berries
¼ cup sugar or more to taste
¼ cup water
2 tablespoons raspberry liqueur or eau-de-vie (optional)
1 tablespoon fresh lemon juice or more to taste
½ teaspoon ground cinnamon or more to taste

Put the berries in a large sauté pan or skillet with the ¼ cup sugar, water, and optional liqueur or eau-de-vie. Cook over medium heat for 15 minutes, or until the fruit is soft enough to mash with a spoon and most of the liquid has evaporated. Add the 1 tablespoon lemon juice and ½ teaspoon cinnamon, then taste and adjust the flavor with additional sugar, lemon juice, or cinnamon as needed.

Transfer the mixture to a blender or food processor and puree until smooth. Strain the fruit through a fine-meshed sieve, cover, and refrigerate until cold, about 2 hours; this should be a very thick puree. It may be used as an ingredient in another recipe, or by itself as a sauce.

Plum, Apple, Pear, or Prune Puree or Sauce Substitute 12 chopped pitted large plums or dried prunes, or 8 peeled, cored, and chopped large apples or pears for the berries.

Uncooked Fruit Puree (Coulis)
Makes about 2 cups

4 cups fresh berries, or 2 cups diced fresh fruit
2 tablespoons sugar or more to taste
1 teaspoon fresh lemon juice

Puree the berries or fruit in a blender or food processor. Strain the puree through a fine-meshed sieve. Stir in the 2 tablespoons sugar and the lemon juice. Adjust the amount of sugar if necessary. Cover and refrigerate until needed. This puree may be used as an ingredient in another recipe, or by itself as a sauce.

Mayonnaise
Makes 1½ cups

1 teaspoon Dijon mustard
2 egg yolks
Salt and white pepper to taste
2 cups peanut or other vegetable oil
2 tablespoons white wine vinegar or fresh lemon juice

Using a whisk or an electric beater, beat the mustard, egg yolks, salt, and pepper in a medium bowl until thick. Gradually whisk the oil into the egg mixture, starting with 1 drop at a time; when 2 or 3 tablespoons of the oil have been whisked into the eggs, you can pour in the rest of the oil in a fine stream while whisking constantly. Add the vinegar or lemon juice to the mixture 1 teaspoon at a time, whisking constantly until smooth. Cover and store up to 1 week in the refrigerator.

Oven-dried Tomatoes Preheat the oven to 250°F. Cut plum (Roma) tomatoes in half lengthwise and sprinkle with salt and pepper. Place on a baking sheet, cut-side up; bake until almost dry, 45 to 60 minutes.

Cream Puffs
Makes about twenty-four 2-inch puffs

½ cup milk
½ cup water
½ cup (1 stick) unsalted butter
1 cup unbleached all-purpose flour
2 tablespoons sugar
4 eggs

Preheat the oven to 400°F. Line 2 baking sheets with baking parchment or grease them. In a medium saucepan, combine the milk, water, and butter and bring to a boil over medium-high heat. Add the flour and sugar all at once and stir the mixture until it comes away from the side of the pan, 2 or 3 minutes. Add the eggs one at a time, stirring until each is blended. Remove from heat and let stand for 5 minutes.

Place the mixture in a pastry bag fitted with a 1-inch plain tip. Pipe twenty-four 1½-inch-diameter portions 2 inches apart on the prepared pans. Bake for 10 minutes, then reduce heat to 350°F and bake for 10 to 15 minutes, or until golden.

Basic

▰▰▰▰▰▰▰▰▰▰▰▰

Phyllo Triangles
Makes 32 triangles

6 sheets phyllo dough
2 cups (4 sticks) unsalted butter, melted
1 cup sugar

Preheat the oven to 375°F. Line a baking sheet with parchment paper or aluminum foil. Place 1 sheet of phyllo dough on a large cutting board. Keep the remaining dough covered with a towel to keep it moist. Lightly brush the phyllo with melted butter and sprinkle with some of the sugar. Repeat to make 6 layers of phyllo. Cut the dough in half lengthwise, then divide each half into 8 equal squares. Cut each square in half diagonally, making 32 triangles.

Transfer the triangles to the prepared pan. Cover the pastry with another sheet of parchment or foil and set a second pan on top. (The additional pan helps the triangles to keep their shape and helps to caramelize the phyllo dough.) Bake the triangles for 8 to 10 minutes, or until golden brown. The pastry burns easily, so watch carefully. Remove the top pan and paper or foil and let the pastries cool completely.

Pie Crust
Makes one 9-inch crust pie, or two 9-inch pie shells

2¼ cups unbleached all-purpose flour
½ teaspoon salt
¾ cup vegetable shortening
5 to 6 teaspoons ice water

In a medium bowl, combine the flour and salt. Using a pastry blender or 2 knives, cut half of the shortening into the flour. Cut the remaining half of the shortening into the flour until the mixture resembles coarse meal. Add the ice water 1 tablespoon at a time, mixing it in lightly with a fork. As soon as the dough holds its shape, stop adding water and gently gather the dough into a ball with your hands. Divide the dough in half, wrap each half in plastic wrap, and place in the refrigerator for at least 1 hour or up to 3 days.

When ready to use, preheat the oven to 425°F. Lightly dust a work surface with flour. Unwrap one of the balls of dough and press it down with the heel of your hand to flatten it slightly. Lightly dust a rolling pin with flour and roll the pastry into a circle ⅛ inch thick and 2 inches larger than the pie pan. Roll the pastry around the rolling pin, place the rolling pin across the pie pan, and unroll the pastry into the pan. Press it gently into the bottom and sides of the pan. Trim any extra pastry from the pan rim.

For a 2-crust pie: Repeat the process to roll out the top crust, and fill and seal the pie according to the recipe directions.

For a pie shell: Flute the edge of the dough by pinching and twisting it with your fingers. Prick the bottom and sides of the dough liberally with a fork. Line the pie shell with aluminum foil or parchment paper, and weight with dried beans or pie weights. Repeat with the remaining ball of dough.

For a fully baked shell: Bake for 10 to 15 minutes, or until just lightly browned.

For a partially baked shell (to be baked again with the filling added): Bake the shell for 5 to 7 minutes, or until just set and barely colored.

Simple Syrup
Makes about 1½ cups

2 cups sugar
1 cup water

In a medium, heavy saucepan combine the sugar and water and cook over high heat until the sugar dissolves and the mixture reaches a full boil, about 3 minutes. Remove from heat, let cool, and store in a covered container in the refrigerator for up to 3 weeks.

Pulled Sugar

4 pounds sugar
2 cups water
¼ cup apple cider vinegar
¼ cup red or another color of paste or liquid food coloring
¼ cup blue or another color of paste or liquid food coloring

In a medium, heavy saucepan, combine the sugar, water, and vinegar and cook over medium-high heat until the mixture is a light golden color. Pour onto a baking sheet and let cool enough to handle. It will be like taffy.

Pick up one end of the mixture and pull it over itself again and again, working it until it becomes shiny. Cut it into 2 pieces and add one coloring to one and the second coloring to the other. Knead each piece to blend in the coloring. Form into 2 strips of equal length. Lay one strip on top of the other and press them together. Holding each end, pull that strip until it is stretched double the original length. Fold the strip in half, pressing the inside edges together. Pull the strip to double its length again. Repeat this process, stretching and then folding the strip over itself again and again, until the colors have ribboned themselves throughout the piece.

Cut or pull off a piece suitable to the shape you wish to form: small for flowers and other small designs, larger for ribbons and fluted shapes. Stretch this piece until it is thin, and form it into the shape or ribbon desired. Repeat with the remaining pieces. Let set until cool and firm. It may be necessary to work under a heat lamp to keep the sugar strip pliable while you are pulling it.

Basic

■■■■■■■■■■■■■

Spun Sugar

1 cup sugar
½ cup hot water
⅛ teaspoon cream of tartar

In a small, heavy saucepan, combine all the ingredients. Place over medium-high heat until the mixture reaches 310°F, or just begins to turn an amber color. Remove from heat and let the syrup cool for a few minutes.

Spray a heavy baking sheet with vegetable-oil spray, then wipe the baking sheet with a paper towel to remove any excess. Working quickly, dip a fork into the hot syrup and wave it over the baking sheet. The strands of syrup will begin hardening almost immediately. With practice you can form them into a lattice design or swirls, or even make into a lacy dome by forming them over an inverted oiled bowl.

Chicken Stock
Makes 12 cups

6 quarts water
5 pounds chicken bones, skin, and trimmings
2 carrots, peeled and cut into chunks
1 large onion, halved
3 garlic cloves, halved
3 celery stalks, halved
3 fresh thyme sprigs, or 1 teaspoon dried thyme
6 fresh parsley sprigs
3 bay leaves
12 black peppercorns

In a large stockpot, combine the water and the chicken bones, skin, and trimmings. Bring to a boil, then reduce heat to a simmer, skimming off the foam that rises for the first 10 to 15 minutes. Cook for 1 hour, then add the remaining ingredients. Raise the heat to bring the liquid to a boil, reduce heat to low, and simmer the stock for 3 hours.

Strain the stock through a fine-meshed sieve and let cool to room temperature, then refrigerate. Remove and discard the congealed layer of fat on the surface. Store in the refrigerator up to 3 days. To keep longer, bring the stock to a boil every 3 days, or freeze it for up to 3 months.

Veal or Beef Stock
Makes 12 cups

8 pounds veal or beef bones and trimmings
2 onions, halved
2 carrots, peeled and halved
2 celery stalks, halved
3 garlic cloves, halved

8 quarts water
3 fresh thyme sprigs, or 1 teaspoon dried thyme
6 fresh parsley sprigs
2 bay leaves
12 peppercorns

Preheat the oven to 400°F. Put the bones and trimmings in a roasting pan and roast until they are browned, about 45 minutes, turning occasionally. Add the vegetables to the pan and roast 20 minutes longer, or until the vegetables are browned.

Place the bones and vegetables in a stockpot and pour off any fat. Add 1 quart of the water to the pan and place on the stove over high heat. Stir to scrape up the brown bits clinging to the bottom of the pan. Pour this liquid into the stockpot with the remaining 7 quarts water and the herbs and spices, and bring to a boil. Reduce the heat so that the stock is barely simmering, and skim the surface of the scum that will rise for the first 10 to 15 minutes. Simmer the stock for 5 to 6 hours.

Strain the stock through a fine-meshed sieve, and discard the solids. Let cool, then cover and refrigerate. Remove and discard the congealed layer of fat on the surface. Store in the refrigerator for up to 3 days. To keep longer, bring the stock to a boil every 3 days, or freeze it for up to 3 months.

Pasta with Mushrooms and Foie Gras; *Debra Ponzek, Montrachet*

Basic

Fish Stock
Makes 12 cups

16 cups water
1 cup dry white wine
4 pounds fish trimmings such as skin, bones, and heads
2 tablespoons fresh lemon juice
1 onion, halved
2 celery stalks, halved
4 fresh parsley sprigs
2 fresh thyme sprigs, or 1 teaspoon dried thyme
6 peppercorns

In a large stockpot, bring the water and wine to a boil. Rinse all the fish trimmings under cold running water, add to the stockpot, and bring to a boil. Reduce heat to a simmer and cook for 1 hour.

Add the remaining ingredients to the pot. Bring the mixture to a boil, then reduce heat to a simmer and cook for 1½ to 2 hours. Strain the stock through a fine-meshed sieve, pressing on the solids with the back of a large spoon. Discard the solids and let the stock cool. Cover and refrigerate for up to 3 days. To keep longer, bring the stock to a boil every 3 days, or freeze it for up to 3 months.

Shrimp or Lobster Stock: Follow the preceding recipe, using 4 pounds shrimp shells or lobster shells in place of the fish trimmings.

Vegetable Stock
Makes 12 cups

4 large leeks, carefully washed
2 large carrots, peeled and sliced
4 large celery stalks, sliced
4 large yellow onions, sliced
5 garlic cloves
6 fresh parsley sprigs
4 fresh thyme sprigs, or 1 teaspoon dried thyme
2 bay leaves
16 cups water
½ teaspoon white peppercorns
1 teaspoon black peppercorns
Salt to taste

Place all the ingredients except the salt in a large stockpot. Slowly bring the liquid to a boil over medium heat, reduce heat to a simmer, and cook, partially covered, for 1½ hours. Strain through a fine-meshed sieve, pressing the liquid from the solids with the back of a large spoon. Let cool, then cover and refrigerate for up to 3 days. To keep longer, bring to a boil every 3 days, or freeze for up to 3 months

Duck, Rabbit, Lamb or Venison Stock

3 pounds duck, rabbit, Lamb or venison trimmings (bones, skin, fat, and/or anything else you can trim away) and meat
4 quarts (16 cups) water
1 onion, halved
1 carrot, peeled and halved
2 celery stalks, including leaves, cut into sections
3 fresh thyme sprigs, or 1 teaspoon dried thyme
3 fresh parsley sprigs
6 black peppercorns

Preheat the oven to 450°F. Put the trimmings and meat in a shallow roasting pan and roast for 30 minutes, or until browned.

Bring the water to a boil over high heat. Add the trimmings and meat to the water and reduce heat to medium. When the water comes back to a boil, skim frequently until the scum stops rising, then add the remaining ingredients and simmer, uncovered, for at least 6 hours. Add additional water if the stock level falls below the level of the ingredients.

Strain and discard the solids. Let the stock cool to room temperature, then refrigerate. Remove and discard the congealed fat layer from the top. Store in the refrigerator for up to 3 days. To keep longer, bring to a boil every 3 days, or refrigerate for up to 3 months.

Rich Stock: Multiply the amount of rich stock specified in the recipe by 1½, and pour that amount of the kind of stock specified into a small saucepan. Bring to a boil over high heat. Cook the stock to reduce it by one third. If the stock was not salt-free, add a few slices of raw potato or some uncooked rice before reducing the stock; the starchy substance will absorb much of the salt.

Basic

▰▰▰▰▰▰▰▰▰▰▰

Veal Demi-Glace
Makes 2 cups

Demi-glace is unsalted meat stock that has been degreased and then reduced over medium-low heat until it becomes rich and syrupy. The concentrated flavor adds richness and depth to sauces and stews. Traditional demi-glace is thickened with flour and must simmer gently with much tending, but this quick version is lighter and can be made more quickly because it is thickened at the end with arrowroot or cornstarch.

2 tablespoons vegetable oil
1 large onion, diced
2 celery stalks, diced
1 carrot, peeled and sliced
½ cup diced ham
3 tablespoons tomato paste
1 fresh thyme sprig
1 bay leaf
6 peppercorns
10 cups veal stock (see page 228)
½ cup Madeira
2 to 3 teaspoons arrowroot or cornstarch mixed with 2 tablespoons cold water
Salt and freshly ground black pepper to taste
1 tablespoon unsalted butter

Heat the oil in a large saucepan over medium heat. Stir in the onion, celery, carrot, and ham. Cover and cook over low heat for 10 minutes. Uncover the pan and stir in the tomato paste, thyme, bay leaf, and peppercorns. Whisk in the stock and Madeira, and bring to a boil over high heat.

Once the mixture has started to boil, reduce heat to medium high and cook the sauce to reduce to 2 cups. Depending on the rate at which the liquid is boiling, this may take anywhere from 30 minutes to 1 hour. Strain the liquid through a fine-meshed sieve into a 2-cup measuring cup. If it has not reduced enough, pour the liquid back into the pan and keep boiling. If it has reduced too much, add enough water to make 2 cups.

Pour the liquid back into the pan and bring it back to a simmer. Whisk in the arrowroot or cornstarch mixture 1 teaspoon at a time, returning the sauce to a simmer after each addition, until the sauce reaches the desired consistency. Add salt and pepper. If using the sauce immediately, swirl in the butter. If not serving immediately, do not whisk in the butter, but remove the pan from heat and place dots of the butter on the surface of the sauce to prevent a skin from forming. Whisk in the butter when reheating the sauce. To store, cover and refrigerate for up to 5 days or freeze for up to 3 months.

Terrine of Squab Breast and Wild Mushrooms; *Klaus Helmin, Tivoli*

Basic

▪▫▪▫▪▫▪▫▪▫▪▫▪▫▪

Charred Rare Tuna with Radish Salad and Soy-Ginger Vinaigrette; *Anne Gingrass, Postrio*

To Julienne Cut the food to be julienned into thin strips about 1 to 2 inches long and ⅛ inch wide. Fine julienne is ¹⁄₁₆ inch wide.

Cleaning Leeks Trim the top of the leek, leaving some green or removing it altogether, depending on the recipe. Discard the outer leaves and trim the root. Split the leek in quarters or halves almost through the root, depending on size. Rinse the leek down to the root under cold running water, separating the leaves to rinse between them, and reassemble the layers for cooking.

Peeling and Seeding Tomatoes With a sharp knife, cut an X in the blossom end (opposite the stem end) of the tomatoes. Using a slotted spoon, place the tomatoes in rapidly boiling water to cover for 10 seconds. Lift out and plunge the tomatoes in a bowl of ice water. When the tomatoes are cool enough to handle, lift out with slotted spoon and core the tomatoes, then slip off the skins. To seed the tomatoes, cut each tomato in half and hold it upside down over the sink, shaking the tomato and squeezing it slightly to discard the seeds.

Preparing Artichoke Hearts Soak the artichokes in cool water for 10 minutes. Drain, then remove any tough, discolored outer leaves, usually found around the base of the stem end. Cut off the stem. Working in circular fashion around the artichoke, cut off all of the leaf tips with a pair of scissors. With a large, sharp knife, cut off the top quarter of the artichoke and discard.

Cook the trimmed artichokes in boiling water to cover, to which 1 or 2 tablespoons of lemon juice or vinegar and ½ to 1 teaspoon of salt have been added. Cook until a knife inserted in the base of an artichoke goes in easily, about 30 minutes. Drain the artichokes upside down in a colander. When cool enough to handle, peel off all of the artichoke leaves and pull out small purple-tinged core of thin leaves. Use a spoon to scrape out the hairy choke in the center and discard. Trim the edges of the heart.

Roasting Garlic With a sharp knife, cut the top quarter off a head of unpeeled garlic. Rub the head with olive oil. Place in a baking dish in a 350°F oven and roast for 1 hour. Remove from the oven. When cool enough to handle, separate the cloves from the head and squeeze the roasted garlic pulp or puree from each.

Handling Bell Peppers and Chilies

Bell peppers now come in a rainbow of colors, and there are literally hundreds of varieties of chilies. Here are some general rules common to all:

Handling Fresh Chilies Precautions should be exercised in handling fresh hot chilies, since they contain potent oils. Either wear rubber gloves, or wash your hands thoroughly with soap and hot water after handling chilies and never touch your skin until you've washed your hands. Also wash the knife and cutting board in hot, soapy water. Do not handle hot chilies under running water, since that spreads the oil vapors upward to your eyes.

Seeding and Deribbing Either cut out the ribs and seeds with a paring knife, or cut away the flesh, leaving a skeleton of ribs and seeds to discard. For the second method, cut a slice off the bottom of the pepper or chili so that it will stand up on the cutting board. Holding the pepper or chili with your free hand, slice its natural curvature in sections. You will be left with all the flesh and none of the seeds and ribs. The flesh may now be cut as indicated in the recipe.

Roasting and Peeling Cut a small slit near the stem end of each whole pepper or chili to ensure that it will not explode. Roast the peppers or chilies in one of the following ways:

- For a large number of peppers or chilies, and to retain the most texture, lower them gently into 375°F (almost smoking) oil and fry until the skin blisters. Turn them with tongs when one side is blistered, since they will float to the surface of the oil. This method is also the most effective if the vegetables are not perfectly shaped, since it is difficult to get the heat from the broiler into the folds of peppers and some chilies.

- Place the peppers or chilies 6 inches from a preheated broiler, turning them with tongs until all surfaces are charred.

- Place the peppers or chilies on the cooking rack of a hot charcoal or gas grill and turn them until the skin is charred.

- Place a wire cake rack over a gas or electric burner set at the highest temperature and turn the peppers or chilies with tongs until all surfaces are charred.

- Place the peppers or chilies on a rack on a baking sheet in a preheated 550°F oven until they are totally blistered. Use this method only for a sauce or a recipe in which the peppers or chilies are to be pureed.

Cool the peppers or chilies by one of the following methods:

- Place them in ice water. This stops the cooking action immediately and cools them enough to peel them within 1 minute. The peppers or chilies will stay relatively firm.

- Place the peppers or chilies in a paper bag, close it, and let them cool. This also effectively separates the flesh from the skin, but it will be about 20 minutes before they are cool enough to handle, and they will soften somewhat during that time.

Finally, pull the skin off and remove the seeds.

Cleaning Dried Chilies Remove the stem, then pull the chili apart lengthwise, splitting it in half. Brush the seeds from both halves and the chili is ready to cook. If it is dusty, rinse it under cold water.

Basic

■■■■■■■■■■■■■

The '21' Club Crab Cakes; *Michael Lomonaco, The '21' Club*

Toasting Nuts Place shelled nuts in large dry skillet over low to medium heat. Cook, stirring and turning constantly with a spoon or spatula, until the nuts are heated through and just beginning to change color; do not let them turn brown. Remove the pan from heat immediately and spread the nuts on a large plate or a tray lined with paper towels to cool.

Or, spread the nuts in a single layer in a shallow pan. Bake in a preheated 350°F oven, shaking the sheet occasionally, until the nuts or seeds are golden, 5 to 12 minutes, depending on size. Let cool.

Toasting and Peeling Hazelnuts Toast hazelnuts in the oven as described above for 7 or 8 minutes, or until the papery skin begins to flake. Roll the hazelnuts in a clean dish towel and let cool for several minutes. Rub the hazelnuts vigorously inside the towel until part of the skins have rubbed off. Pour them into a colander and stir them over the sink to release more of the skins.

Peeling and Deveining Shrimp With a small sharp knife, slit through the inner curve of the shell from front to back. Remove the shell by peeling it off. The tail shell may be removed as well or left attached.

To devein peeled raw or cooked shrimp, make a shallow slit along the outside curve with a small knife, then pull out and discard the black vein that runs from the head to the tail. Rinse deveined shrimp quickly under cold water. Pat dry with paper towels.

To butterfly peeled raw shrimp, cut from the outer curved side down to but not all the way through the inner curve. Spread the shrimp open and flatten gently with the flat side of the knife. The tail shell may be left on or discarded, depending on the recipe.

Caramelizing Sugar Combine 3 parts granulated sugar and 1 part water in a small, heavy saucepan. Bring to a simmer over medium heat, swirling the pan occasionally until the sugar crystals have dissolved and the liquid is clear, about 3 to 4 minutes.

Cover the pan, raise the heat to medium high, and boil, undisturbed, for 2 minutes, or until the bubbles look thick. Remove the lid. Within a few seconds, the syrup will begin to color. Swirl the pot by its handle, since the syrup will color first directly over the heat. When the syrup is almost the desired color, remove the pan from the heat and continue to swirl. It will darken another shade or two from the residual heat of the pan.

If lining a mold, immediately pour the caramel into the center of the mold and rotate the mold to spread the caramel in an even layer.

To clean the pan in which the caramel was made, fill the pan with water to the top of the hardened caramel and place it over high heat. Stir it as the water comes to a boil, and the pan will be virtually clean.

Melting Chocolate Chop the chocolate into small pieces with a heavy knife or in a food processor. If using a food processor, break the chocolate into chunks with a heavy knife first.

Melt the chocolate in a double boiler placed over barely simmering water, stirring just until smooth. Or, place the chocolate in a microwaveable bowl and microwave on 100 percent for 20 seconds, stir, and repeat as necessary; or place in a preheated 250°F oven, then turn off the heat immediately. Stir after 3 minutes and return to the warm oven if necessary.

Handling Phyllo Dough Phyllo dough is available in 1-pound packages in the freezer section of supermarkets. A package of phyllo contains approximately 18 to 24 sheets, each sheet measuring about 12 by 20 inches. The phyllo should be defrosted completely for at least 8 hours at room temperature before opening. It can also be defrosted in a microwave oven at medium (50 percent) power; remove the phyllo from the outer carton but leave it inside the sealed inner plastic pouch. Defrost for 3 to 5 minutes, depending on the power of the microwave.

When handling phyllo, you should try to work as quickly as possible, so it is important to have all ingredients ready. If using only part of the dough at a time, cover the remaining phyllo with a slightly damp towel or plastic wrap, or put the phyllo that you aren't immediately using in the refrigerator, tightly wrapped in plastic wrap.

Making Ice Cream Without a Machine
While there are a number of inexpensive ice cream machines on the market, it is possible to make ice creams and sorbets without any sort of ice cream machine. Here are two methods:

Food Processor Method Freeze mixture in ice cube trays for 45 minutes to 1 hour, or until the cubes are almost frozen. Empty the ice cube trays into a blender or food processor and process, using on-and-off pulsing motions, until the mixture is smooth. Put back into the ice cube trays and freeze for another 30 minutes. Process again and scrape the ice cream into a plastic container or mixing bowl. Freeze again until solid. When you are ready to serve, let sit at room temperature for several minutes to soften slightly.

Electric Mixer Method Freeze the mixture in a mixing bowl until the outer 2 to 3 inches is frozen. Remove from the freezer and beat with an electric mixer until smooth. Repeat 2 more times, then allow to freeze completely. When you are ready to serve, let sit at room temperature for several minutes to soften slightly.

Roasted Baby Rack of Lamb with Stuffed Sweet Mini-Peppers and Eggplant Cake; *Gabino Sotelino, Ambria*

Menus for Entertaining

▼▼▲▼▲▼▲▼▲▼▲▼▲▼▲▼

The chefs in this book created their dishes with their own menus in mind, and without knowing what the other chefs would contribute. These chefs know best how to combine their own dishes. Still, these dishes are ours for the making. And that task includes combining them into menus.

The sample menus that follow are based on seasonal and regional or ethnic themes, which are the best way to ensure foods peacefully coexisting on our table.

Here, then, from plain to fancy, are some suggestions for combining the recipes in this book into menus for a variety of occasions.

Miami, Florida

Spring Lunch

Goat Cheese Cobbler, page 68
Tuna Tartare, page 28
Spring Lamb with Vegetables, page 140
Napoleon of Tropical Fruit, page 214

Summer Picnic

Cheese Grits Cake, page 36
Salmon Salad with Avocado Vinaigrette and Corn Salsa, page 104
Country-Style Pork Ribs in Green Chili Sauce, page 123
Lemon Angel Food Chiffon, page 191

Thanksgiving Feast

Corn Flan with Smoked Salmon, page 26
Baked Vidalia Onion with Chive Blossom Vinaigrette, page 14
Venison with Rhubarb and Spelt-Corn Relish, page 146
Apple Tart, page 188
Gâteau Chocolat Fondant, page 204

Christmas Celebration

Eggplant and Roasted–Red Pepper Terrine, page 34
Roasted Foie Gras with Risotto, page 40
Pork Tenderloin with Apple-Onion Confit, page 124
Mascarpone Caramel Cream with Berries and White Chocolate–Raspberry Brittle,
   page 152
Chocolate-Rum Truffle Cake, page 200

New Year's Buffet

The '21' Club Crab Cakes, page 10
Rabbit Ravioli in a Potato Crust with Red Pepper Oil, page 18
Grilled Swordfish Tostada, page 42
Smoked Duck Hash, page 112
Pesto-crusted Salmon Skewers with Wild Mushroom Risotto and Arugula-Basil
   Vinaigrette, page 102
Sun-dried Cherry Charlotte with Green Tea Ice Cream, page 192
Alsatian Sour Cream Coffee Cake, page 179

Flavors of Italy

Pasta with Mushrooms and Foie Gras, page 14
Gamberoni alla Griglia, page 82
Italian Flat Bread, page 19
Saddle of Lamb with Pesto and Fingerling Potato, Baby Artichoke,
   and Oven-dried Tomato Ragout, page 136
Tiramisù, page 180

Bistro Fare

Onion Tart, page 52
Peppered Salmon Niçoise, page 12
Braised Lamb Shanks with Carrots, Leeks, and Coriander Sauce, page 138
Maple Sugar Crème Caramel, page 154

New World Dinner

Sweet and Sour Quail Peruvian Style, page 8
Tamale Tart with Roasted-Garlic Custard and Crabmeat, page 24
Shrimp Enchiladas on Black Bean Sauce, page 106
Apple Dumpling with Cinnamon-Rum Sauce, page 210

Romantic Supper

Deviled Oysters with Sour Mango Slaw and Tabasco Butter Sauce,
　　page 38
Ballottine of Sole Sauce Émeraude, page 22
Langoustine Purse with Mango, Leeks, and Ginger, with a Port Wine
　　Sauce, page 78
Hazelnut and Roasted-Almond Mousse Cake, page 196

Caribbean Sun Splash

Stone Crab Salad with Baby-Tomato Confit, page 30
Fresh-cracked Conch with Vanilla-Rum Sauce and Spicy Black
　　Bean Salad, page 32
Creole Spiny Lobster, page 76
Key Lime Pie, page 182
Chocolate–Macadamia Nut Meringue with Tropical Fruit Cream, page 156

Pacific Rim Dinner

Grilled Chinese Eggplant with Balsamic Vinaigrette, page 10
Lobster with Avocado and Tangy Honey Sauce, page 16
Kasu-marinated Sturgeon with Grilled Rice Cakes, Umaboshi
　　Plum Vinaigrette, and Beet Oil, page 100
Sweet Dim Sum Box, page 174

Southern Hospitality

Scallop and Leek Flan, page 84
Deviled Oysters with Sour Mango Slaw and Tabasco Butter
　　Sauce, page 38
Veal Steak Sauté with Jerky Sauce, page 120
Rum Banana and Maple Ice Cream Sandwich, page 164

Dinner for "Foodies"

Rabbit Ravioli in a Potato Crust with Red Pepper Oil, page 18
Minced Chicken in Lettuce Cups, page 50
Corn Pancake with Thinly Sliced Salmon, Caviar, and Watercress
　　Sauce, page 20
Sweetbreads with Camomile and Morels, page 122
Chocolate Parfait, page 159

Veal Steak Sauté with Jerky Sauce; *Larry Forgione, An American Place*

Glossary

The chefs represented in *Great Chefs—Great Cities* use ingredients from all over the globe. Most of these ingredients are familiar to all cooks. But some are more exotic, flown in from distant markets to make their appearance on supermarket shelves and produce counters. Now that shoppers have become accustomed to the many varieties of peppers and mushrooms in the stores, the burgeoning interest in Asian and Pacific ingredients is introducing lemongrass, galangal, and nori. The world is at our market basket.

This glossary collects information about many of the ingredients used by the chefs, explaining what they are, where they are usually found, and what other ingredients, if any, can be substituted.

Boston, Massachusetts

A

Ahi Tuna:
Yellowtail tuna, often used for sushi and sashimi.

Aïoli:
Garlic mayonnaise. Some chefs complement the garlic with roasted pureed red bell pepper, basil, or lemon zest.

Asiago:
A firm, sharp grating cheese made from cow's milk.

Arborio rice:
A medium-grain rice imported from Italy and used primarily in making risotto or risotto-based dishes.

Alligator:
A large reptile from Louisiana and Florida swamps that yields a mild white meat used in regional dishes. Deboned frogs' legs or chicken breast can be substituted.

Anaheim chilies:
Also called California green chilies or *chiles verdes*. When canned, they are called mild green chilies. Anaheim chilies are dark green, about 7 inches long and 1½ inches wide, and are mild to hot in flavor. When they ripen in the fall, they turn red and are sweeter and milder. Their large size makes Anaheims ideal for stuffing.

Ancho chilies:
Dried poblano chilies, anchos come from California (where they're sometimes incorrectly called pasilla chilies) and Mexico, and range from dark red to almost black. They are about 4½ inches long and 3 inches wide and are moderately hot, with a smoky undertaste. They are wrinkled but should still be pliable if fresh. Pasilla chilies, though difficult to find, may be substituted.

Andouille sausage:
Spicy smoked pork sausage, a Cajun specialty.

Annatto (achiote):
Dark brick-red seeds from the annatto tree, which are often made into a paste; these are especially popular in the Yucatán for adding color and an earthy flavor to food.

Almond flour:
A fine flour of crushed almonds available from confectioners' supply stores. Almond flour can be made at home by grinding almonds as finely as possible, although the result will still be coarser than true almond flour; you may also substitute unbleached all-purpose flour with a small amount of almond extract added.

Almond paste:
A thick paste made of finely ground almonds, sugar, and water. Almond paste can be formed into sheets or molded into shapes. It is similar to marzipan, but marzipan is made from almond paste, confectioners' sugar, flavoring, and sometimes egg white.

Arrowroot:
A powder made from a tropical tuber and used as a thickening agent. Substitute twice the amount of cornstarch to achieve the same transparency in a thickened sauce. Arrowroot should be mixed with cold water before being added to hot liquid.

Asian eggplants:
Long, slender eggplants with a thin purple skin.

Azuki bean paste:
A thick puree of cooked azuki beans, which are reddish beans with a mild nutty flavor. The prepared paste can be bought in Asian markets.

B

Balsamic vinegar:
Imported from Italy and prized for its mild, almost sweet flavor, balsamic vinegar is made from unfermented grape juice that has been aged for at least ten years. Balsamic vinegar may be used in sauces and salad dressings, and as a topping for fresh strawberries.

Beurre blanc:
A white butter sauce made of a reduction of white wine and shallots thickened with butter, and possibly finished with fresh herbs or other seasonings.

Black Friar plums:
A large eastern plum with dark red skin and deep yellow flesh. When cooked, the puree becomes a blushing pink.

Black sesame seeds:
The seeds of the sesame plant, most familiar as the small pale seeds used on breads, also come in black. The black seeds are a little more pungent and bitter than the white seeds.

Black trumpet mushrooms:
Also called black chanterelles, these have the same shape and size as their orange cousins, and must be cooked before eating.

Bouquet garni:
A small bundle of herbs, usually bay leaf, parsley, and thyme, used to flavor stocks, braises, and other preparations.

C

Caperberries:
A large green berry resembling a gooseberry, from the same plant that yields capers (capers are the flower buds of this plant). Caperberries are found in the gourmet section of groceries, and are usually pickled. They are often used as a garnish for mixed drinks. Each caperberry contains many small seeds.

Caul fat:
A lacy fat from the belly of animals. It is used as a covering or binding for foods to be cooked, especially small sausages.

Caviar:
Fish roe that has been preserved by being salted.

Beluga: Large light to dark gray eggs of the largest of the sturgeon species. Beluga eggs have a delicate skin and are rated "O" for the darkest eggs, "OO" for eggs of medium tone, and "OOO" for the lightest eggs.

Osetra: Dark brown to golden large eggs with a delicate skin.

Sevruga: Smaller eggs with a fine dark gray color.

American sturgeon: Very similar to osetra in taste, size, and color, this caviar is from sturgeon harvested in the southern states in tributaries of the Mississippi River.

Salmon roe: Large, bright red eggs from Atlantic Ocean salmon, prized for their color as well as for their flavor.

Golden whitefish: Tiny golden eggs with a delicate flavor, used primarily as a garnish.

Cèpes:
See porcini.

Chanterelles:
Called "trumpets" due to their shape, most available chanterelles are an exotic golden color, although the colors range from creamy white to black. The flavor is delicate, with almost peachy tones.

Chipotle chilies:
Jalapeño chilies that have been dried, smoked, and often pickled, chipotles are usually a dark shade of brown and have a hot, smoky taste. If packed in tomato sauce, chipotles may be called *mara* and are a dark brick red.

Chocolate

Unsweetened: Also referred to as baking or bitter chocolate, this is the purest of all cooking chocolates. A hardened chocolate liquor (which is the essence of the cocoa bean, not an alcohol), it contains no sugar and is usually packaged in a bar of eight blocks weighing 1 ounce each. Unsweetened chocolate must contain 50 to 58 percent cocoa butter.

Bittersweet: This chocolate is slightly sweetened with sugar, in amounts that vary depending on the manufacturer. It must contain 35 percent chocolate liquor and is used whenever an intense chocolate taste is desired. Bittersweet chocolate may be used interchangeably with semisweet chocolate in cooking and baking.

Semisweet: Sweetened with sugar, semisweet chocolate, unlike bittersweet, may have flavorings such as vanilla added to it. It is available in bar form as well as in chips and pieces.

Milk: A mild-flavored chocolate used primarily for candy bars but rarely (except for milk chocolate chips) in cooking. It may have as little as 10 percent chocolate liquor, but must contain 12 percent milk solids.

Unsweetened cocoa powder: Powdered chocolate that has had a portion of the cocoa butter removed.

Dutch process cocoa powder: Cocoa powder that has been treated to reduce its acidity. It has a more mellow flavor than regular cocoa, but it burns at a lower temperature.

White chocolate: Ivory in color, white chocolate is technically not chocolate at all: It is made from cocoa butter, sugar, and flavoring. It is difficult to work with, and should be used only in recipes that are specifically designed for it.

Chouriço sausage:
Highly spiced Portuguese garlic pork sausage. Similar sausages are the chorizo of the Southwest and the chaurice of French Louisiana.

Chayote (also called mirliton or christophine):
Originally a staple of the Mayas and the Aztecs, this pear-shaped gourd with a pale green furrowed skin is grown in California, Louisiana, and Florida. Widely available in supermarkets, chayote squash may be stored, wrapped in plastic, in the refrigerator for up to 30 days. It can be boiled, sautéed, stuffed and baked, or used raw in salads.

Chinese chives:
Flatter and wider than other chives, these look almost like blades of grass; they are available in Asian markets. Regular chives may be substituted.

Cilantro:
Also called fresh coriander or Chinese parsley, cilantro is used as extensively in Asian cooking as it is in Southwestern cuisine. It resembles flat-leaf Italian parsley, but is much more flavorful and aromatic. Its pungent scent has been compared to a combination of caraway and cumin.

Clarified butter:
Butter from which the milk solids and water have been removed, leaving pure butterfat that can be heated to a higher temperature without smoking or scorching.

Conch:
A shellfish native to the warm waters of the Caribbean and used in the cuisine of south Florida. Conch meat must be tenderized by being pounded before it is cooked.

Coriander seeds:
The seed of fresh coriander, which is also known as cilantro or Chinese parsley.

Couscous:
Although it resembles a grain, couscous, a staple of North African cooking, is actually a pasta made from semolina and is usually cooked by steaming. It is now also available precooked and dehydrated and is usually sold as "instant" couscous.

Crayfish (crawfish):
Small crustaceans that resemble tiny lobsters, usually measuring between 3½ and 5½ inches long. Long used in Louisiana's Cajun cuisine, they are now farm raised and are commercially available, March through June. Frozen crayfish tail meat is available year round.

Crabmeat:
Meat from any of a large variety of saltwater crustaceans with a hard shell and five pairs of legs with front pincers. Blue crabs are native to the East Coast, while the much larger Dungeness crab is found on the West Coast. The best fresh crabmeat comes in "lump" form.

Crème fraîche:
While its tangy, tart flavor is similar to that of sour cream, crème fraîche is thinner and is used in cooking because it does not curdle when heated as do sour cream and yogurt.

Cremini mushrooms:
These mushrooms resemble white, or common, mushrooms but are a medium brown in color and have a dense, earthy flavor. They may be used interchangeably with white mushrooms in almost all dishes.

D

Daikon sprouts:
The soft green sprouts of the daikon plant. Found in the vegetable or salad section of groceries.

Daikon:
A long, thin white radish used in Asian cuisines. Daikon is found in the vegetable or salad section of groceries.

E

Enoki mushrooms:
These Japanese mushrooms have thin pale stems, about 3 inches long, and small ivory buttonlike heads. Available year round, they may be used without washing or other preparation, but the base holding the mushroom stalks together should be trimmed away.

F

Fermented black beans:
Strongly flavored salt-preserved soybeans available in Asian markets either whole or ground into a paste.

Fish sauce, Thai:
One of the basic flavorings of Thai cuisine, called *nam pla* in Thailand, fish sauce is the pungent, salty liquid poured off small fish fermented in brine. It is available in Asian markets.

Flat-leaf (Italian) parsley:
A variety of parsley with large leaves and a stronger, more pungent flavor than curly-leaf parsley.

Fondant, plain:
A creamy sugar base used to make many confections and to ice cakes. Fondant can be made at home, but it is far easier to buy it from a confectioners' supply store.

Foie gras:
The oversized liver of force-fed geese or ducks, foie gras is considered one of the most luxurious of foods. Fresh foie gras should be soaked in tepid water for 1 hour. Then it should be patted dry, the lobes gently separated, and any connecting tubes and visible blood vessels removed and discarded.

Frisée (curly endive):
A green with decorative curly edges, frisée is used in salads and as a garnish.

Feuilles de Brigue:
A thin round dough found in Middle Eastern groceries, feuilles de Brigue is slightly sweet and not as flaky as phyllo or puff pastry.

G

Ganache:
A filling or coating made from heavy cream and chocolate. It is also used to make chocolate truffles.

Garlic, elephant:
Not really garlic, but a garlic-flavored member of the onion family. Available in many supermarkets and specialty produce stores.

Galangal, fresh:
A relative of ginger, this rhizome is pale yellow and quite hot. It is usually pounded in a mortar with other ingredients.

Ginger, fresh:
The rhizome of the ginger plant has a thin, light tan skin and golden flesh. It is available in most grocery stores year round.

Goat cheese:
Called *chèvre* in French, goat cheese ranges in flavor from mild and tangy in its fresh form to sharp when it is aged.

Gorgonzola:
A creamy blue-veined cheese from Italy, similar in taste to Stilton.

Ground fish paste (anchovy cream):
A strongly flavored paste made by pureeing anchovies with a little cream. It is available in specialty markets.

Guava Puree:
A thick puree made from dried guava fruit; it is available frozen from confectioners' supply stores.

Güero chilies:
Also called Hungarian yellow wax chilies, these hot chilies are yellow or yellow-green in color when immature and red when ripe.

H

Haricots verts:
Tender, long, and very thin green beans used in French cuisine and now becoming popular in America. They are available in specialty produce markets. Baby Blue Lake beans may be substituted.

Hazelnut puree (praline noisette):
A paste made of finely ground hazelnuts. While fresh hazelnuts may be stored in the freezer or the refrigerator, hazelnut puree should be used immediately. Available from confectioners' supply stores.

Harissa:
A paste of ground red chilies, olive oil, and garlic, sold in Middle Eastern groceries.

J

Jalapeño chilies:
Fairly small, dark green hot chilies about 2 inches long and 1 inch wide. Jalapeños are widely available. Serranos are a common substitute, although the heat from jalapeños is immediate while serranos provide more of an afterburn. Jalapeños can vary in the level of heat, and those with striations on the skin are older and usually hotter. It's better to start with less than the amount called for, and add more to taste.

Japanese cucumbers:
Very long, thin cucumbers available in specialty produce markets or Asian markets. Regular cucumbers can be substituted.

K

Kalamata olives:
A robustly flavored brine-cured Greek black olive packed with some vinegar. Liguria or Lugano olives are a good substitute, but Kalamatas are widely available.

Kasu:
A paste made of the lees from the process of making sake. It is available at Asian markets.

Kosher salt:
Also known as coarse salt or pickling salt, kosher salt is pure refined rock salt that does not contain magnesium carbonate. It is less salty than table salt and has larger grains. Use ½ to 1 teaspoon of table salt for each tablespoon of kosher salt specified.

L

Langoustines:
Small European lobsters used for their sweet tail meat. Jumbo shrimp may be substituted.

Lemongrass:
Technically an herb, lemongrass is characterized by a strong citrus flavor with a spicy finish similar to that of ginger. The 6- to 8-inch bulb-like base of fresh lemongrass stalks is used extensively in the cuisines of Thailand and Vietnam and may be found in some Asian markets. Also called citronella.

Linguiça sausage:
A garlicky pork sausage from Portugal. Other cured garlic sausages can be substituted.

Lobster:
The American, Atlantic, or Maine lobster is a crustacean with a jointed body and two large pincer claws. The larger claw is used for crushing and the smaller one is used for catching its prey. The spiny, or rock, lobster, found in warmer waters from South Africa to the eastern Pacific, lacks the large claws of its northern relative.

M

Malt powder (malted milk):
A deep tan powder of dried milk and malted cereal, available in groceries; Ovaltine may be substituted.

Mango:
A tropical fruit, the mango is now available in many supermarkets throughout the United States. A ripe mango has a smooth yellow to red skin and smells sweet; the yellow flesh is both sweet and tart. The skin should be peeled and the flesh cut away from the pit in strips. Papaya can be substituted in many recipes.

Mango puree:
A thick puree made from diced mango fruit; it is available frozen from confectioners' supply stores.

Marzipan:

A confection made from almond paste, confectioners' sugar, flavoring, and sometimes egg white. Marzipan is often used for shaped candies, such as fruit or flowers, or as a coating for cakes.

Masa harina:

Finely ground cornmeal used in place of raw masa dough to make tamale dough and corn tortillas. Available in Latino markets and many supermarkets.

Mascarpone:

A soft, fresh Italian cheese with a high fat content used primarily in desserts and for cheese tortas. If it is not available, combining equal parts of cream cheese and unsalted butter will produce a similar product.

Maui onions:

Large mild onions grown in Hawaii; similar to Vidalia onions.

Medjool dates:

Large and very moist dates, now being grown in California (most dates sold in the United States are the Deglet Noor variety).

Mirin (sweet sake):

A sweet rice wine sold in Asian markets and some groceries. Sweet sherry may be substituted.

Mirliton:

See chayote.

Miso:

This thick soybean paste is made by salting and fermenting soybeans with rice or barley. It is available at Asian markets.

Morels:

These spring mushrooms are about 1 inch long with a tall, hollow, pitted cap. The colors range from gray to brown to black, depending on where they are found. Their flavor is rich, nutty, and meaty when cooked, and they should never be eaten raw. Morels are also available dried.

Mushroom soy sauce:

A mushroom-flavored sauce available in Asian markets. Regular soy sauce may be substituted; soaking dried mushrooms in soy sauce will yield a similar mushroom-flavored sauce.

N

Nairagi:

A striped marlin with pink to orange-red flesh. Ahi tuna or swordfish may be substituted.

Nori:

A dark seaweed, most commonly used to wrap sushi rolls. It is available from Asian markets.

O

Ogo (red and green seaweed):

A Hawaiian highly prized seaweed. Ogo comes in many colors and flavors; some is used like a spice, some like a vegetable.

Old Bay seasoning:

This brand-name seasoning is available in most groceries. It contains celery salt, mustard, red and black pepper, bay leaf, cloves, allspice, ginger, mace, cardamom, cinnamon, and paprika, and is used on seafood, meats, and vegetables.

Oyster mushrooms:

Sometimes referred to as "the shellfish of the woods," oyster mushrooms are delicate and translucent, with a silky consistency. The cap is scalloped, and they have a graceful appearance similar to that of a calla lily. The pale gray color may have hints of blue, yellow, and pink. Despite a slight aroma of anise, oyster mushrooms have a mild shellfish or oyster flavor.

P

Pancetta:

An unsmoked Italian bacon sold in cylindrical form and used in dishes as a flavoring.

Papaya:

A mottled yellow and green tropical fruit with yellow flesh and shiny round black seeds. Papayas have a musky flavor with a slight citrus tang and are used primarily for desserts. They must be ripe when used or they will be bitter and acid.

Parchment paper:

A white heat-resistant paper sold in rolls at cookware stores. It is used in cooking to line baking pans and baking sheets, to cook foods *en papillote,* and to loosely cover delicate foods like fish fillets during poaching.

Pasilla chilies:

Named for *pasa,* which means "raisin" in Spanish, this long, thin chili is also called *chilaca* when fresh, brown, and ripe, and *negro* when dried and black. Pasillas are mild to hot in taste, are used in *moles,* and may be substituted for ancho chilies.

Passion fruit:
A yellow, brown, or purple tropical fruit with a perfumelike scent. The juice is available as frozen concentrate or fresh in supermarkets and specialty produce stores.

Passion fruit puree:
A thick puree made from diced passion fruit; it is available frozen from confectioners' supply stores.

Paste food coloring:
Available from confectioners' supply stores, paste food colors are more intense than the liquid food colors commonly found in supermarkets and can be used like paints to obtain bright colors.

Phyllo (filo) dough:
This tissue-paper-thin pastry is made from a flour and water dough. Phyllo sheets are used in layers and brushed with butter or oil before baking. They are widely available in packages in the frozen section of supermarkets.

Pilaf:
A dish of grain that has been sautéed briefly in butter or oil, then simmered in stock or water with various seasonings.

Pistachio paste:
A paste of ground pistachios available from confectioners' supply stores.

Plantains:
Similar to a banana in both shape and texture, plantains are a member of the same family. The green skin turns black when ripe, and the pinkish flesh must be cooked to be edible.

Plum (Roma) tomatoes:
Small plum-sized red tomatoes frequently used in Italian cuisine because their thick, meaty flesh is excellent for drying and for making sauces. Regular red tomatoes may be substituted.

Poblano chilies:
Large tapered chilies about 4 inches long, 2½ inches wide, and shiny dark green in color. Poblanos are mild to hot. When used in sauces, they may be interchanged with green Anaheim chilies, though the flavor will be different.

Polenta:
Coarsely ground yellow or white cornmeal. Polenta is traditionally combined with stock or water and cooked slowly until thick. It may be served creamy, or it may be chilled, cut into shapes, and grilled.

Porcini mushrooms:
Popular the world over, these short, fat bolete mushrooms are rusty brown with thick, bulbous stems. Porcini do not have gills under the cap, but rather a mass of minuscule tubes. Their flavor is earthy, rich, and reminiscent of hazelnuts, and is intensified when the mushrooms are used in dried form. Fresh porcini are also known as *cèpes.*

Portobello mushrooms:
Huge mushrooms with caps from 3 to 6 inches in diameter. The brown gills underneath the cap should be cut away before the mushrooms are cooked or they will give a dark brown color to the dish.

Praline paste:
A paste made by cooking brown sugar until it has caramelized and thickened; chopped nuts are added. It is available from confectioners' supply stores.

Prune puree:
A thick puree made from cut-up prunes moistened with water or other liquid. It is available in cans from confectioners' supply stores and some specialty foods stores.

Puff pastry:
Flaky pastry that rises up to ten times its original height when baked. It is made from flour, water, butter, and salt. The distinctive flakiness results from adding the butter during a series of at least six rollings, turnings, and foldings that trap layers of butter and air between the layers of the pastry; when baked, the butter melts and the air

expands as steam, puffing up the pastry. It can be prepared at home, or purchased frozen.

Pumpkin seeds:
Also called *pepitas,* these are the husked inner seeds of the pumpkin. The seeds are roasted and eaten as a snack or garnish. When ground they can be used as a thickener and flavoring agent.

Q

Quenelle:
While a traditional French quenelle is a dumpling based on ground meat or seafood and bound with egg, in contemporary American cooking they may be any sort of pureed and bound food that tops a liquid; the term is used almost interchangeably with dumpling.

Queso fresco:
Also called *ranchero seco,* this is a white Mexican cheese made with rennet. It is similar to farmer's cheese but is slightly saltier. White Cheddar or a mixture of farmer's and feta cheeses may be substituted.

R

Radicchio:
A member of the chicory family developed in Italy. The head ranges in size from that of a golf ball to that of a grapefruit. The beautifully white-veined leaves may be any shade from bright red to dark maroon, and the flavor is rather bitter. In Italy radicchio is served as a salad, or is braised, grilled, or wilted and often served with a splash of vinegar and oil.

Rattlesnake beans:
Small dried beans used in Southwestern cuisine. Dried black-eyed peas may be substituted.

S

Scotch bonnet (habanero) chilies:
The hottest of all chilies, these tiny crinkled red or yellow peppers are available in supermarkets and specialty produce markets.

Serrano chilies:
Tapered, thin bright-green chilies that are similar to but smaller than jalapeños. Serranos may be substituted for jalapeños.

Shallots:
A member of the onion family, their flavor is milder than that of the onion and less pungent than garlic. Shallots are usually about ½ to 1 inch long, oval in shape, and may come as one bulb or a pair. They are excellent in sauces, salad dressing, and roasted whole.

Shiitake mushrooms:
The second most widely cultivated mushroom in the world, shiitakes have a distinctive woodsy, smoky flavor, are moist and fleshy when fresh, and need to be soaked to soften when dried. They are medium to large, with an umbrella-shaped, floppy tan to dark brown cap with edges that tend to roll inward. Use only the caps and discard the tough, fibrous stems.

Short-grain rice:
High in starch and gluten, short-grain rice is used to make the sticky rice of many Asian cuisines.

Shrimp paste:
A pungent paste found in Asian markets. A little goes a long way; keep the remainder refrigerated.

Sichimi:
A Japanese spice blend, made of red bell peppers, orange peel, sesame seeds, seaweed, and poppy seeds.

Smoked Pig Jowl:
A southern favorite, smoked pig, or hog, jowl is used to season dishes such as black-eyed peas and is also eaten as a meat.

Soy, dark:
A heavier and more pungent soy sauce than the soy sauce available in most groceries. Available in Asian markets.

Star anise:
Anise-flavored, eight-pointed dried brown seed pods available in Asian markets or specialty foods stores.

Stone crab:
A south Florida favorite, the stone crab is an ivory-colored crab with an extremely hard shell. The large dark-tipped claws are used in many regional dishes.

Sweetbreads:
The thymus glands of calves, sold in pairs. They have a very delicate flavor and weigh about 1 pound per pair.

T

Pear tomatoes:
Small yellow or red tomatoes with a distinctive teardrop shape, found in specialty produce markets. Cherry tomatoes can be substituted.

Thai chili paste:
A fiery hot paste of Thai chili peppers found in Asian markets. It is made with or without garlic.

Toasted sesame oil:
A strongly flavored oil made from toasted sesame seeds. Available in Asian markets and many supermarkets.

Tomatillos:
Tomatillos look like tomatoes with a papery brown husk. They are small and green even when ripe, and are available at specialty produce markets and some supermarkets. Although they will not have the same lemony taste, green tomatoes are the best substitute.

Turmeric:
A yellow rhizome that is a member of the ginger family. Available fresh in Asian markets, or as a bright yellow powder in supermarkets.

U

Umaboshi plums:
Small pickled plums used in Japanese cuisine and available in Asian markets.

V

Vanilla beans:
The pods of a relative of the orchid, vanilla beans are green and have no flavor when picked; they are then cured by a process of sweating and drying. Once cured, the long, wrinkled black beans are either bundled whole for export or processed into extract.

Venison:
The meat of large game animals; usually used to refer to deer meat.

Vidalia onions:

These large sweet onions, named for the Vidalia, Georgia, area in which they are grown, are so mild they can be eaten raw like an apple. They are similar to Maui onions, with which they are interchangeable. Other mild onions may be substituted, but reduce the amount used.

W

Wasabi powder:

Ground dried wasabi root, available in Asian markets. It is mixed with a small amount of water to form a thick paste called wasabi, which is often served with Japanese foods such as sashimi.

Z

Zest:

The thin, brightly colored outer part of citrus rind. It contains volatile oils, making it ideal for use as a flavoring.

Mail-Order Sources

▝▖▝▖▝▖▝▖▝▖▝▖▝▖▝▖▝▖▝▖

Most of the ingredients called for in this book are available in supermarkets, specialty foods stores, natural foods stores, confectioners' and restaurant supply stores, and ethnic markets in large cities. If you don't have access to such stores, or you can't find a specific item, almost anything you need may be found in the following list.

Aidells Sausage Company
1625 Alvarado Street
San Leandro, CA 94577-2636
415-285-6660

A wide array of traditional and specialty sausages of the highest quality, reasonably priced.

American Spoon Foods
P.O. Box 566
Petoskey, MI 49770
800-222-5886

Chef Larry Forgione and his partner Justin Rashid package a wonderful line of dried fruits and other ingredients for cooking, including dried cranberries and cherries, and many regional American specialties from other companies.

Auricchio Cheese, Inc.
5810 Highway NN
Denmark, WI 54208
414-863-2123

An excellent source of fine Italian cheeses, from fresh Mascarpone to Parmesan.

Balducci's
P.O. Box 10373
Newark, NJ 07193-0373
800-225-3822

The mail-order division of the famed New York gourmet market, with everything from fresh pastas and excellent sauces to prime meats, desserts, and such foods as pâté de foie gras, capon, quail, pheasant, squid, venison, and imported and domestic caviars.

Boyajian, Inc.
385 California Street
Newton, MA 02160
617-965-5800

Poussin, turkey, caviar, wonderful citrus and garlic oils, imported and domestic caviars, and smoked fish.

Broken Arrow Ranch
P.O. Box 530
Ingram, TX 78025
800-962-4263

Mike Hughes was the pioneer of farm-raised game in Texas, and his venison, bear, and other products are superb.

Casa Lucas Market
2934 24th Street
San Francisco, CA 94110
415-826-4334

Dried chilies, fresh epazote, and other ingredients for Mexican cuisine.

Chesapeake Express Ltd.
1129 Hope Road
Centreville, MD 21617
410-758-0913

This company is one of the few to ship jumbo soft-shell crabs as well as fresh lump crabmeat and authentic Maryland crab cakes.

Chickory Farms
723 Hilary Street
New Orleans, LA 70118
800-605-4550

All manner of mushrooms, both cultivated and wild, as well as truffles, fine cheeses, handmade chocolates, and specialty produce.

Clambake Celebrations
9 West Road
Orleans, MA 02653
800-423-4038

The source for an entire New England clambake in a pot, as well as other types of eastern seafood.

Dallas Mozzarella Company
2944 Elm Street
Dallas, TX 75226
800-798-2954

Paula Lambert's delicious array of
Italian and Texan cheeses.

D'Artagnan
399–419 St. Paul Avenue
Jersey City, NJ 07306
800-327-8246

The only source in this country for fresh
foie gras, D'Artagnan also offers fresh
game birds and meats, sausages, free-
range poultry, duck fat, smoked duck,
and pâté de foie gras.

Dodge Cove Marine Farm, Inc.
P.O. Box 211
Newcastle, ME
207-563-8168

An excellent source for farmed oysters,
mussels, lobster, fresh fish, and other
Maine delicacies.

Ducktrap River Fish Farm
R.R. 2, P.O. Box 378
Lincolnville, ME 04849
800-828-3825

Smoked seafood, including smoked
scallops, mussels, and shrimp, made
Ducktrap famous with New England
food aficionados, and it remains the
source for some of the best available
nationally.

The Farm at Mt. Walden
P.O. Box 515
The Plains, VA 22171
800-64-TROUT

This small smokehouse in the foothills
of the Shenandoahs offers fine smoked
trout, as well as hot-smoked salmon.

Foggy Ridge Gamebird Farm
213 Highland Road
Warren, ME 04864
207-273-2357

The farm will ship a wide range of
game birds such as pheasant, grouse,
Guinea hen, squab, wild duck, and wild
turkey.

Fresh Island Fish Company, Inc.
R.R. I, P.O. Box 373B
Wailuku, HI 96793
808-244-9633

Hawaiian fish and shellfish.

G.B. Ratto, International Grocers
821 Washington Street
Oakland, CA 94607
510-832-6503

Write for a catalogue of their chocolate,
nuts, flavor extracts, and spices.

Gray's Grist Mill
P.O. Box 442
Adamsville, RI 02801
508-636-6075

This small mill sells white flint cornmeal for true Rhode Island johnnycakes,
as well as brown-bread flour and various pancake and muffin mixes.

Gwaltney's
P.O. Box 1
Smithfield, VA 23431
800-292-2773

While many people substitute prosciutto
in recipes calling for Smithfield ham,
there is really no comparable product.
The hams are available cooked and
presliced.

Harrington Ham Company
Main Street
Richmond, VT 05477
802-434-4311

A well-known source of Vermont-style
cob-smoked hams, country bacon, and
other smoked specialties.

Hawaiian Exotic Fruit Company
P.O. Box 1089
Pahoa, HI 96778

Organic tropical produce.

Hawaiian Vintage Chocolate Company
4614 Kilauea Avenue, Ste. 435
Honolulu, HI 96816
808-735-8494

Couverture chocolate from Hawaiian
beans.

Horton's Downeast Foods, Inc.
P.O. Box 430
Waterboro, ME 04087
207-247-6900

Write for this catalogue of smoked
seafood specialties, including mussels.

Jamison Farm
171 Jamison Lane
Latrobe, PA 15650-9400
800-237-5262

While every supermarket carries lamb,
very few specialty butchers carry the
kind of free-range organically fed lamb
that can be shipped from this
Pennsylvania farm.

John Dewar & Company
753 Beacon Street
Newton, MA 02159
617-442-4292

Another good source of specialty meats,
venison, and game birds.

Mail-Order Sources

▼▼▼▼▼▼▼▼▼▼

Kreuz Market
208 South Commerce Street
Lockhart, TX 78644
512-398-2361

They will ship their famous smoked sausages, which are 95 percent beef and 5 percent pork.

Legal Seafood
33 Everett Street
Allston, MA 02134
800-343-5804

This firm gained regional fame by offering the finest quality of seafood in its restaurants. In addition to shipping clambakes, you can count on them for many varieties of fish and shellfish as well as excellent chowder and bluefish pâté.

Leonard Solomon's Wines & Spirits, L & L Distributing
1456 North Dayton
Chicago, IL 60622
312-915-5911
Fax 312-915-0466

Grains including spelt, rattlesnake and other beans, oils, vinegars, crème fraîche, salmon, smoked fish, pâtés, caviars, special sausages, smoked duck breast, pastrami, imported cheeses, Amazon spices, frozen purees, and vanilla beans.

L'Esprit de Campagne
P.O. Box 3130
Winchester, VA 22604
703-955-1014

Dried vine-ripened tomatoes in various forms, including halves marinated in extra-virgin olive oil with herbs; pureed; and sprinkles. The company also offers dried apples, cherries, blueberries, and cranberries, all unsulphured and with no preservatives.

Marblehead Lobster Company
Beacon and Orne Streets
Marblehead, MA 01945
617-631-0787

Another fine source for fresh lobsters of all sizes.

Mo Hotta, Mo Betta
P.O. Box 4136
San Luis Obispo, CA 93403
800-462-3220
Fax 805-545-8389

Write for their catalogue of hot sauces; Asian, Latin American, Indian, African, and Caribbean spices and sauces; wasabi powder; dried mushrooms; barbecue sauces; jerk sauces; and condiments.

Montdomaine Cellars
R.R. 6, P.O. Box 188A
Charlottesville, VA 22902
800-829-4633

Wines from the land of Thomas Jefferson, including Chardonnay, Cabernet Sauvignon, Merlot, blush, Viogies, Marsanne, and Cabernet Franc.

Mook Seafarm, Inc.
HC 64, P.O. Box 041
Damariscotta, ME 04543
207-563-1456

Some of the best fresh mussels, clams, and oysters in the country.

More Than Gourmet
115 W. Bartges Street
Akron, OH 44311
800-860-9392

Demi-Glace Gold® and Glace de Poulet Gold® two clasic French sauces of four star quality that are made in the classic manner of Escoffier. An ultimate shortcut for the home cook

Mystique
Friendship Street
Waldoro, ME 04572
207-832-5136

One of the region's best goat cheese makers, with a tart yet creamy product.

Papaya Orchards of Hawaii, Inc.
800 Leilani Street
Hilo, HI 96720
800-678-6248

Frozen passion fruit, papaya, and guava purees; fresh papaya.

Pine Acres Rabbitry
299 East Main Street
Norton, MA 02766
508-285-7391

It is still difficult to find good fresh rabbits in many parts of the country, and these are meaty and delicate.

The Pork Shop of Vermont
P.O. Box 99
Hinesburg, VT 05461
802-482-3617

Smoked hams, bacon, and other products, cured without nitrates or other preservatives.

Royal Hawaiian Sea Farms
P.O. Box 3167
Kailua-Kona, HI 96745
808-329-5468

Hawaiian sea vegetables, including limu and ogo.

Salumeria Italiana
151 Richmond Street
Boston, MA 02109
617-523-8743

Replicate a meal in Boston's North End with products from one of the area's best-known purveyors of Italian foodstuffs.

Schartner's Mountain View Fruit and Berry Farm
R.R. 220, P.O. Box 82
Thorndike, ME 04986
207-568-3668

This farm ships many heirloom apple and pear varieties as well as other fruits.

Stonington Lobster Co-op
P.O. Box 87
Indian Point Road
Stonington, ME 04681
207-367-2286

This firm gathers its wares from a number of different suppliers, and offers fresh crabmeat in addition to lobster.

S. Wallace Edwards & Sons, Inc.
P.O. Box 25
Surry, VA 23883
800-290-9213

Hickory-smoked aged Virginia hams, bacon, and Surry sausages, as well as dry-cured duck breast and Virginia seafood including crab cakes, smoked tuna, and Chesapeake Bay oysters.

Sweet Celebrations
P.O. Box 39426
Edina, MN 55439
800-328-6722
Fax 612-943-1688

Write for their catalogue of confectioners' supplies, including chocolate and other ingredients, and equipment. Specializing in cake decorating and candy making.

Take Home Maui, Inc.
121 Dickenson Street
Lahaina, HI 96761
800-545-MAUI

Maui onions, macadamia nut products, papayas, pineapples.

Unique Foods
520 Executive Drive
Willow Brook, IL 60521
800-789-6474
Fax 708-789-1843

Fresh and smoked sausages, wild game, lamb, mushrooms, and herbs.

Albert Uster Imports, Inc.
9211 Gaither Road
Gaithersburg, MD 20877
800-231-8154

A professional source for bakery equipment and supplies, including edible gold dust.

Vermont Butter & Cheese Company, Inc.
Pitman Road, P.O. Box 95
Websterville, VT 05678
802-479-9371

A source for crème fraîche and European-style cheeses, including fromage blanc and Mascarpone.

Wilton Enterprises, Inc.
2240 West 75th Street
Woodridge, IL 60515
708-963-7100, ext. 320

Pastry and cake decorating supplies, paste food colors, and icing ingredients.

Wolfe's Neck Farm Foundation
10 Burnett Road
Freeport, ME 04032
207-865-4469

Organic Black Angus beef.

York Hill Farm
York Hill Road
New Sharon, ME 04955
207-778-9741

A small goat cheese producer, with a line that includes a Roman-style capriano.

GREAT CHEFS — GREAT CITIES

Credits

The Book

Publisher	
Author	
Editor	
Production Services	
Book Design	
Recipe Development	
Photography	
Public Relations	

Great Chefs Publishing

John Shoup
John DeMers
Carolyn Miller
Mimi Luebbermann
Linda Anne Nix
Larry Escudier
Dwain Richard, Jr.
Carolyn Buster
Eric Futran
Linda Anne Nix

Home Video

CD ROM

The Television Series

Presenter	
Announcer	
Writer	
Camera/Lighting	
Camera Assistant	
Field Audio	
Editor	
Assistant Editor	
Post Production Audio	
Culinary Advisor	
Graphic Design	
Computer Animation	
Theme Music	
Performed By	

Great Chefs Video

Great Chefs Television

Mary Lou Conroy
Andres Calandria
John Beyer
Dave Landry
Paul Combel
Mark Schenck
Charles C. Sainz
George Matulik
Maria D. Estevez
Andres Calandria
Nick Maucele
Chan Patterson
Escudier & Richard
Imagetech
John Oddo, music
Earl Brown, lyrics
Glenn Drewes, trumpet
Gerry Niewood, tenor sax
John Oddo, piano
Jay Leonhart, bass
Joe Cocuzzo, drums

Multicom Publishing, Seattle

Original Music	
Recording Studio	
Engineer	
Additional Footage	
Hotel Accommodations	
Transportation	
Public Relations	
Closing Sequence	
Assistant to the Executive Producer	
Associate Producer	
Producer/Director	
Executive Producer	

Charlie Byrd, guitar
Rick Whitehead, guitar
Jeff Meyerriecks, guitar
Chuck Redd, vibes
Ken Peplowski, clarinet
Ultrasonics
Steve Reynolds
Fabulous Footage, Toronto ONT
KCTS, Seattle WA
KERA, Dallas TX
PVS, Washington, D.C.
WHYY Philadelphia PA
Cheeca Lodge, Islamorada FL
Heathman Hotel, Portland OR
Ritz-Carlton, Houston TX
Sheraton Seattle, Seattle WA
Bryan Dupepe, Sr.
Deborah Howard
Linda Anne Nix
Maurice Delechelle
Cybil W. Curtis
Charles C. Sainz
John Beyer
John Shoup

Index

Chef's biographies in bold-face type

chocolate
  bavarian cream, 200
  bittersweet
    in flourless cake, 204
    in sauce, 223
    shavings, 154, 198
    in triangles, 159
    cake, 159
    flourless, 204–205
    and rum truffle cake, 200–202
  chips
    in frozen soufflés, 183
    in sour cream coffee cake, 179
  cookies
    crumbs, 182
    with pistachio cream and chocolate
      sauce, 178
  dark, shavings, 159
  dome, frozen soufflés under a,
    182–183
  filling, 184
  ganache, 156, 178, 200, 207
  melting, 237
  meringue, macadamia nut and, with
    tropical fruit cream, 156–157
  milk
    in domes, 182
    for finish, 157
  mousse
    for parfait, 159
    white, 206, 214
  oil rigs and spouts, 206
  parfait, 159
  sauce, 184, 223
    for garnish, 159, 164, 174, 180,
      182, 192, 199
  white, 223
  wild berry and, 206
  semisweet
    in bavarian cream, 200
    in domes, 182
    in ganache, 156, 200
    in glaze, 156
    in meringue, 156
    in mousse, 159
    for oil rigs and spouts, 206
    in sauce, 184, 206, 223
    in tart filling, 184
    in torte, 206
    in truffles, 201
  tart, 184
  torte, double, with Mascarpone
    mousse and wild berry-chocolate
    sauce, 206–207
  triangles, 159
  truffles, 201
  unsweetened, in sauce, 223
  white
    brittle, raspberry and, 152

curls, 214, 215
  in domes, 182
  for finish, 157
  in fruit curd, 214
  in mousse, 206, 214
  sauce, 223
  shavings, 159
  in triangles, 159
Christmas menu, 240
christophine. *See* chayote
Chu, Lawrence, **50**, 51
cilantro
  compote, corn and, 110
  in green chile sauce, 123
  in radish salad, 65
  in roasted pepper puree, 96
  in salsa, 16, 25, 56
  sour cream, 72
  in yellow curry paste, 145
cinnamon-rum sauce, 210
cinnamon sticks, for garnish, 210
Citrus (restaurant), 66
citrus-honey consommé, 170
Clark, Patrick, 132, **133**
cobbler, goat cheese, 68–69
cocoa powder, 159, 178, 180, 196, 200,
  201, 206
coconut, dried, in frozen soufflés, 182
cod, lobster with, 77
coffee
  in chocolate cake, 159
  in mocha butter cream, 201
  syrup, 180
coffee cake, Alsatian sour cream, 179
Coffee Cottage, 180, 182
Cognac, 146, 190
Coiro, Melanie, 154, **155**
compote
  corn-cilantro, 110
  eggplant, 94
conch, with vanilla-rum sauce and spicy
  black bean salad, 32–33
confit
  apple-onion, 124
  baby-tomato, 30
crispy leek, 60
  pork, 134
consommé, citrus-honey, 170
cookies
  butter, 164
  chocolate, 178
  hazelnut, 177
  See also wafers
coriander sauce, lamb with, 138
coriander seeds, in yellow curry paste,
  145
corn
  baby, 86
  compote, with cilantro, 110

flan, with smoked salmon, 26–27
  in lobster sauce, 76
  nage of mushrooms and, 86
  pancakes, with salmon, caviar, and
    watercress sauce, 20–21
  in relish, 36, 146–147
  in salsa, 16, 105
  with scallops, 86
  shrimp rellenos with, 72–73
cornmeal, in lemon chess pie, 185. *See
  also* polenta
Cost, Bruce, **144**, 145
Coston, Pat, 188, **189**
coulis
  berry, 224
  cucumber, 48
  fruit, 224
  mango, 48
  mango-ginger, 166
  raspberry, 208
  See also puree
couscous, 95, 142
crab. *See* shellfish, crab
cranberries, 124, 179
crawfish, with spicy black bean sauce,
  90
cream
  chive, 85
  heavy (whipping)
    on apple and pecan gratin, 170
    in beurre blanc, 46, 96
    in caramel cream, 188
    for caramelized apples, 190
    in caramel sauce, 222
    in Chantilly cream, 216
    in charlotte aux fruits, 186
    in chocolate bavarian cream, 200
    in chocolate ganache, 156, 200, 207
    in chocolate mousse, 159, 206, 214
    in chocolate sauce, 184, 223
    in chocolate truffles, 201
    with chocolat fondant gâteau, 204
    in corn flan, 26
    in crème fraîche, 220
    in deviled oysters, 38
    in frozen soufflés, 182
    in goat cheese-macaroni soufflé,
      135
    in Gratin Dauphinois, 119
    in ice cream, 158, 192, 220
    in jerky sauce, 120
    on Key lime pie, 182
    on lemon chess pie, 185
    in lemon chiffon, 191
    in lemon custard, 203
    in lemon sauce, 203
    with lobster, 16
    on maple sugar crème caramel, 154
    in Mascarpone caramel cream, 152

Mesa Grill, 43
mesclun. *See* greens, baby
Miami, xi, 32, 76, 214
Miami Beach, 31, 64, 161
Michela's, 116, 171
Midwest, 5. *See also specific states and cities*
mignonette, lemon vodka, 46
Militello, Mark, 32–33, **76**, 77
Milwaukee, 169
mint
    for garnish, 158, 168, 170, 176, 178, 185, 188, 192, 199, 203, 207, 214, 216
    oil, 223
    in tuna tartare, 28
mirepoix, 114
mirin. *See* sake
mirliton, and corn relish, 36. *See also* chayote
miso, 91
mocha butter cream, 201
Molzan, Bruce, 68–69, **96**, 97, 159
Montrachet, 15
Moroccan lamb, 138–139
Moroccan-style Sea Bass in a Golden Balloon, 94
Morrone, George, **28**, 29
mousse
    cake, hazelnut and roasted-almond, 196–197
    chocolate, 159
    white chocolate, 206, 214
    hazelnut, 196
    lemon and berry, 203
    Mascarpone, 206
    strawberry, 208
mousseline, sole, 22–23
mushrooms
    chanterelle, terrine of squab breast and, 51
    cremini, risotto, 102
    enoki
        for garnish, 100
        with sashimi, 55
    field
        nage of corn and, 86
        with scallops, 86
    morel
        in polenta, 86
        risotto, 102
        with scallops, 86
        sweetbreads with, 122–123
    oyster
        in polenta, 86
        with scallops, 86
        terrine of squab breast and, 51
    porcini
        in polenta, 86

    with scallops, 86
    portobello
        ragout with, 44
        with rib-eye steaks, 148
    shiitake
        in alligator stir-fry, 90
        with chicken, 50
        nage of corn and, 86
        with pasta and foie gras, 14
        in polenta, 86
        with pork tenderloin, 124
        risotto, 102
        with scallops, 86
        terrine of squab breast and, 51
    white
        nage of corn and, 86
        sauce, 118
        with scallops, 86
    wild
        in polenta, 86
        ragout, 44
        risotto, 102
        squab breast and, terrine of, 51
mussels. *See* shellfish, mussels
mustard seeds, in marinade, 116
Myers's rum, 64, 180, 200, 201

N

nage, mushroom-corn, 86
nairagi, sashimi of smoked, with ogo salad, 54–55
napoleon, of tropical fruit, 214–215
Nava, 72, 103
nectarines, for garnish, 216
New Mexico, 4
New Orleans, xi, 5, 36, 62, 84, 112, 119, 178, 179, 180, 182, 184, 186, 217
New World dinner menu, 241
New Year's buffet menu, 240
New York, xi, 10, 15, 18, 23, 27, 35, 43, 46, 49, 58, 80, 83, 95, 120, 122, 130, 165, 177, 191, 199, 205
Nola, 84
noodles
    rice stick, fried, 50–51
    Thai yellow curry, with beef, 144
    See also pasta
nori, 100
Northern states, 5. *See also specific states and cities*
nuts
    almond(s)
        and apple tart, 190
        extract, 198, 200
        flour, 198
        frangipane (cream), 190
        for garnish, 91

        glazed, 196, 197
        heart, 198–199
        marzipan and azuki bean paste egg rolls, 174
        paste, 166, 190
        roasted, and hazelnut mousse cake, 196–197
        in rum bananas, 164
        in sour cream coffee cake, 179
        in maple ice cream sandwich, rum banana and, 164–165
    hazelnut(s)
        in cookies, 177
        for garnish, 68
        mousse, 196
        paste, 184, 196
        and roasted-almond mousse cake, 196–197
        in salad, 68
        in tarts, 168
        toasting and peeling, 236
    macadamia, and chocolate meringue, with tropical fruit cream, 156–157
    peanuts
        for garnish, 50
        with Thai yellow curry noodles, 144
    pecan(s)
        and apple gratin, 170–171
        in bread pudding, 176
        in tart shell, 184
    pine
        in almond heart, 198
        for garnish, 199
        in pesto, 136
        in pesto sauce, 102
        in tuna tartare, 28
    pistachio(s)
        cream, 178
        for garnish, 178
        paste, 174, 178
        sauce, 174
        in white chocolate mousse, 206
    toasting, 236

O

O'Brien, Shari, 190
Ocean Grand, The, 99, 156
O'Connell, Patrick, **172**, 173
ogo salad, smoked nairagi sashimi with, 54–55
oil
    annatto, 98
    basil, 223
    beet, 101
    curry, 78

NOTES

NOTES

NOTES